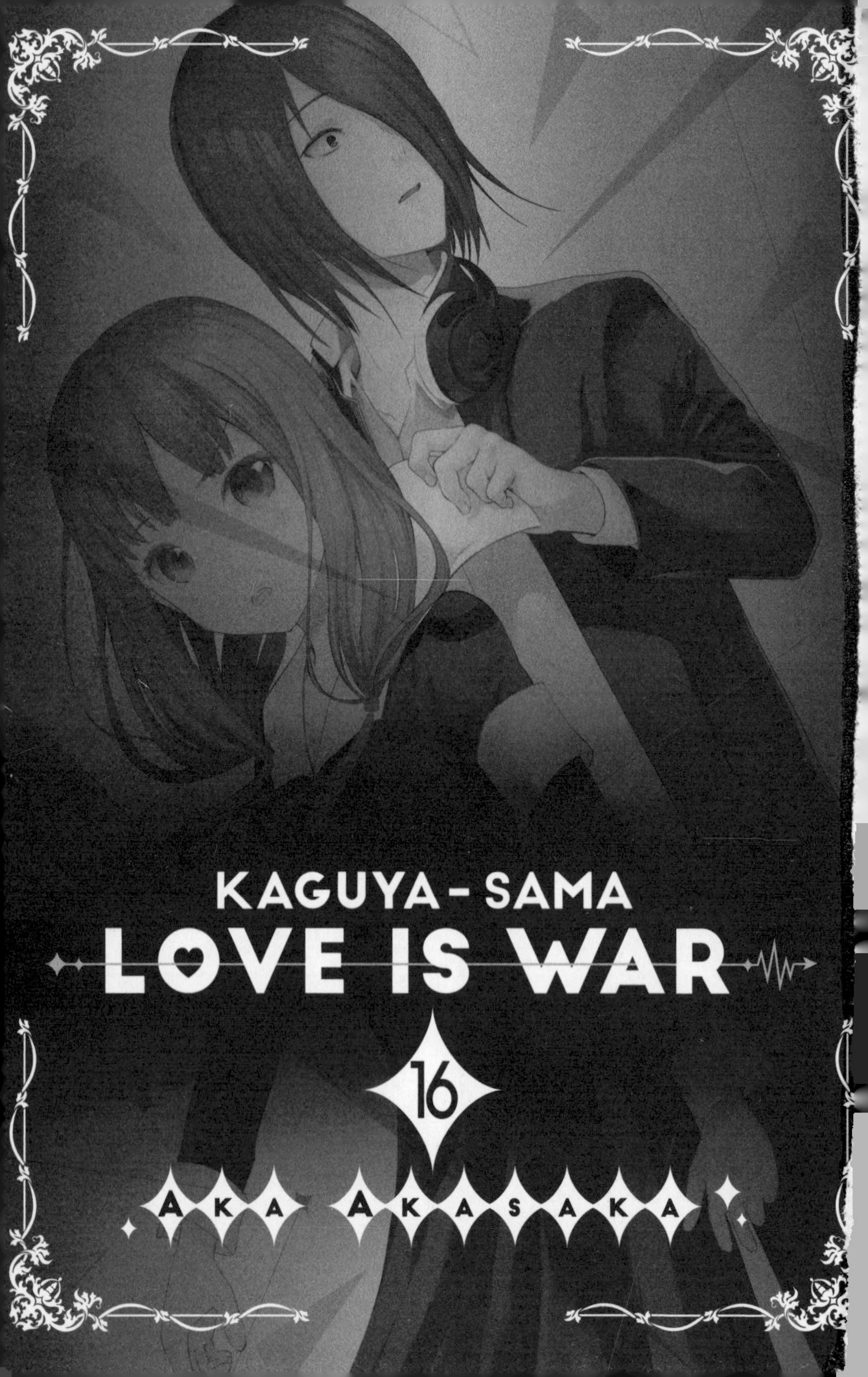
KAGUYA-SAMA
LOVE IS WAR
16
AKA AKASAKA

Meet the Characters!

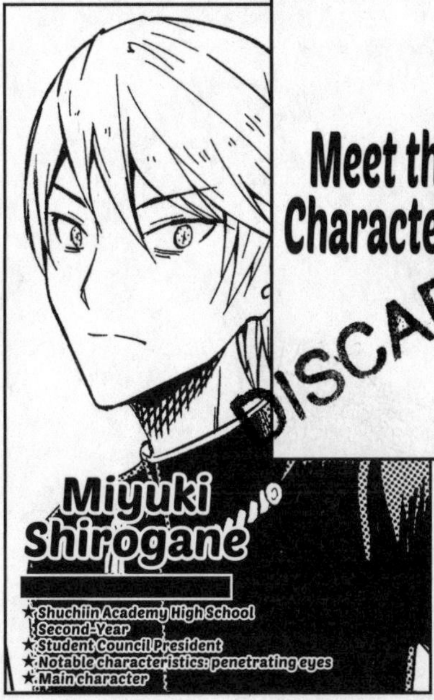
Miyuki Shirogane
★ Shuchiin Academy High School Second-Year
★ Student Council President
★ Notable characteristics: penetrating eyes
★ Main character

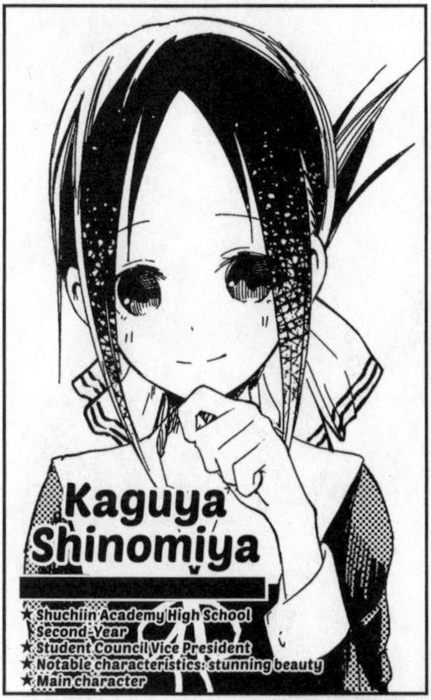
Kaguya Shinomiya
★ Shuchiin Academy High School Second-Year
★ Student Council Vice President
★ Notable characteristics: stunning beauty
★ Main character

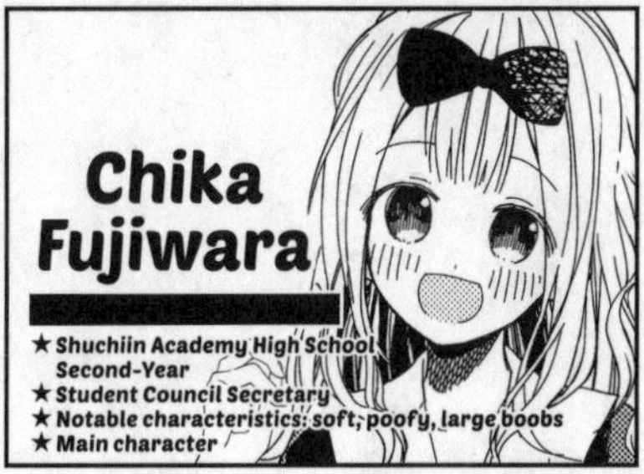
Chika Fujiwara
★ Shuchiin Academy High School Second-Year
★ Student Council Secretary
★ Notable characteristics: soft, poofy, large boobs
★ Main character

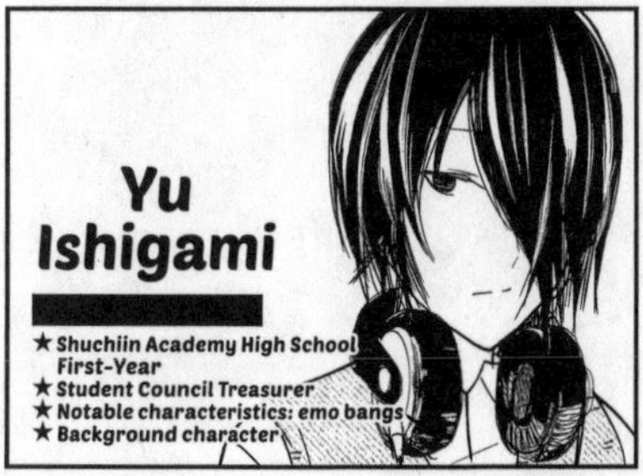
Yu Ishigami
★ Shuchiin Academy High School First-Year
★ Student Council Treasurer
★ Notable characteristics: emo bangs
★ Background character

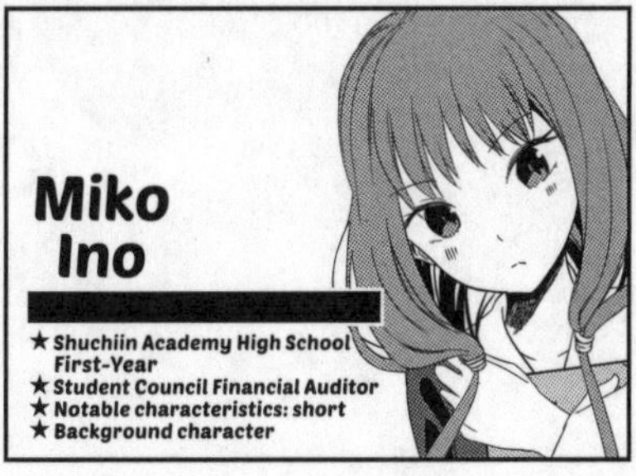
Miko Ino
★ Shuchiin Academy High School First-Year
★ Student Council Financial Auditor
★ Notable characteristics: short
★ Background character

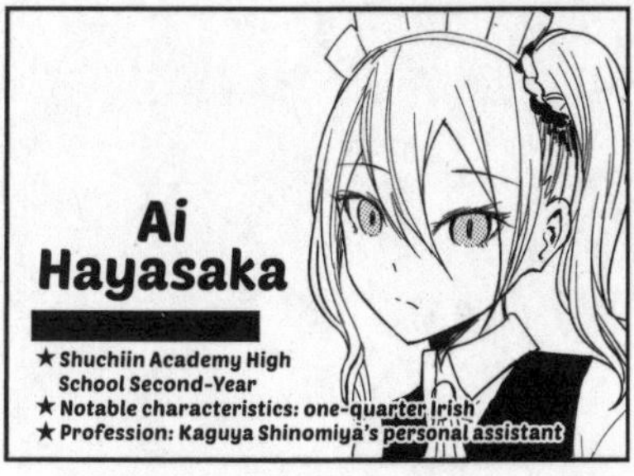
Ai Hayasaka
★ Shuchiin Academy High School Second-Year
★ Notable characteristics: one-quarter Irish
★ Profession: Kaguya Shinomiya's personal assistant

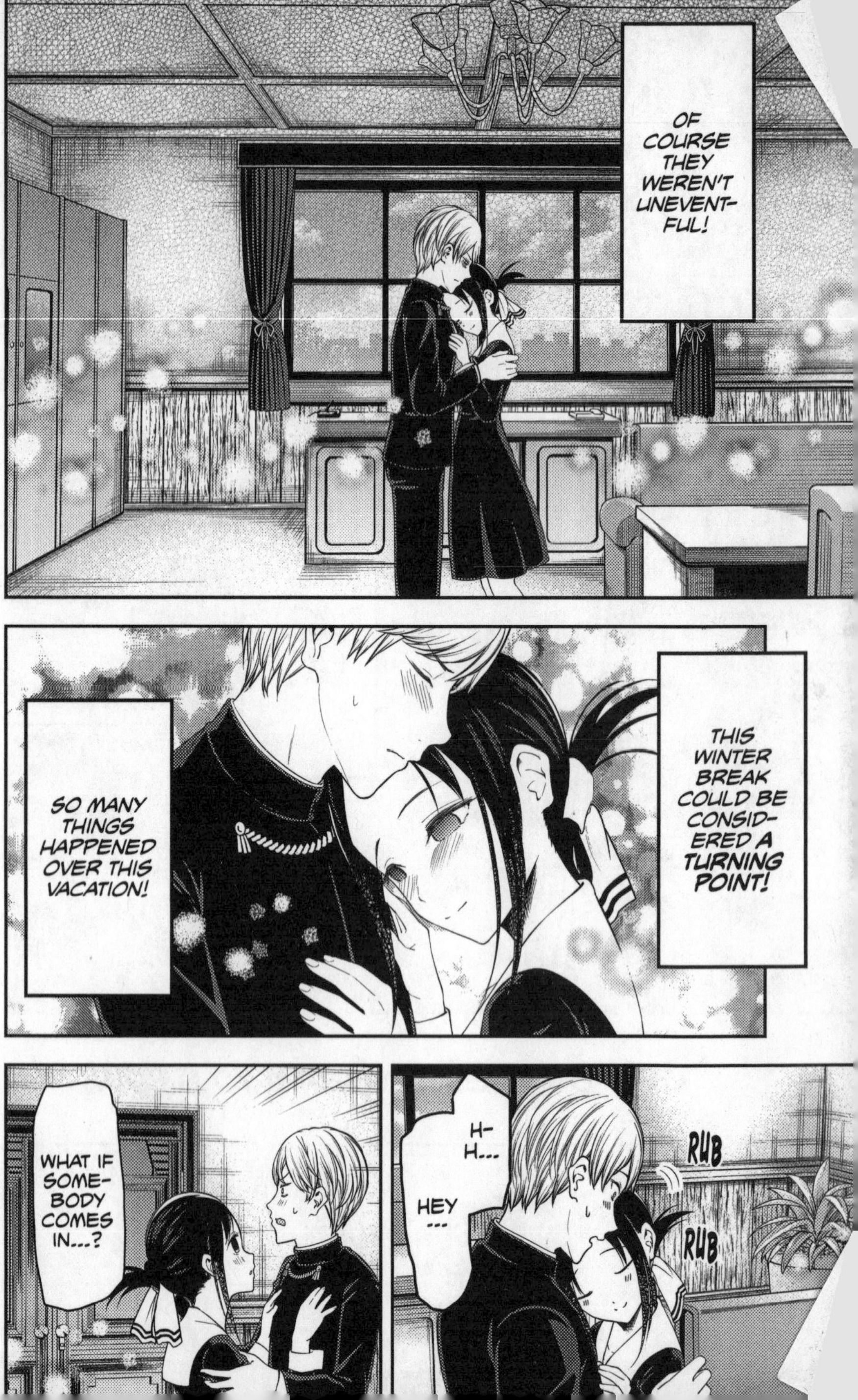
OF COURSE THEY WEREN'T UNEVENTFUL!
THIS WINTER BREAK COULD BE CONSIDERED A TURNING POINT!
SO MANY THINGS HAPPENED OVER THIS VACATION!
RUB
RUB
H-H...
HEY...
WHAT IF SOMEBODY COMES IN...?

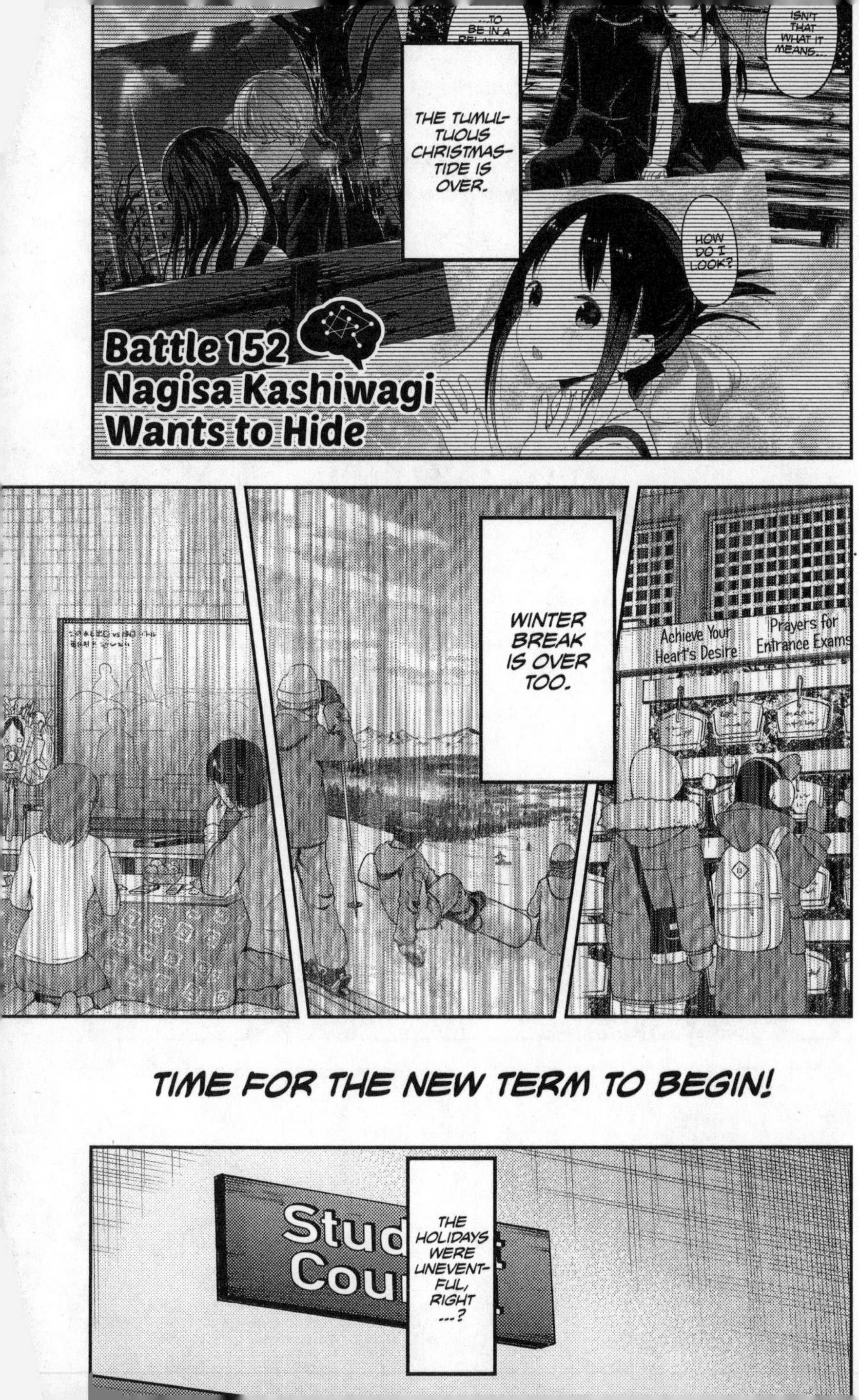
ISN'T THAT WHAT IT MEANS...
...TO BE IN A
THE TUMULTUOUS CHRISTMASTIDE IS OVER.
HOW DO I LOOK?
Battle 152
Nagisa Kashiwagi Wants to Hide
WINTER BREAK IS OVER TOO.
Prayers for Entrance Exams
Achieve Your Heart's Desire
TIME FOR THE NEW TERM TO BEGIN!
THE HOLIDAYS WERE UNEVENTFUL, RIGHT...?

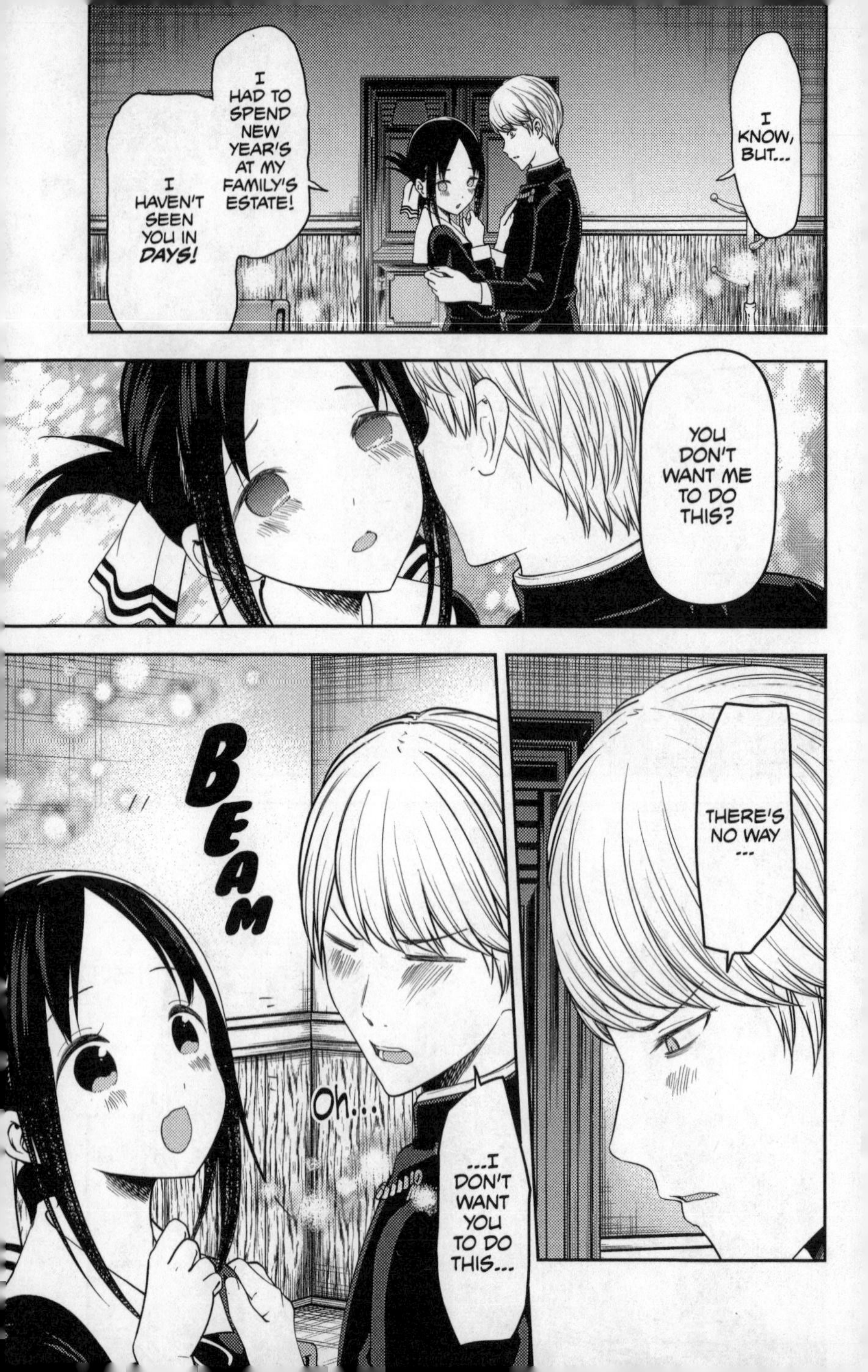
I KNOW, BUT...
I HAD TO SPEND NEW YEAR'S AT MY FAMILY'S ESTATE!
I HAVEN'T SEEN YOU IN DAYS!
YOU DON'T WANT ME TO DO THIS?
THERE'S NO WAY ...
...I DON'T WANT YOU TO DO THIS...
Oh...
BEAM

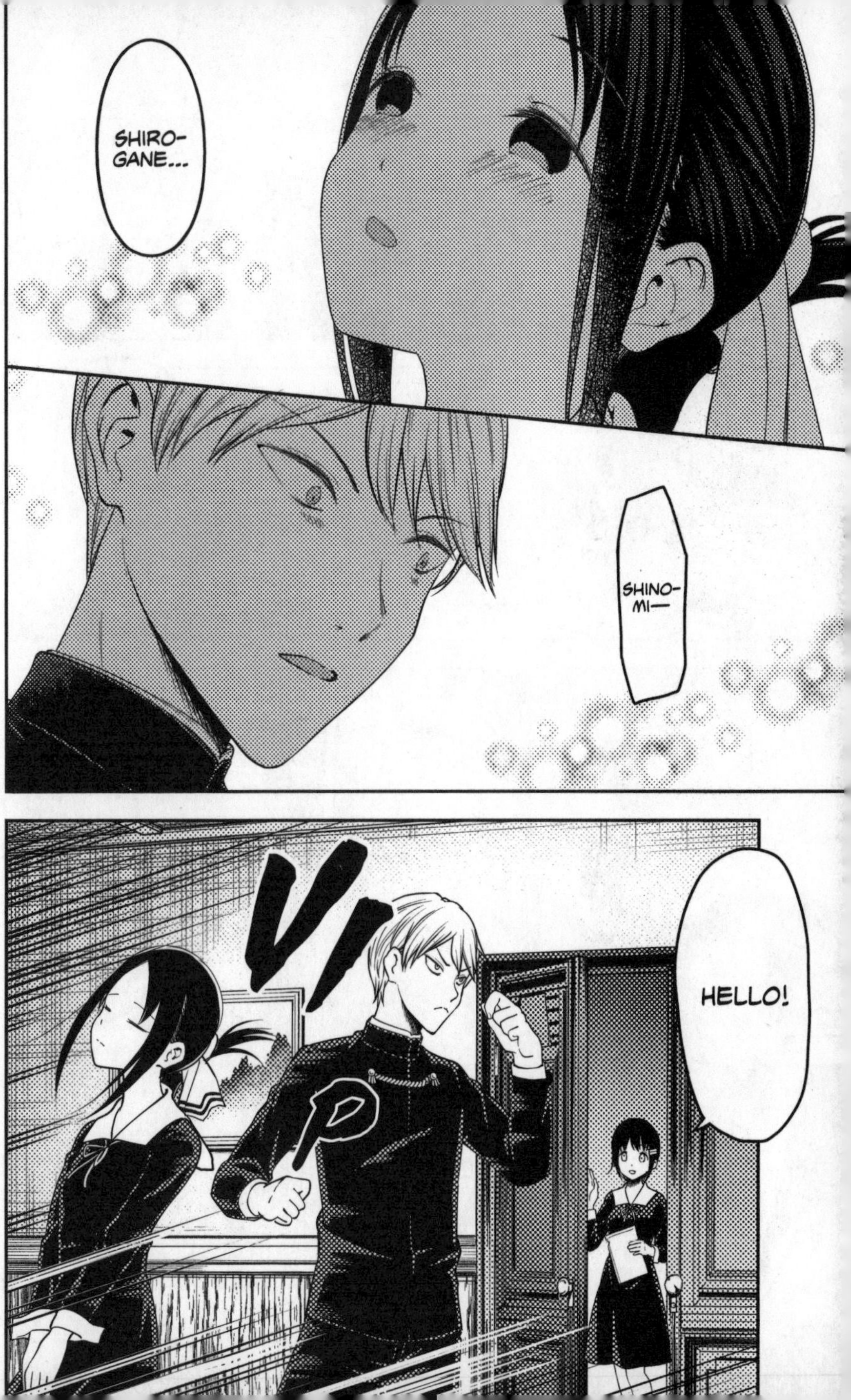
SHIRO-GANE...
SHINO-MI—
HELLO!
V
P

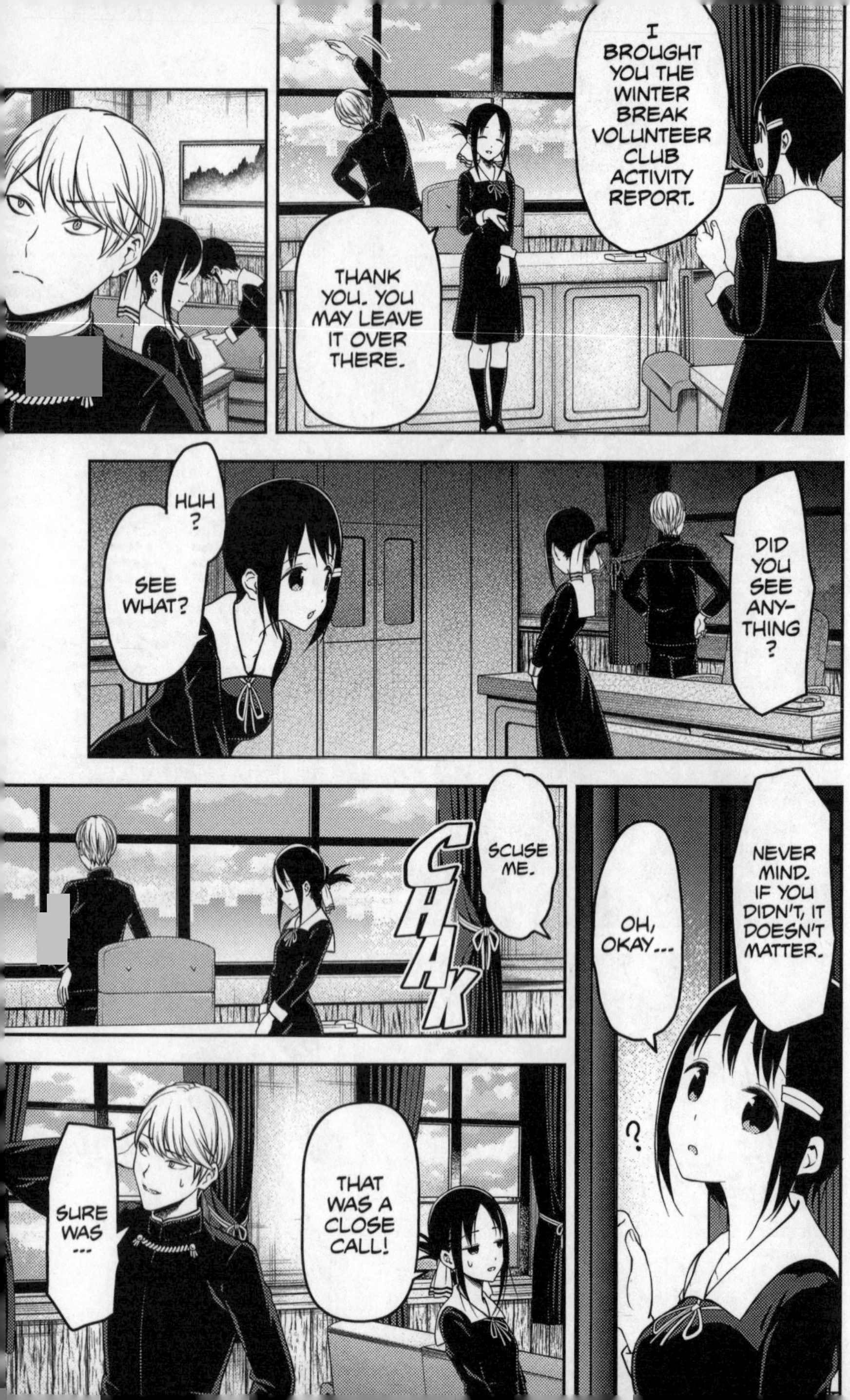
I BROUGHT YOU THE WINTER BREAK VOLUNTEER CLUB ACTIVITY REPORT.
THANK YOU. YOU MAY LEAVE IT OVER THERE.
DID YOU SEE ANYTHING?
HUH? SEE WHAT?
NEVER MIND. IF YOU DIDN'T, IT DOESN'T MATTER.
OH, OKAY...
?
SCUSE ME.
CHAK
THAT WAS A CLOSE CALL!
SURE WAS...

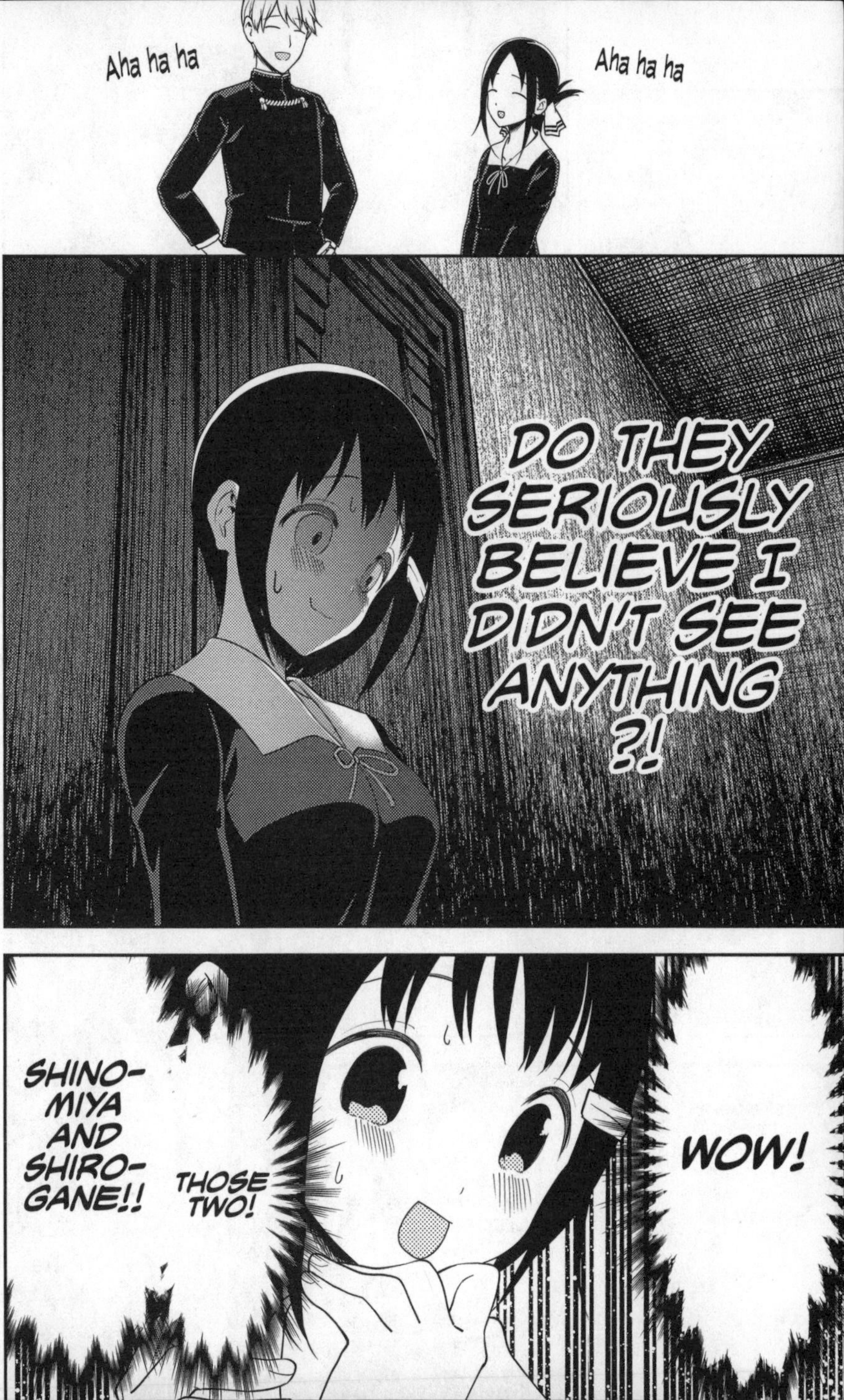
Aha ha ha
Aha ha ha
DO THEY SERIOUSLY BELIEVE I DIDN'T SEE ANYTHING ?!
WOW!
THOSE TWO!
SHINO-MIYA AND SHIRO-GANE!!

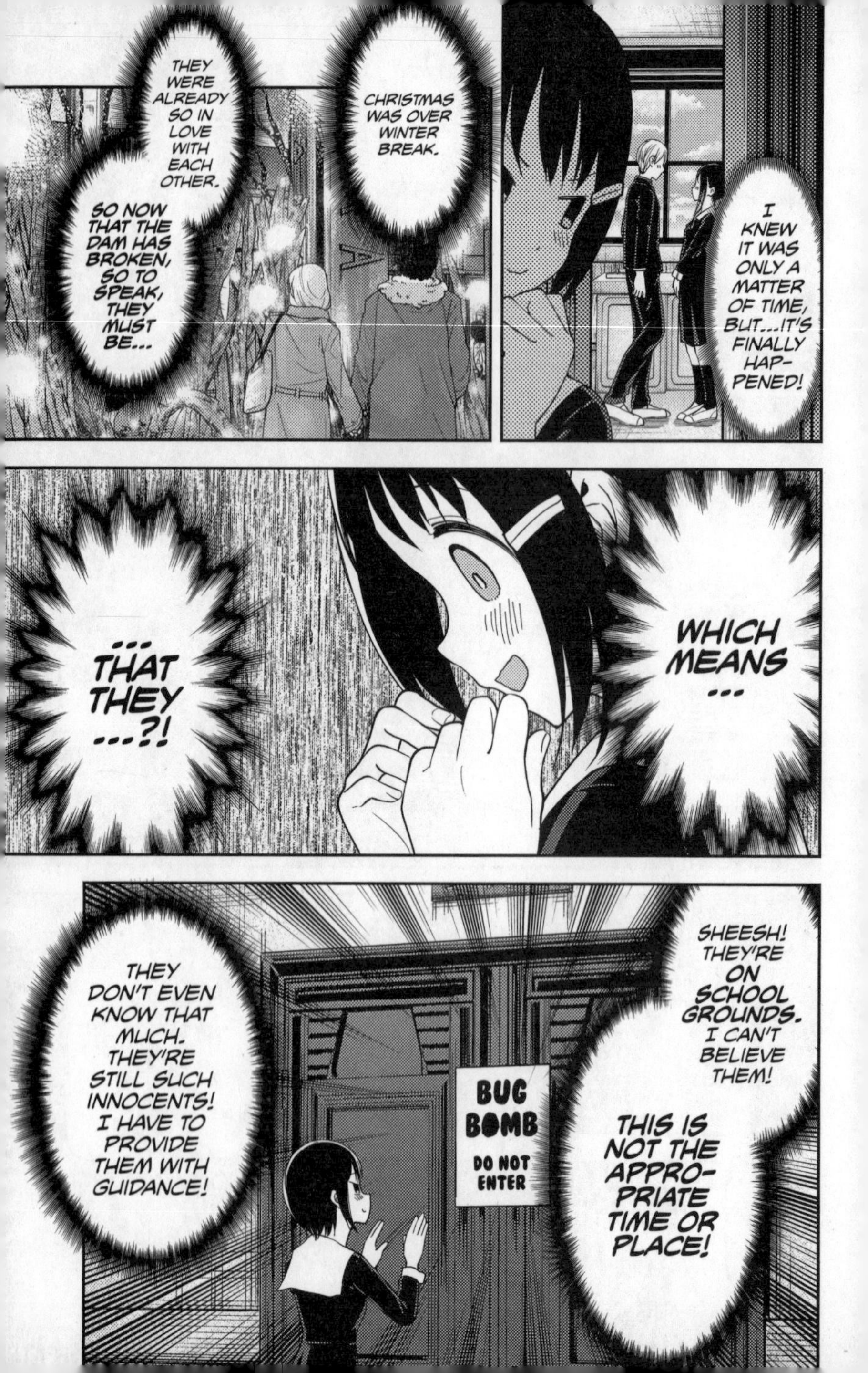
I KNEW IT WAS ONLY A MATTER OF TIME, BUT...IT'S FINALLY HAP-PENED!
CHRISTMAS WAS OVER WINTER BREAK.
THEY WERE ALREADY SO IN LOVE WITH EACH OTHER.
SO NOW THAT THE DAM HAS BROKEN, SO TO SPEAK, THEY MUST BE...
WHICH MEANS...
...THAT THEY...?!
SHEESH! THEY'RE ON SCHOOL GROUNDS. I CAN'T BELIEVE THEM!
THIS IS NOT THE APPRO-PRIATE TIME OR PLACE!
BUG BOMB
DO NOT ENTER
THEY DON'T EVEN KNOW THAT MUCH. THEY'RE STILL SUCH INNOCENTS! I HAVE TO PROVIDE THEM WITH GUIDANCE!

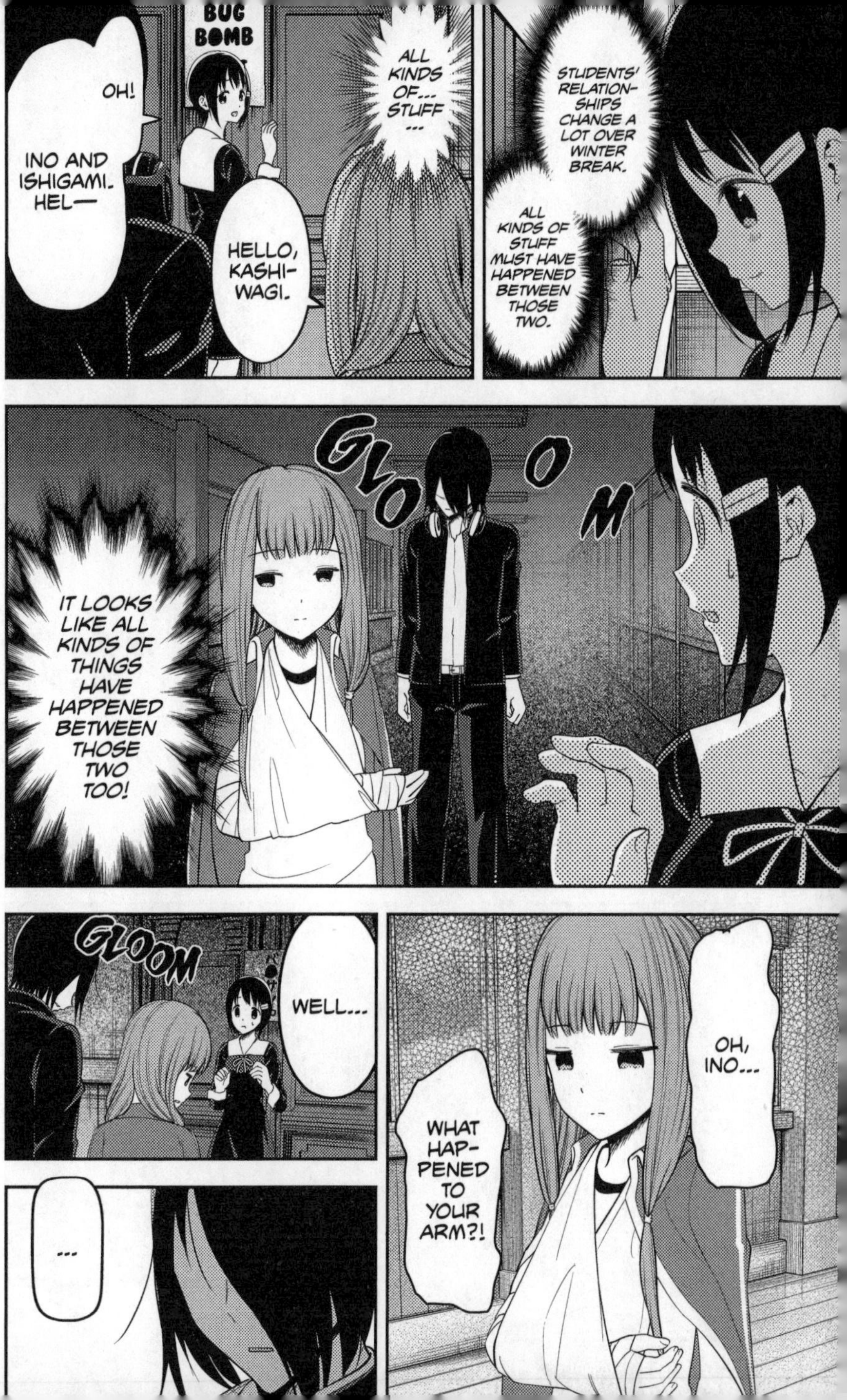
STUDENTS' RELATIONSHIPS CHANGE A LOT OVER WINTER BREAK.
ALL KINDS OF STUFF MUST HAVE HAPPENED BETWEEN THOSE TWO.
BUG BOMB
ALL KINDS OF... STUFF ...
OH!
INO AND ISHIGAMI. HEL—
HELLO, KASHIWAGI.
GLOOOM
IT LOOKS LIKE ALL KINDS OF THINGS HAVE HAPPENED BETWEEN THOSE TWO TOO!
OH, INO...
WHAT HAPPENED TO YOUR ARM?!
GLOOM
WELL...
...

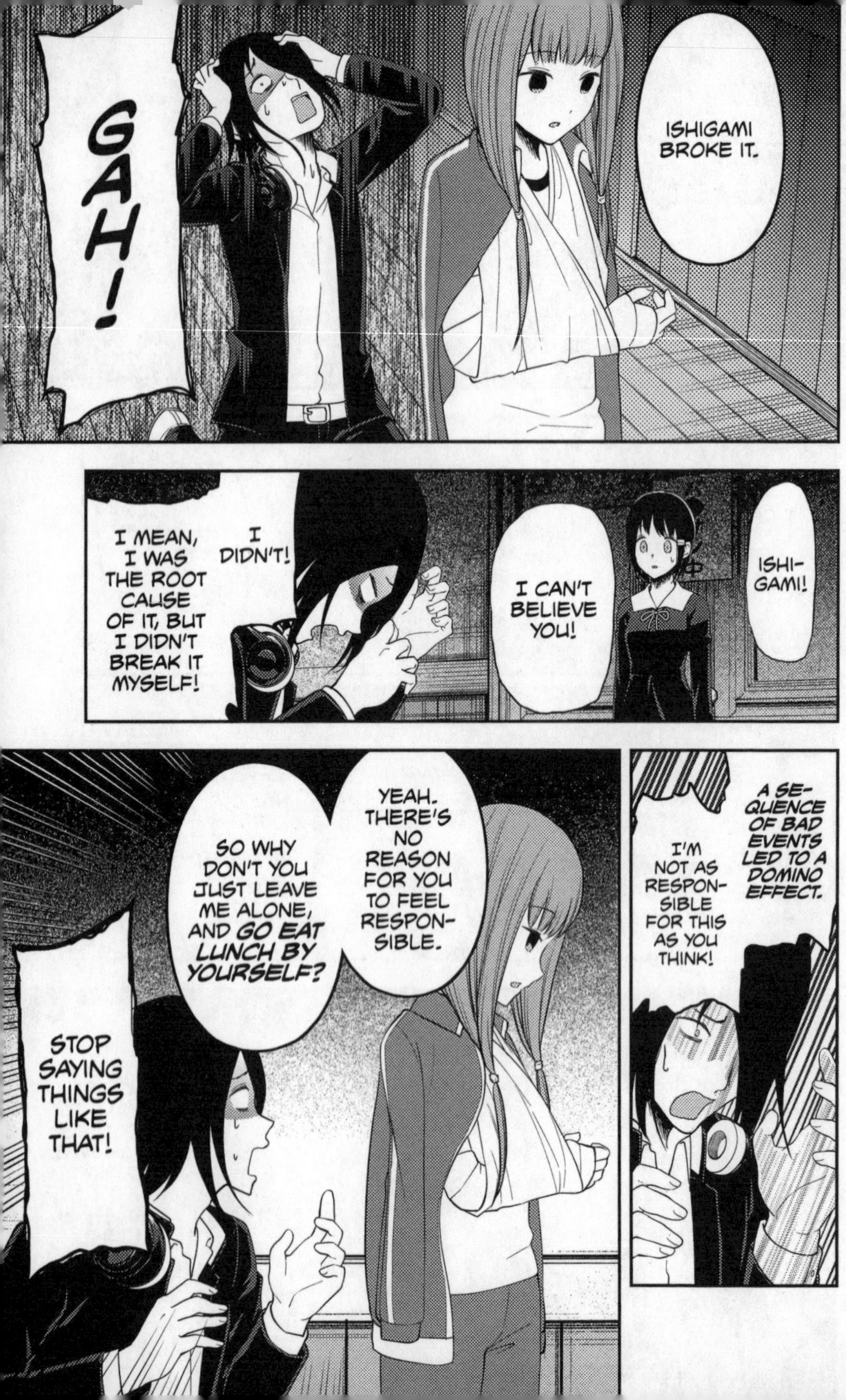
ISHIGAMI BROKE IT.
GAH!
ISHI-GAMI!
I CAN'T BELIEVE YOU!
I DIDN'T!
I MEAN, I WAS THE ROOT CAUSE OF IT, BUT I DIDN'T BREAK IT MYSELF!
A SEQUENCE OF BAD EVENTS LED TO A DOMINO EFFECT.
I'M NOT AS RESPONSIBLE FOR THIS AS YOU THINK!
YEAH. THERE'S NO REASON FOR YOU TO FEEL RESPONSIBLE.
SO WHY DON'T YOU JUST LEAVE ME ALONE, AND *GO EAT LUNCH BY YOURSELF?*
STOP SAYING THINGS LIKE THAT!

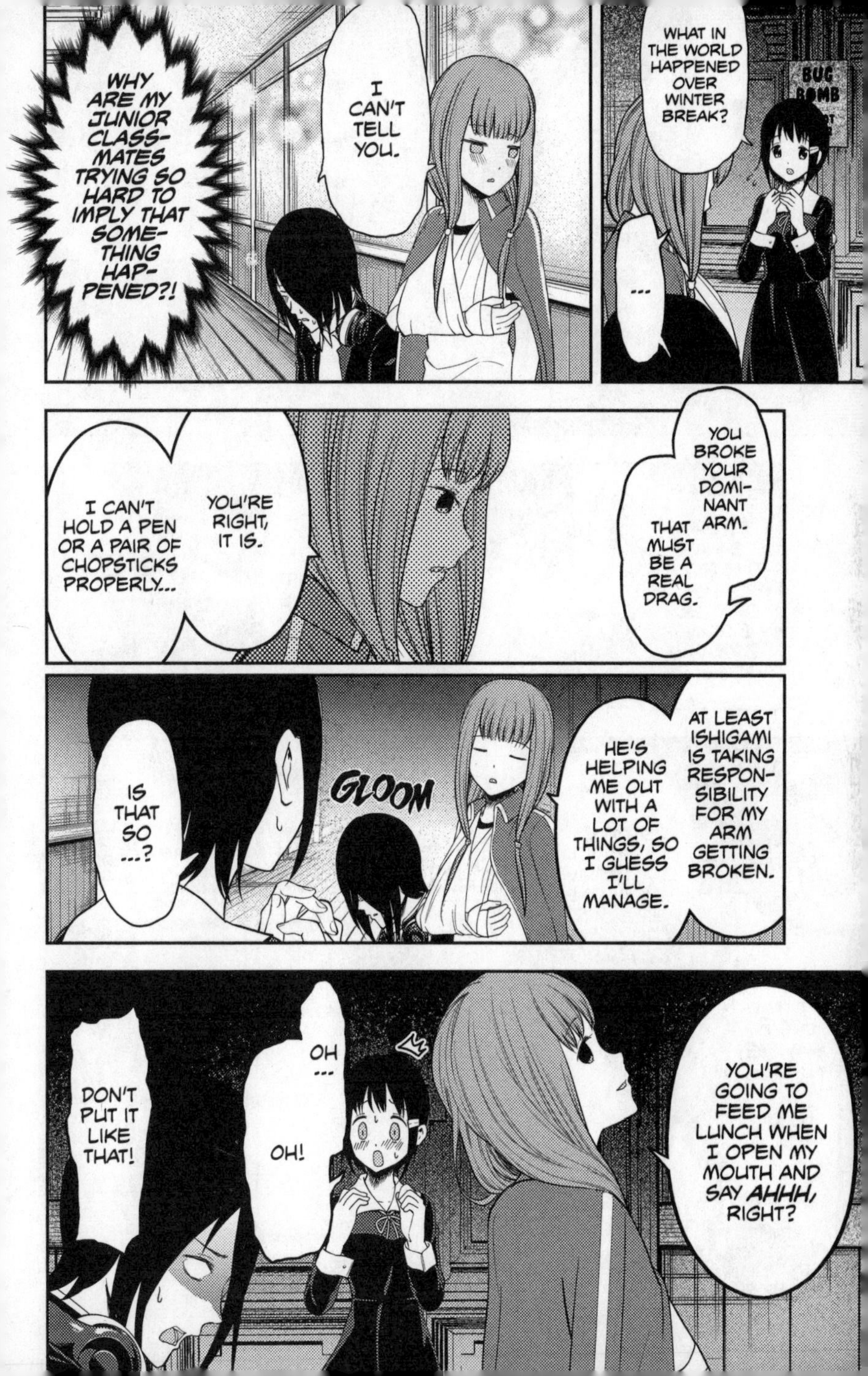

WHAT IN THE WORLD HAPPENED OVER WINTER BREAK?
BUG BOMB
...
I CAN'T TELL YOU.
WHY ARE MY JUNIOR CLASSMATES TRYING SO HARD TO IMPLY THAT SOMETHING HAPPENED?!
YOU BROKE YOUR DOMINANT ARM.
THAT MUST BE A REAL DRAG.
YOU'RE RIGHT, IT IS.
I CAN'T HOLD A PEN OR A PAIR OF CHOPSTICKS PROPERLY...
AT LEAST ISHIGAMI IS TAKING RESPONSIBILITY FOR MY ARM GETTING BROKEN.
HE'S HELPING ME OUT WITH A LOT OF THINGS, SO I GUESS I'LL MANAGE.
GLOOM
IS THAT SO...?
YOU'RE GOING TO FEED ME LUNCH WHEN I OPEN MY MOUTH AND SAY *AHHH*, RIGHT?
OH...
OH!
DON'T PUT IT LIKE THAT!

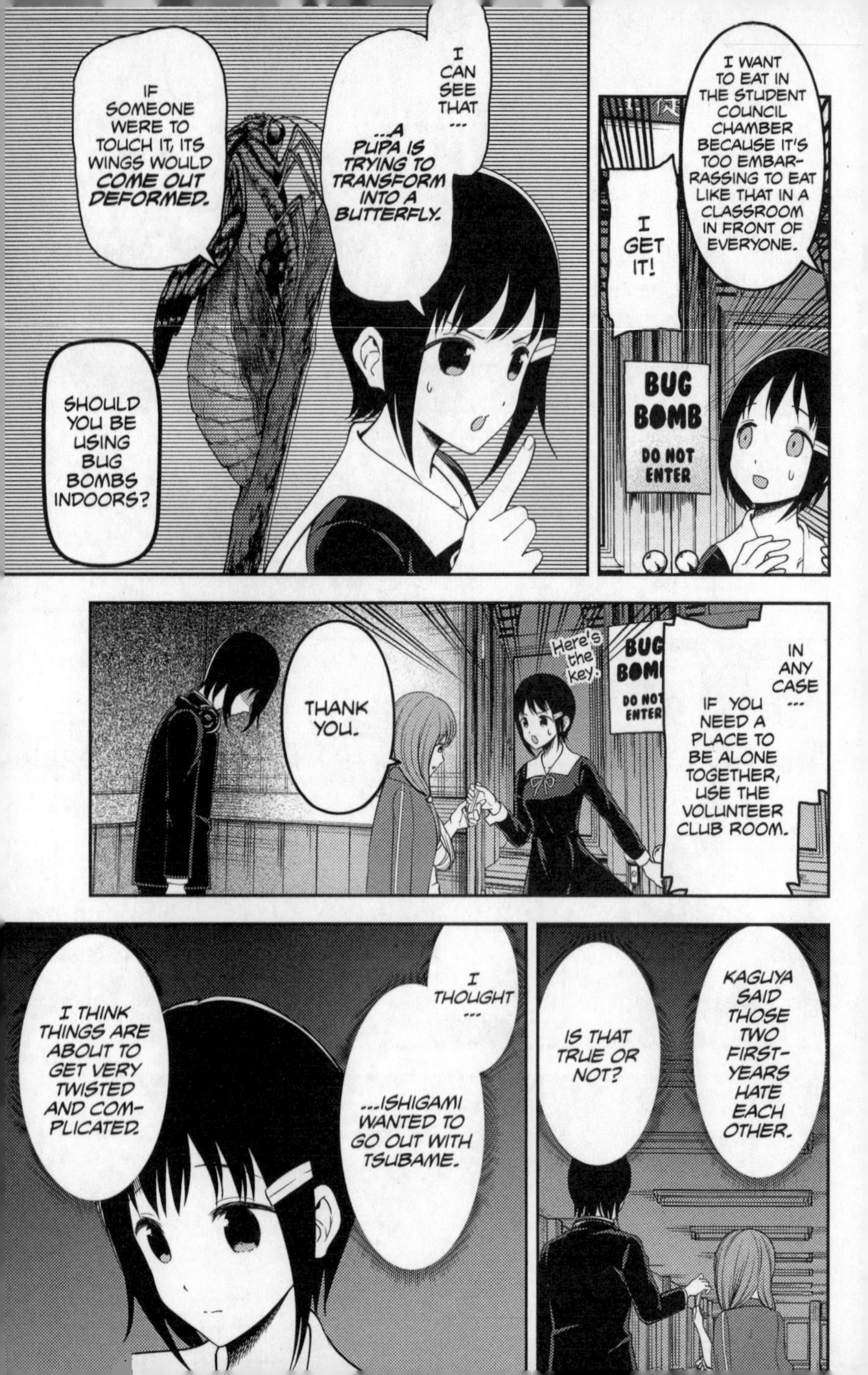
I WANT TO EAT IN THE STUDENT COUNCIL CHAMBER BECAUSE IT'S TOO EMBARRASSING TO EAT LIKE THAT IN A CLASSROOM IN FRONT OF EVERYONE.
I GET IT!
BUG BOMB
DO NOT ENTER
I CAN SEE THAT ---
...A PUPA IS TRYING TO TRANSFORM INTO A BUTTERFLY.
IF SOMEONE WERE TO TOUCH IT, ITS WINGS WOULD COME OUT DEFORMED.
SHOULD YOU BE USING BUG BOMBS INDOORS?
IN ANY CASE ---
IF YOU NEED A PLACE TO BE ALONE TOGETHER, USE THE VOLUNTEER CLUB ROOM.
Here's the key.
THANK YOU.
KAGUYA SAID THOSE TWO FIRST-YEARS HATE EACH OTHER.
IS THAT TRUE OR NOT?
I THOUGHT ---
...ISHIGAMI WANTED TO GO OUT WITH TSUBAME.
I THINK THINGS ARE ABOUT TO GET VERY TWISTED AND COMPLICATED.

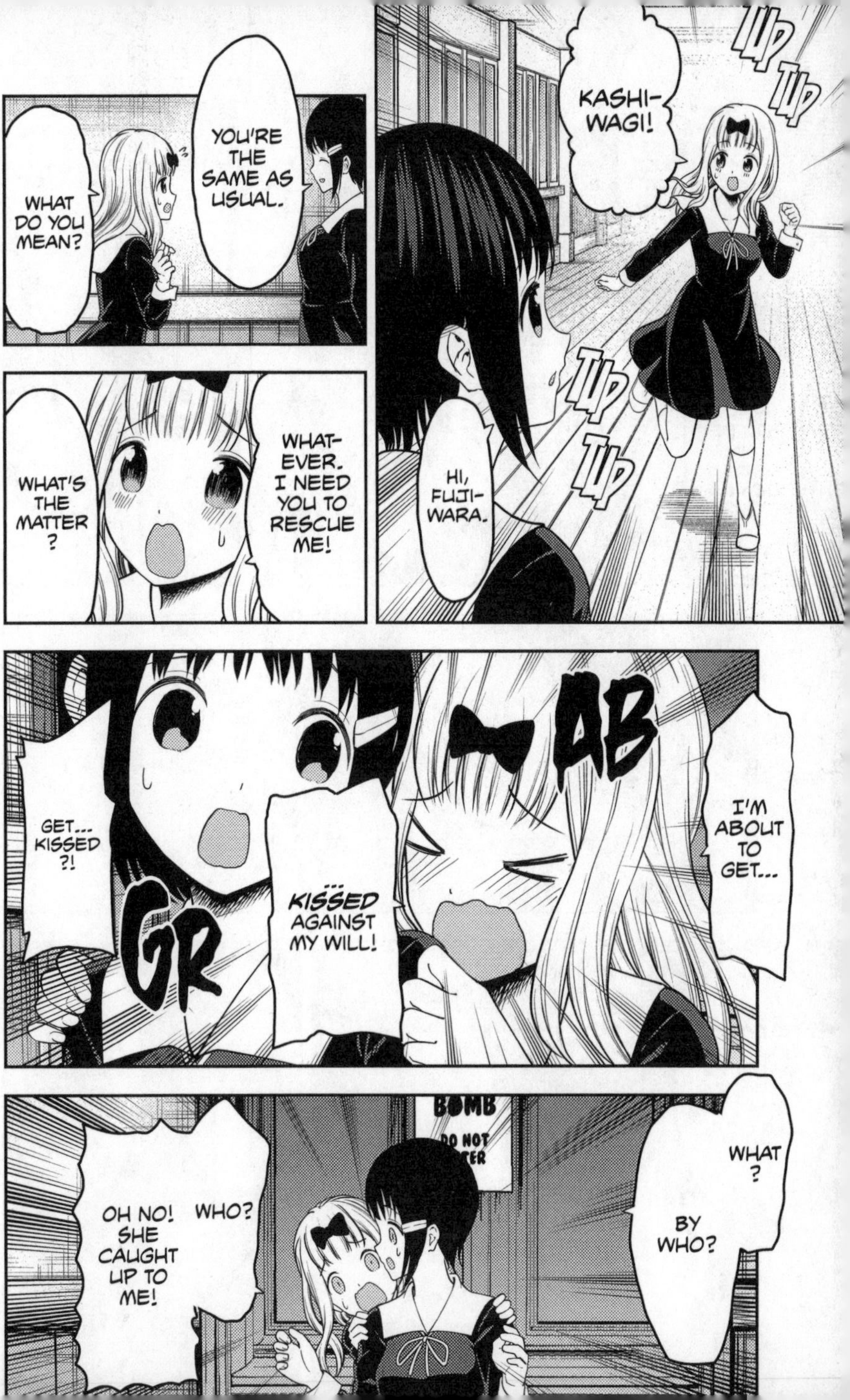
KASHI-WAGI!
TUP TUP
TUP TUP
HI, FUJI-WARA.
YOU'RE THE SAME AS USUAL.
WHAT DO YOU MEAN?
WHAT-EVER. I NEED YOU TO RESCUE ME!
WHAT'S THE MATTER?
AB
I'M ABOUT TO GET...
...KISSED AGAINST MY WILL!
GR
GET... KISSED?!
WHAT?
BY WHO?
BOMB
DO NOT
WHO?
OH NO! SHE CAUGHT UP TO ME!

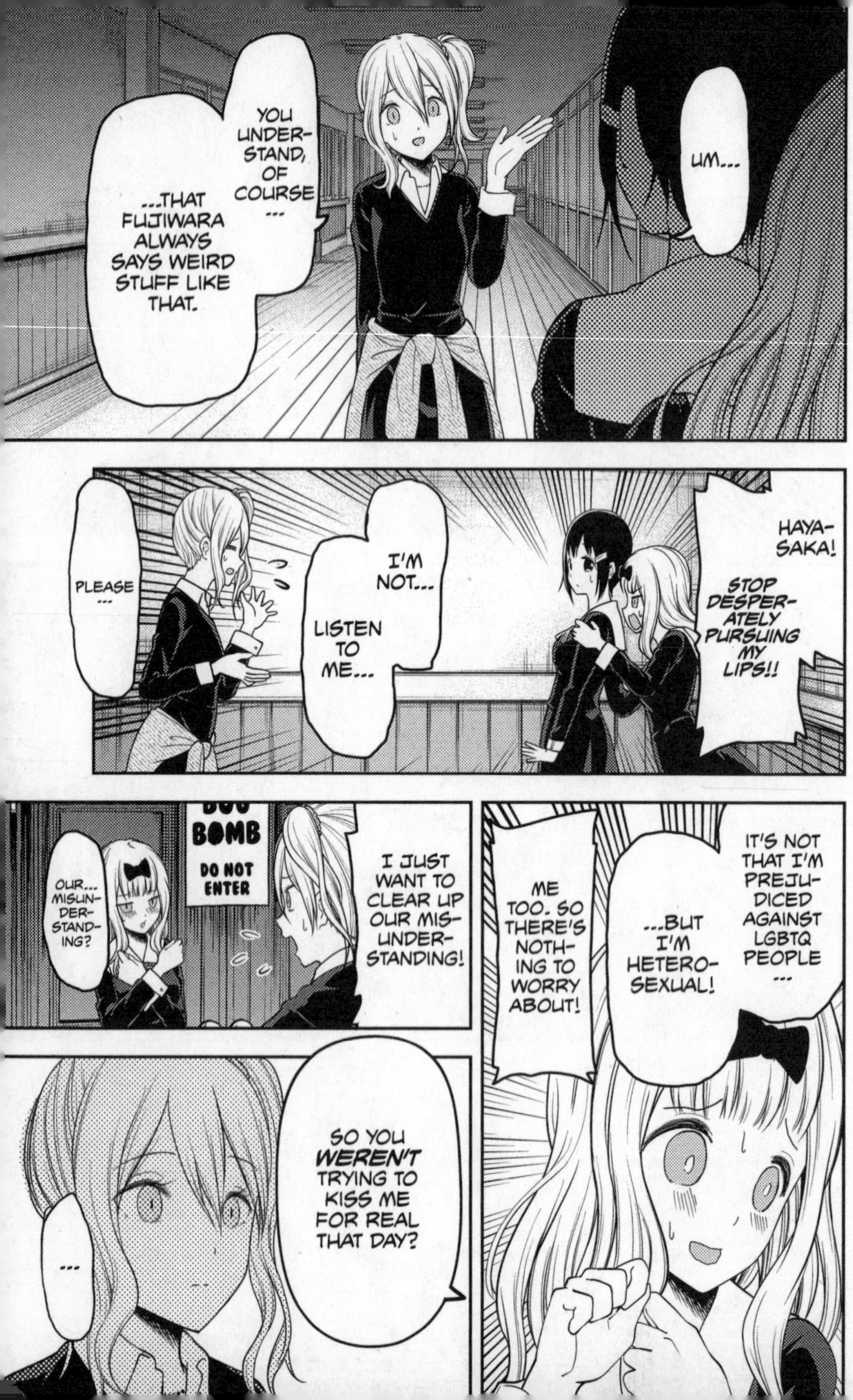
UM...
YOU UNDERSTAND, OF COURSE...
...THAT FUJIWARA ALWAYS SAYS WEIRD STUFF LIKE THAT.
HAYA-SAKA!
STOP DESPERATELY PURSUING MY LIPS!!
I'M NOT...
LISTEN TO ME...
PLEASE...
IT'S NOT THAT I'M PREJUDICED AGAINST LGBTQ PEOPLE...
...BUT I'M HETEROSEXUAL!
ME TOO. SO THERE'S NOTHING TO WORRY ABOUT!
I JUST WANT TO CLEAR UP OUR MISUNDERSTANDING!
BOMB
DO NOT ENTER
OUR... MISUNDERSTANDING?
SO YOU WEREN'T TRYING TO KISS ME FOR REAL THAT DAY?
...

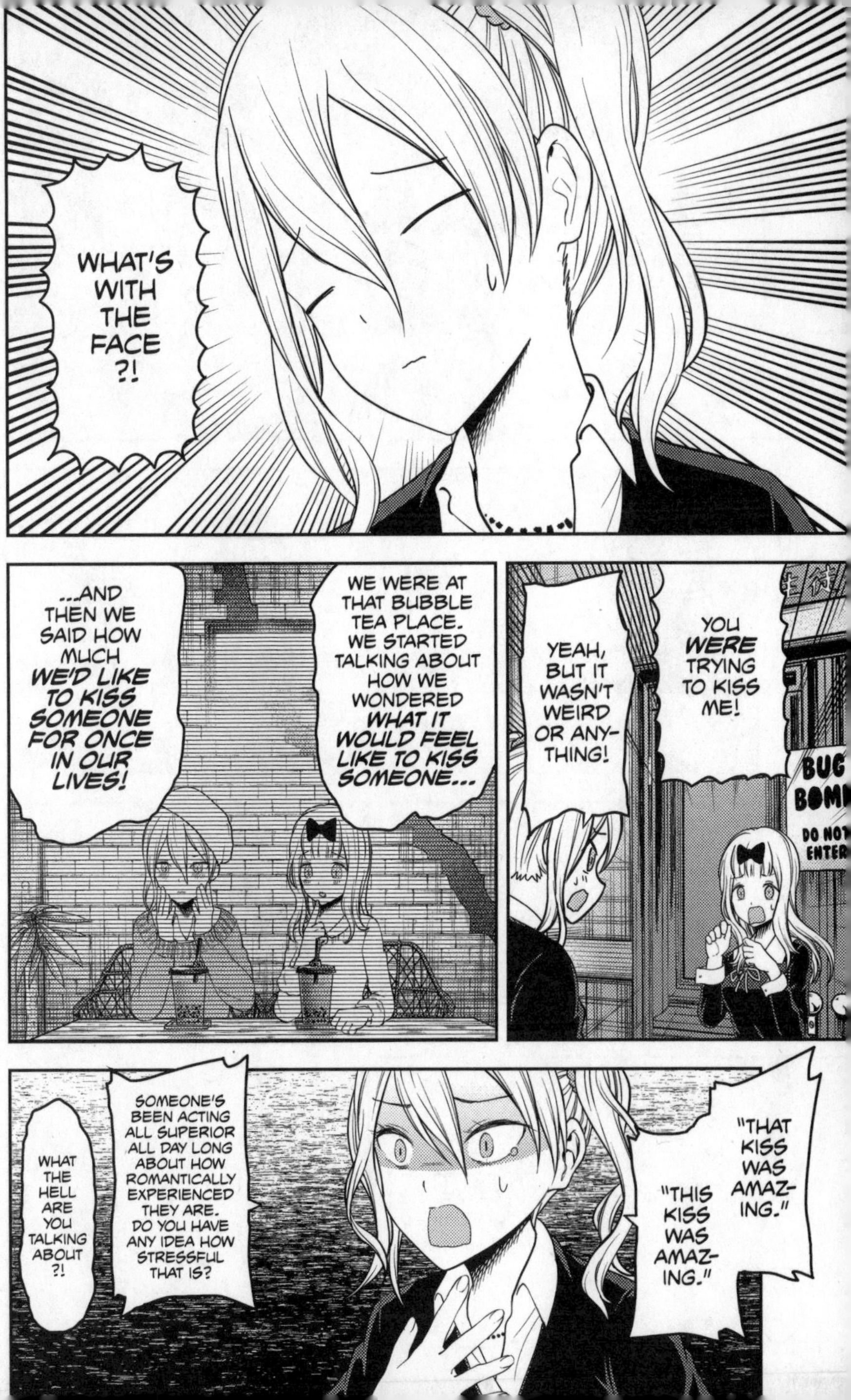
WHAT'S WITH THE FACE ?!
YOU WERE TRYING TO KISS ME!
YEAH, BUT IT WASN'T WEIRD OR ANY-THING!
BUG
WE WERE AT THAT BUBBLE TEA PLACE. WE STARTED TALKING ABOUT HOW WE WONDERED WHAT IT WOULD FEEL LIKE TO KISS SOMEONE...
...AND THEN WE SAID HOW MUCH WE'D LIKE TO KISS SOMEONE FOR ONCE IN OUR LIVES!
"THAT KISS WAS AMAZ-ING."
"THIS KISS WAS AMAZ-ING."
SOMEONE'S BEEN ACTING ALL SUPERIOR ALL DAY LONG ABOUT HOW ROMANTICALLY EXPERIENCED THEY ARE. DO YOU HAVE ANY IDEA HOW STRESSFUL THAT IS?
WHAT THE HELL ARE YOU TALKING ABOUT ?!

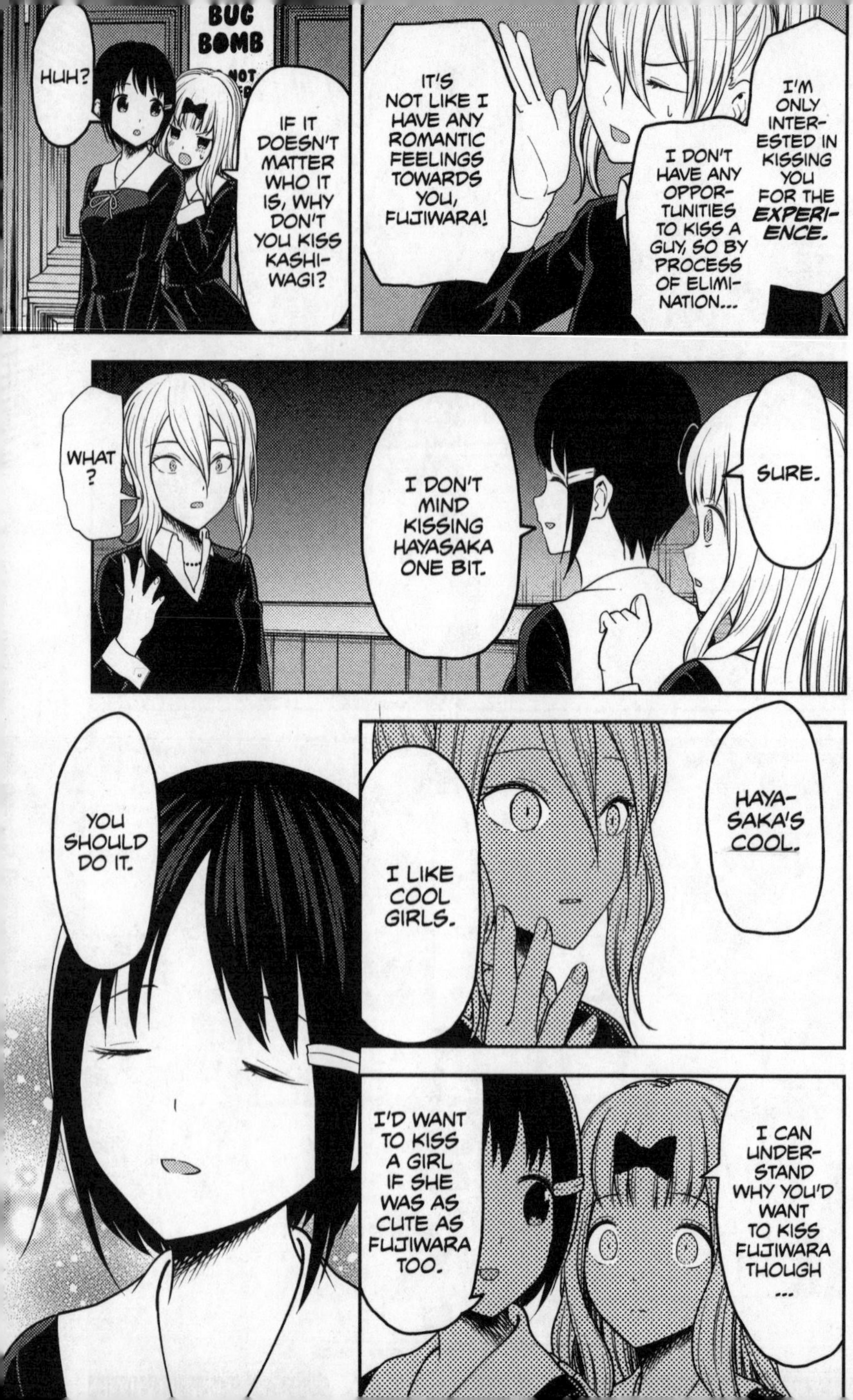
I'M ONLY INTERESTED IN KISSING YOU FOR THE EXPERIENCE.
I DON'T HAVE ANY OPPORTUNITIES TO KISS A GUY, SO BY PROCESS OF ELIMINATION...
IT'S NOT LIKE I HAVE ANY ROMANTIC FEELINGS TOWARDS YOU, FUJIWARA!
BUG BOMB
IF IT DOESN'T MATTER WHO IT IS, WHY DON'T YOU KISS KASHIWAGI?
HUH?
SURE.
I DON'T MIND KISSING HAYASAKA ONE BIT.
WHAT?
HAYASAKA'S COOL.
I LIKE COOL GIRLS.
I CAN UNDERSTAND WHY YOU'D WANT TO KISS FUJIWARA THOUGH...
I'D WANT TO KISS A GIRL IF SHE WAS AS CUTE AS FUJIWARA TOO.
YOU SHOULD DO IT.

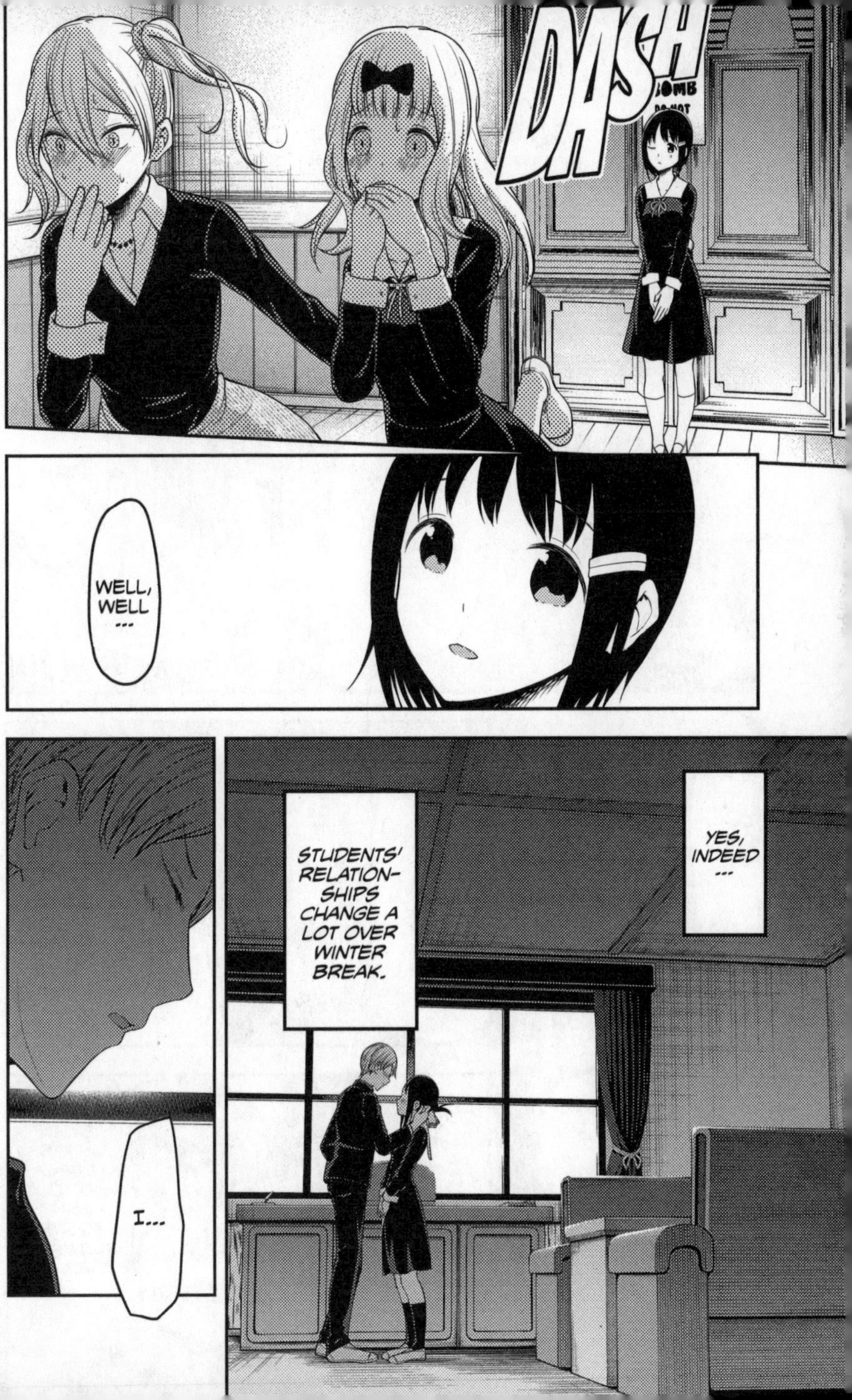
DASH
WELL, WELL ...
YES, INDEED ...
STUDENTS' RELATION-SHIPS CHANGE A LOT OVER WINTER BREAK.
I...

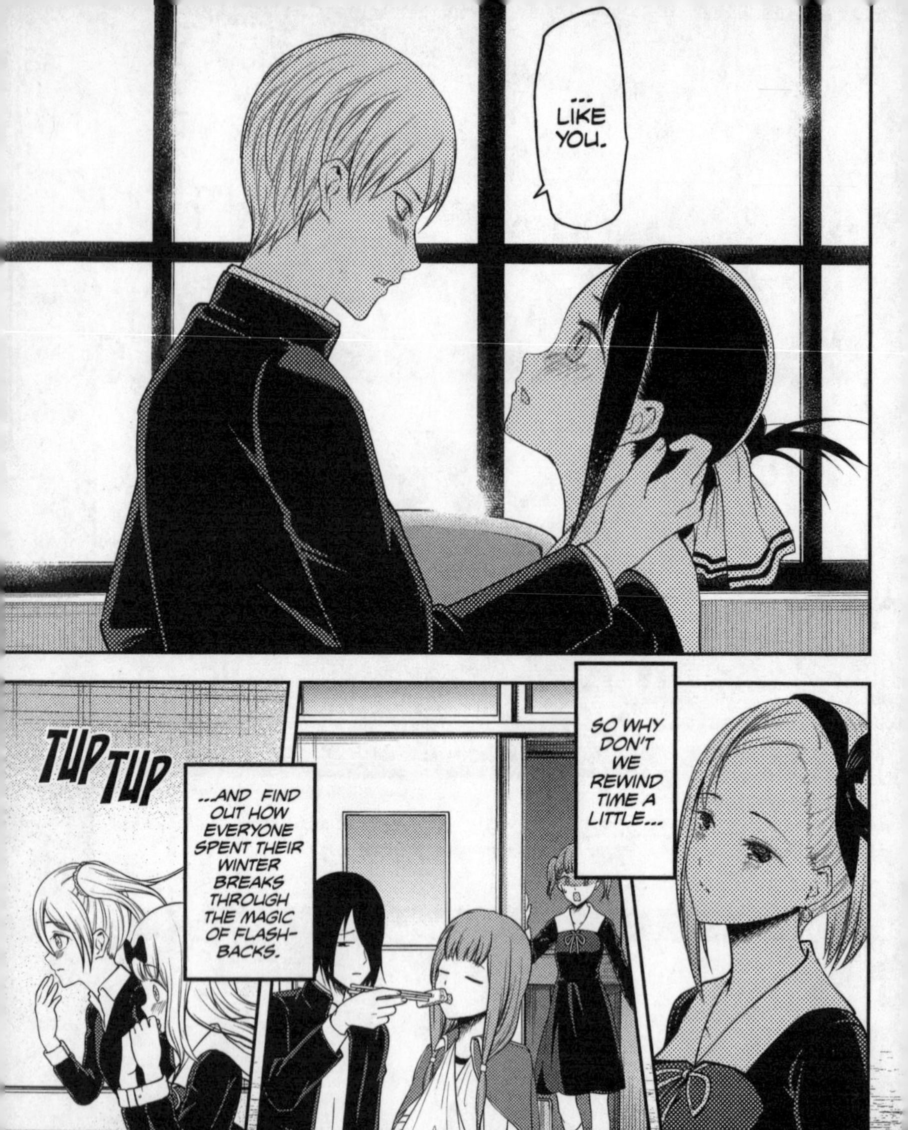
...LIKE YOU.
SO WHY DON'T WE REWIND TIME A LITTLE...
...AND FIND OUT HOW EVERYONE SPENT THEIR WINTER BREAKS THROUGH THE MAGIC OF FLASHBACKS.
TUP TUP

FLASHBACK #1: YU ISHIGAMI'S CHRISTMAS

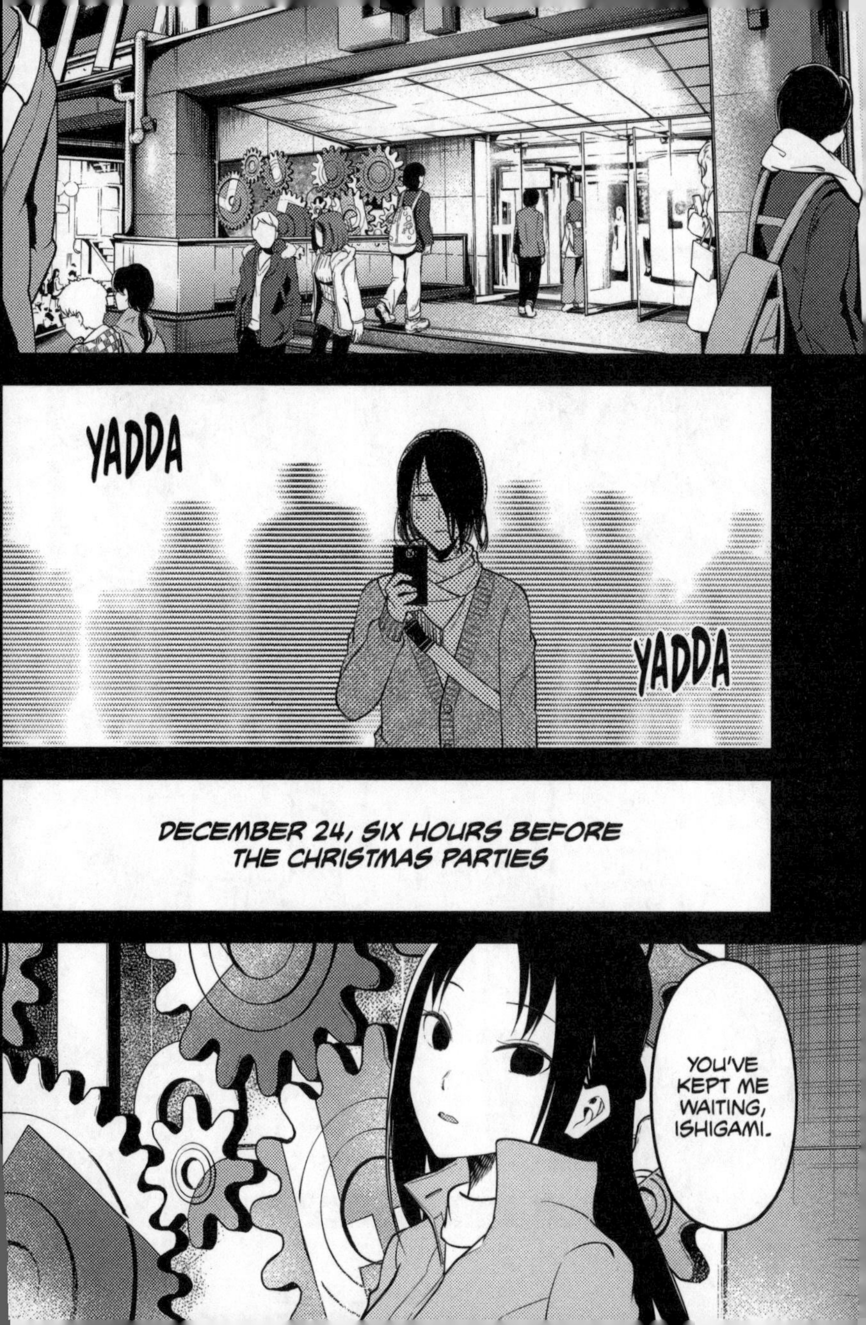
YADDA
YADDA
DECEMBER 24, SIX HOURS BEFORE THE CHRISTMAS PARTIES
YOU'VE KEPT ME WAITING, ISHIGAMI.

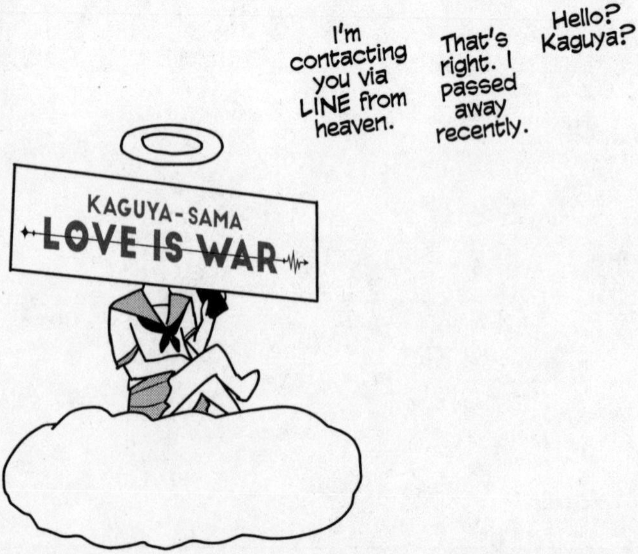
Hello? Kaguya?
That's right. I passed away recently.
I'm contacting you via LINE from heaven.
KAGUYA-SAMA
LOVE IS WAR

KAGUYA-SAMA
LOVE IS WAR

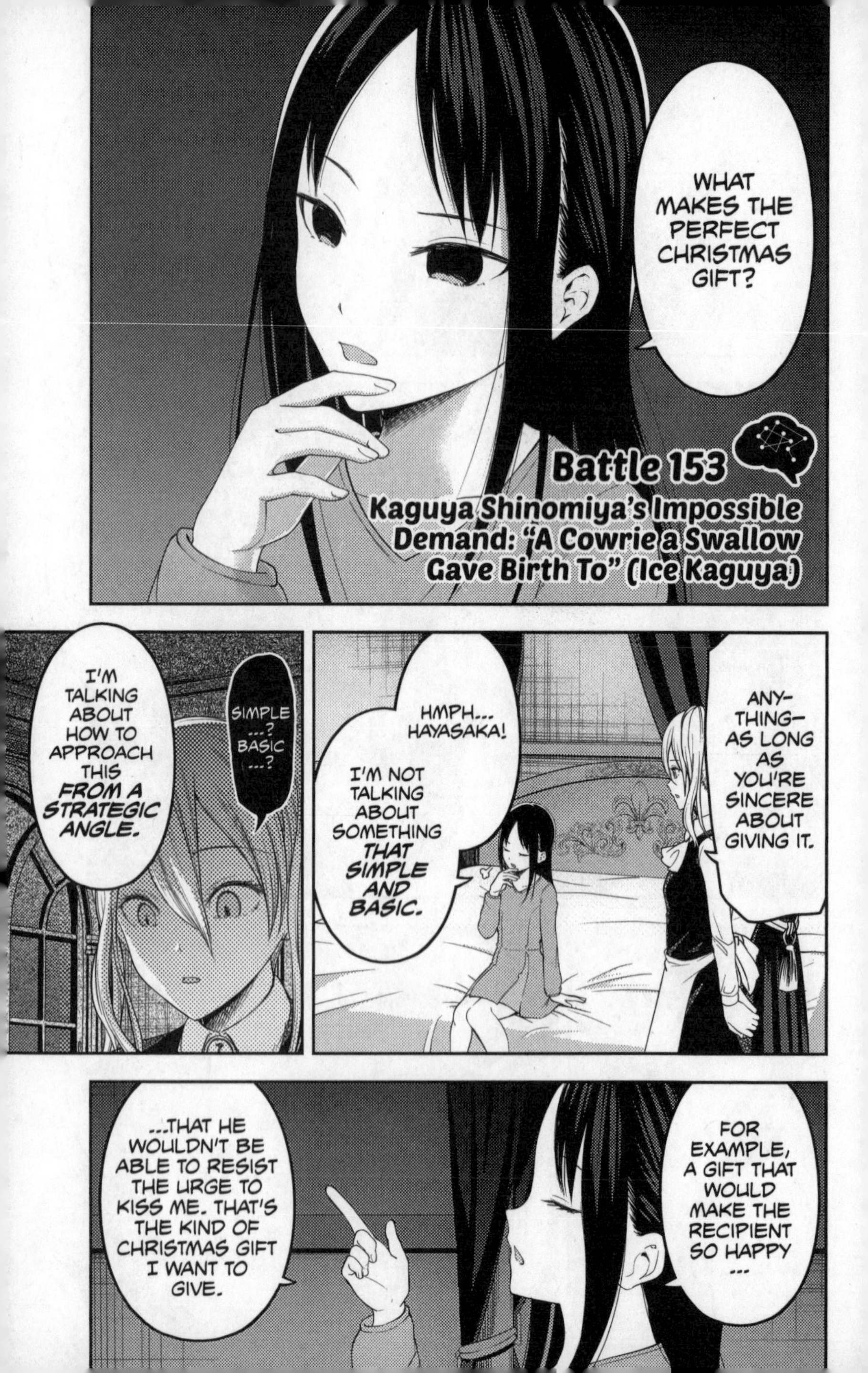
WHAT MAKES THE PERFECT CHRISTMAS GIFT?
Battle 153
Kaguya Shinomiya's Impossible Demand: "A Cowrie a Swallow Gave Birth To" (Ice Kaguya)
ANY-THING— AS LONG AS YOU'RE SINCERE ABOUT GIVING IT.
HMPH... HAYASAKA!
I'M NOT TALKING ABOUT SOMETHING ***THAT SIMPLE AND BASIC.***
SIMPLE ...? BASIC ...?
I'M TALKING ABOUT HOW TO APPROACH THIS ***FROM A STRATEGIC ANGLE.***
FOR EXAMPLE, A GIFT THAT WOULD MAKE THE RECIPIENT SO HAPPY ...
...THAT HE WOULDN'T BE ABLE TO RESIST THE URGE TO KISS ME. THAT'S THE KIND OF CHRISTMAS GIFT I WANT TO GIVE.

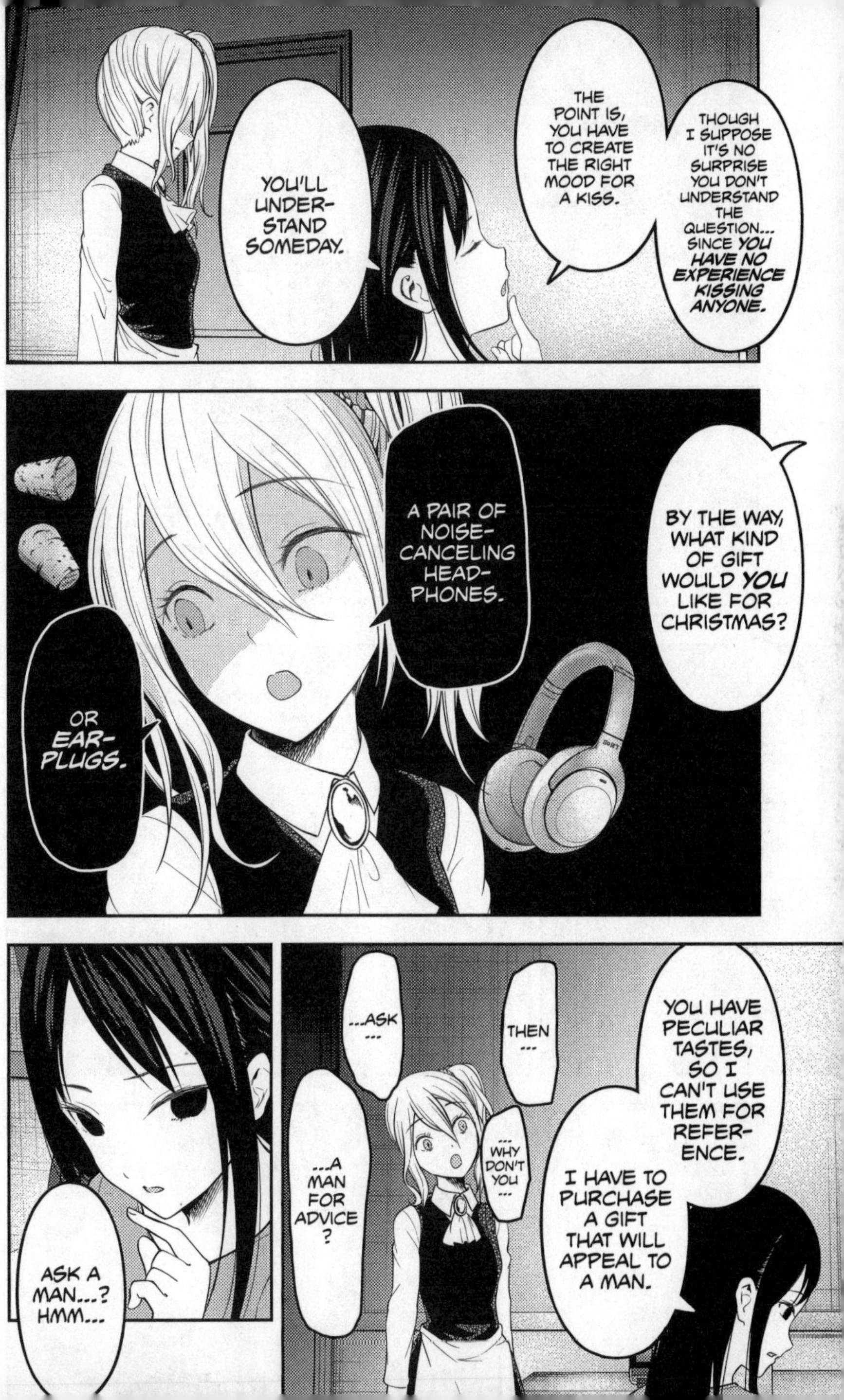
THOUGH I SUPPOSE IT'S NO SURPRISE YOU DON'T UNDERSTAND THE QUESTION... SINCE *YOU HAVE NO EXPERIENCE KISSING ANYONE.*
THE POINT IS, YOU HAVE TO CREATE THE RIGHT MOOD FOR A KISS.
YOU'LL UNDER-STAND SOMEDAY.
BY THE WAY, WHAT KIND OF GIFT WOULD *YOU* LIKE FOR CHRISTMAS?
A PAIR OF NOISE-CANCELING HEAD-PHONES.
OR *EAR-PLUGS.*
YOU HAVE PECULIAR TASTES, SO I CAN'T USE THEM FOR REFER-ENCE.
I HAVE TO PURCHASE A GIFT THAT WILL APPEAL TO A MAN.
THEN ...
...WHY DON'T YOU ...
...ASK ...
...A MAN FOR ADVICE ?
ASK A MAN...? HMM...

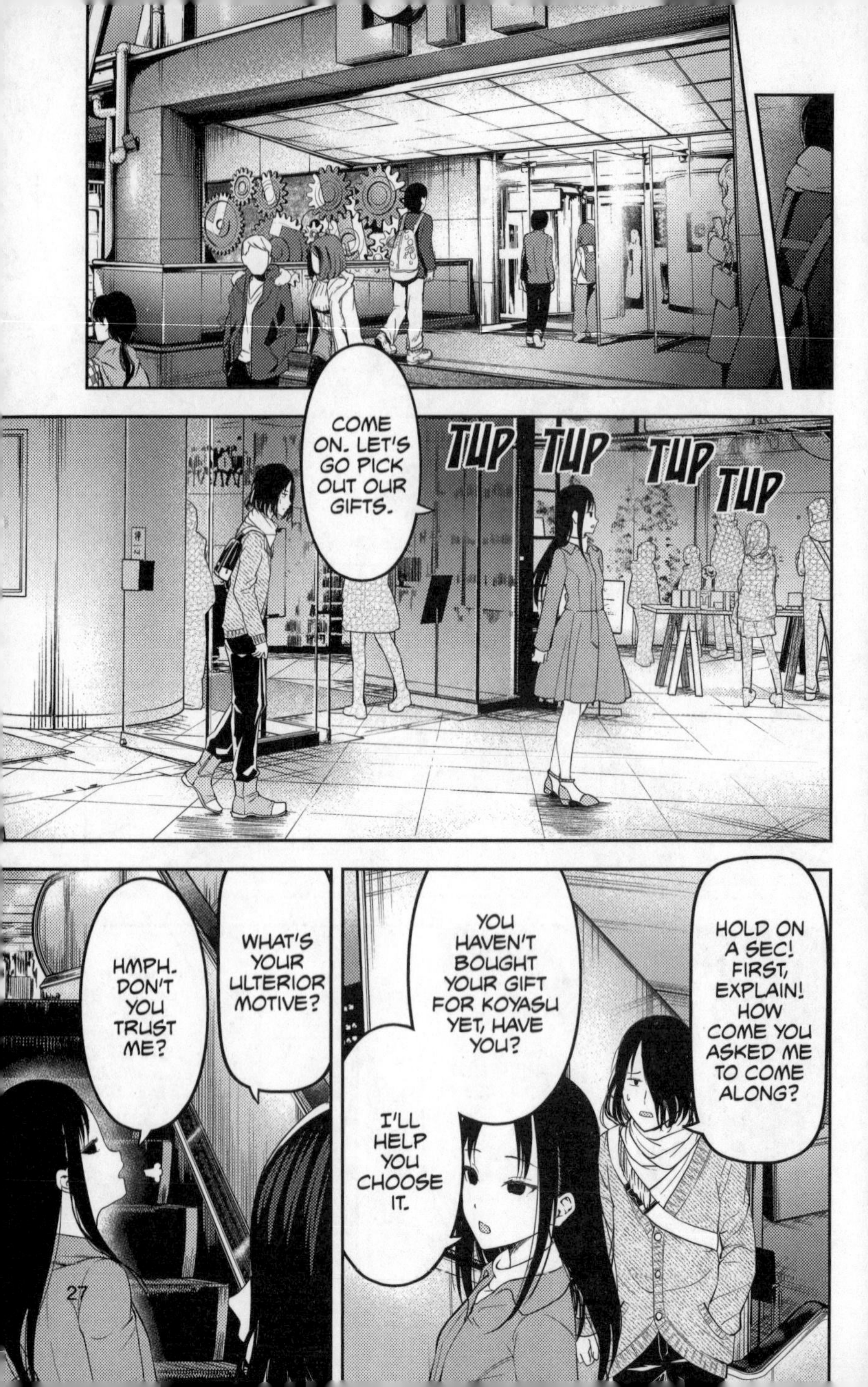
TUP TUP TUP TUP
COME ON. LET'S GO PICK OUT OUR GIFTS.
HOLD ON A SEC! FIRST, EXPLAIN! HOW COME YOU ASKED ME TO COME ALONG?
YOU HAVEN'T BOUGHT YOUR GIFT FOR KOYASU YET, HAVE YOU?
I'LL HELP YOU CHOOSE IT.
WHAT'S YOUR ULTERIOR MOTIVE?
HMPH. DON'T YOU TRUST ME?

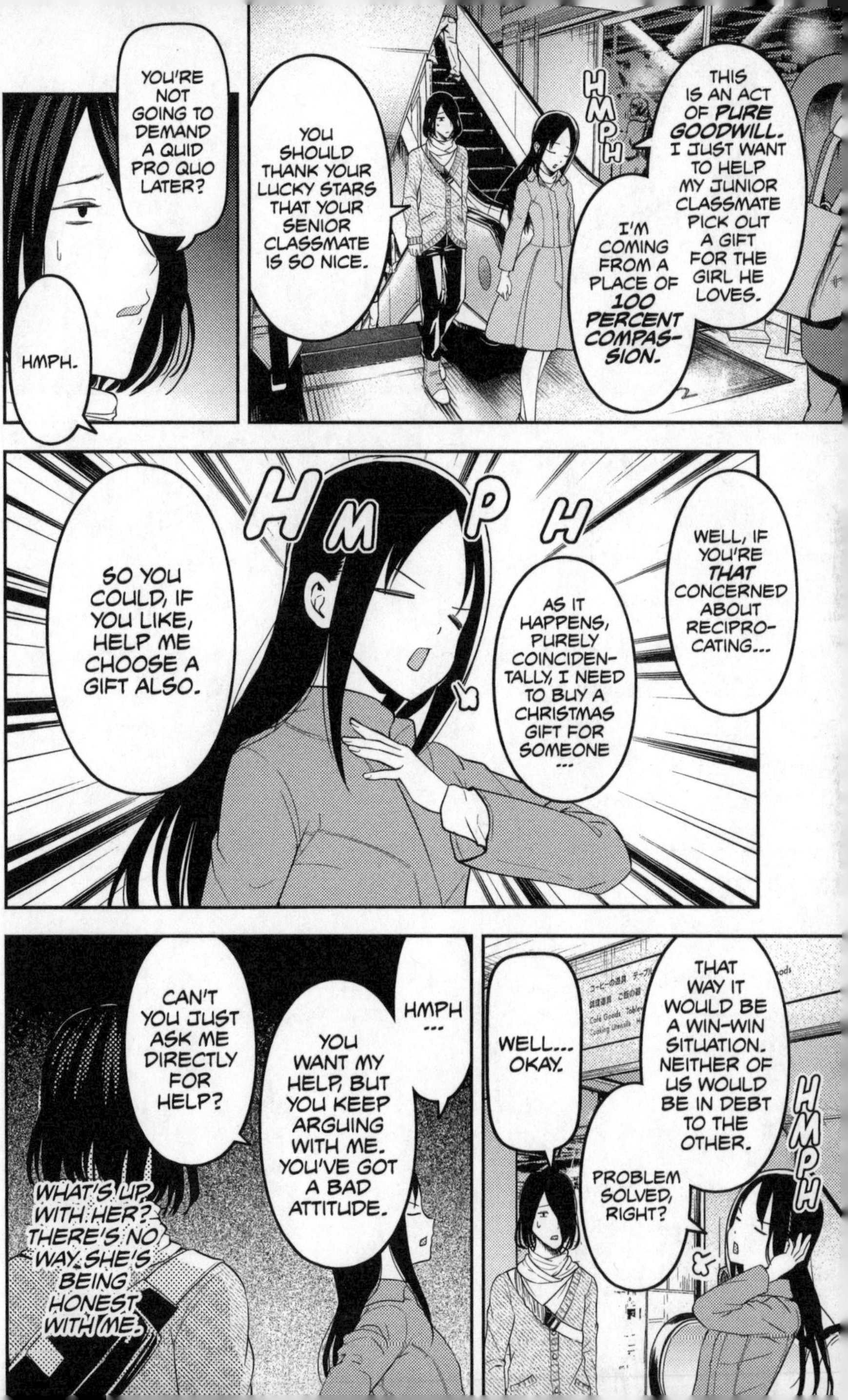
THIS IS AN ACT OF PURE GOODWILL. I JUST WANT TO HELP MY JUNIOR CLASSMATE PICK OUT A GIFT FOR THE GIRL HE LOVES.
I'M COMING FROM A PLACE OF 100 PERCENT COMPASSION.
HMPH
YOU SHOULD THANK YOUR LUCKY STARS THAT YOUR SENIOR CLASSMATE IS SO NICE.
YOU'RE NOT GOING TO DEMAND A QUID PRO QUO LATER?
HMPH.
WELL, IF YOU'RE THAT CONCERNED ABOUT RECIPROCATING...
AS IT HAPPENS, PURELY COINCIDENTALLY, I NEED TO BUY A CHRISTMAS GIFT FOR SOMEONE...
HMPH
SO YOU COULD, IF YOU LIKE, HELP ME CHOOSE A GIFT ALSO.
THAT WAY IT WOULD BE A WIN-WIN SITUATION. NEITHER OF US WOULD BE IN DEBT TO THE OTHER.
HMPH
PROBLEM SOLVED, RIGHT?
WELL... OKAY.
HMPH...
YOU WANT MY HELP, BUT YOU KEEP ARGUING WITH ME. YOU'VE GOT A BAD ATTITUDE.
CAN'T YOU JUST ASK ME DIRECTLY FOR HELP?
WHAT'S UP WITH HER? THERE'S NO WAY SHE'S BEING HONEST WITH ME.

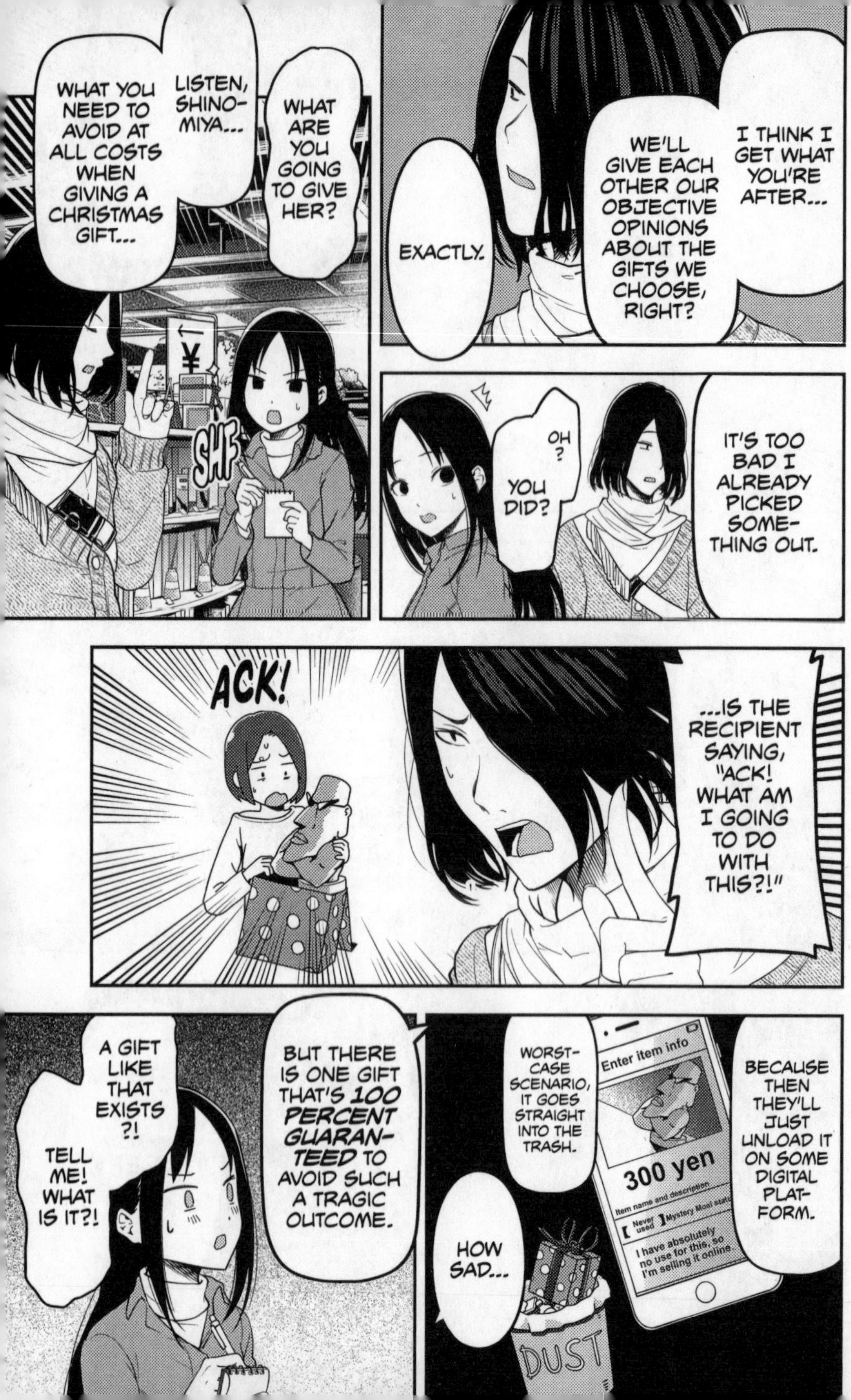
I THINK I GET WHAT YOU'RE AFTER...
WE'LL GIVE EACH OTHER OUR OBJECTIVE OPINIONS ABOUT THE GIFTS WE CHOOSE, RIGHT?
EXACTLY.
IT'S TOO BAD I ALREADY PICKED SOME-THING OUT.
OH? YOU DID?
WHAT ARE YOU GOING TO GIVE HER?
LISTEN, SHINO-MIYA...
WHAT YOU NEED TO AVOID AT ALL COSTS WHEN GIVING A CHRISTMAS GIFT...
SHF
...IS THE RECIPIENT SAYING, "ACK! WHAT AM I GOING TO DO WITH THIS?!"
ACK!
BECAUSE THEN THEY'LL JUST UNLOAD IT ON SOME DIGITAL PLAT-FORM.
Enter item info
300 yen
Item name and description
[Never used] Mystery Moai stat
I have absolutely no use for this, so I'm selling it online.
WORST-CASE SCENARIO, IT GOES STRAIGHT INTO THE TRASH.
HOW SAD...
DUST
BUT THERE IS ONE GIFT THAT'S 100 PERCENT GUARAN-TEED TO AVOID SUCH A TRAGIC OUTCOME.
A GIFT LIKE THAT EXISTS?!
TELL ME! WHAT IS IT?!

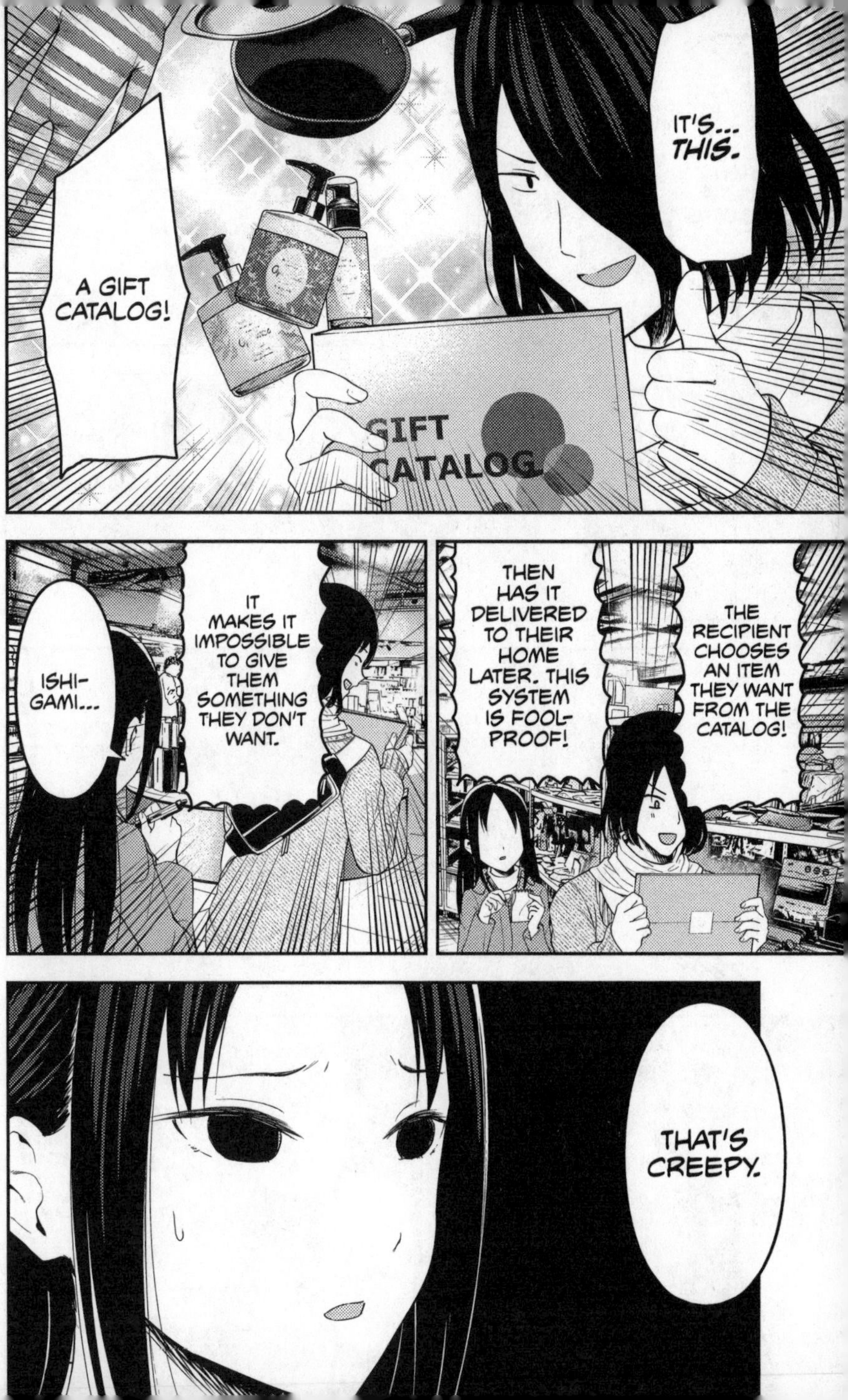

IT'S... THIS.
A GIFT CATALOG!
GIFT CATALOG
THE RECIPIENT CHOOSES AN ITEM THEY WANT FROM THE CATALOG!
THEN HAS IT DELIVERED TO THEIR HOME LATER. THIS SYSTEM IS FOOL-PROOF!
IT MAKES IT IMPOSSIBLE TO GIVE THEM SOMETHING THEY DON'T WANT.
ISHI-GAMI...
THAT'S CREEPY.

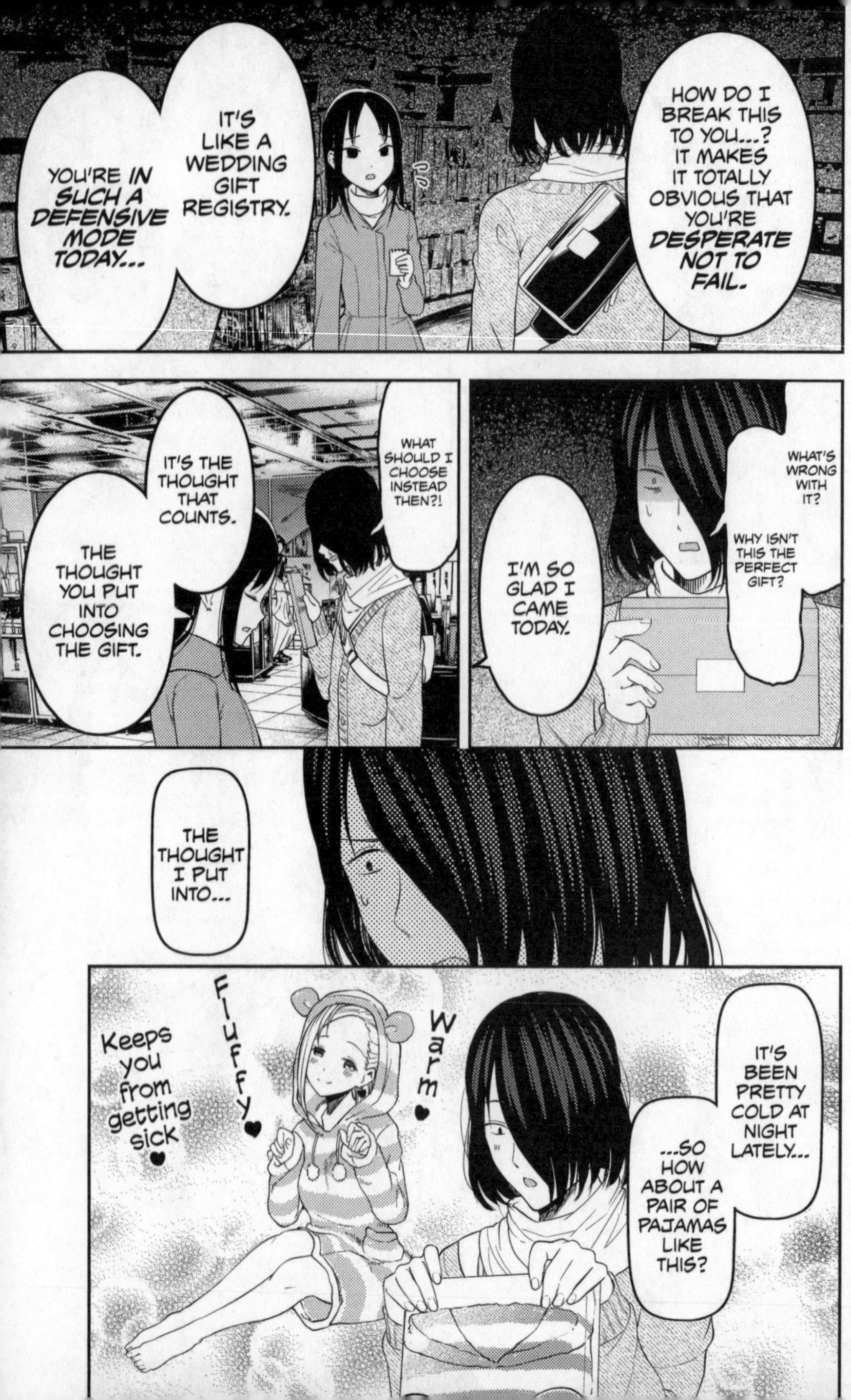
HOW DO I BREAK THIS TO YOU...? IT MAKES IT TOTALLY OBVIOUS THAT YOU'RE DESPERATE NOT TO FAIL.
IT'S LIKE A WEDDING GIFT REGISTRY.
YOU'RE IN SUCH A DEFENSIVE MODE TODAY...
WHAT'S WRONG WITH IT?
WHY ISN'T THIS THE PERFECT GIFT?
I'M SO GLAD I CAME TODAY.
WHAT SHOULD I CHOOSE INSTEAD THEN?!
IT'S THE THOUGHT THAT COUNTS.
THE THOUGHT YOU PUT INTO CHOOSING THE GIFT.
THE THOUGHT I PUT INTO...
IT'S BEEN PRETTY COLD AT NIGHT LATELY...
...SO HOW ABOUT A PAIR OF PAJAMAS LIKE THIS?
Warm
Fluffy
Keeps you from getting sick

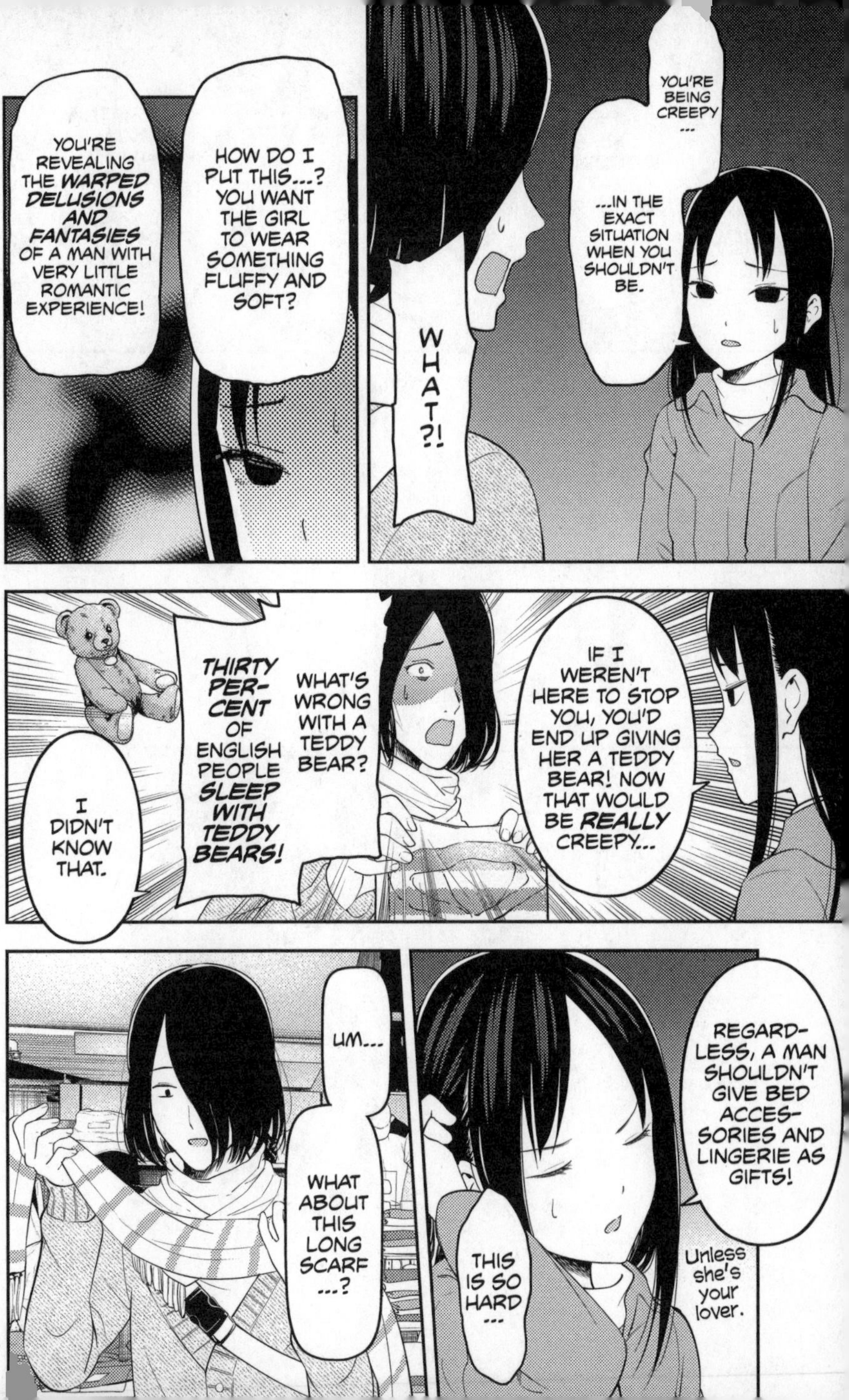
YOU'RE BEING CREEPY...
...IN THE EXACT SITUATION WHEN YOU SHOULDN'T BE.
WHAT?!
HOW DO I PUT THIS...? YOU WANT THE GIRL TO WEAR SOMETHING FLUFFY AND SOFT?
YOU'RE REVEALING THE WARPED DELUSIONS AND FANTASIES OF A MAN WITH VERY LITTLE ROMANTIC EXPERIENCE!
IF I WEREN'T HERE TO STOP YOU, YOU'D END UP GIVING HER A TEDDY BEAR! NOW THAT WOULD BE REALLY CREEPY...
WHAT'S WRONG WITH A TEDDY BEAR?
THIRTY PERCENT OF ENGLISH PEOPLE SLEEP WITH TEDDY BEARS!
I DIDN'T KNOW THAT.
REGARDLESS, A MAN SHOULDN'T GIVE BED ACCESSORIES AND LINGERIE AS GIFTS!
Unless she's your lover.
THIS IS SO HARD...
UM...
WHAT ABOUT THIS LONG SCARF...?

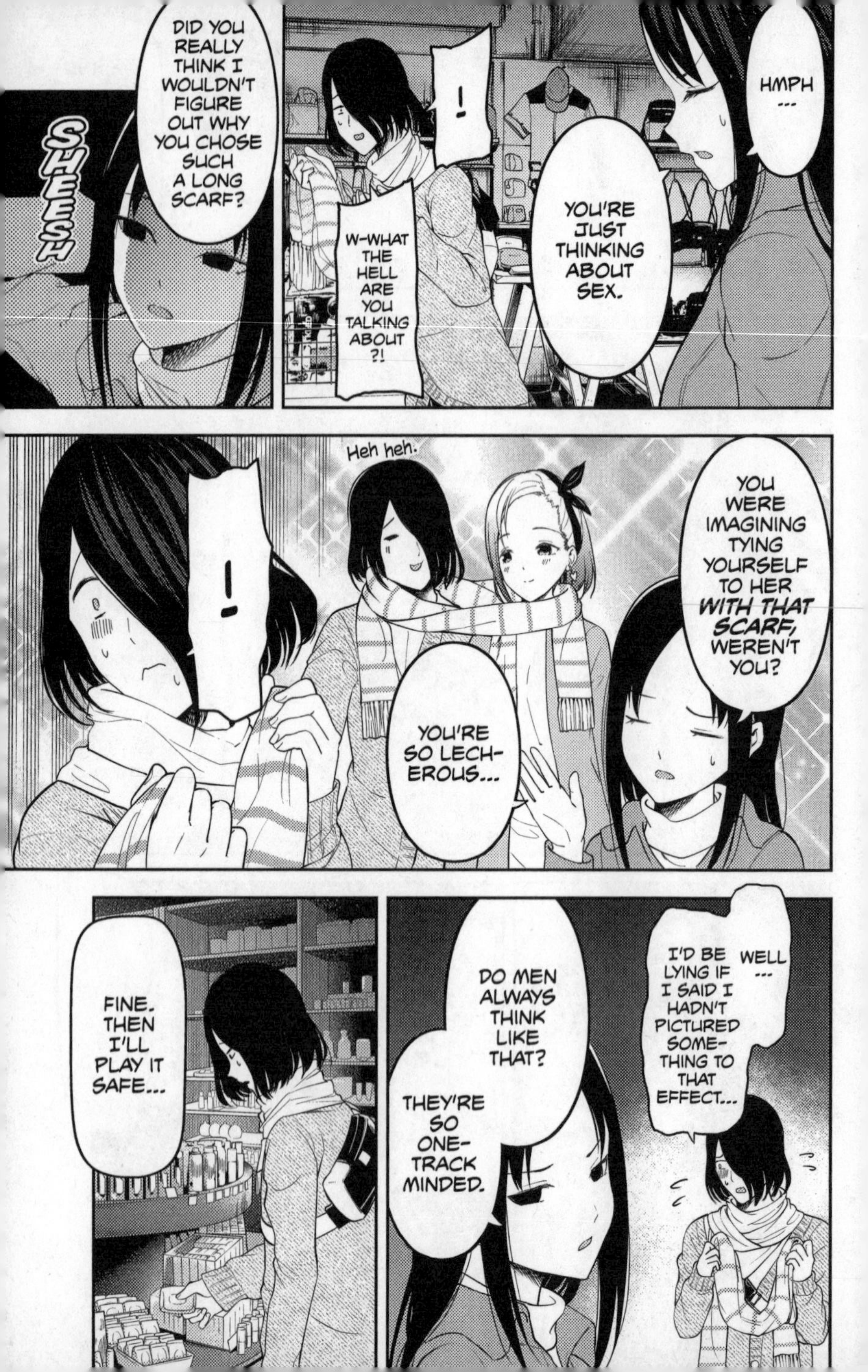
HMPH ---
YOU'RE JUST THINKING ABOUT SEX.
!
W-WHAT THE HELL ARE YOU TALKING ABOUT?!
SHEESH
DID YOU REALLY THINK I WOULDN'T FIGURE OUT WHY YOU CHOSE SUCH A LONG SCARF?
YOU WERE IMAGINING TYING YOURSELF TO HER *WITH THAT SCARF,* WEREN'T YOU?
Heh heh.
YOU'RE SO LECH-EROUS...
!
WELL ---
I'D BE LYING IF I SAID I HADN'T PICTURED SOME-THING TO THAT EFFECT...
DO MEN ALWAYS THINK LIKE THAT?
THEY'RE SO ONE-TRACK MINDED.
FINE. THEN I'LL PLAY IT SAFE...

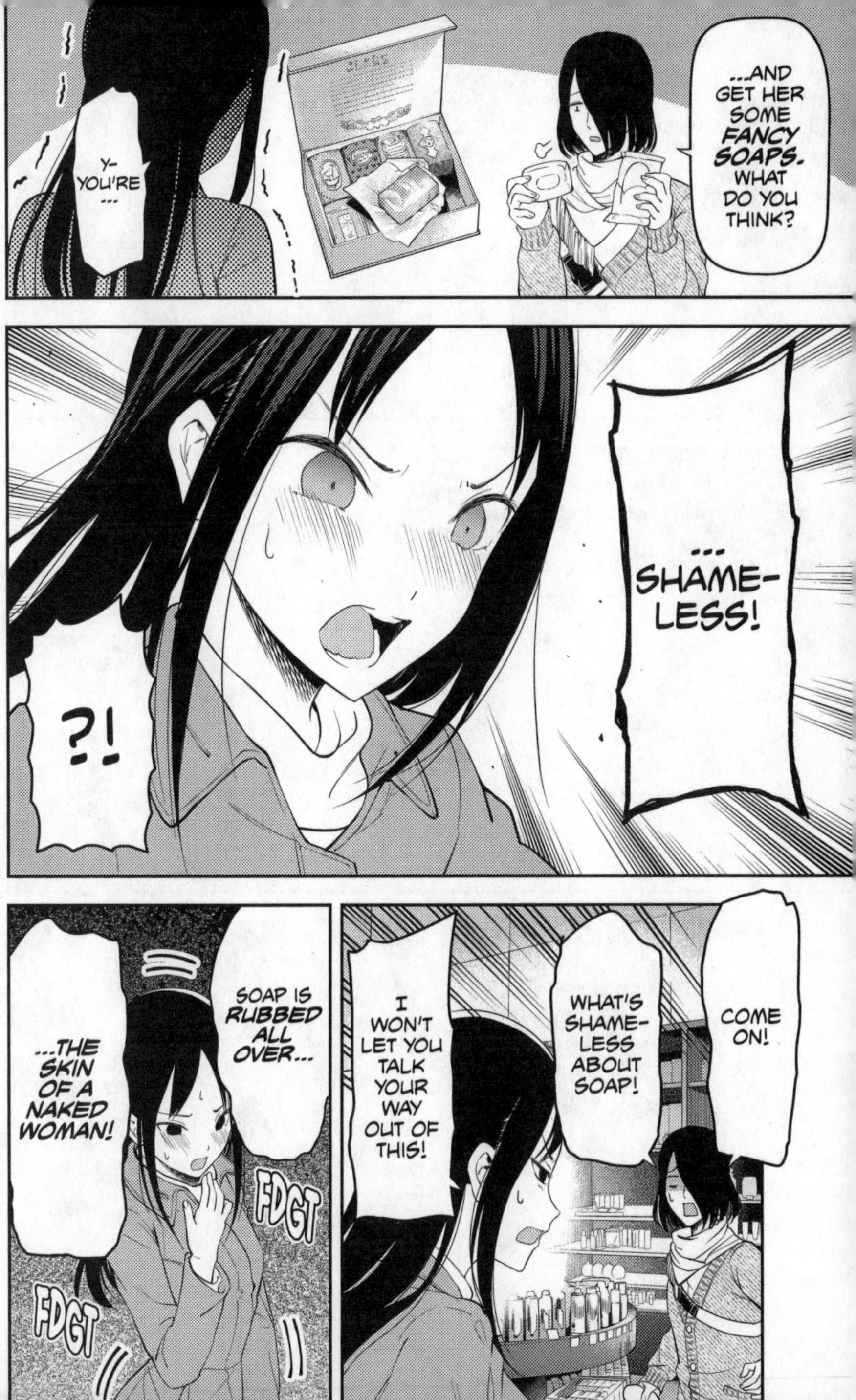
...AND GET HER SOME FANCY SOAPS. WHAT DO YOU THINK?
Y- YOU'RE ...
... SHAME-LESS!
?!
COME ON!
WHAT'S SHAME-LESS ABOUT SOAP!
I WON'T LET YOU TALK YOUR WAY OUT OF THIS!
SOAP IS RUBBED ALL OVER...
...THE SKIN OF A NAKED WOMAN!
FDGT
FDGT

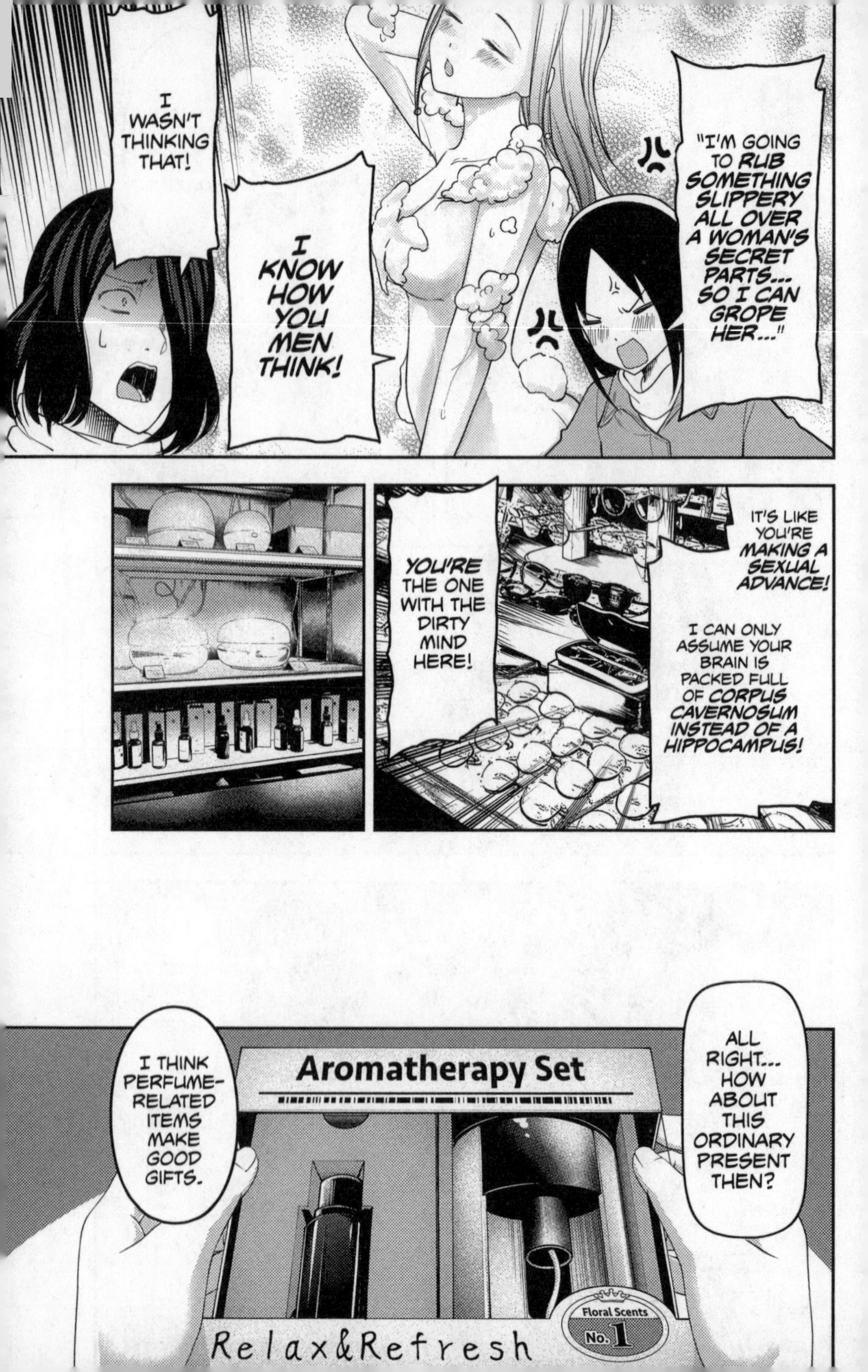
"I'M GOING TO RUB SOMETHING SLIPPERY ALL OVER A WOMAN'S SECRET PARTS... SO I CAN GROPE HER..."
I KNOW HOW YOU MEN THINK!
I WASN'T THINKING THAT!
IT'S LIKE YOU'RE MAKING A SEXUAL ADVANCE!
I CAN ONLY ASSUME YOUR BRAIN IS PACKED FULL OF CORPUS CAVERNOSUM INSTEAD OF A HIPPOCAMPUS!
YOU'RE THE ONE WITH THE DIRTY MIND HERE!
ALL RIGHT... HOW ABOUT THIS ORDINARY PRESENT THEN?
Aromatherapy Set
I THINK PERFUME-RELATED ITEMS MAKE GOOD GIFTS.
Floral Scents
No. 1
Relax&Refresh

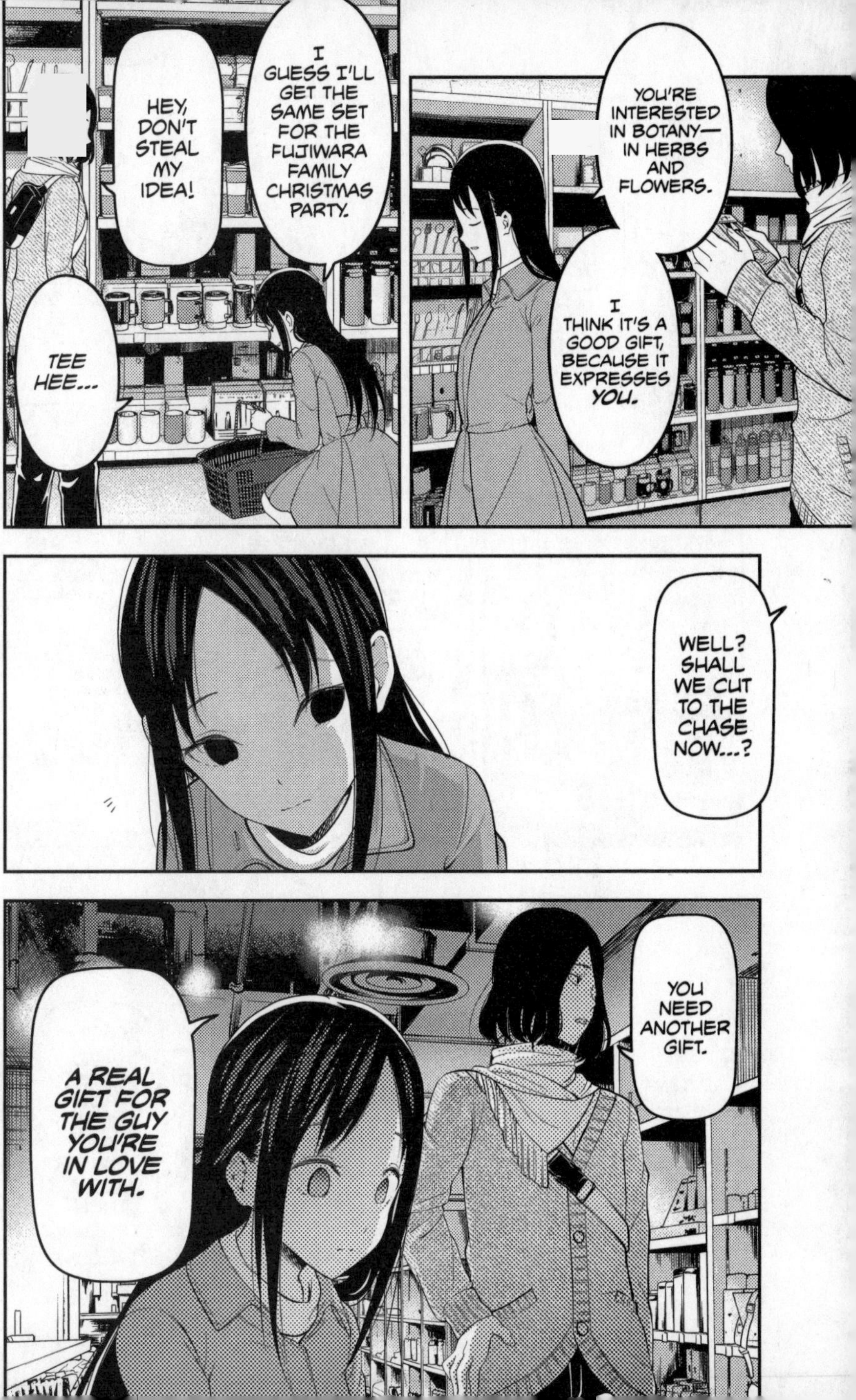
YOU'RE INTERESTED IN BOTANY—IN HERBS AND FLOWERS.
I THINK IT'S A GOOD GIFT, BECAUSE IT EXPRESSES *YOU*.
I GUESS I'LL GET THE SAME SET FOR THE FUJIWARA FAMILY CHRISTMAS PARTY.
HEY, DON'T STEAL MY IDEA!
TEE HEE...
WELL? SHALL WE CUT TO THE CHASE NOW...?
YOU NEED ANOTHER GIFT.
A REAL GIFT FOR THE GUY YOU'RE IN LOVE WITH.

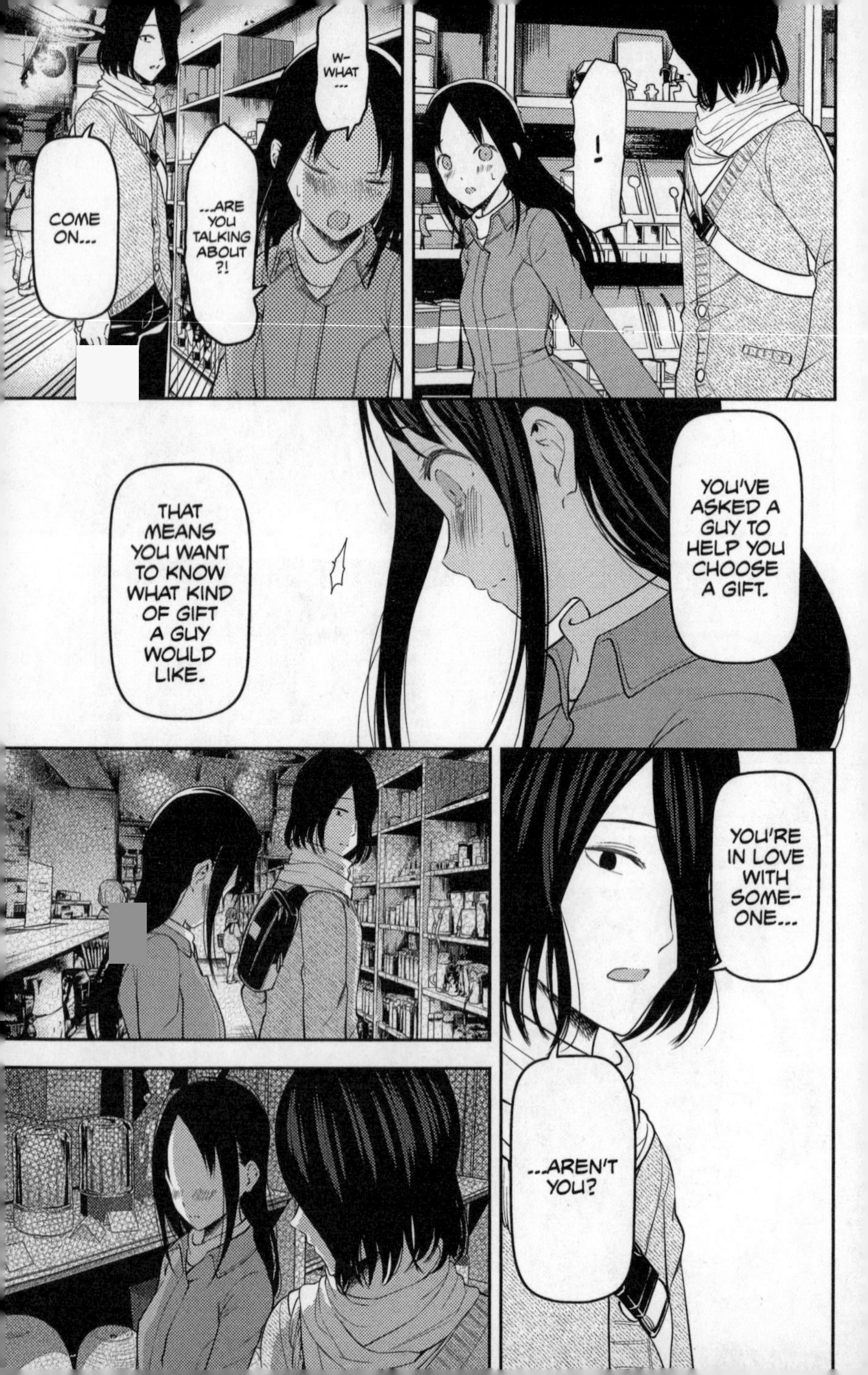
!
W-WHAT...
...ARE YOU TALKING ABOUT?!
COME ON...
YOU'VE ASKED A GUY TO HELP YOU CHOOSE A GIFT.
THAT MEANS YOU WANT TO KNOW WHAT KIND OF GIFT A GUY WOULD LIKE.
YOU'RE IN LOVE WITH SOMEONE...
...AREN'T YOU?

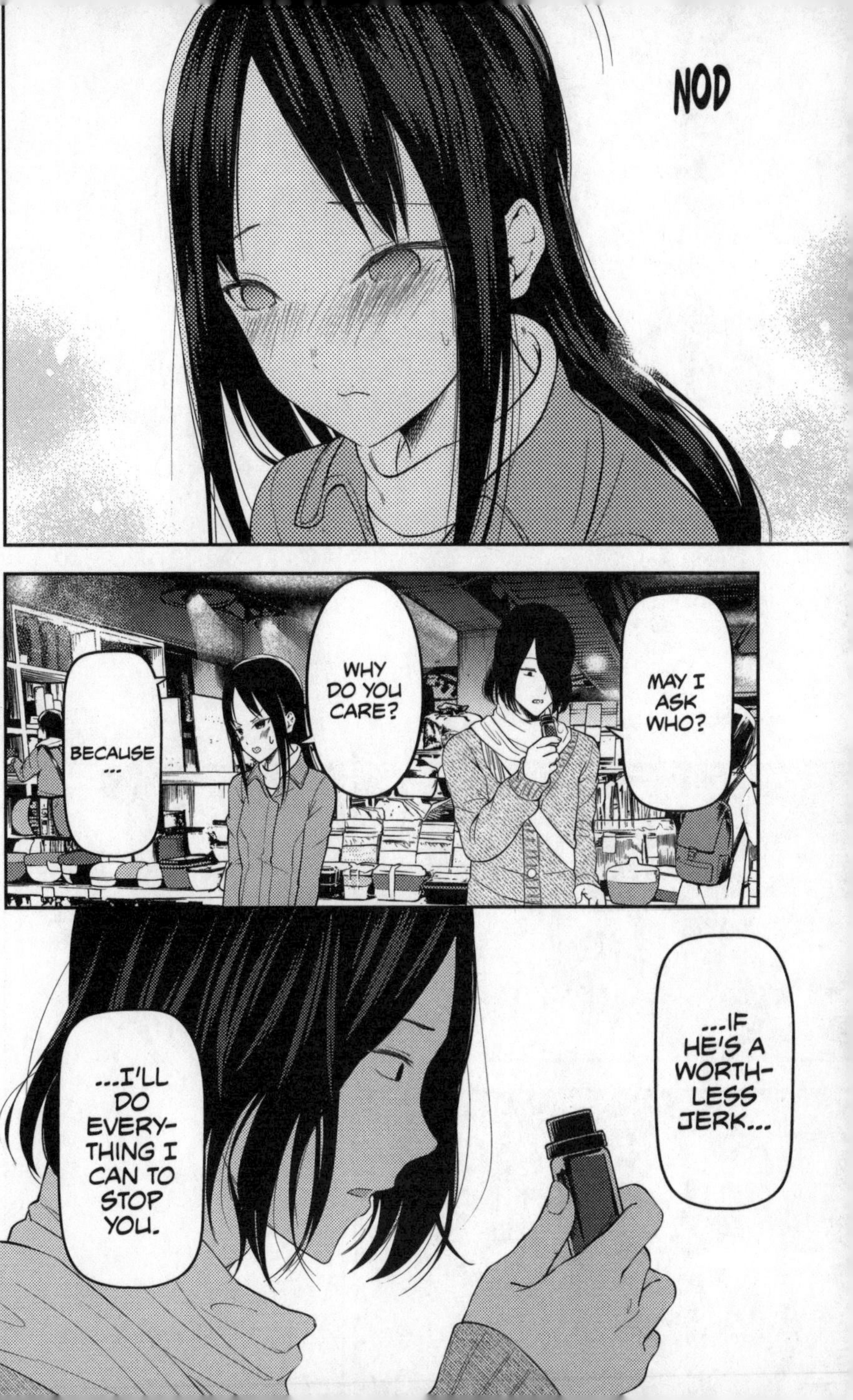
NOD
MAY I ASK WHO?
WHY DO YOU CARE?
BECAUSE...
...IF HE'S A WORTHLESS JERK...
...I'LL DO EVERYTHING I CAN TO STOP YOU.

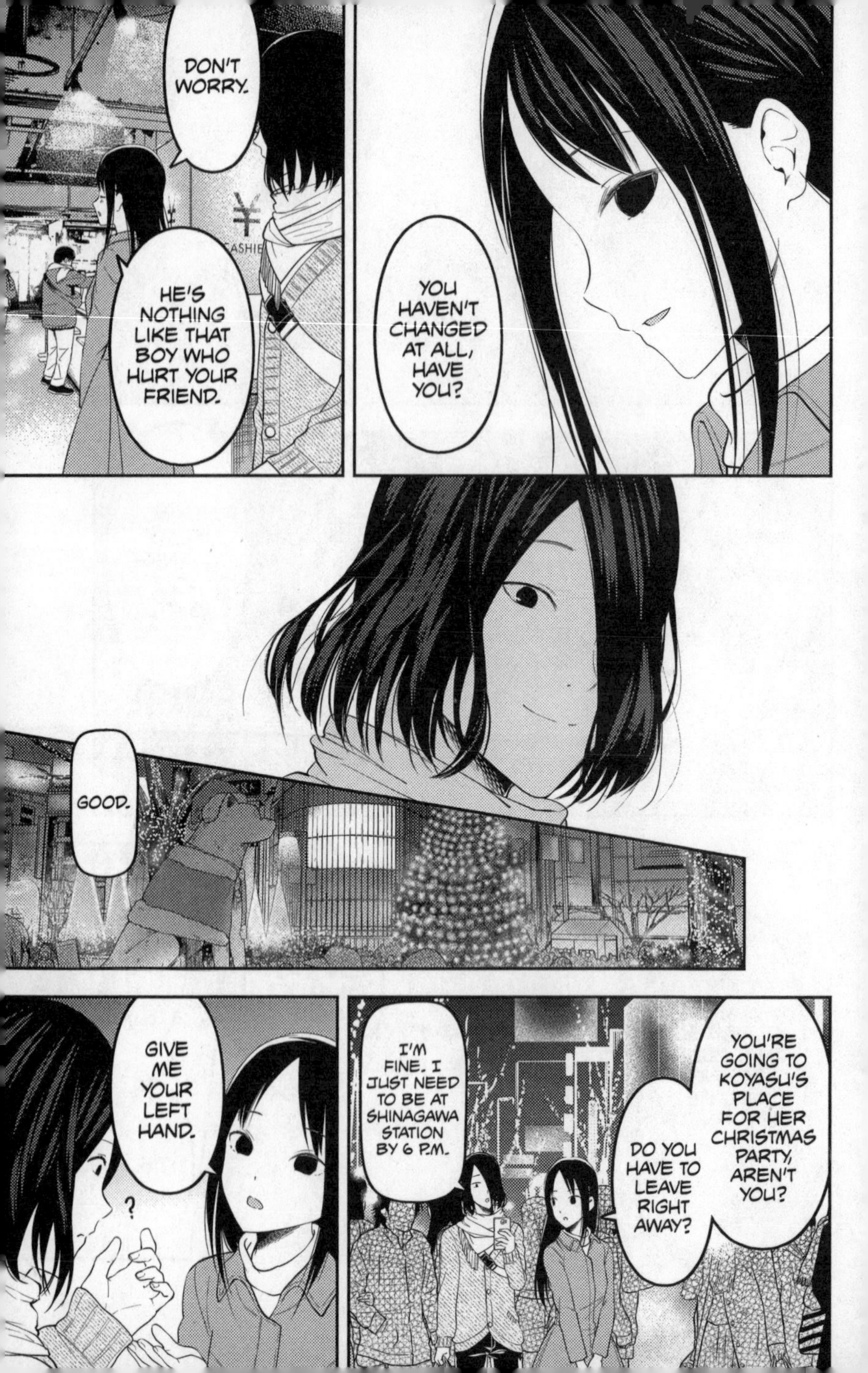
YOU HAVEN'T CHANGED AT ALL, HAVE YOU?
DON'T WORRY.
HE'S NOTHING LIKE THAT BOY WHO HURT YOUR FRIEND.
GOOD.
YOU'RE GOING TO KOYASU'S PLACE FOR HER CHRISTMAS PARTY, AREN'T YOU?
DO YOU HAVE TO LEAVE RIGHT AWAY?
I'M FINE. I JUST NEED TO BE AT SHINAGAWA STATION BY 6 P.M.
GIVE ME YOUR LEFT HAND.
?

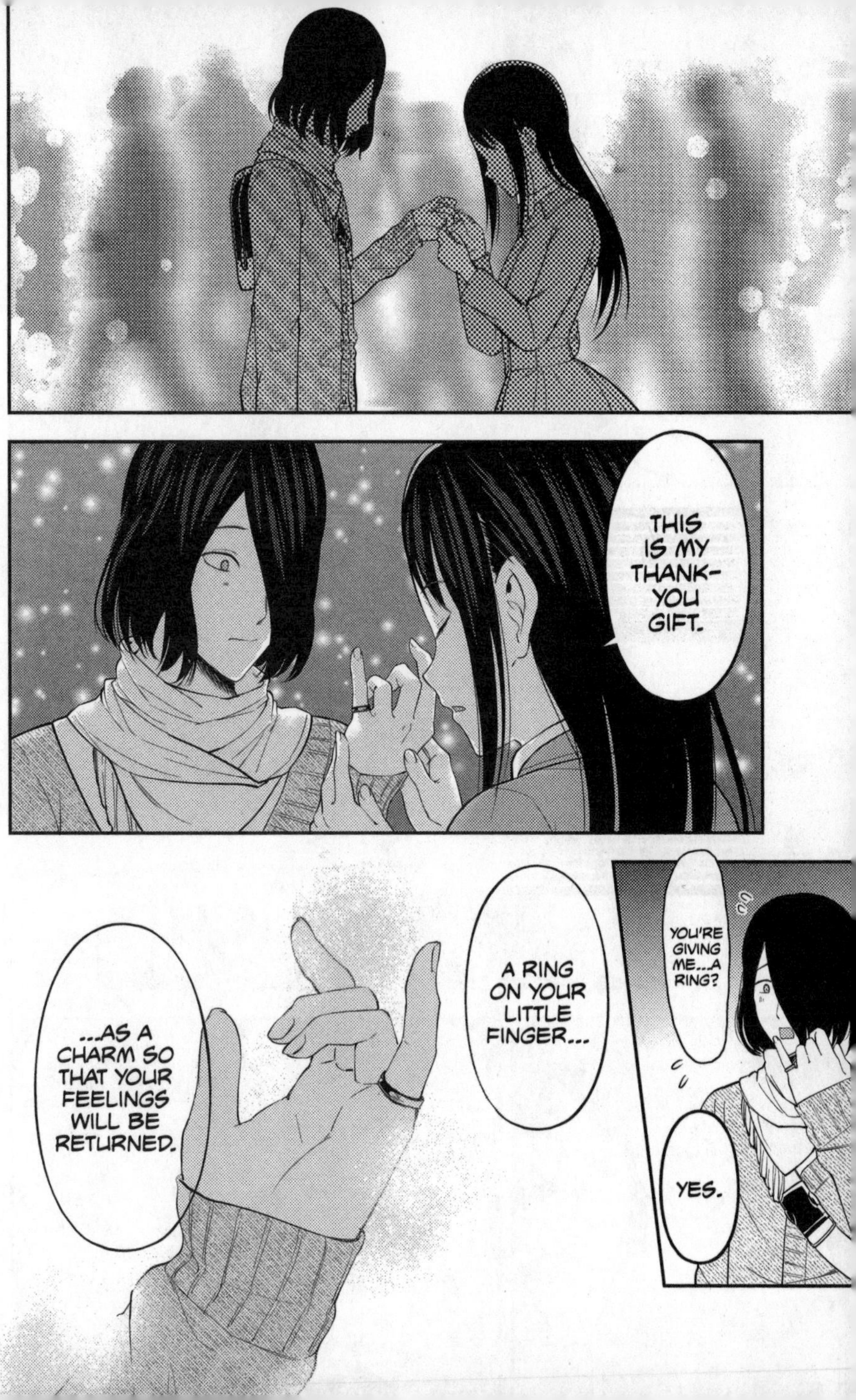
THIS IS MY THANK-YOU GIFT.
YOU'RE GIVING ME...A RING?
YES.
A RING ON YOUR LITTLE FINGER...
...AS A CHARM SO THAT YOUR FEELINGS WILL BE RETURNED.

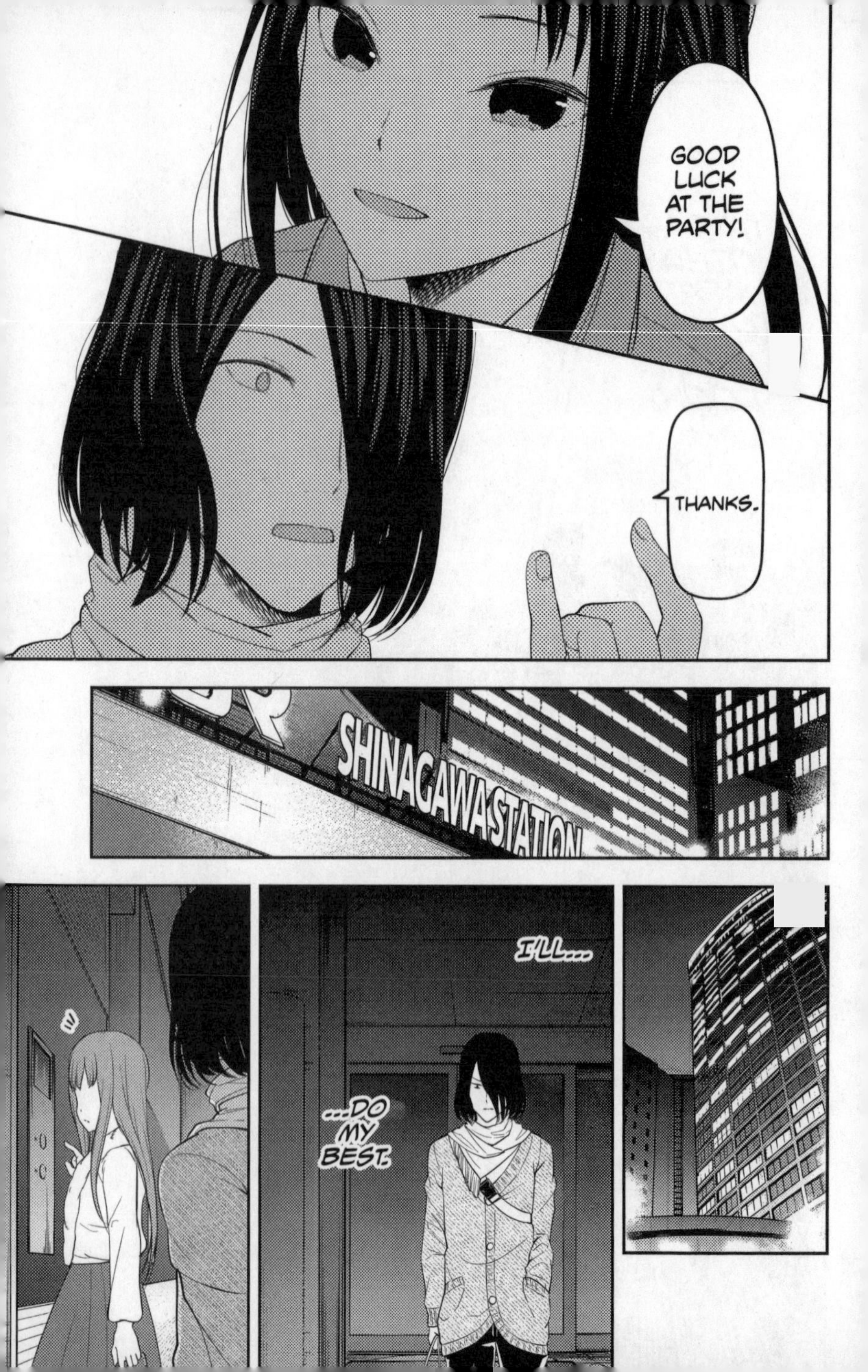
GOOD LUCK AT THE PARTY!
THANKS.
SHINAGAWA STATION
I'LL...
...DO MY BEST.
!!

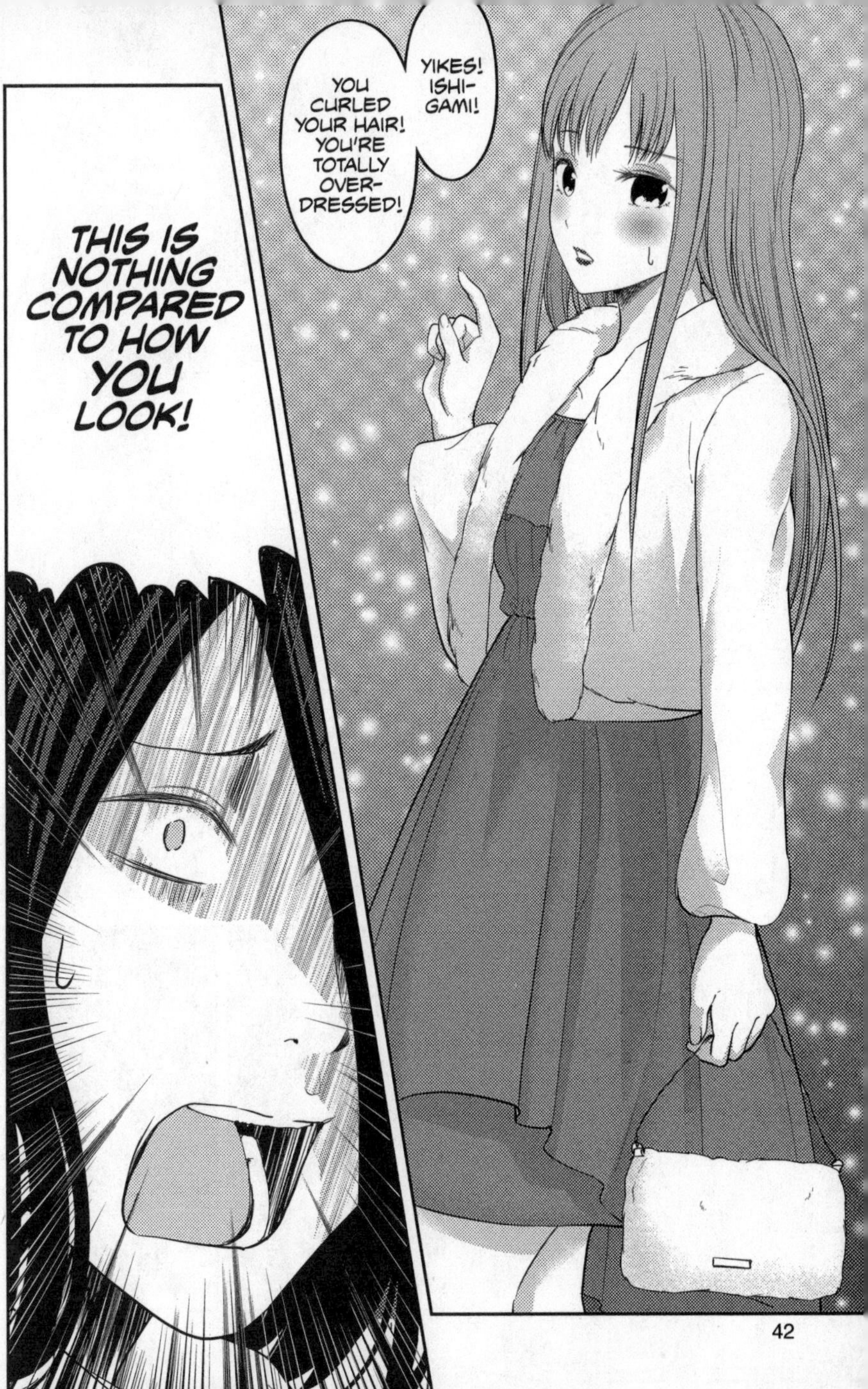
YIKES! ISHI-GAMI!
YOU CURLED YOUR HAIR! YOU'RE TOTALLY OVER-DRESSED!
THIS IS NOTHING COMPARED TO HOW YOU LOOK!

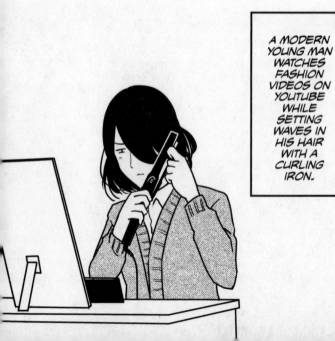

A MODERN YOUNG MAN WATCHES FASHION VIDEOS ON YOUTUBE WHILE SETTING WAVES IN HIS HAIR WITH A CURLING IRON.

KAGUYA-SAMA
LOVE IS WAR

Battle 154
Kaguya Shinomiya's Impossible Demand: "A Cowrie a Swallow Gave Birth To," Part 2

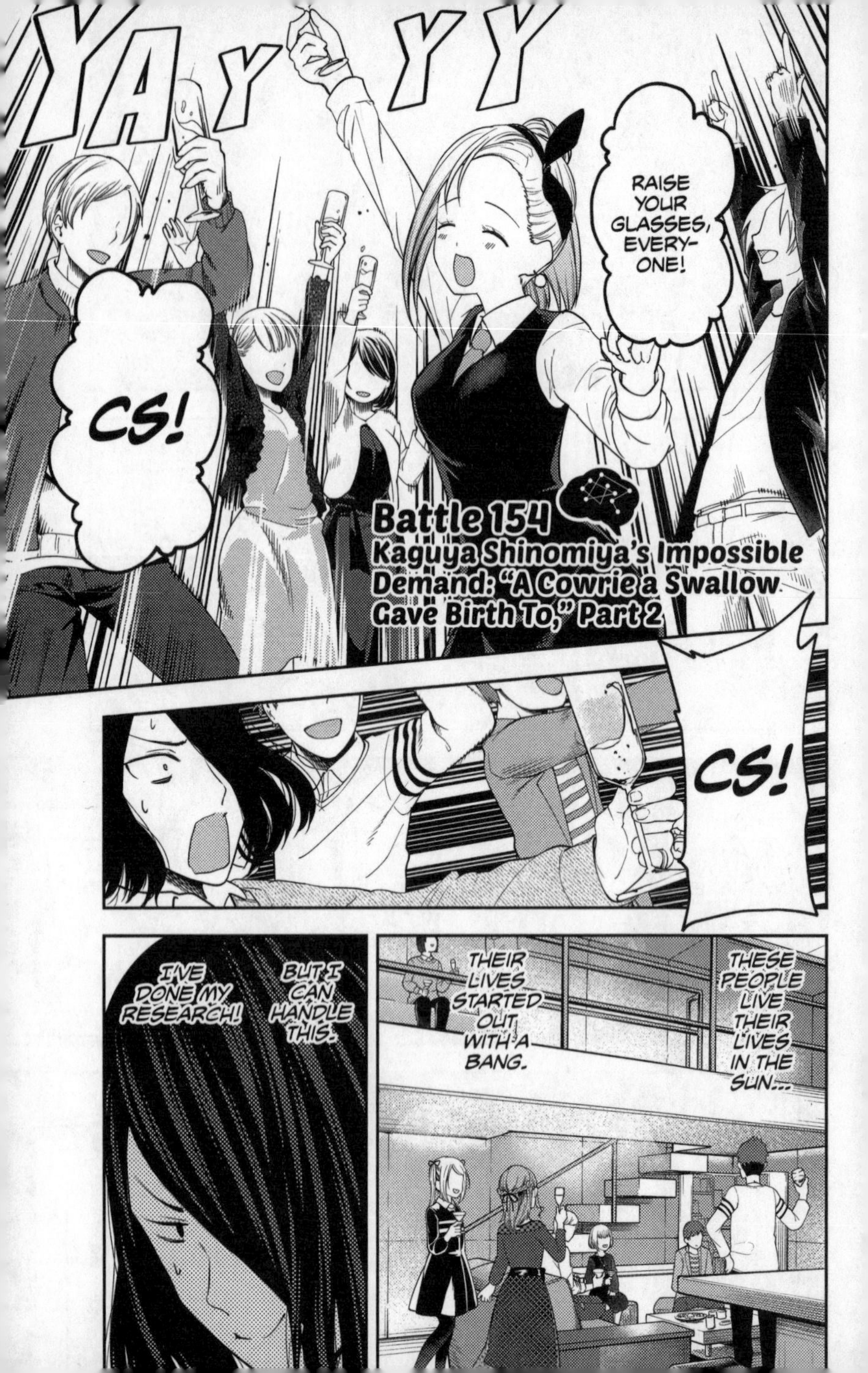
YAYYY
RAISE YOUR GLASSES, EVERYONE!
CS!
CS!
THESE PEOPLE LIVE THEIR LIVES IN THE SUN...
THEIR LIVES STARTED OUT WITH A BANG.
BUT I CAN HANDLE THIS.
I'VE DONE MY RESEARCH!

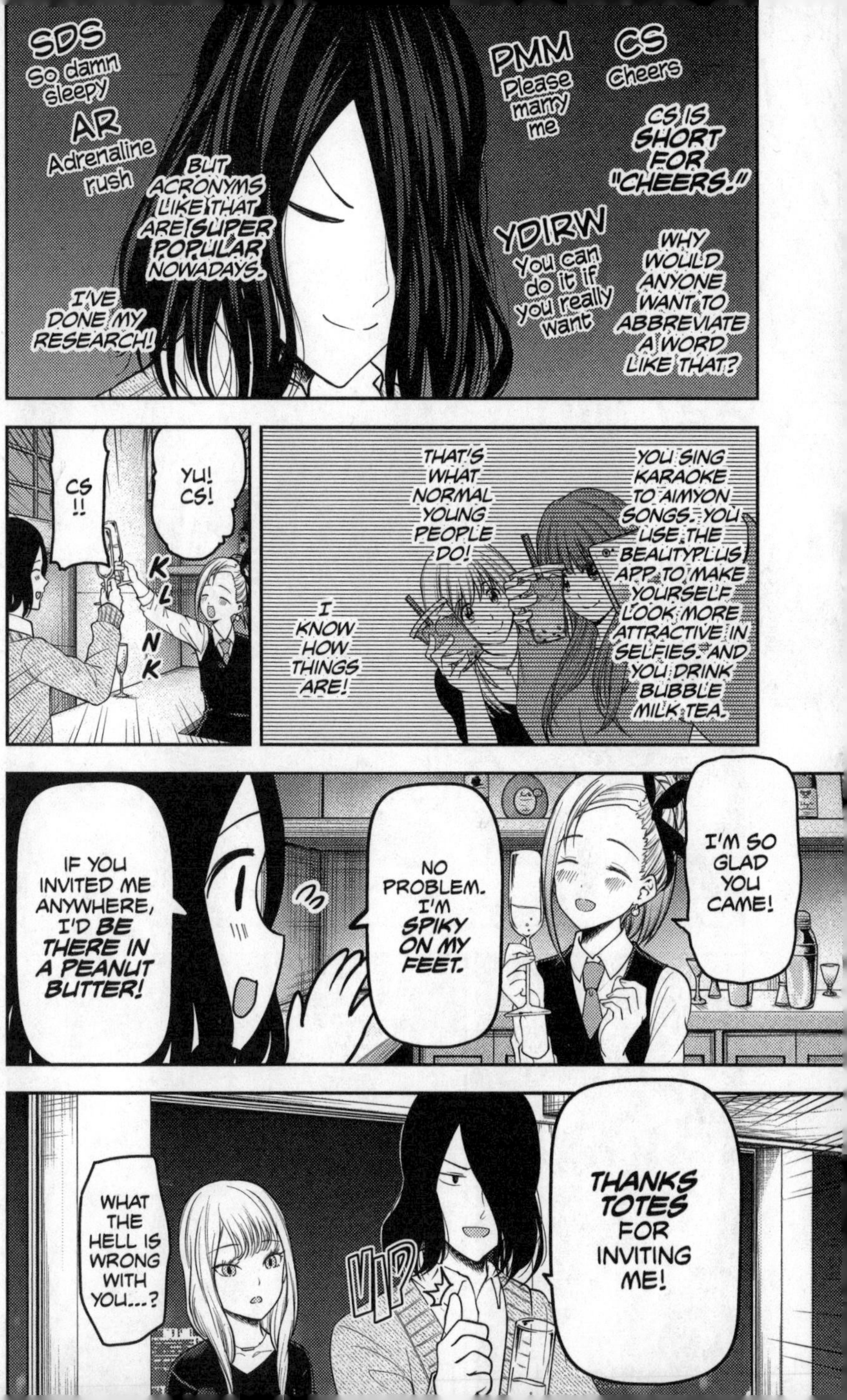
CS
Cheers
PMM
Please marry me
SDS
So damn sleepy
AR
Adrenaline rush
YDIRW
You can do it if you really want
CS IS SHORT FOR "CHEERS."
WHY WOULD ANYONE WANT TO ABBREVIATE A WORD LIKE THAT?
BUT ACRONYMS LIKE THAT ARE SUPER POPULAR NOWADAYS.
I'VE DONE MY RESEARCH!
YOU SING KARAOKE TO AIMYON SONGS. YOU USE THE BEAUTYPLUS APP TO MAKE YOURSELF LOOK MORE ATTRACTIVE IN SELFIES. AND YOU DRINK BUBBLE MILK TEA.
THAT'S WHAT NORMAL YOUNG PEOPLE DO!
I KNOW HOW THINGS ARE!
YU! CS!
CS !!
KLNK
I'M SO GLAD YOU CAME!
NO PROBLEM. I'M SPIKY ON MY FEET.
IF YOU INVITED ME ANYWHERE, I'D BE THERE IN A PEANUT BUTTER!
THANKS TOTES FOR INVITING ME!
WHAT THE HELL IS WRONG WITH YOU...?

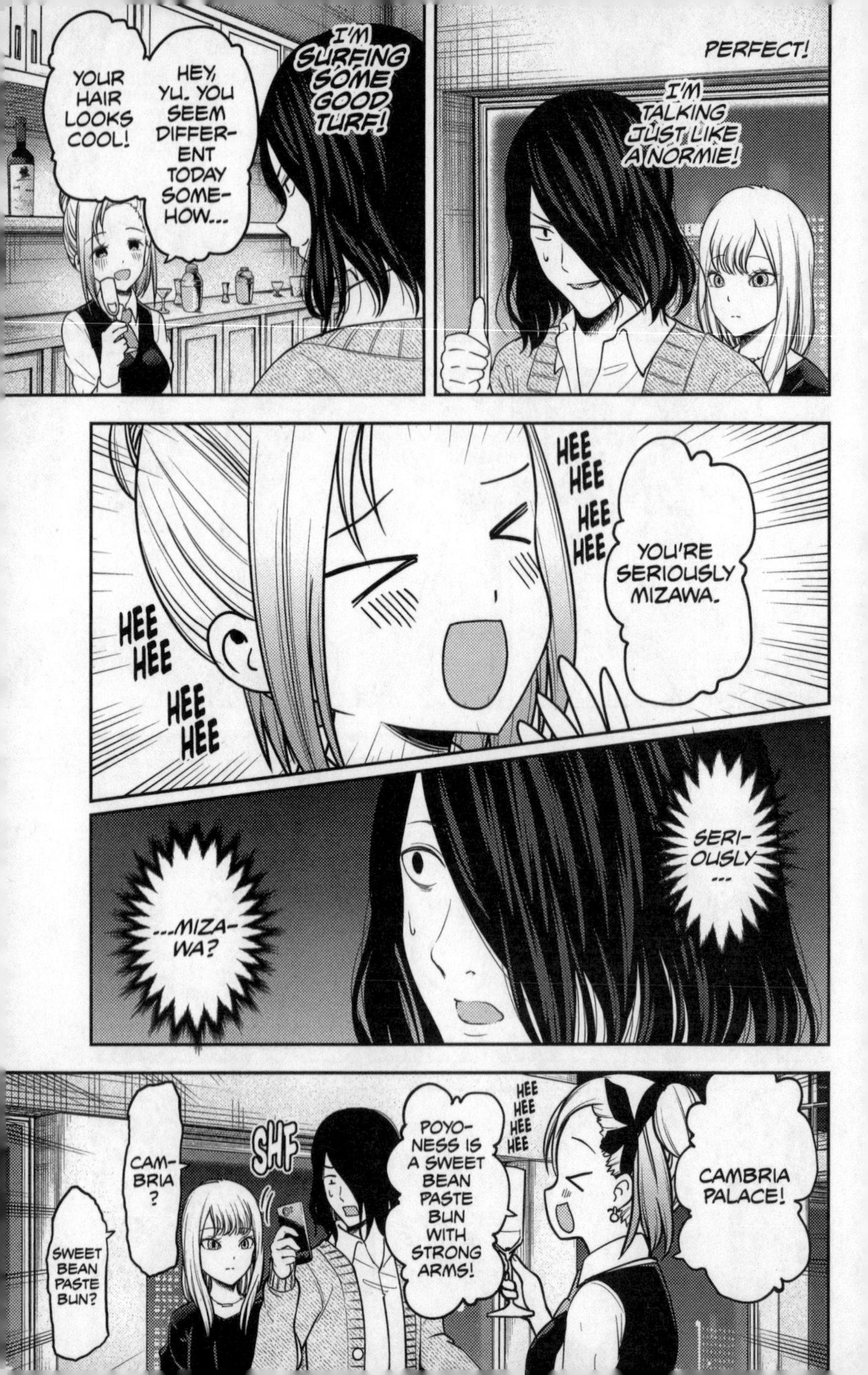
PERFECT!
I'M TALKING JUST LIKE A NORMIE!
I'M SURFING SOME GOOD TURF!
HEY, YU. YOU SEEM DIFFERENT TODAY SOMEHOW...
YOUR HAIR LOOKS COOL!
HEE HEE HEE HEE
YOU'RE SERIOUSLY MIZAWA.
HEE HEE HEE HEE
SERIOUSLY...
...MIZAWA?
CAMBRIA PALACE!
HEE HEE HEE HEE
POYONESS IS A SWEET BEAN PASTE BUN WITH STRONG ARMS!
SHF
CAMBRIA?
SWEET BEAN PASTE BUN?

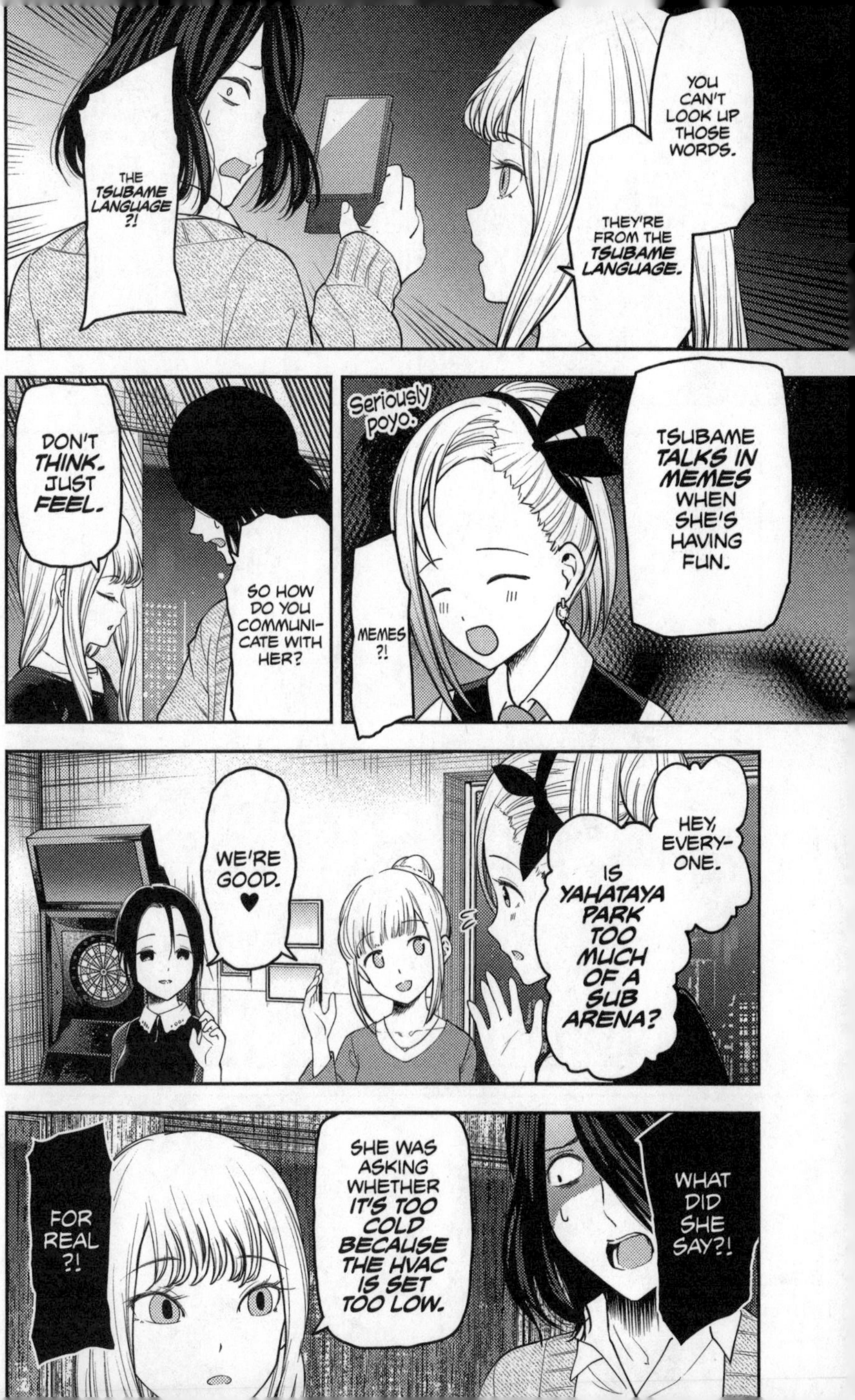
YOU CAN'T LOOK UP THOSE WORDS.
THEY'RE FROM THE TSUBAME LANGUAGE.
THE TSUBAME LANGUAGE?!
TSUBAME TALKS IN MEMES WHEN SHE'S HAVING FUN.
Seriously poyo.
MEMES?!
SO HOW DO YOU COMMUNICATE WITH HER?
DON'T THINK. JUST FEEL.
HEY, EVERYONE.
IS YAHATAYA PARK TOO MUCH OF A SUB ARENA?
WE'RE GOOD. ♥
WHAT DID SHE SAY?!
SHE WAS ASKING WHETHER IT'S TOO COLD BECAUSE THE HVAC IS SET TOO LOW.
FOR REAL?!

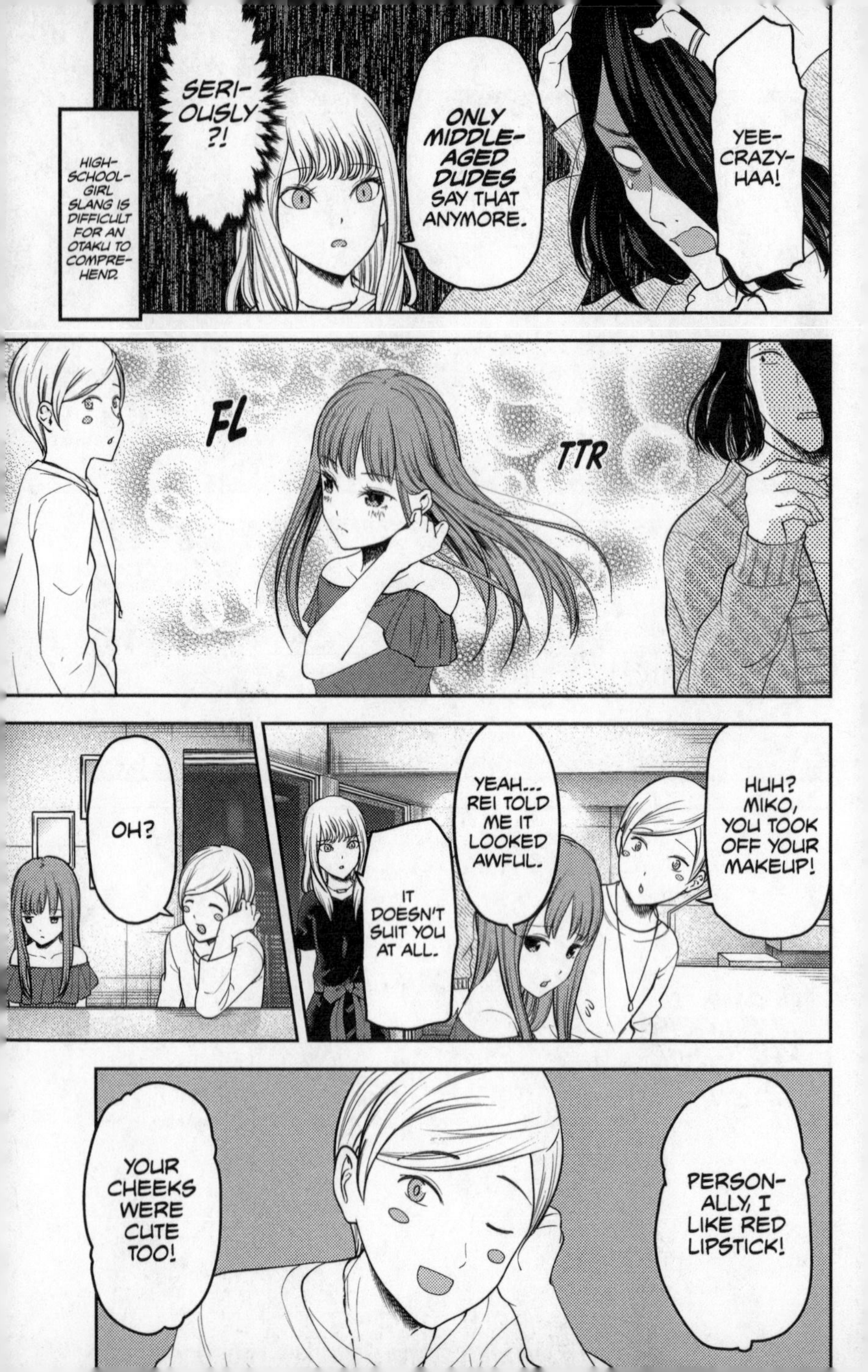
YEE-CRAZY-HAA!
ONLY MIDDLE-AGED DUDES SAY THAT ANYMORE.
SERI-OUSLY?!
HIGH-SCHOOL-GIRL SLANG IS DIFFICULT FOR AN OTAKU TO COMPREHEND.
FL
TTR
HUH? MIKO, YOU TOOK OFF YOUR MAKEUP!
YEAH... REI TOLD ME IT LOOKED AWFUL.
IT DOESN'T SUIT YOU AT ALL.
OH?
PERSON-ALLY, I LIKE RED LIPSTICK!
YOUR CHEEKS WERE CUTE TOO!

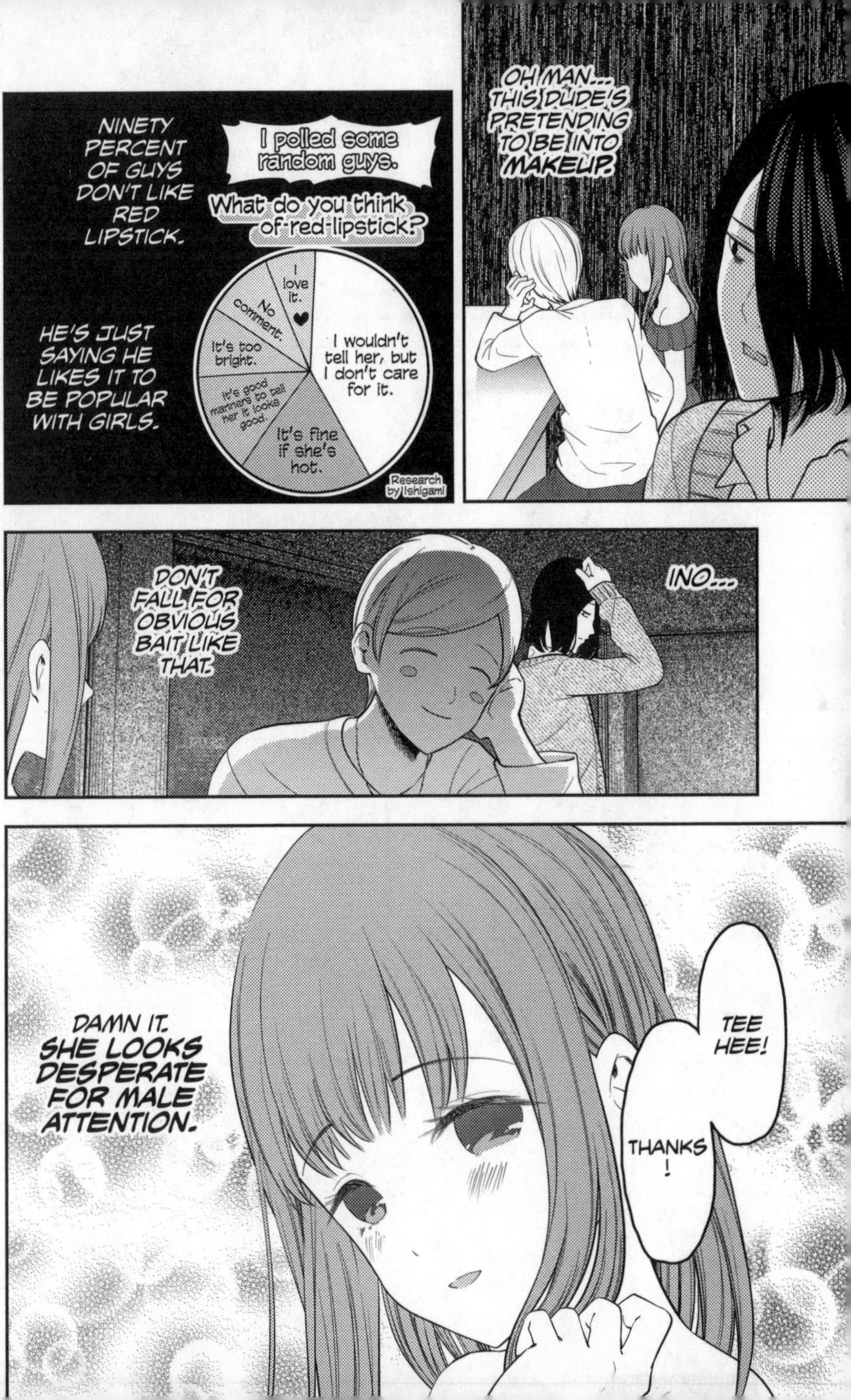
OH MAN... THIS DUDE'S PRETENDING TO BE INTO MAKEUP.
I polled some random guys.
NINETY PERCENT OF GUYS DON'T LIKE RED LIPSTICK.
What do you think of red lipstick?
I love it. ♥
I wouldn't tell her, but I don't care for it.
It's fine if she's hot.
It's good manners to tell her it looks good.
It's too bright.
No comment.
Research by Ishigami
HE'S JUST SAYING HE LIKES IT TO BE POPULAR WITH GIRLS.
INO...
DON'T FALL FOR OBVIOUS BAIT LIKE THAT.
TEE HEE!
THANKS!
DAMN IT. SHE LOOKS DESPERATE FOR MALE ATTENTION.

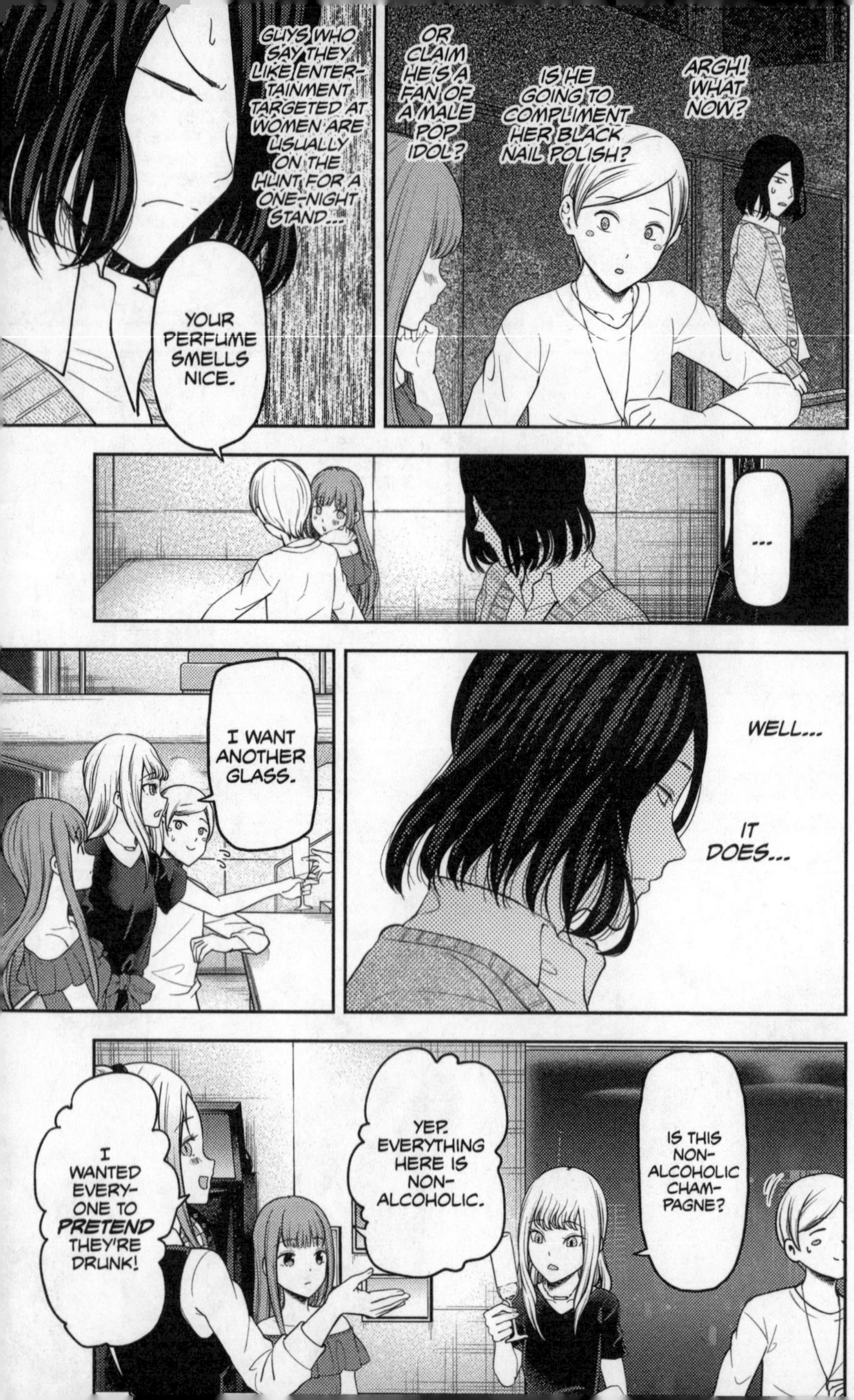
ARGH! WHAT NOW?
IS HE GOING TO COMPLIMENT HER BLACK NAIL POLISH?
OR CLAIM HE'S A FAN OF A MALE POP IDOL?
GUYS WHO SAY THEY LIKE ENTERTAINMENT TARGETED AT WOMEN ARE USUALLY ON THE HUNT FOR A ONE-NIGHT STAND...
YOUR PERFUME SMELLS NICE.
...
WELL...
IT DOES...
I WANT ANOTHER GLASS.
IS THIS NON-ALCOHOLIC CHAMPAGNE?
YEP. EVERYTHING HERE IS NON-ALCOHOLIC.
I WANTED EVERYONE TO PRETEND THEY'RE DRUNK!

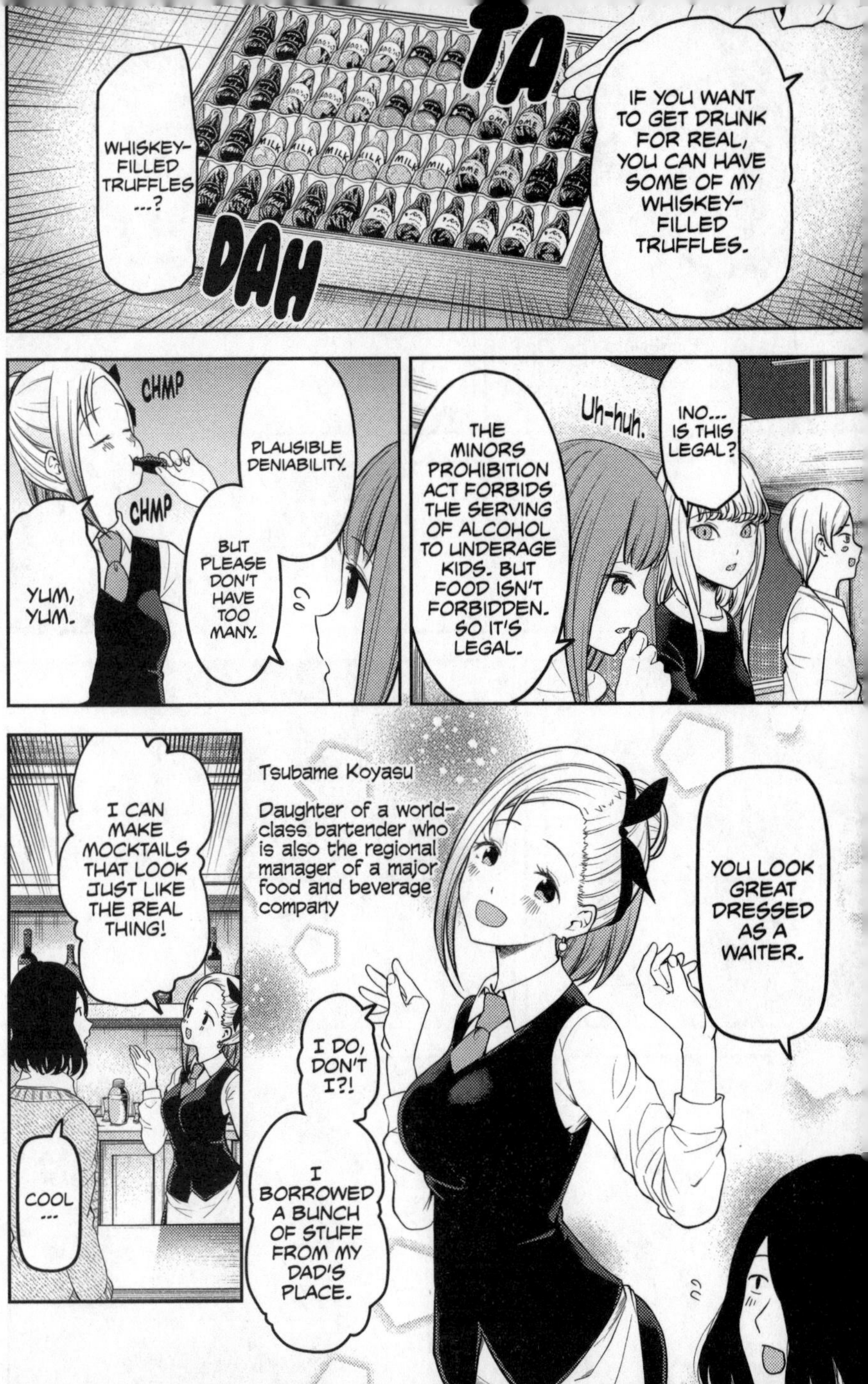
IF YOU WANT TO GET DRUNK FOR REAL, YOU CAN HAVE SOME OF MY WHISKEY-FILLED TRUFFLES.
TA
DAH
WHISKEY-FILLED TRUFFLES ...?
INO... IS THIS LEGAL?
Uh-huh.
THE MINORS PROHIBITION ACT FORBIDS THE SERVING OF ALCOHOL TO UNDERAGE KIDS. BUT FOOD ISN'T FORBIDDEN. SO IT'S LEGAL.
PLAUSIBLE DENIABILITY.
BUT PLEASE DON'T HAVE TOO MANY.
CHMP
CHMP
YUM, YUM.
YOU LOOK GREAT DRESSED AS A WAITER.
I DO, DON'T I?!
I BORROWED A BUNCH OF STUFF FROM MY DAD'S PLACE.
Tsubame Koyasu
Daughter of a world-class bartender who is also the regional manager of a major food and beverage company
I CAN MAKE MOCKTAILS THAT LOOK JUST LIKE THE REAL THING!
COOL ...

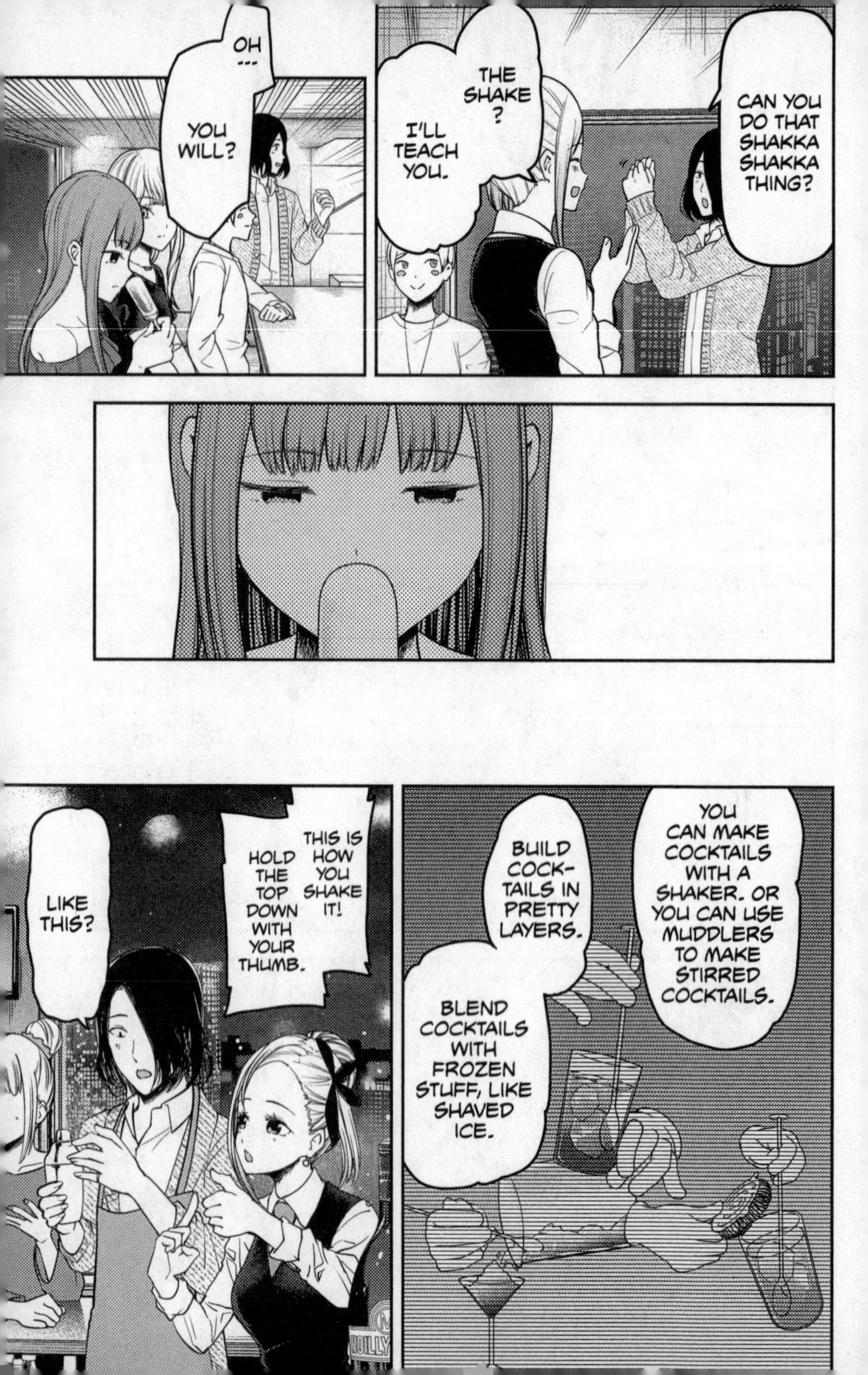
CAN YOU DO THAT SHAKKA SHAKKA THING?
THE SHAKE? I'LL TEACH YOU.
OH... YOU WILL?
YOU CAN MAKE COCKTAILS WITH A SHAKER. OR YOU CAN USE MUDDLERS TO MAKE STIRRED COCKTAILS.
BUILD COCKTAILS IN PRETTY LAYERS.
BLEND COCKTAILS WITH FROZEN STUFF, LIKE SHAVED ICE.
THIS IS HOW YOU SHAKE IT! HOLD THE TOP DOWN WITH YOUR THUMB.
LIKE THIS?

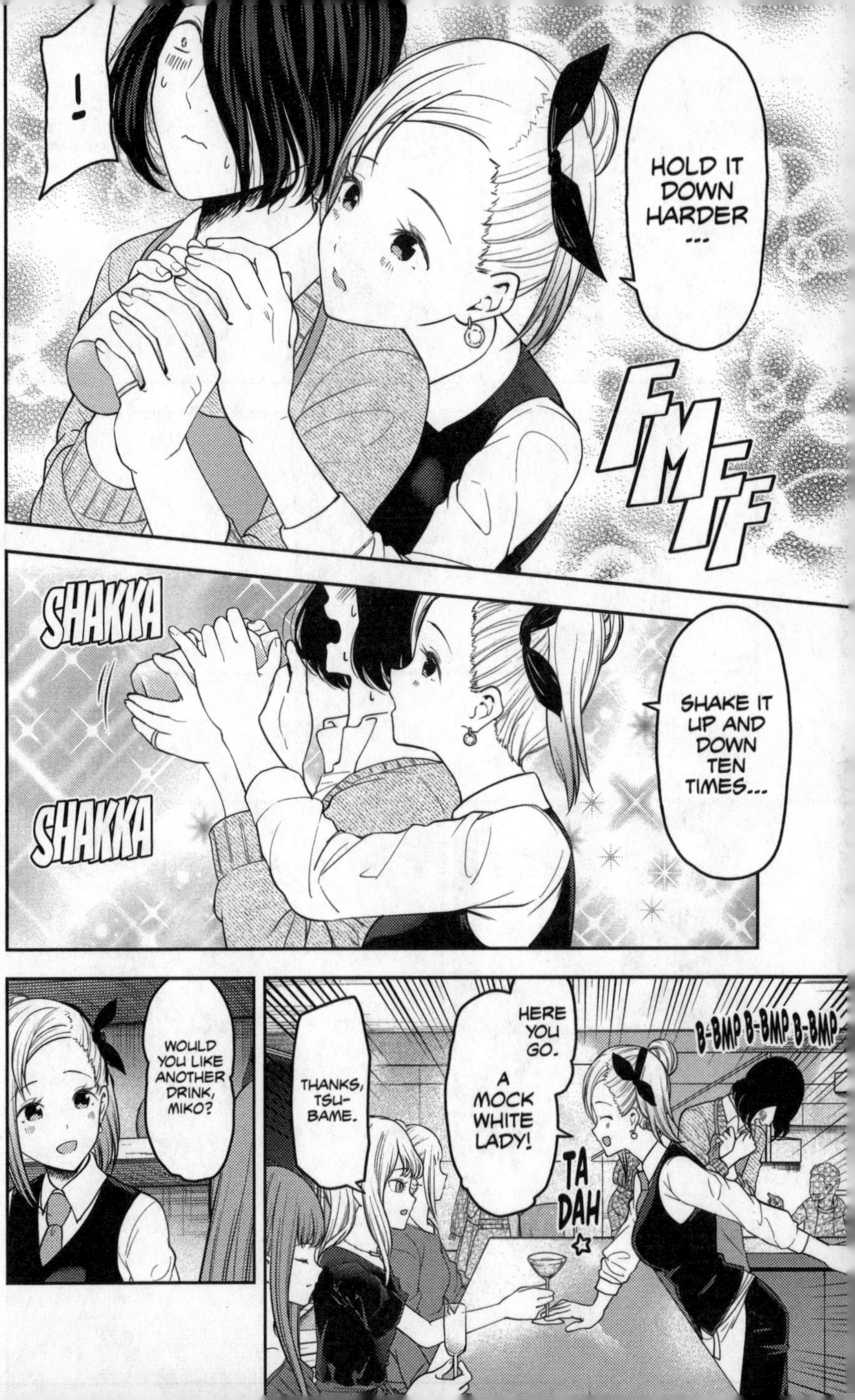
HOLD IT DOWN HARDER ...
FMFF
!
SHAKE IT UP AND DOWN TEN TIMES...
SHAKKA
SHAKKA
B-BMP B-BMP B-BMP
HERE YOU GO.
A MOCK WHITE LADY!
TA DAH
THANKS, TSU-BAME.
WOULD YOU LIKE ANOTHER DRINK, MIKO?

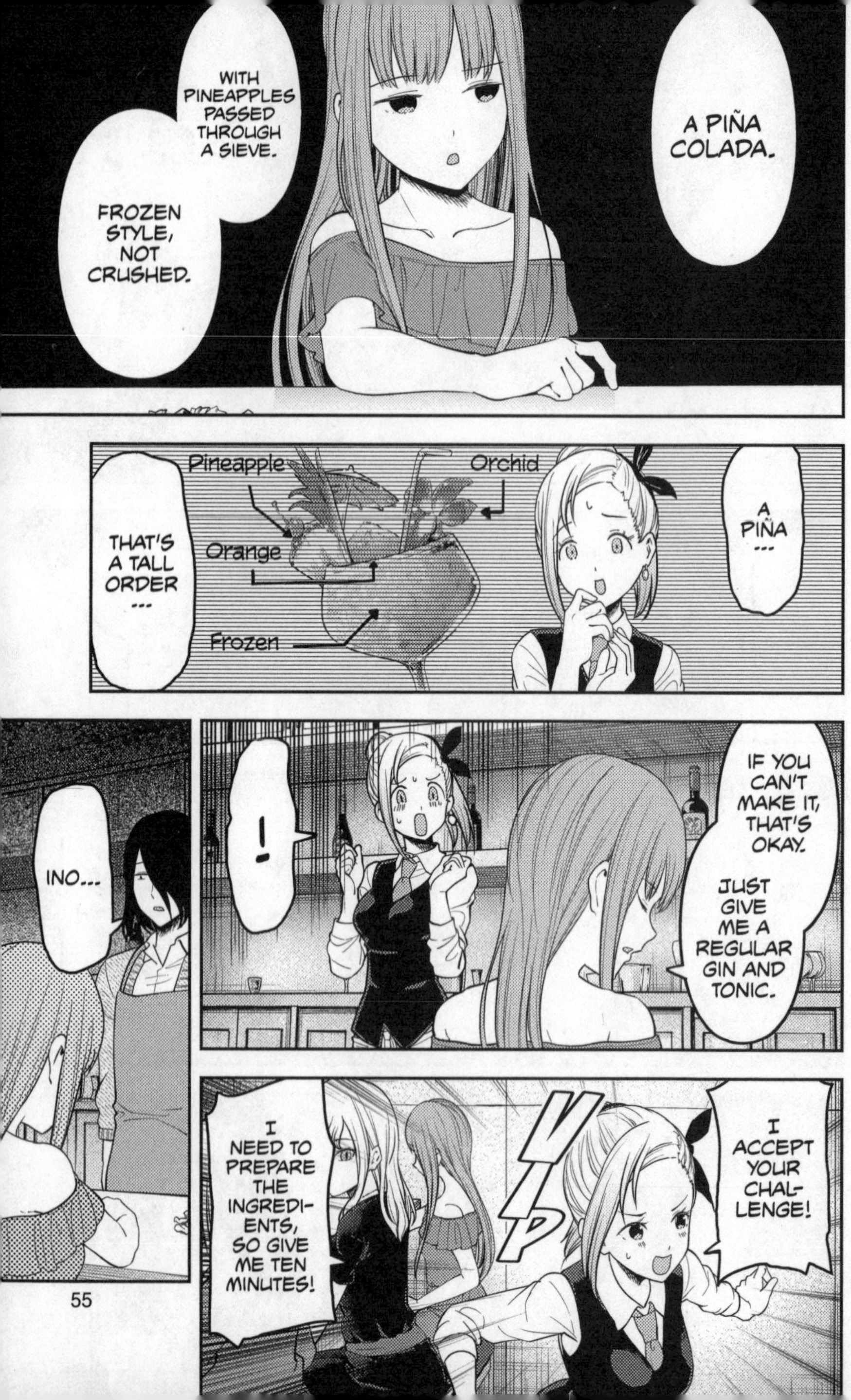
A PIÑA COLADA.
WITH PINEAPPLES PASSED THROUGH A SIEVE.
FROZEN STYLE, NOT CRUSHED.
A PIÑA ---
Orchid
Pineapple
Orange
Frozen
THAT'S A TALL ORDER ---
IF YOU CAN'T MAKE IT, THAT'S OKAY.
JUST GIVE ME A REGULAR GIN AND TONIC.
!
I ACCEPT YOUR CHALLENGE!
I NEED TO PREPARE THE INGREDIENTS, SO GIVE ME TEN MINUTES!
INO...

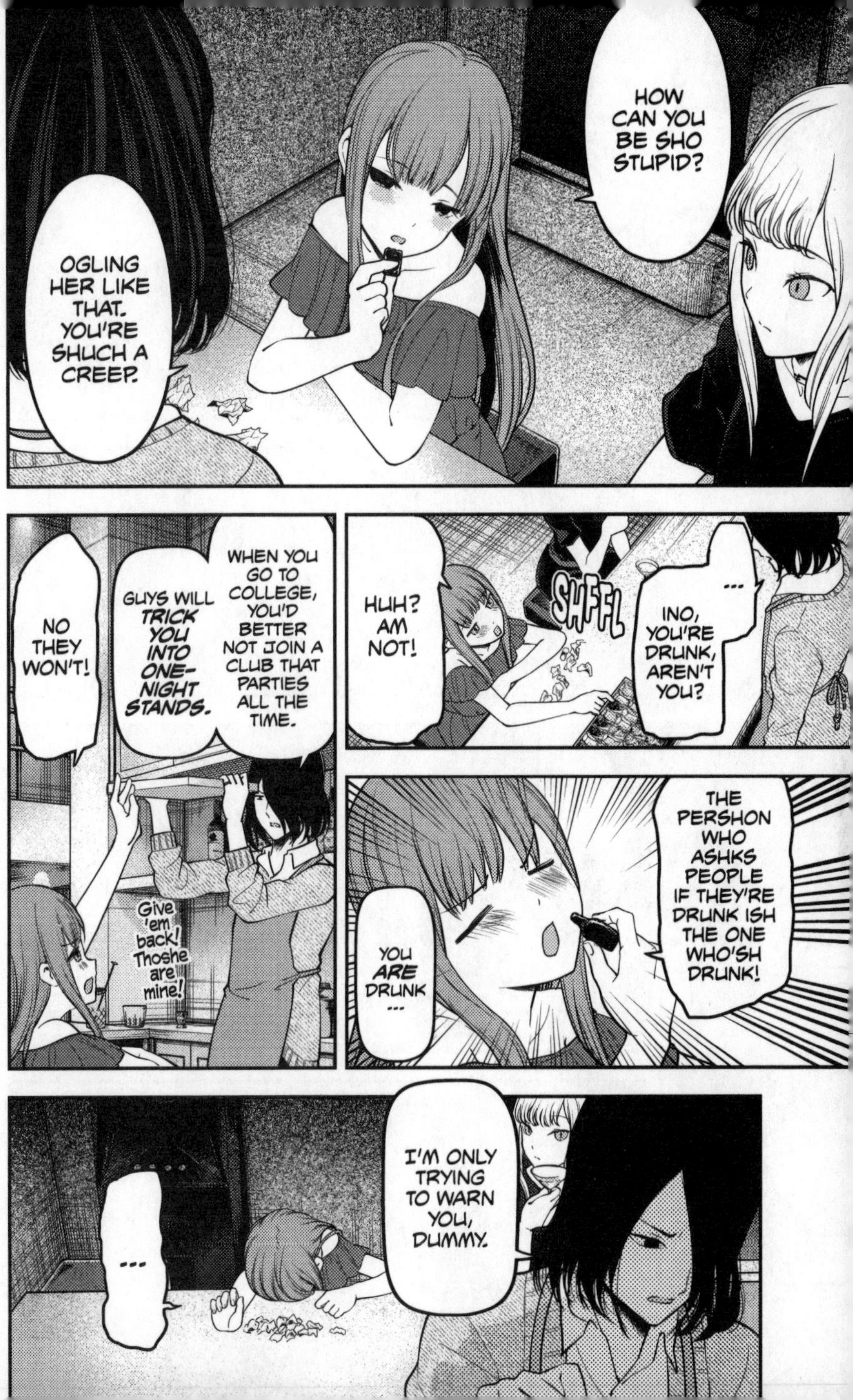
HOW CAN YOU BE SHO STUPID?
OGLING HER LIKE THAT. YOU'RE SHUCH A CREEP.
...
INO, YOU'RE DRUNK, AREN'T YOU?
SHFFL
HUH? AM NOT!
THE PERSHON WHO ASHKS PEOPLE IF THEY'RE DRUNK ISH THE ONE WHO'SH DRUNK!
YOU *ARE* DRUNK ...
WHEN YOU GO TO COLLEGE, YOU'D BETTER NOT JOIN A CLUB THAT PARTIES ALL THE TIME.
GUYS WILL *TRICK YOU INTO ONE-NIGHT STANDS.*
NO THEY WON'T!
Give 'em back! Thoshe are mine!
I'M ONLY TRYING TO WARN YOU, DUMMY.
...

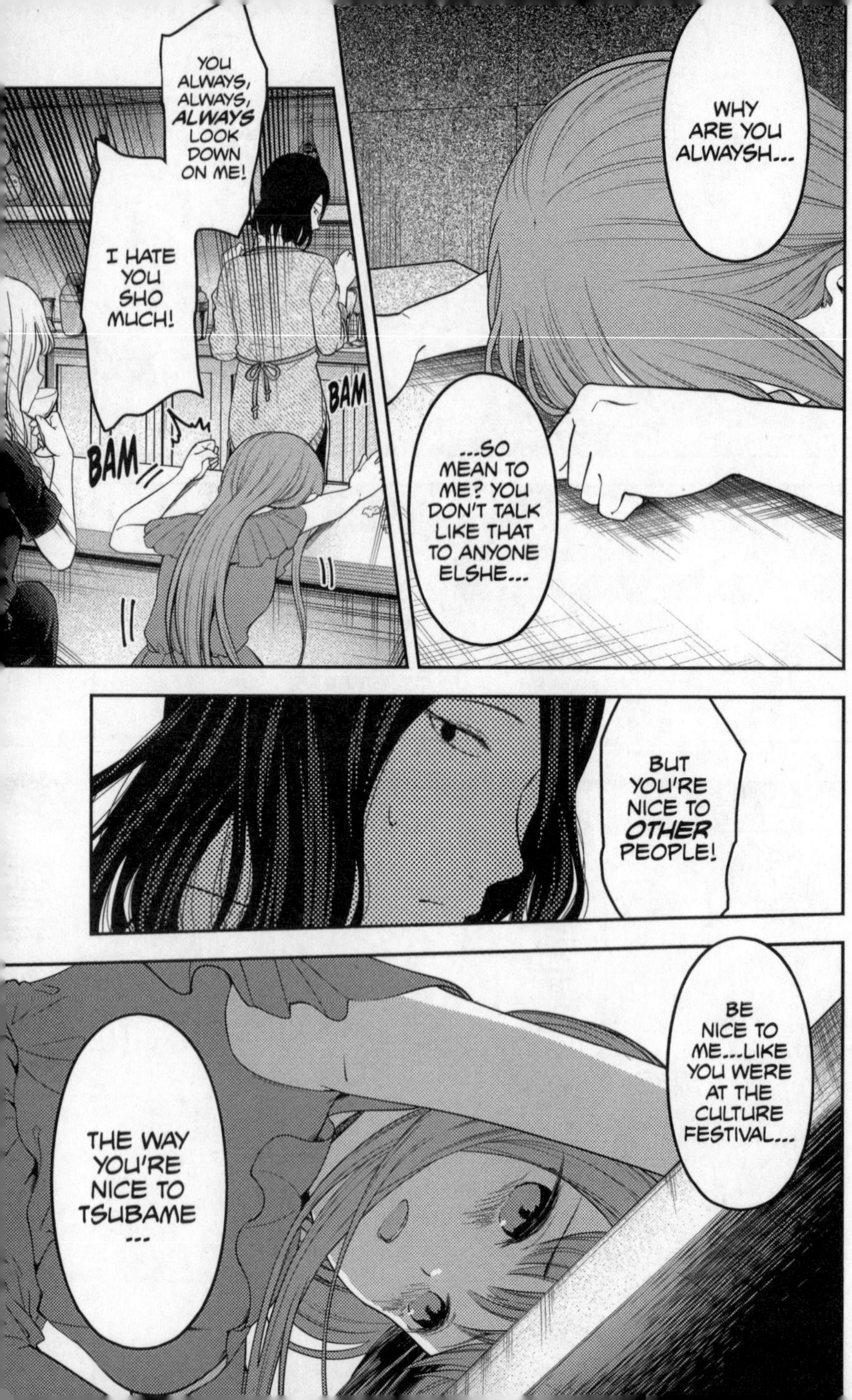
WHY ARE YOU ALWAYSH...
...SO MEAN TO ME? YOU DON'T TALK LIKE THAT TO ANYONE ELSHE...
YOU ALWAYS, ALWAYS, ALWAYS LOOK DOWN ON ME!
I HATE YOU SHO MUCH!
BAM
BAM
BUT YOU'RE NICE TO OTHER PEOPLE!
BE NICE TO ME...LIKE YOU WERE AT THE CULTURE FESTIVAL...
THE WAY YOU'RE NICE TO TSUBAME ...

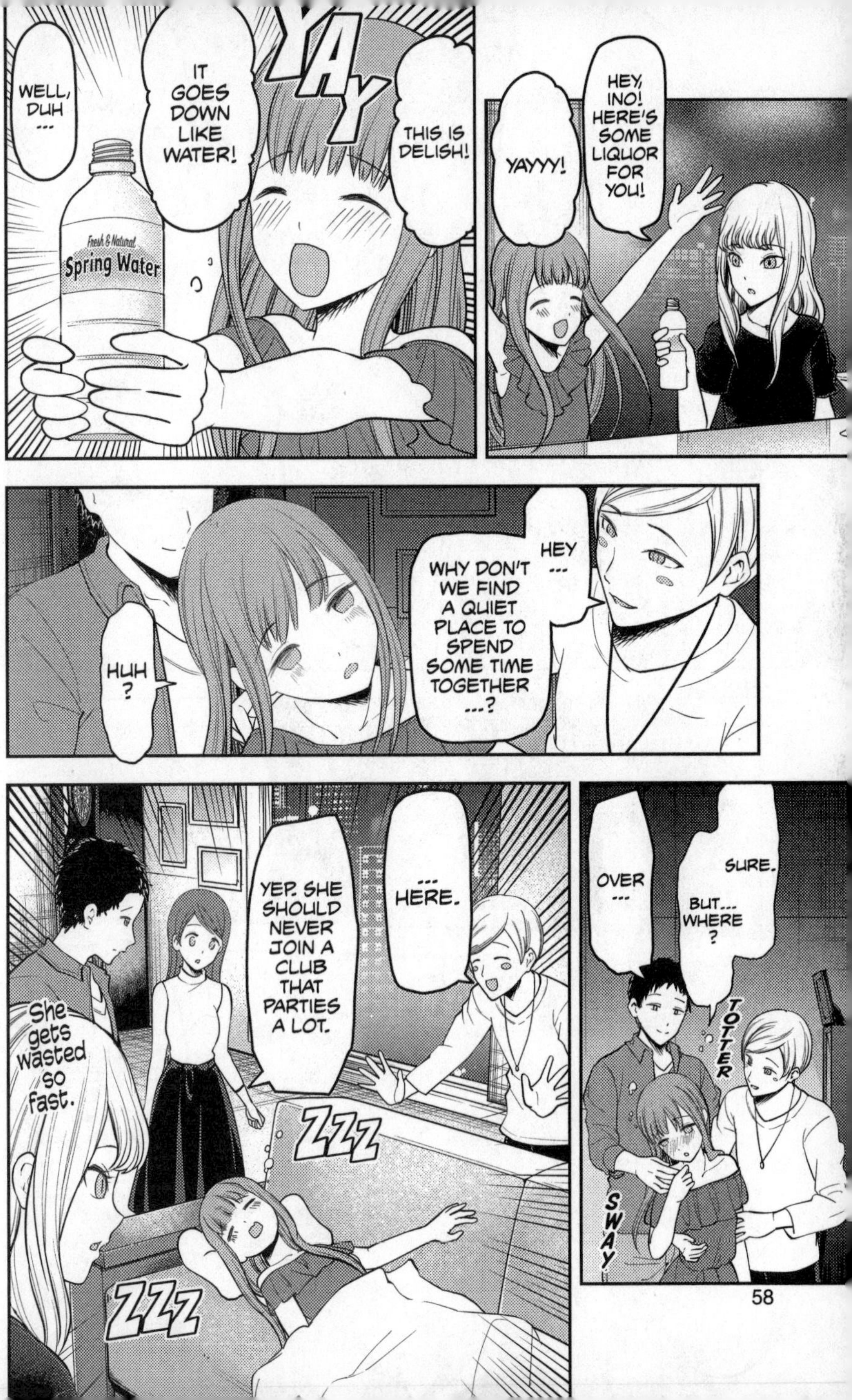
HEY, INO! HERE'S SOME LIQUOR FOR YOU!
YAYYY!
THIS IS DELISH!
YAY
IT GOES DOWN LIKE WATER!
WELL, DUH ...
Fresh & Natural
Spring Water
HEY ...
WHY DON'T WE FIND A QUIET PLACE TO SPEND SOME TIME TOGETHER ...?
HUH ?
SURE.
BUT... WHERE ?
OVER ...
TOTTER
SWAY
... HERE.
YEP. SHE SHOULD NEVER JOIN A CLUB THAT PARTIES A LOT.
She gets wasted so fast.
ZZZ
ZZZ

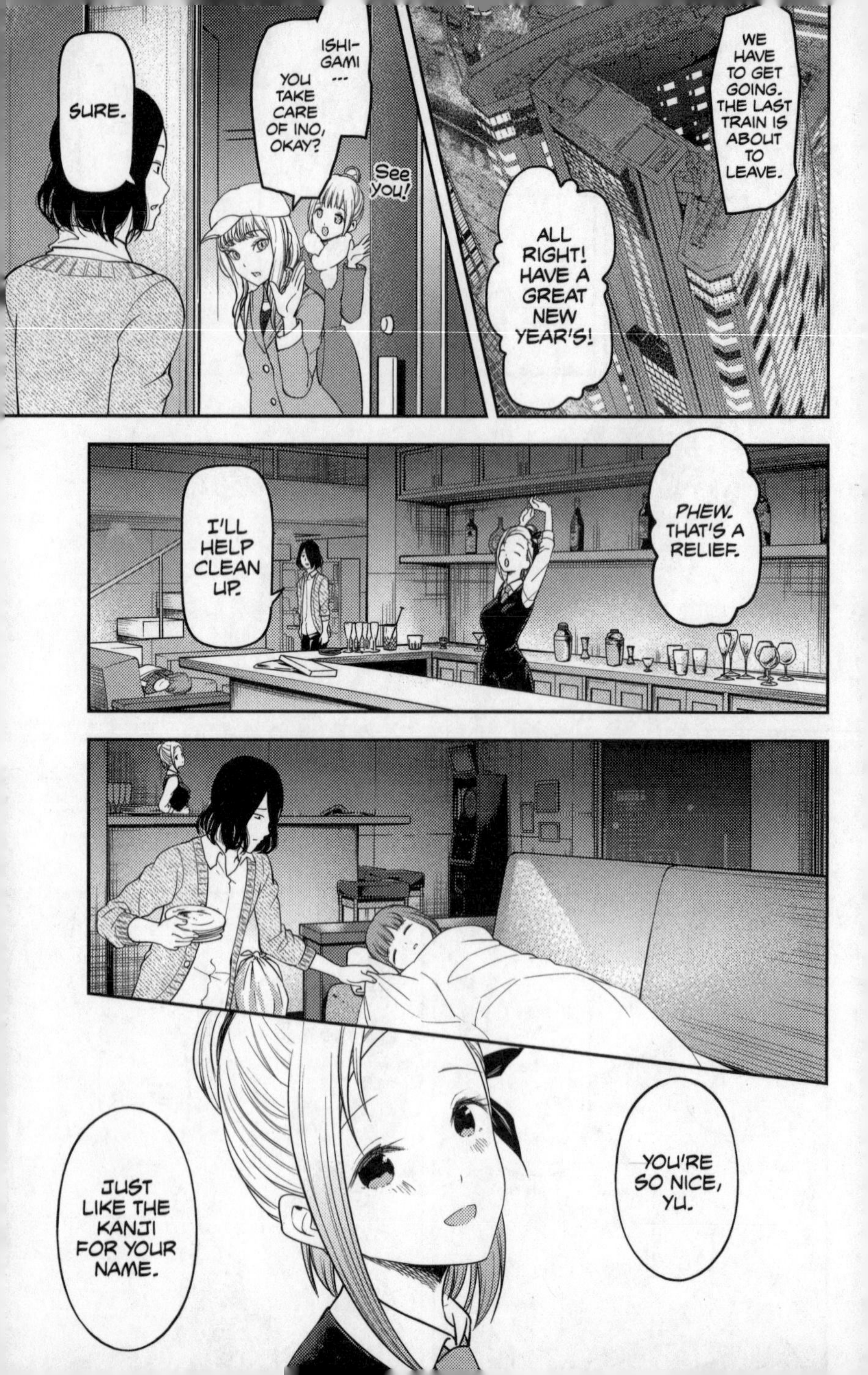
WE HAVE TO GET GOING. THE LAST TRAIN IS ABOUT TO LEAVE.
ALL RIGHT! HAVE A GREAT NEW YEAR'S!
ISHIGAMI--- YOU TAKE CARE OF INO, OKAY?
See you!
SURE.
PHEW. THAT'S A RELIEF.
I'LL HELP CLEAN UP.
YOU'RE SO NICE, YU.
JUST LIKE THE KANJI FOR YOUR NAME.

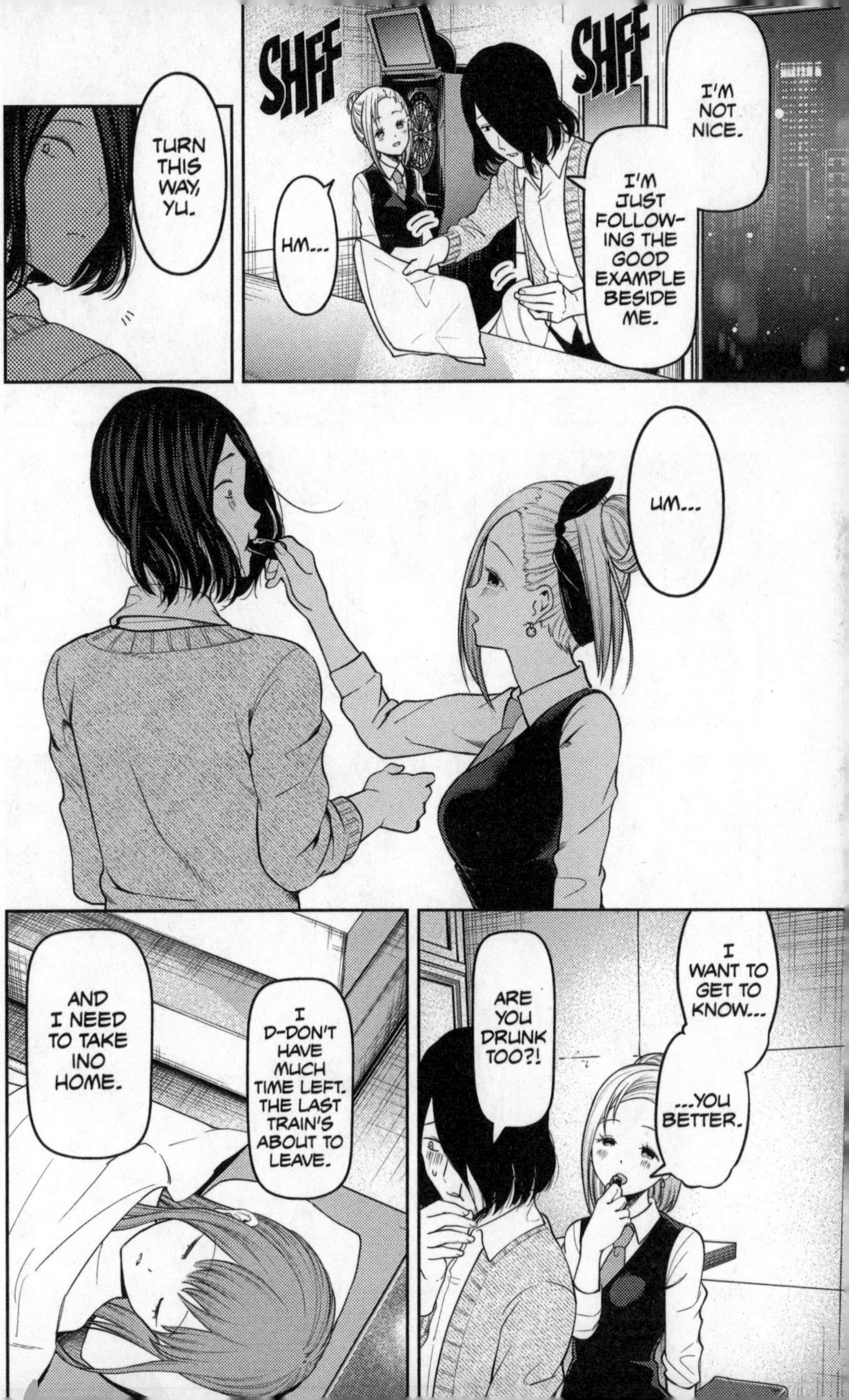
SHFF
I'M NOT NICE.
I'M JUST FOLLOWING THE GOOD EXAMPLE BESIDE ME.
SHFF
HM...
TURN THIS WAY, YU.
UM...
I WANT TO GET TO KNOW...
...YOU BETTER.
ARE YOU DRUNK TOO?!
I D-DON'T HAVE MUCH TIME LEFT. THE LAST TRAIN'S ABOUT TO LEAVE.
AND I NEED TO TAKE INO HOME.

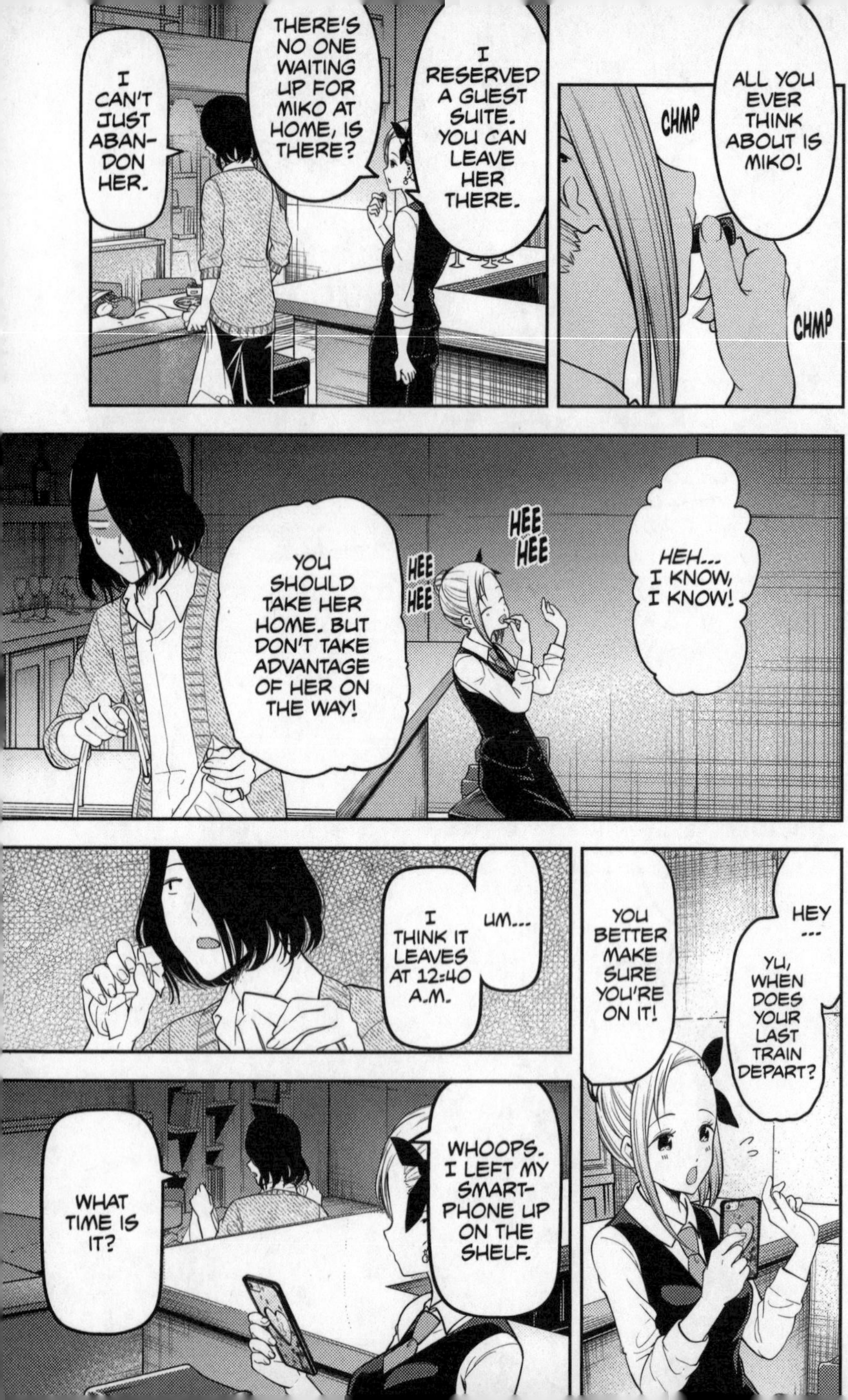
ALL YOU EVER THINK ABOUT IS MIKO!
CHMP
CHMP
I RESERVED A GUEST SUITE. YOU CAN LEAVE HER THERE.
THERE'S NO ONE WAITING UP FOR MIKO AT HOME, IS THERE?
I CAN'T JUST ABAN-DON HER.
HEH... I KNOW, I KNOW!
HEE HEE
HEE HEE
YOU SHOULD TAKE HER HOME. BUT DON'T TAKE ADVANTAGE OF HER ON THE WAY!
HEY...
YU, WHEN DOES YOUR LAST TRAIN DEPART?
YOU BETTER MAKE SURE YOU'RE ON IT!
UM...
I THINK IT LEAVES AT 12:40 A.M.
WHOOPS. I LEFT MY SMART-PHONE UP ON THE SHELF.
WHAT TIME IS IT?

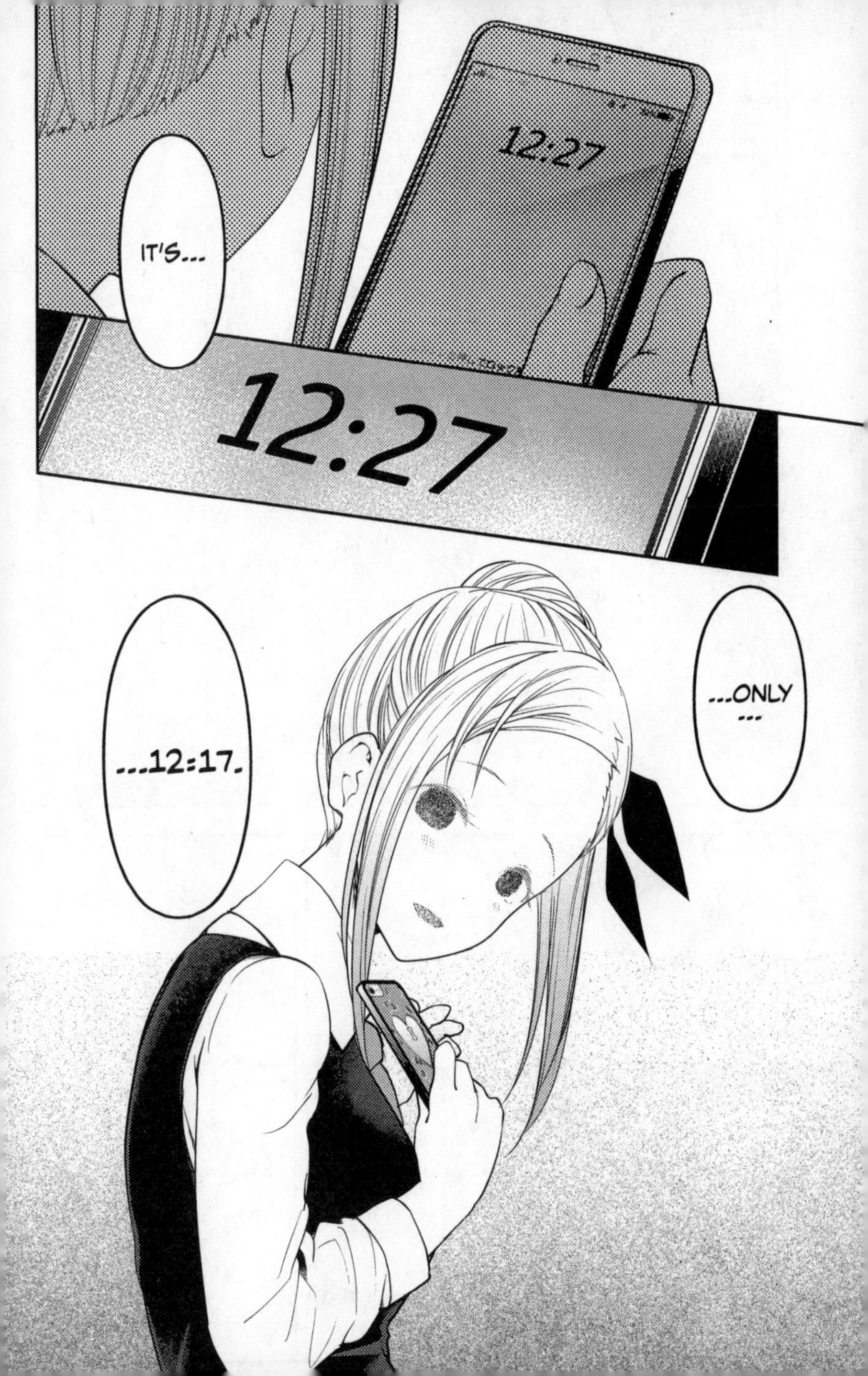
12:27
IT'S...
12:27
...ONLY ...
...12:17.

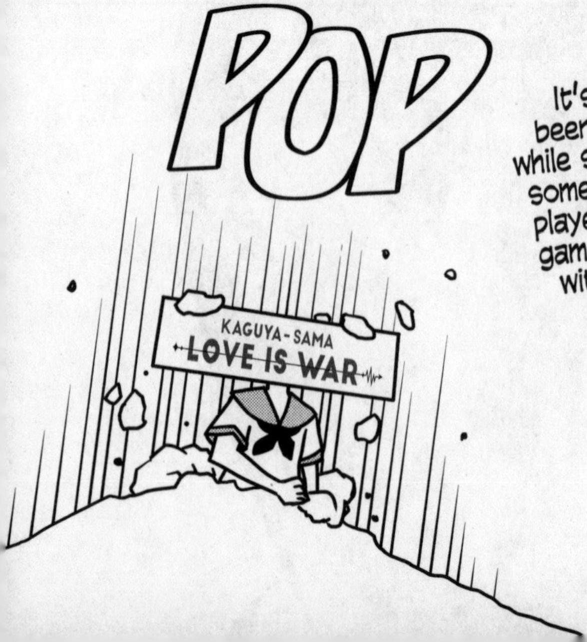
POP
KAGUYA-SAMA
LOVE IS WAR

It's been a while since someone played a game of wits!

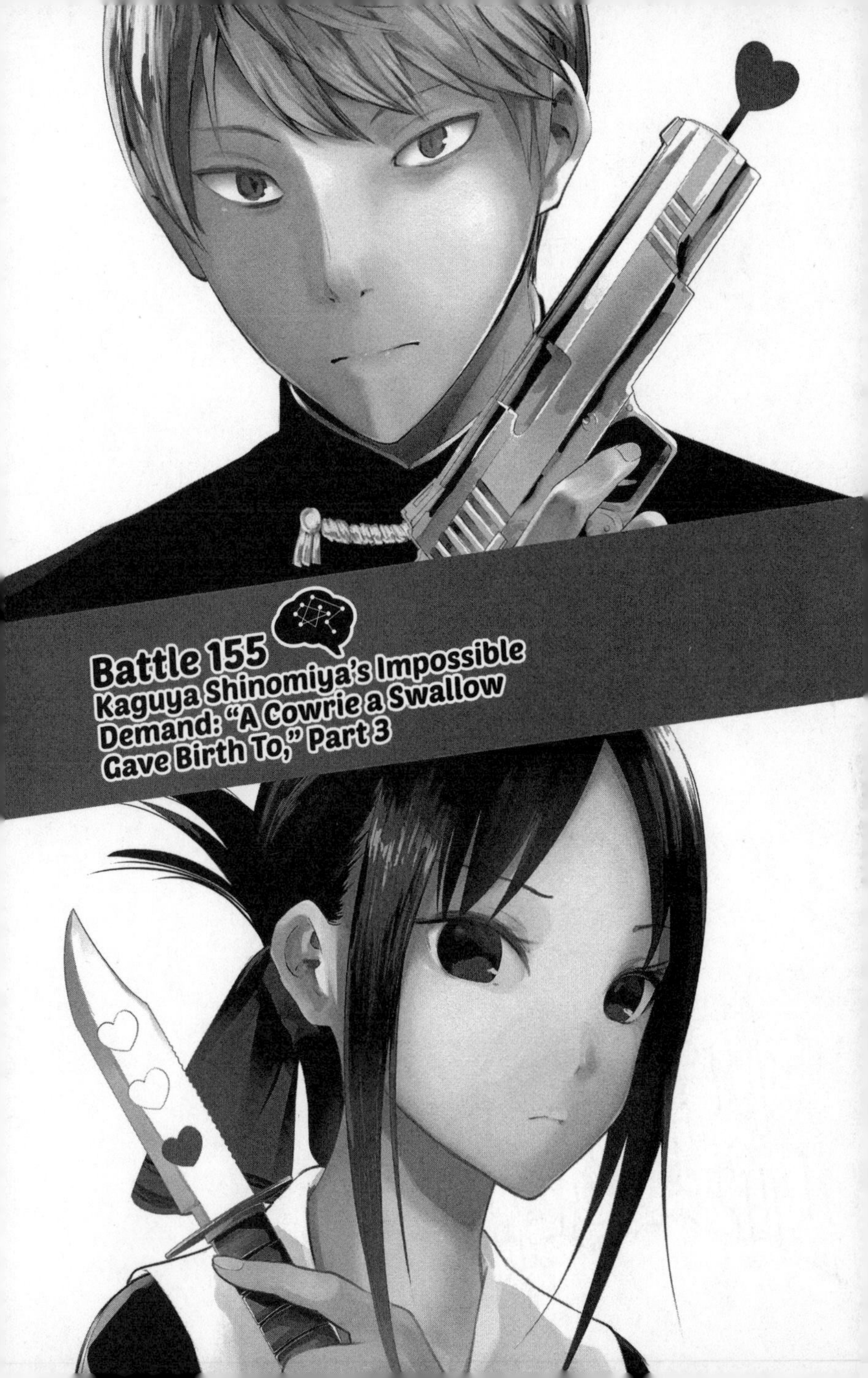
Battle 155
Kaguya Shinomiya's Impossible Demand: "A Cowrie a Swallow Gave Birth To," Part 3

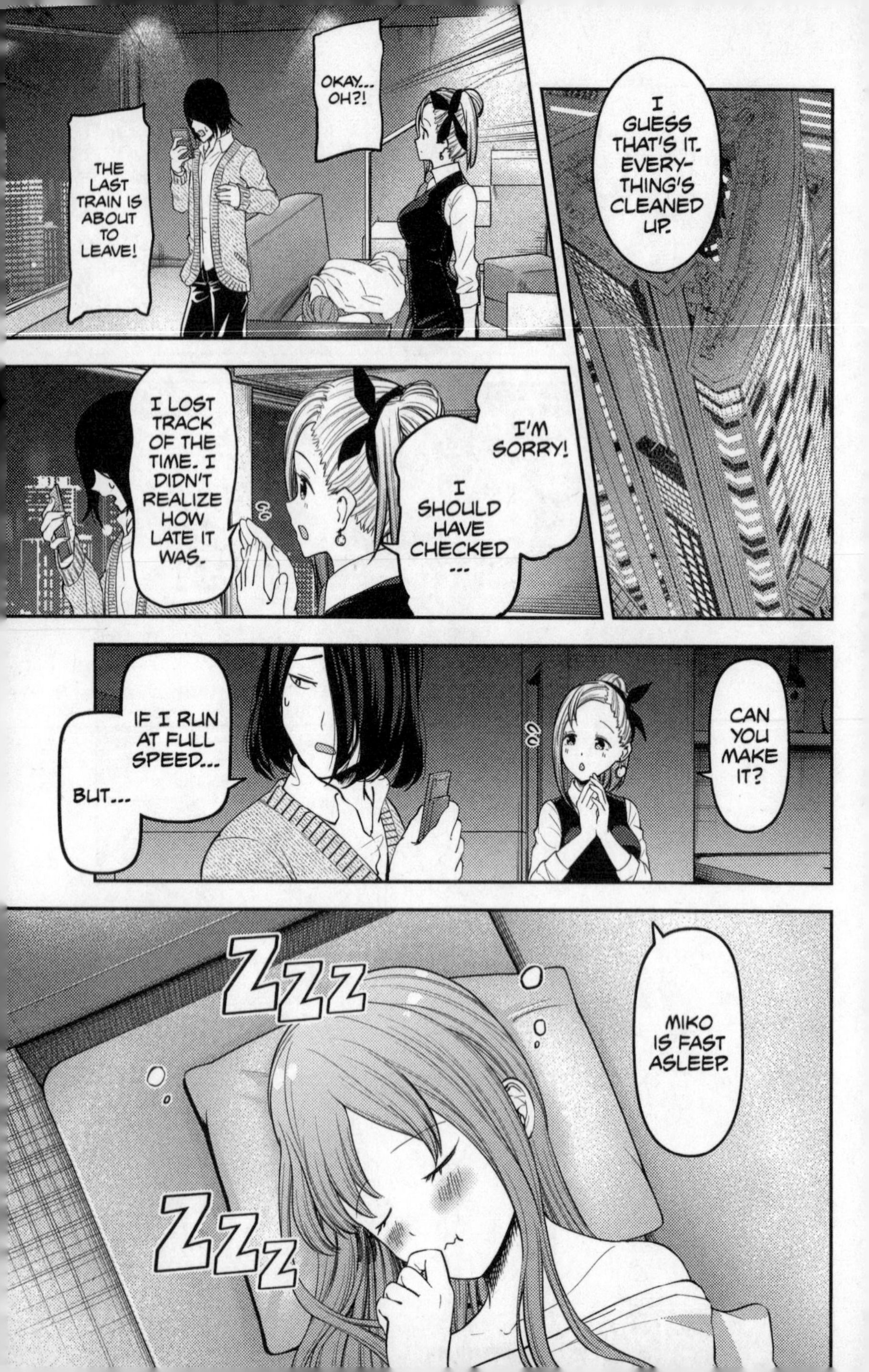
I GUESS THAT'S IT. EVERYTHING'S CLEANED UP.
OKAY... OH?!
THE LAST TRAIN IS ABOUT TO LEAVE!
I'M SORRY!
I SHOULD HAVE CHECKED ...
I LOST TRACK OF THE TIME. I DIDN'T REALIZE HOW LATE IT WAS.
CAN YOU MAKE IT?
IF I RUN AT FULL SPEED...
BUT...
MIKO IS FAST ASLEEP.
ZZZ
ZZZ

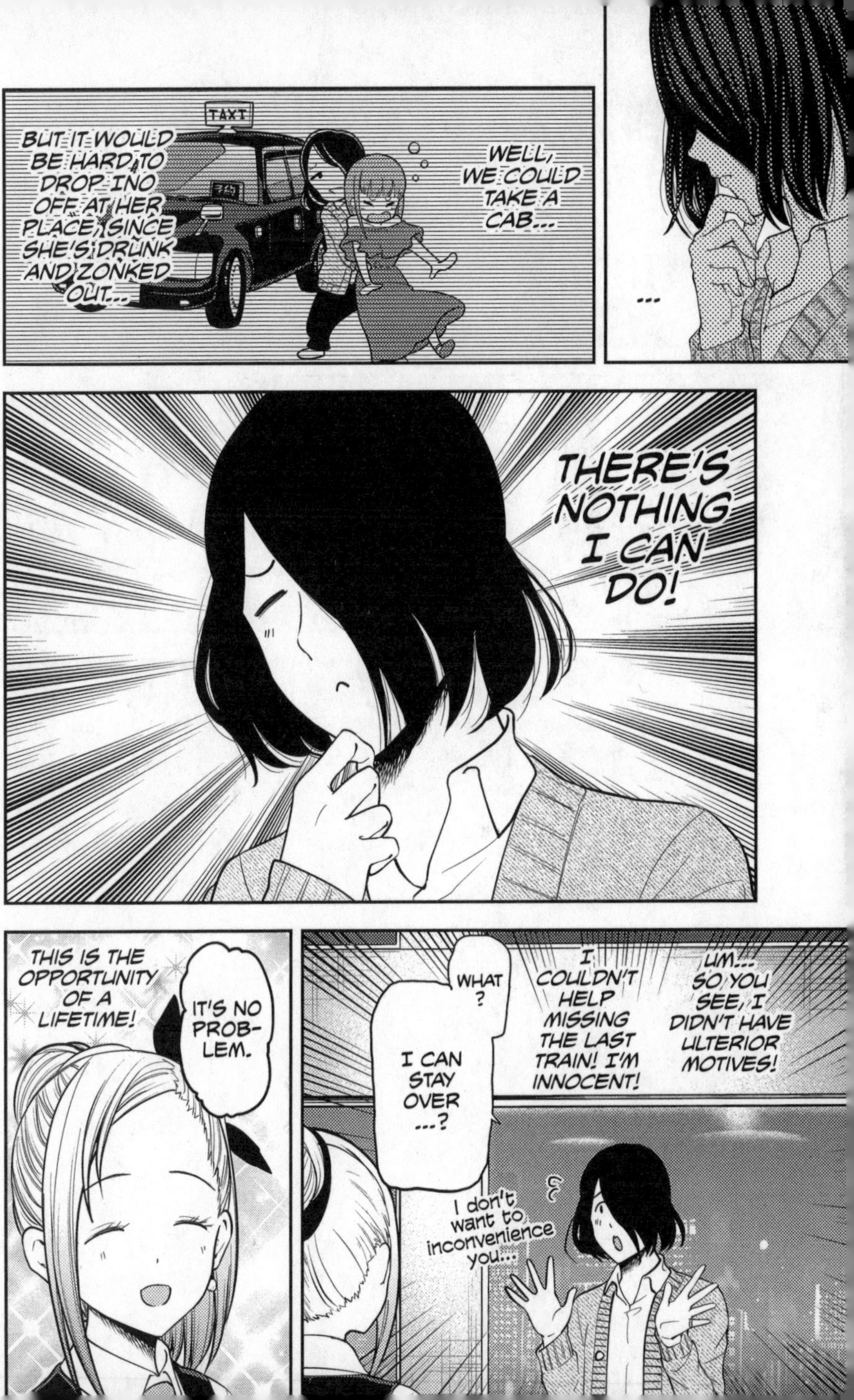
...
WELL, WE COULD TAKE A CAB...
TAXI
BUT IT WOULD BE HARD TO DROP INO OFF AT HER PLACE, SINCE SHE'S DRUNK AND ZONKED OUT...
THERE'S NOTHING I CAN DO!
UM... SO YOU SEE, I DIDN'T HAVE ULTERIOR MOTIVES!
I COULDN'T HELP MISSING THE LAST TRAIN! I'M INNOCENT!
WHAT?
I CAN STAY OVER...?
I don't want to inconvenience you...
IT'S NO PROB-LEM.
THIS IS THE OPPORTUNITY OF A LIFETIME!

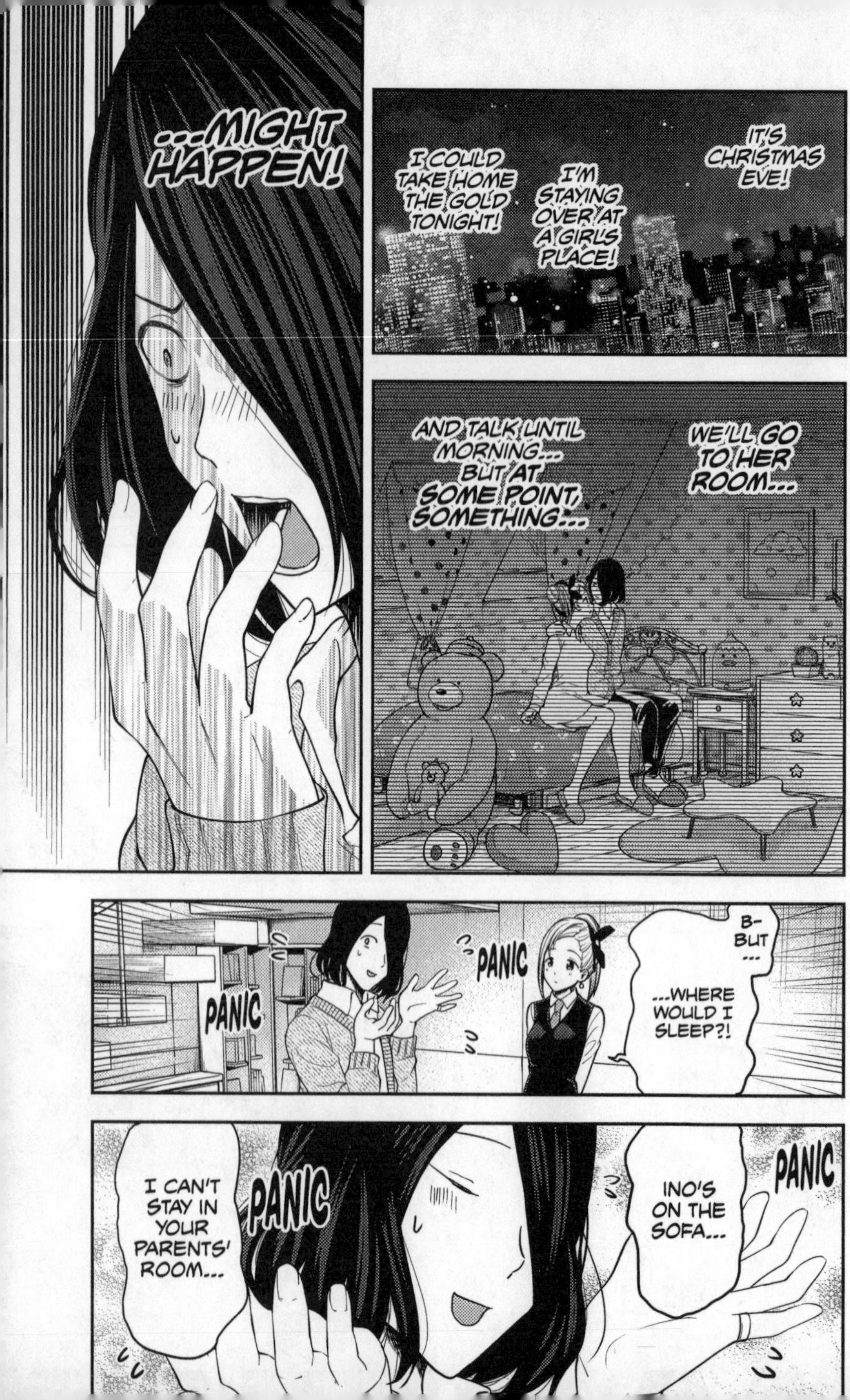
IT'S CHRISTMAS EVE!
I'M STAYING OVER AT A GIRL'S PLACE!
I COULD TAKE HOME THE GOLD TONIGHT!
WE'LL GO TO HER ROOM...
AND TALK UNTIL MORNING... BUT AT SOME POINT, SOMETHING...
...MIGHT HAPPEN!
B-BUT...
...WHERE WOULD I SLEEP?!
PANIC
PANIC
PANIC
INO'S ON THE SOFA...
PANIC
I CAN'T STAY IN YOUR PARENTS' ROOM...

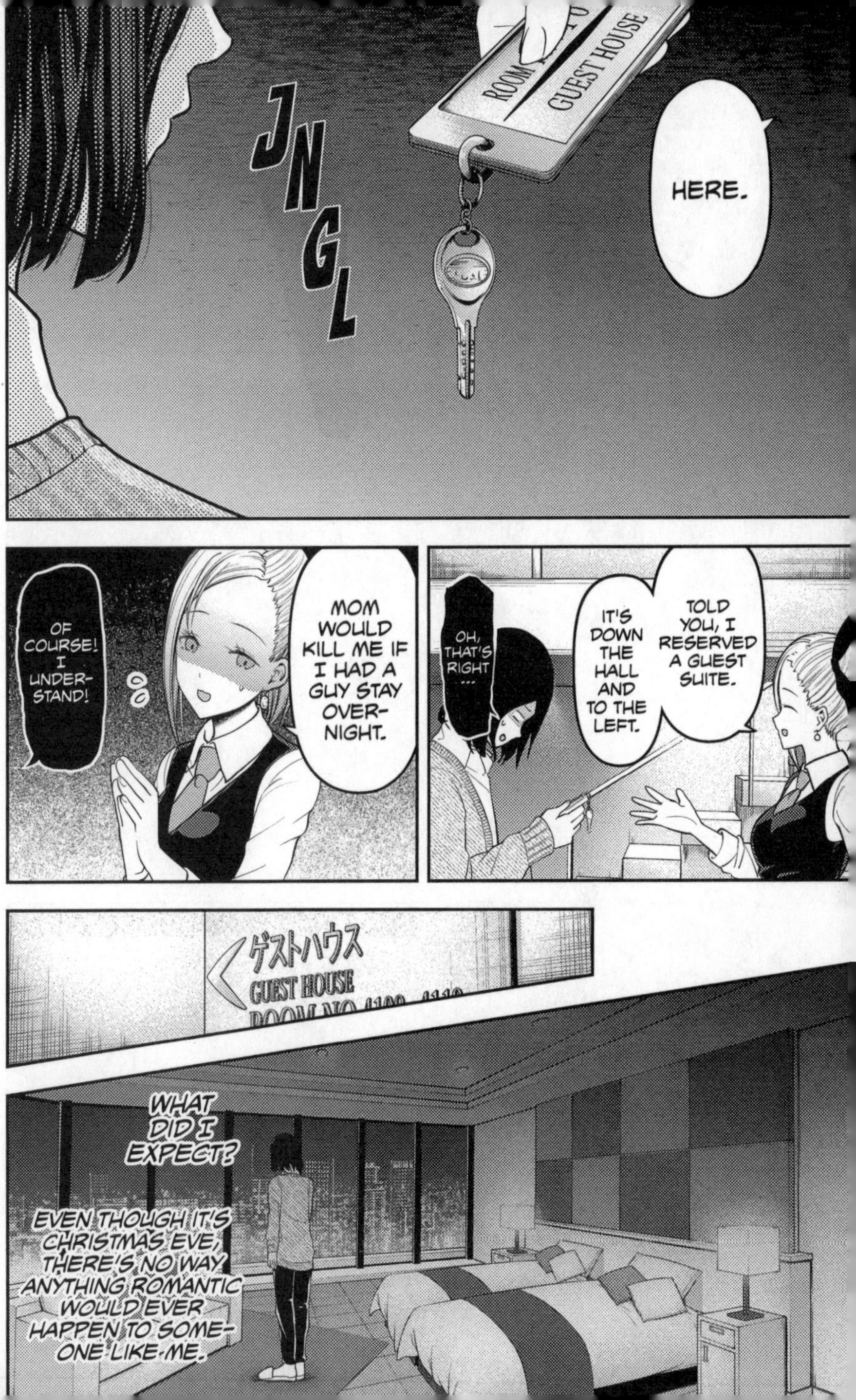
ROOM
GUEST HOUSE
JNGL
HERE.
TOLD YOU, I RESERVED A GUEST SUITE.
IT'S DOWN THE HALL AND TO THE LEFT.
OH, THAT'S RIGHT...
MOM WOULD KILL ME IF I HAD A GUY STAY OVER-NIGHT.
OF COURSE! I UNDER-STAND!
ゲストハウス
GUEST HOUSE
WHAT DID I EXPECT?
EVEN THOUGH IT'S CHRISTMAS EVE, THERE'S NO WAY ANYTHING ROMANTIC WOULD EVER HAPPEN TO SOME-ONE LIKE ME.

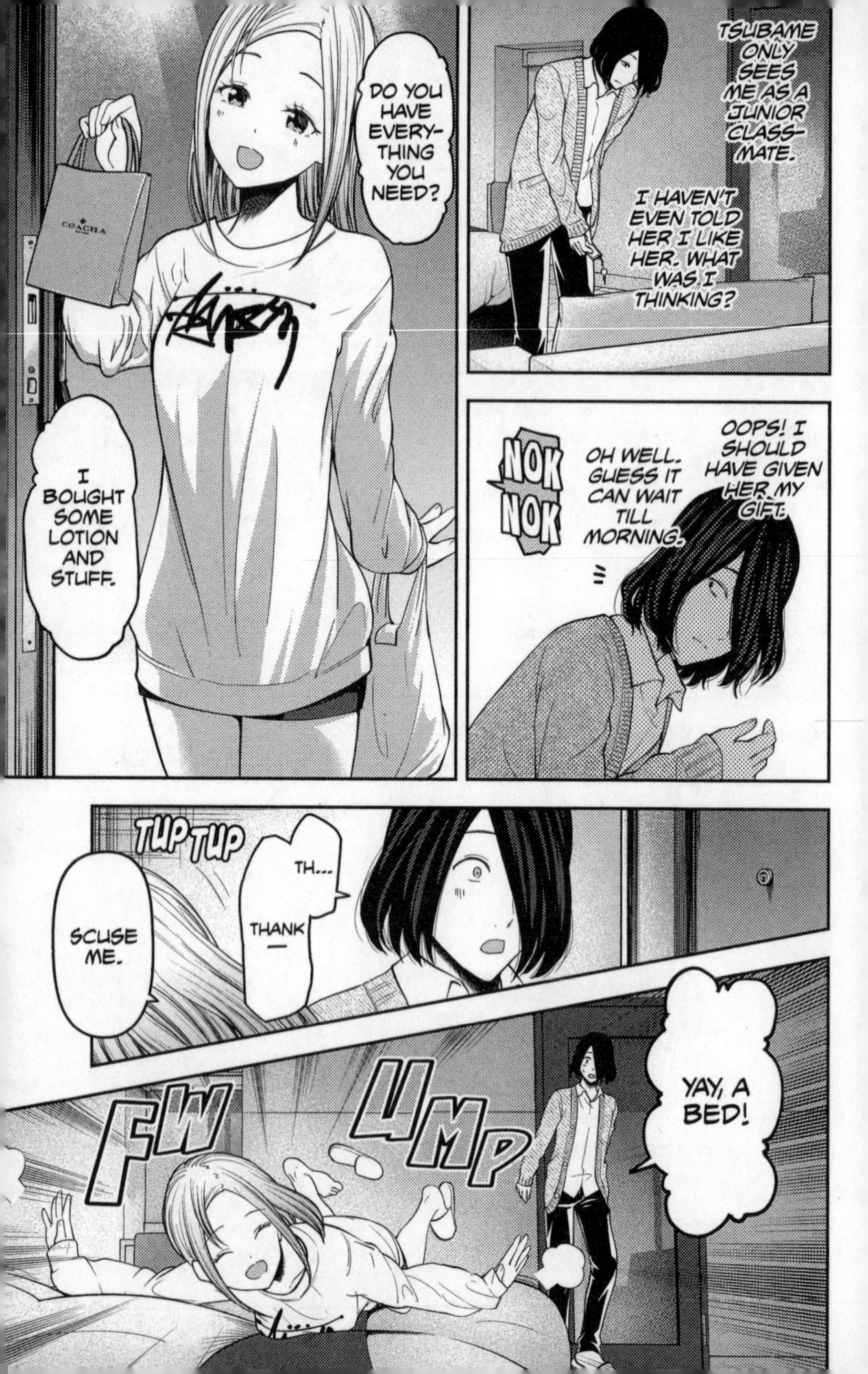
TSUBAME ONLY SEES ME AS A JUNIOR CLASS-MATE.
I HAVEN'T EVEN TOLD HER I LIKE HER. WHAT WAS I THINKING?
OOPS! I SHOULD HAVE GIVEN HER MY GIFT.
OH WELL. GUESS IT CAN WAIT TILL MORNING.
NOK NOK
DO YOU HAVE EVERY-THING YOU NEED?
I BOUGHT SOME LOTION AND STUFF.
TH...
THANK—
SCUSE ME.
TUP TUP
YAY, A BED!
FWUMP

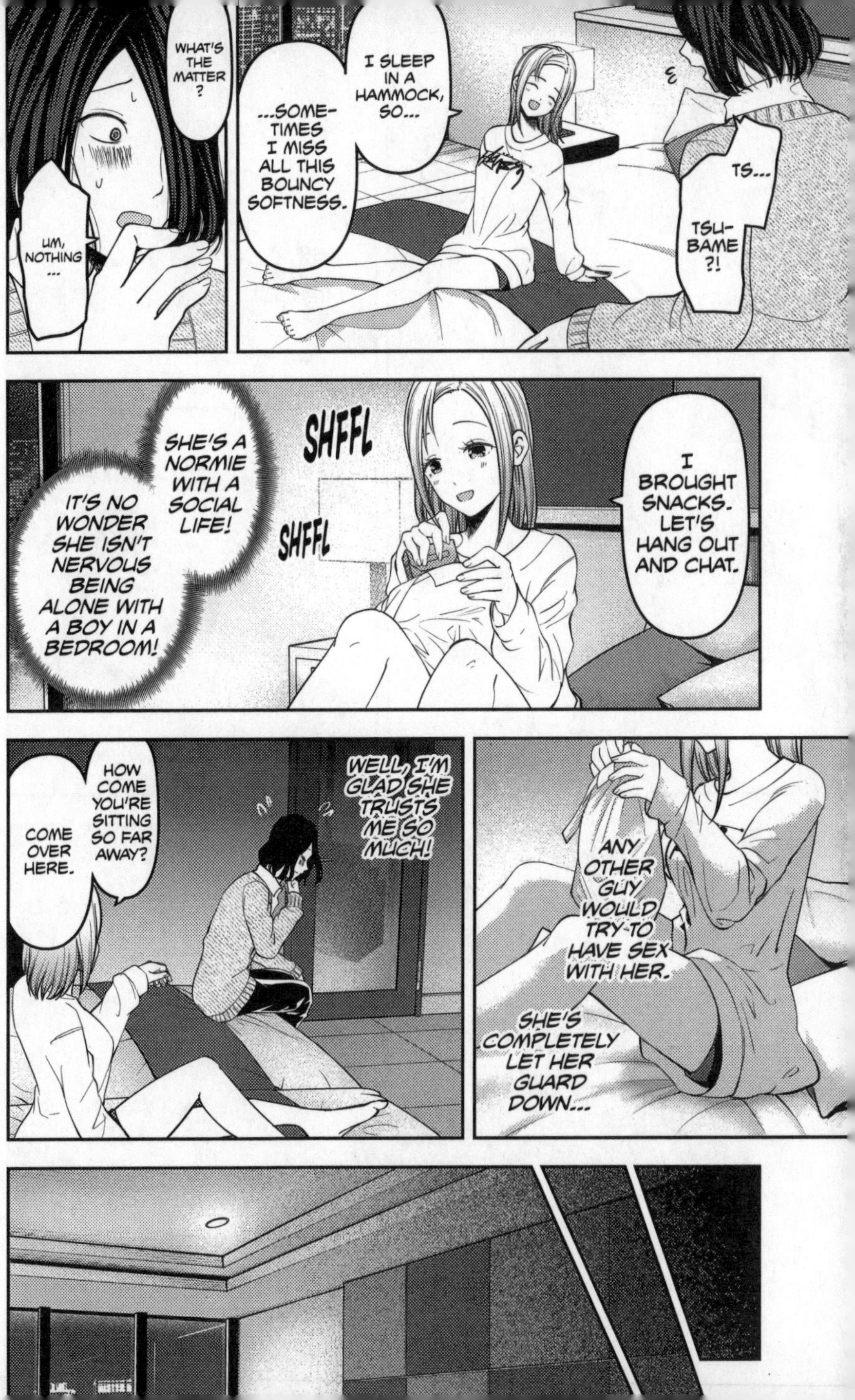
TS...
TSU-BAME?!
I SLEEP IN A HAMMOCK, SO...
...SOME-TIMES I MISS ALL THIS BOUNCY SOFTNESS.
WHAT'S THE MATTER?
UM, NOTHING...
I BROUGHT SNACKS. LET'S HANG OUT AND CHAT.
SHFFL
SHFFL
SHE'S A NORMIE WITH A SOCIAL LIFE!
IT'S NO WONDER SHE ISN'T NERVOUS BEING ALONE WITH A BOY IN A BEDROOM!
ANY OTHER GUY WOULD TRY TO HAVE SEX WITH HER.
SHE'S COMPLETELY LET HER GUARD DOWN...
WELL, I'M GLAD SHE TRUSTS ME SO MUCH!
HOW COME YOU'RE SITTING SO FAR AWAY?
COME OVER HERE.

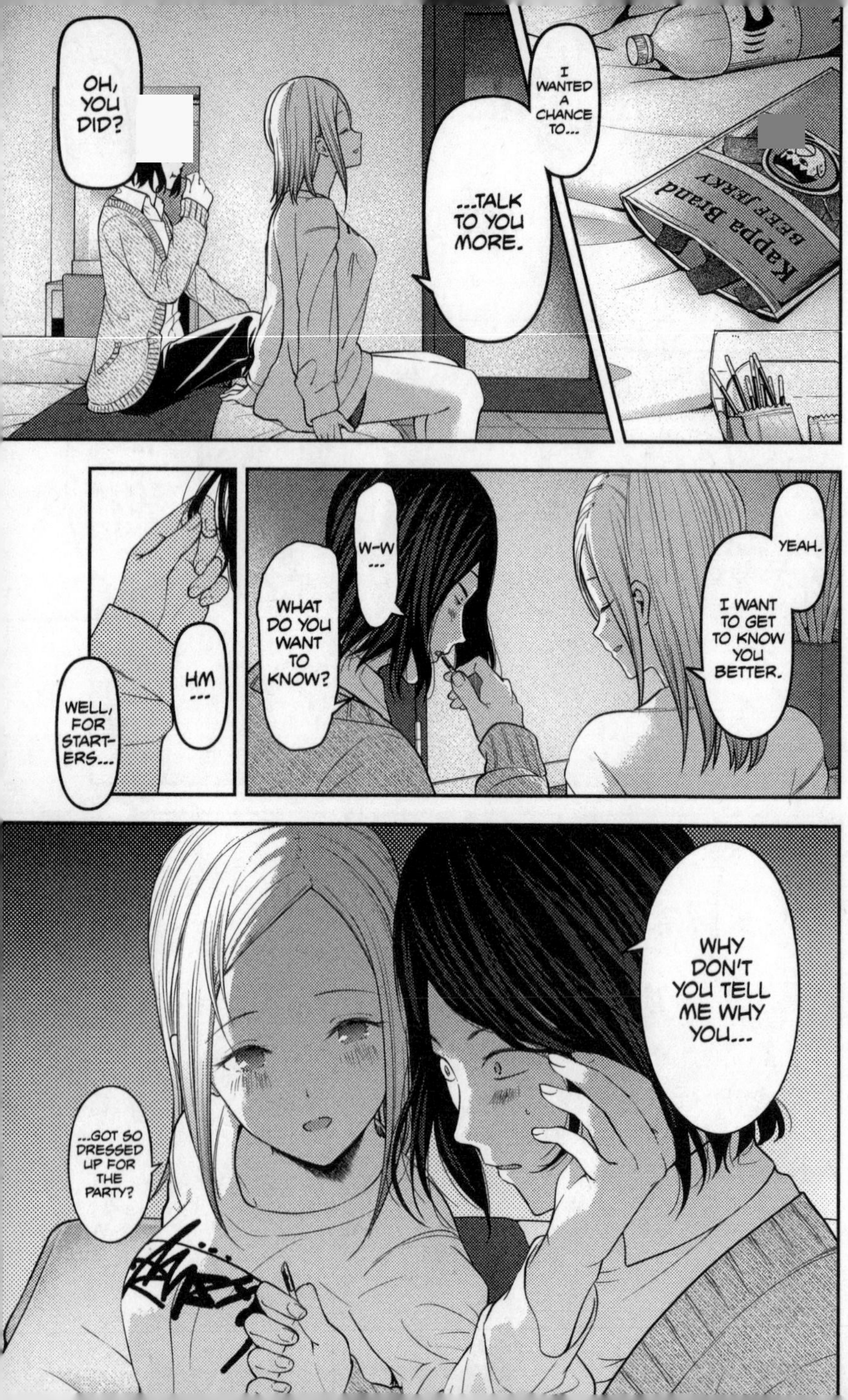
I WANTED A CHANCE TO...
...TALK TO YOU MORE.
Kappa Brand BEEF JERKY
OH, YOU DID?
YEAH.
I WANT TO GET TO KNOW YOU BETTER.
W-W...
WHAT DO YOU WANT TO KNOW?
HM...
WELL, FOR STARTERS...
WHY DON'T YOU TELL ME WHY YOU...
...GOT SO DRESSED UP FOR THE PARTY?

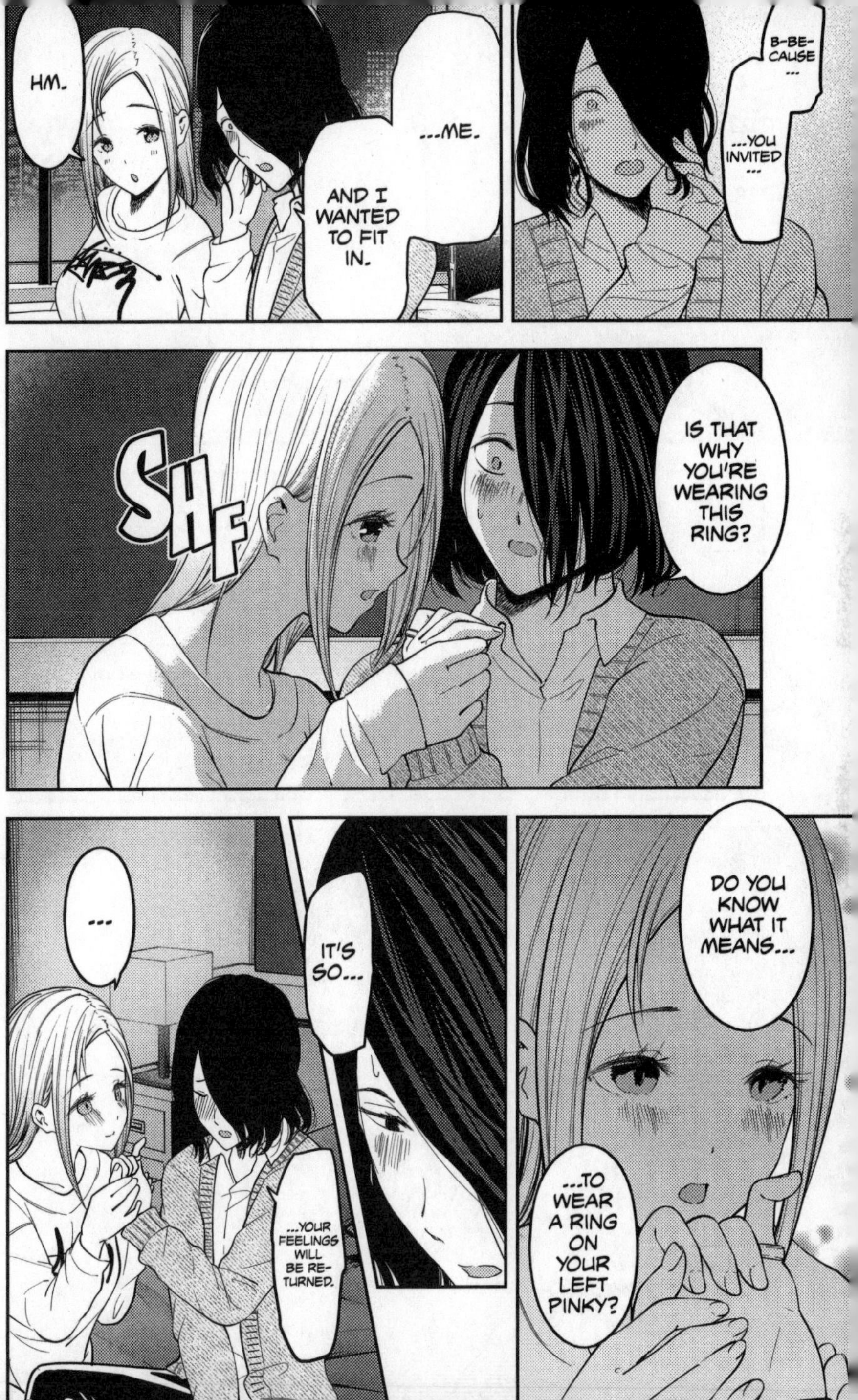
B-BE-CAUSE...
...YOU INVITED...
...ME.
AND I WANTED TO FIT IN.
HM.
IS THAT WHY YOU'RE WEARING THIS RING?
SHF
DO YOU KNOW WHAT IT MEANS...
...TO WEAR A RING ON YOUR LEFT PINKY?
IT'S SO...
...
...YOUR FEELINGS WILL BE RE-TURNED.

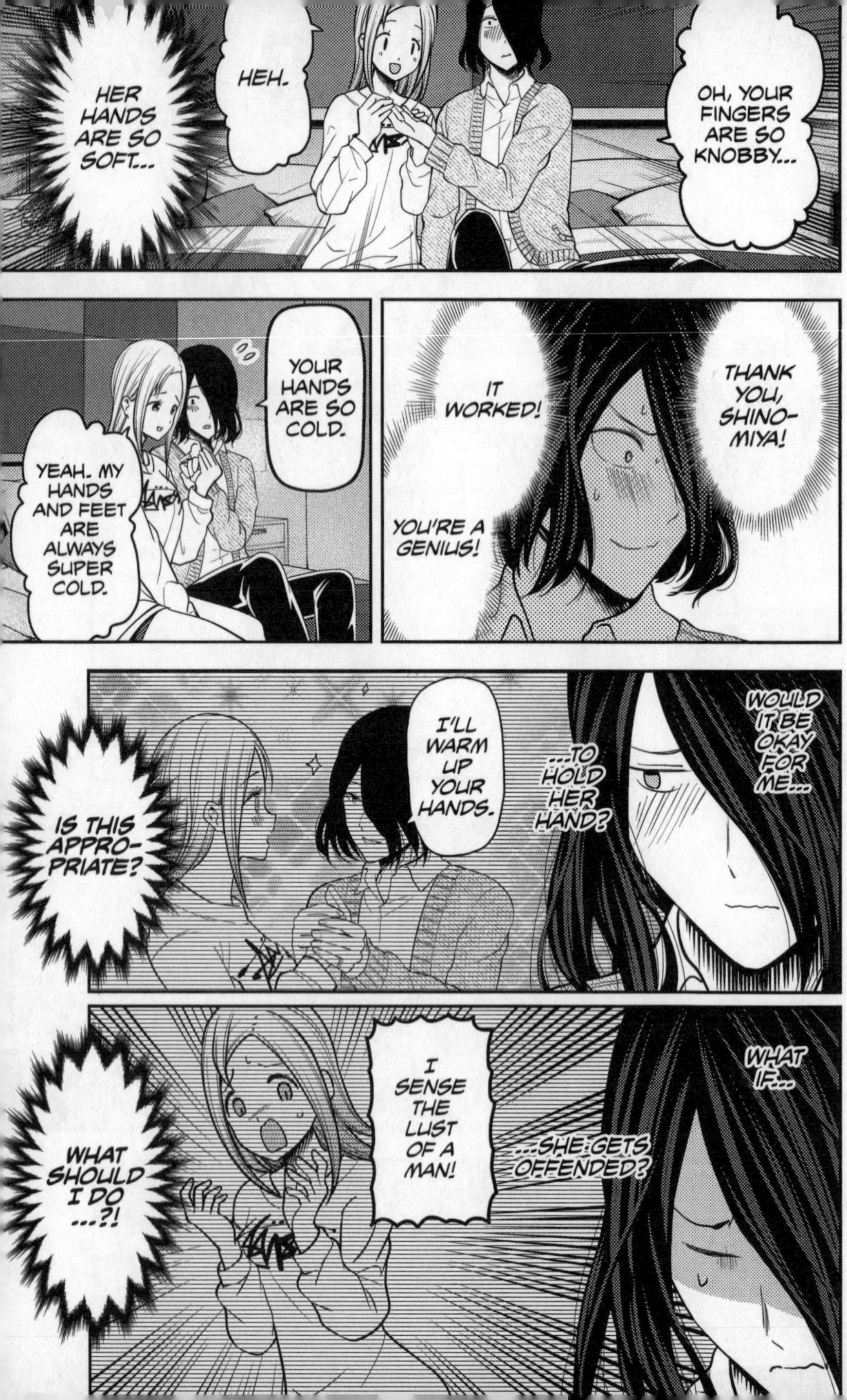
OH, YOUR FINGERS ARE SO KNOBBY...
HEH.
HER HANDS ARE SO SOFT...
THANK YOU, SHINO-MIYA!
IT WORKED!
YOU'RE A GENIUS!
YOUR HANDS ARE SO COLD.
YEAH. MY HANDS AND FEET ARE ALWAYS SUPER COLD.
WOULD IT BE OKAY FOR ME...
...TO HOLD HER HAND?
I'LL WARM UP YOUR HANDS.
IS THIS APPRO-PRIATE?
WHAT IF...
...SHE GETS OFFENDED?
I SENSE THE LUST OF A MAN!
WHAT SHOULD I DO ...?!

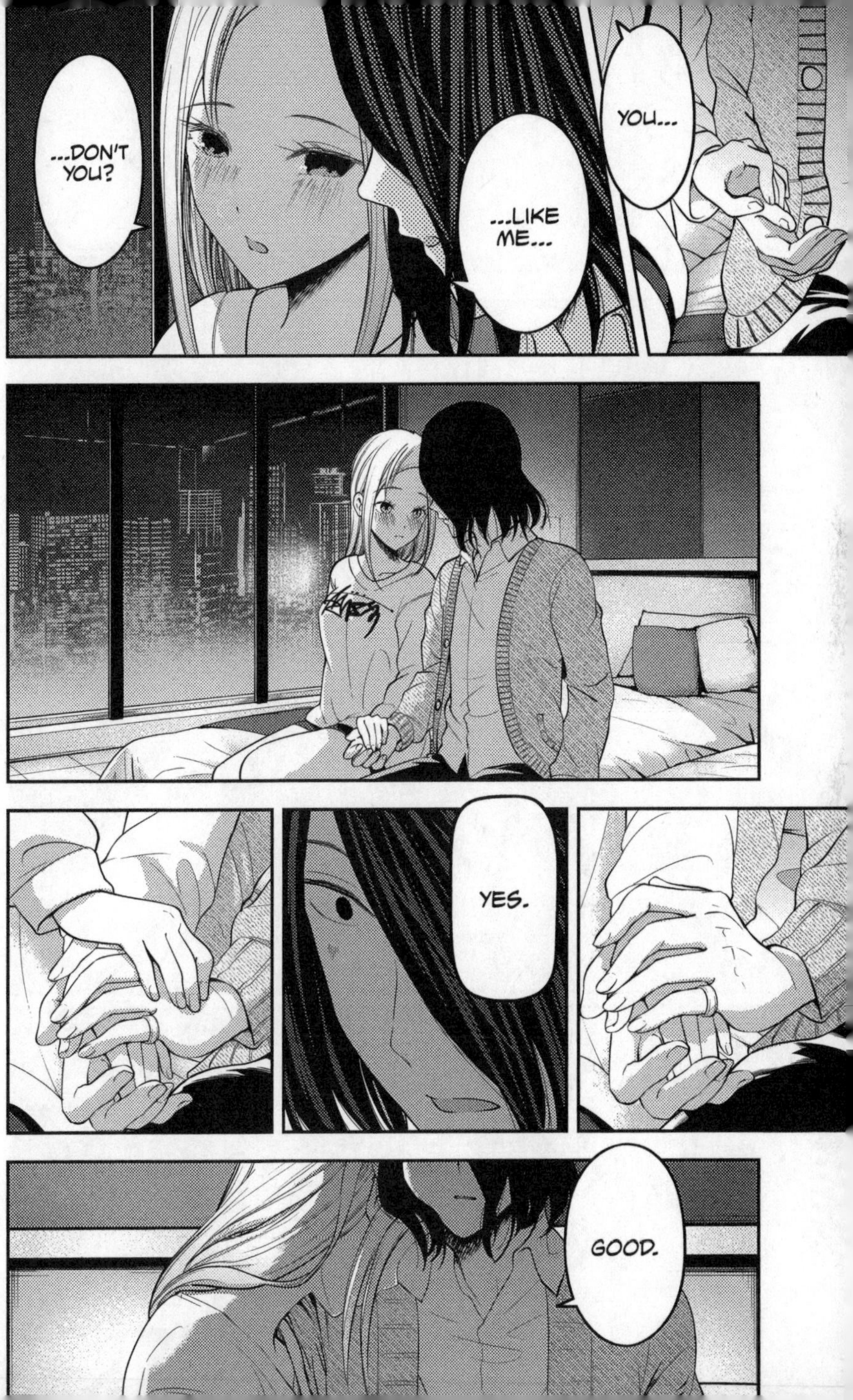
YOU...
...LIKE ME...
...DON'T YOU?
YES.
GOOD.

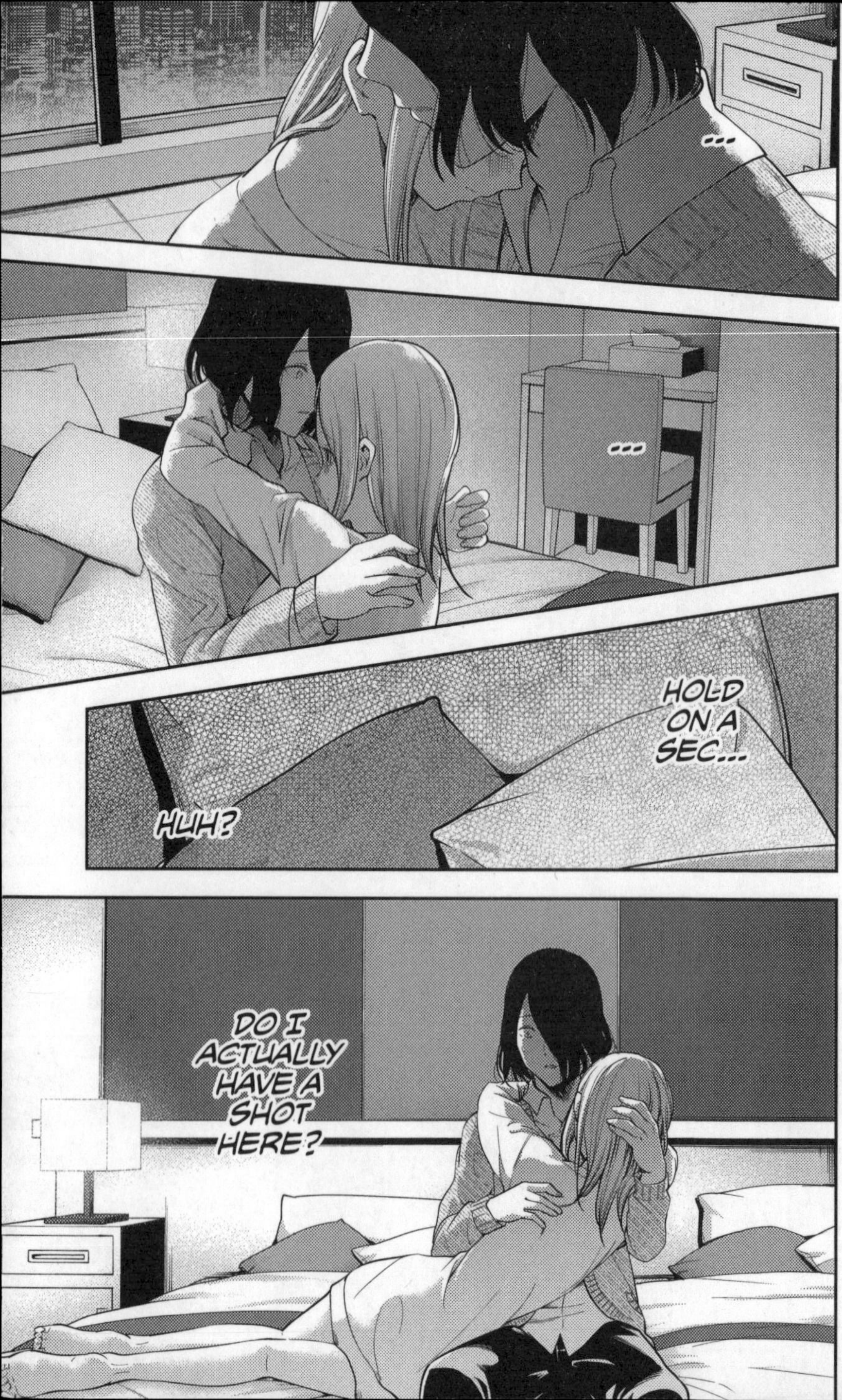
...
...
HOLD ON A SEC...
HUH?
DO I ACTUALLY HAVE A SHOT HERE?

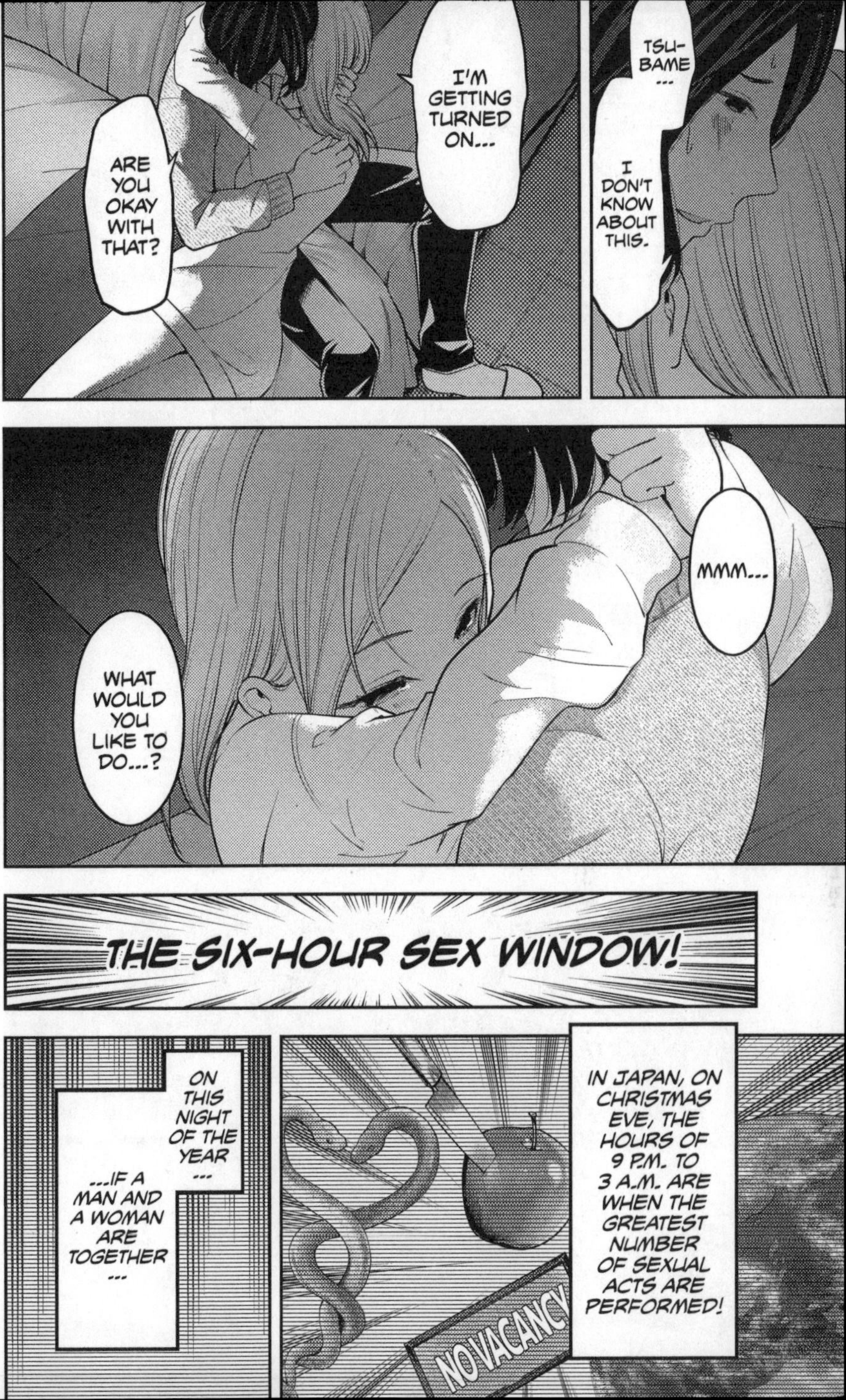
TSU-BAME...
I DON'T KNOW ABOUT THIS.
I'M GETTING TURNED ON...
ARE YOU OKAY WITH THAT?
MMM...
WHAT WOULD YOU LIKE TO DO...?
THE SIX-HOUR SEX WINDOW!
IN JAPAN, ON CHRISTMAS EVE, THE HOURS OF 9 P.M. TO 3 A.M. ARE WHEN THE GREATEST NUMBER OF SEXUAL ACTS ARE PERFORMED!
NO VACANCY
ON THIS NIGHT OF THE YEAR...
...IF A MAN AND A WOMAN ARE TOGETHER...

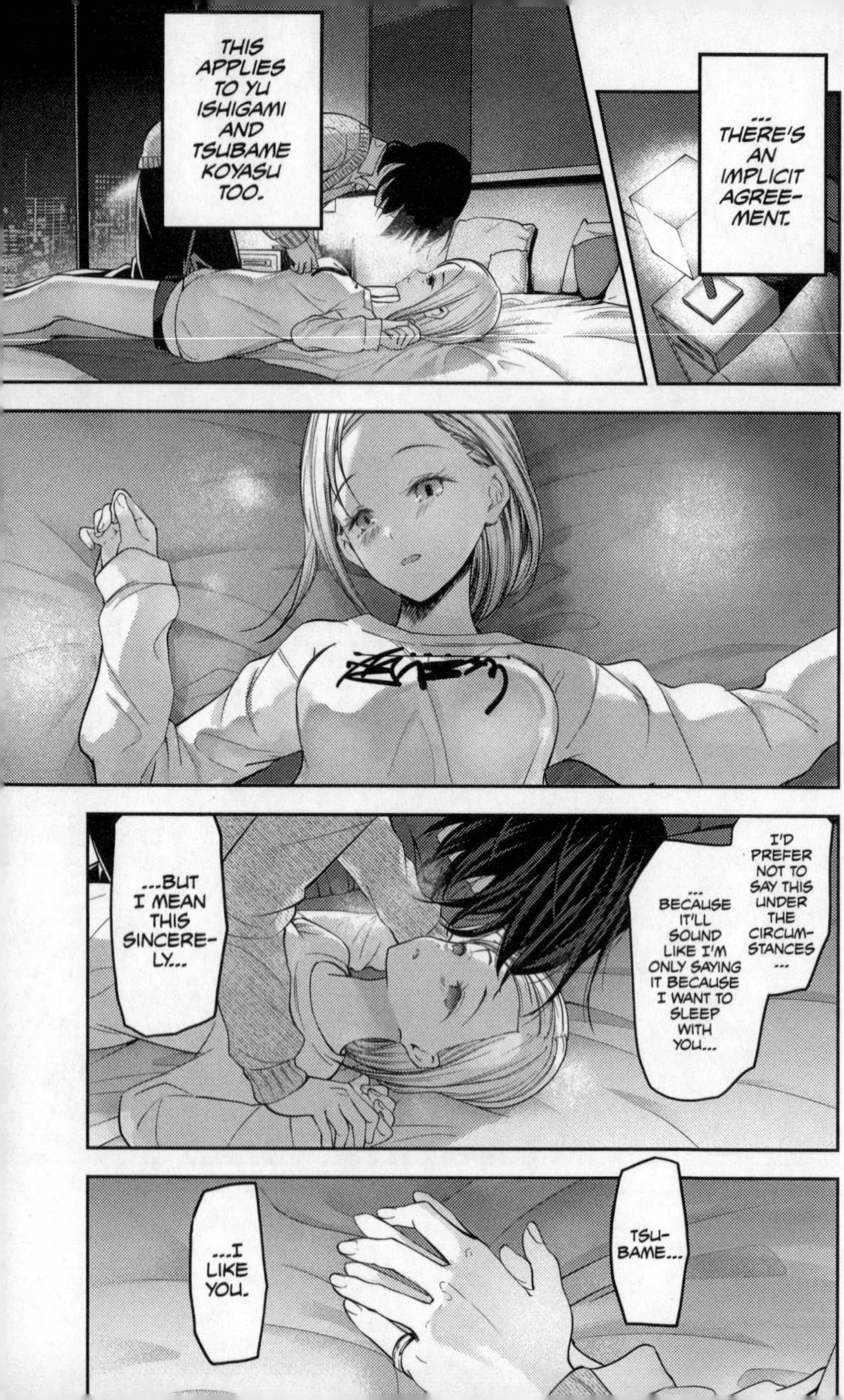
...THERE'S AN IMPLICIT AGREEMENT.
THIS APPLIES TO YU ISHIGAMI AND TSUBAME KOYASU TOO.
I'D PREFER NOT TO SAY THIS UNDER THE CIRCUMSTANCES...
...BECAUSE IT'LL SOUND LIKE I'M ONLY SAYING IT BECAUSE I WANT TO SLEEP WITH YOU...
...BUT I MEAN THIS SINCERELY...
TSUBAME...
...I LIKE YOU.

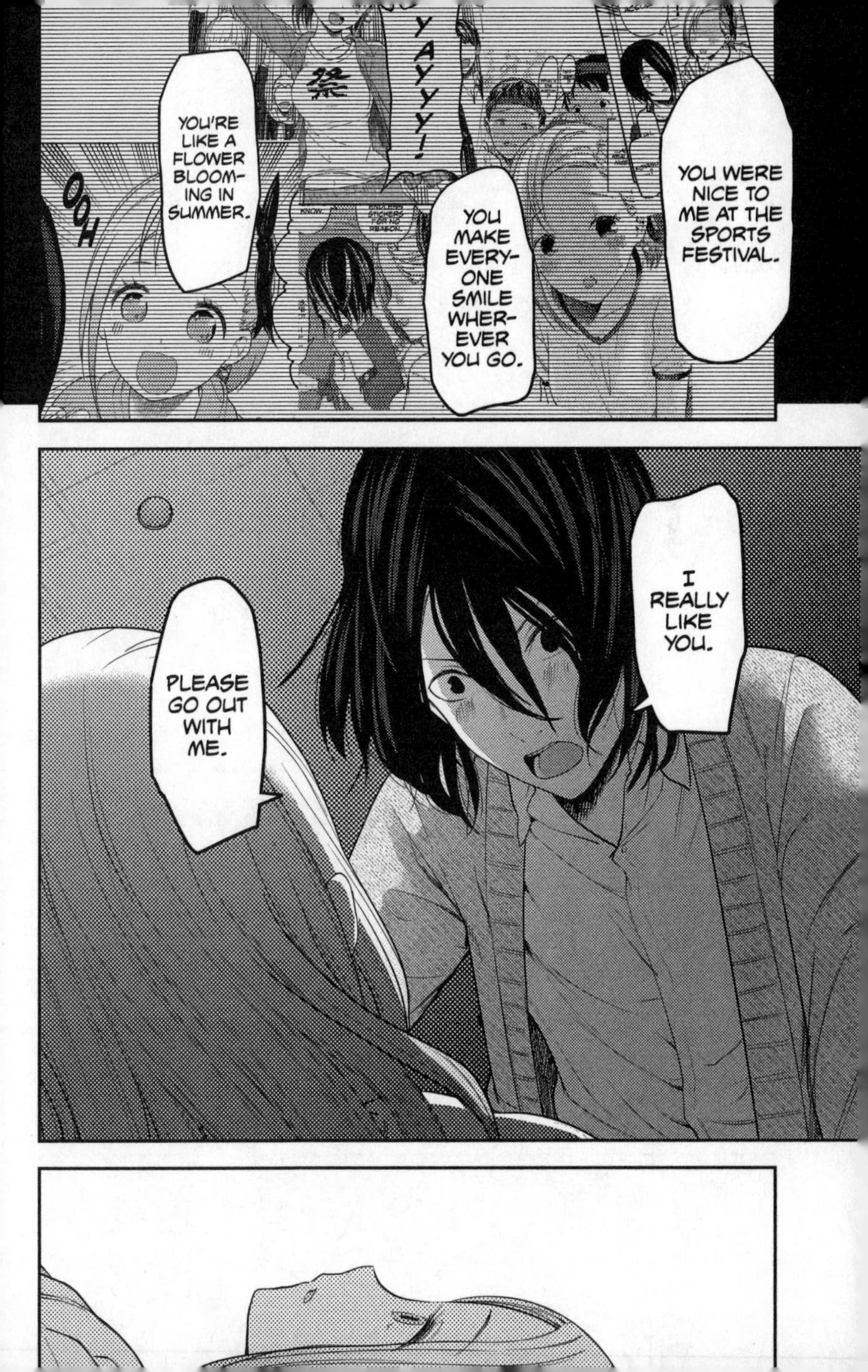
YOU WERE NICE TO ME AT THE SPORTS FESTIVAL.
YOU MAKE EVERY-ONE SMILE WHER-EVER YOU GO.
ENDLESS STICKERS FOR NO REASON.
YAYYY!
KNOW.
YOU'RE LIKE A FLOWER BLOOM-ING IN SUMMER.
OOH
I REALLY LIKE YOU.
PLEASE GO OUT WITH ME.

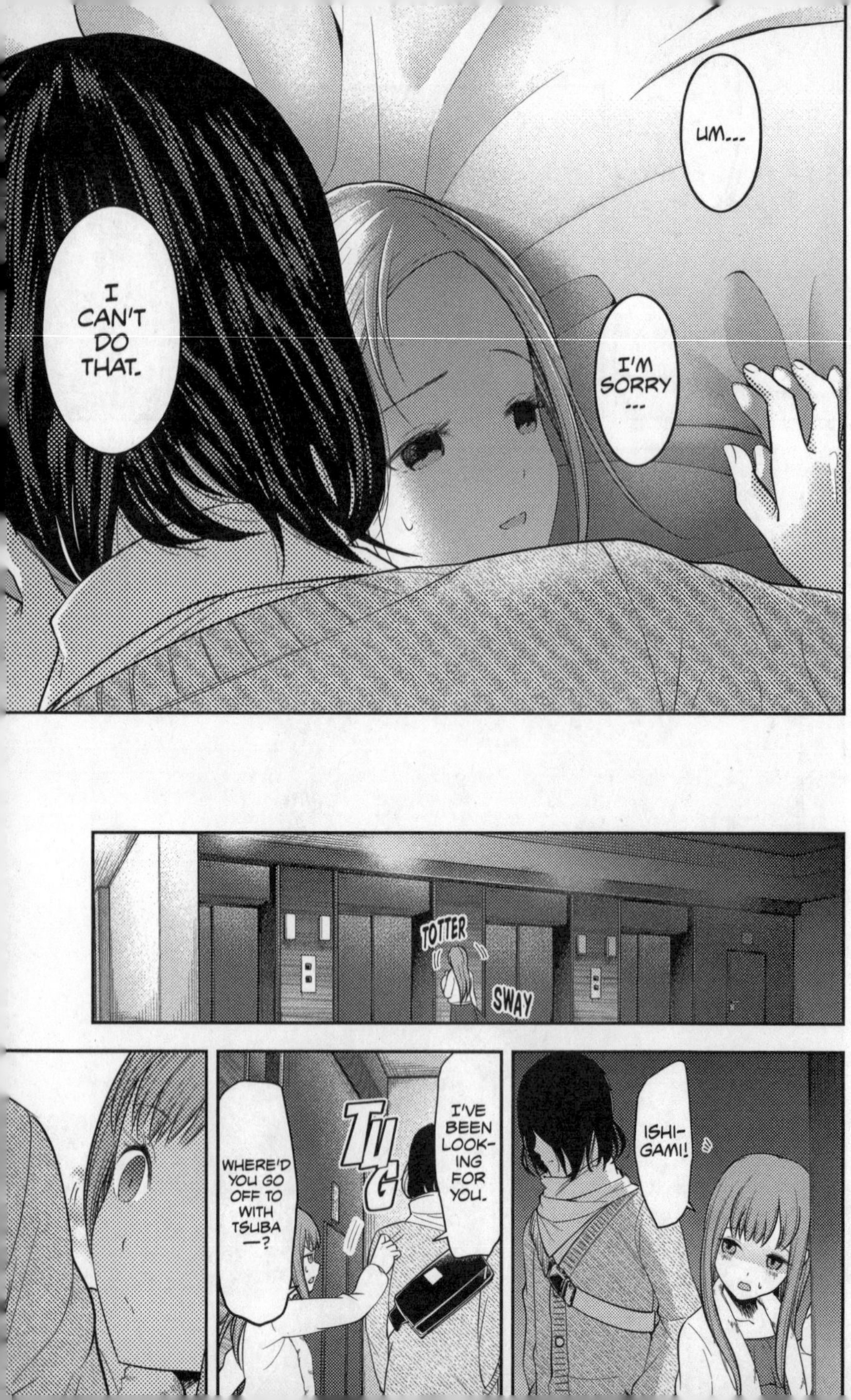
UM...
I'M SORRY...
I CAN'T DO THAT.
TOTTER
SWAY
ISHI-GAMI!
TUG
I'VE BEEN LOOKING FOR YOU.
WHERE'D YOU GO OFF TO WITH TSUBA—?

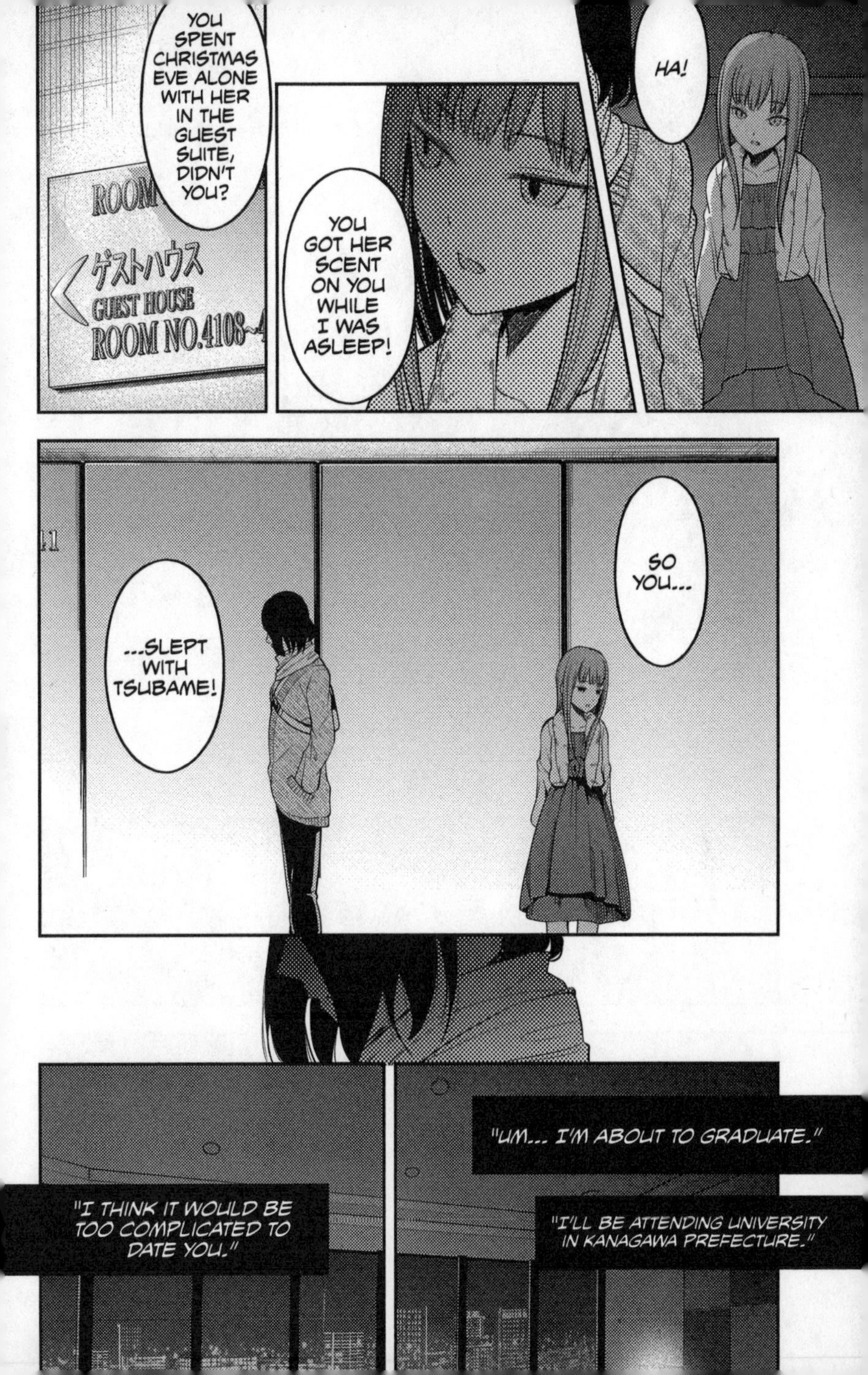
HA!
YOU GOT HER SCENT ON YOU WHILE I WAS ASLEEP!
YOU SPENT CHRISTMAS EVE ALONE WITH HER IN THE GUEST SUITE, DIDN'T YOU?
ROOM
ゲストハウス
GUEST HOUSE
ROOM NO.4108~4
SO YOU...
...SLEPT WITH TSUBAME!
"UM... I'M ABOUT TO GRADUATE."
"I'LL BE ATTENDING UNIVERSITY IN KANAGAWA PREFECTURE."
"I THINK IT WOULD BE TOO COMPLICATED TO DATE YOU."

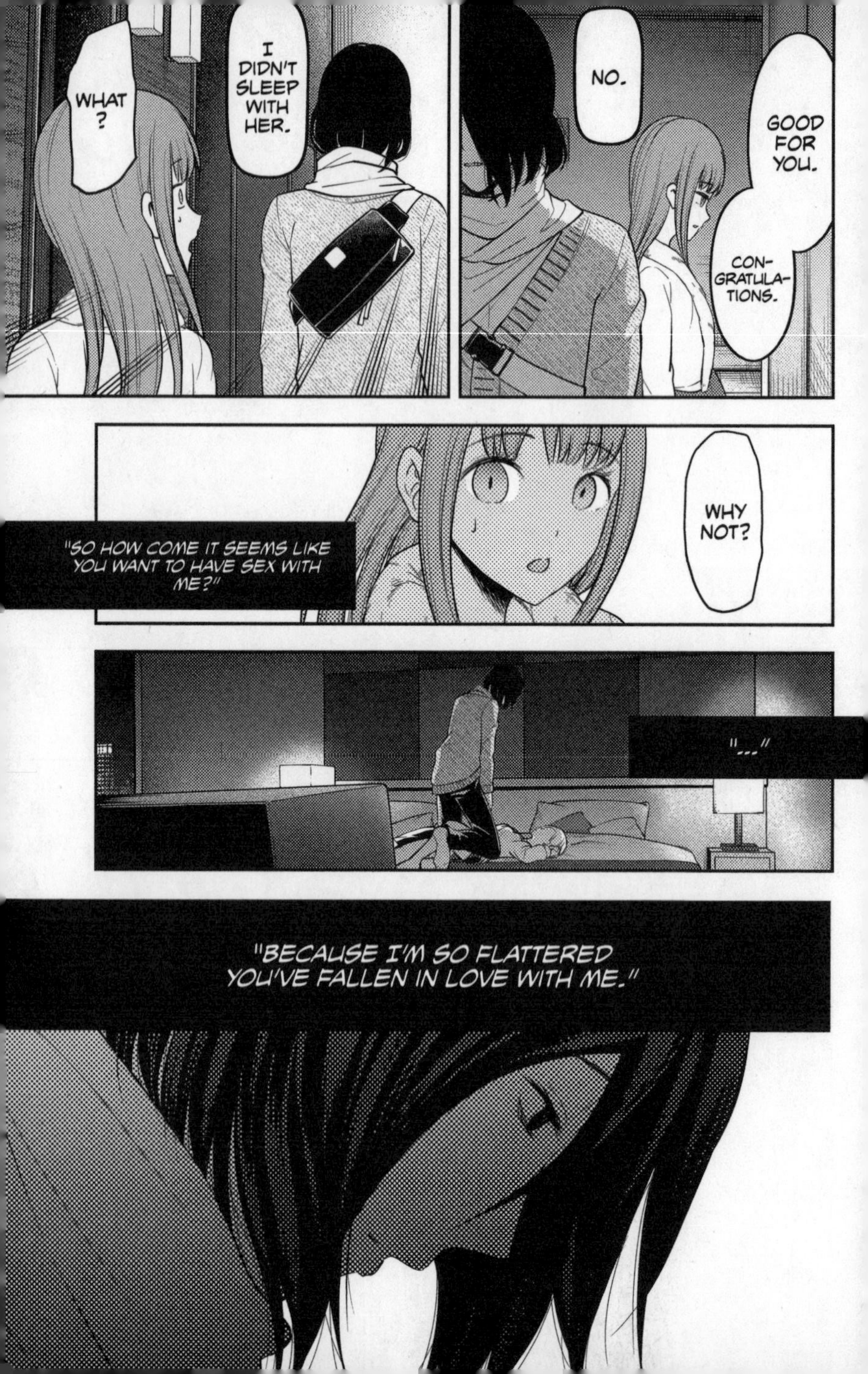
GOOD FOR YOU.
CON-GRATULA-TIONS.
NO.
I DIDN'T SLEEP WITH HER.
WHAT?
WHY NOT?
"SO HOW COME IT SEEMS LIKE YOU WANT TO HAVE SEX WITH ME?"
"..."
"BECAUSE I'M SO FLATTERED YOU'VE FALLEN IN LOVE WITH ME."

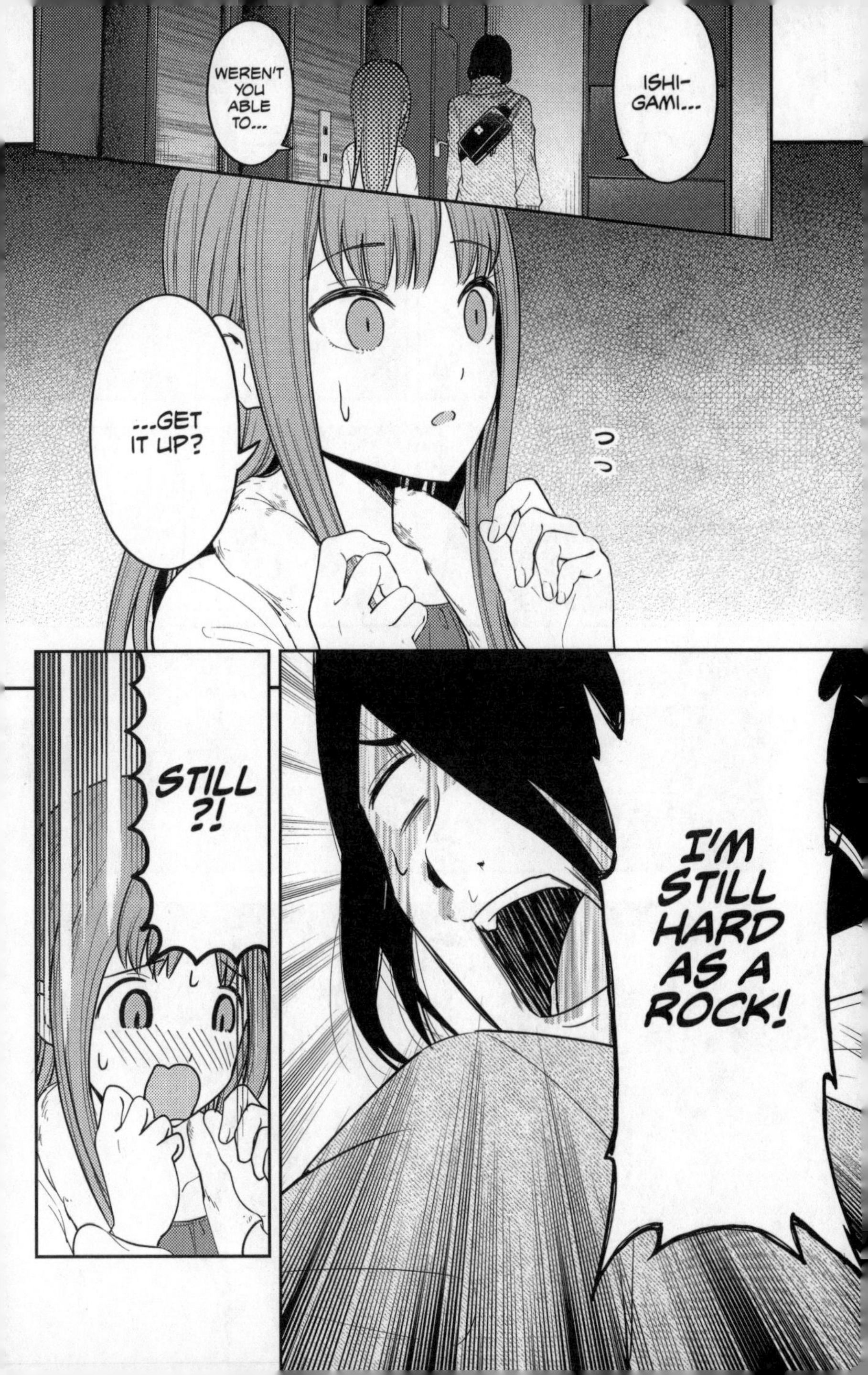
ISHI-GAMI...
WEREN'T YOU ABLE TO...
...GET IT UP?
I'M STILL HARD AS A ROCK!
STILL ?!

WHERE EVERYONE LIVES

KAGUYA: SENGAKUJI, MINATO WARD
SHIROGANE: SANGENJAYA, SETAGAYA WARD
FUJIWARA: SHOTO, SHIBUYA WARD
ISHIGAMI: NAKAMEGURO, MEGURO WARD
INO: DAIKANYAMA, SHIBUYA WARD
KOYASU: KONAN, MINATO WARD

KAGUYA-SAMA

LOVE IS WAR

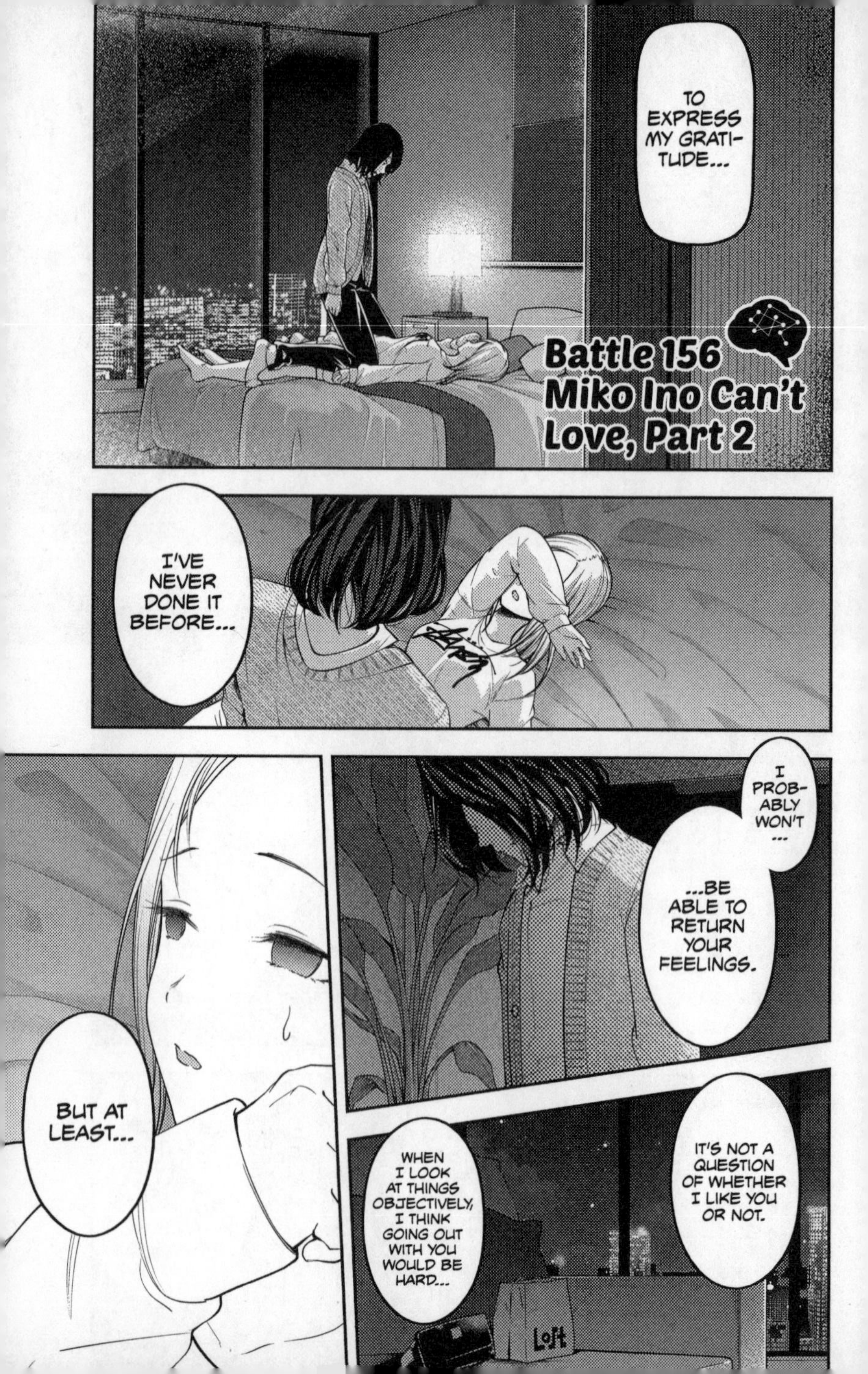
TO EXPRESS MY GRATITUDE...
Battle 156 Miko Ino Can't Love, Part 2
I'VE NEVER DONE IT BEFORE...
I PROBABLY WON'T ...
...BE ABLE TO RETURN YOUR FEELINGS.
IT'S NOT A QUESTION OF WHETHER I LIKE YOU OR NOT.
WHEN I LOOK AT THINGS OBJECTIVELY, I THINK GOING OUT WITH YOU WOULD BE HARD...
Loft
BUT AT LEAST...

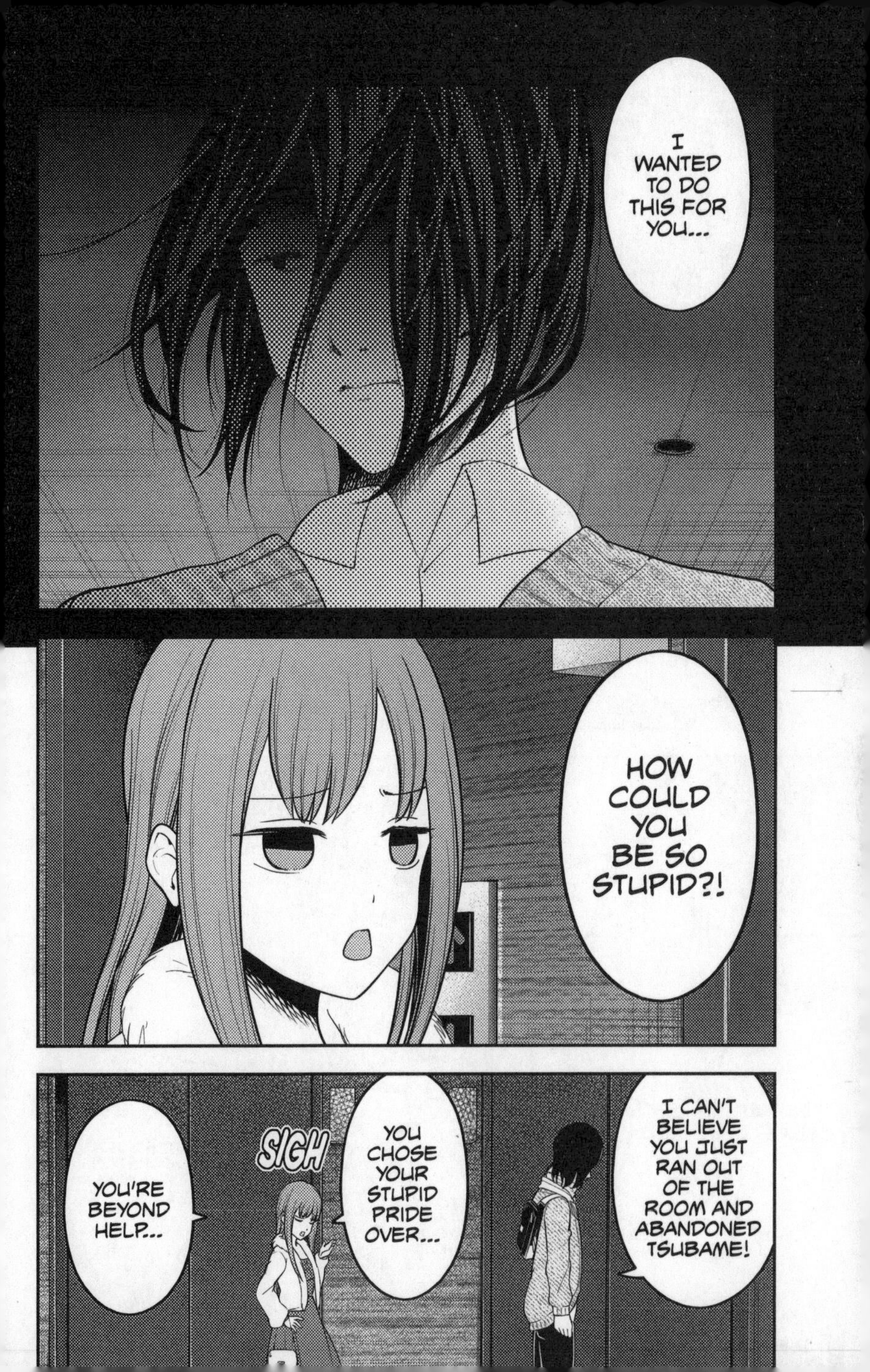
I WANTED TO DO THIS FOR YOU...
HOW COULD YOU BE SO STUPID?!
I CAN'T BELIEVE YOU JUST RAN OUT OF THE ROOM AND ABANDONED TSUBAME!
YOU CHOSE YOUR STUPID PRIDE OVER...
SIGH
YOU'RE BEYOND HELP...

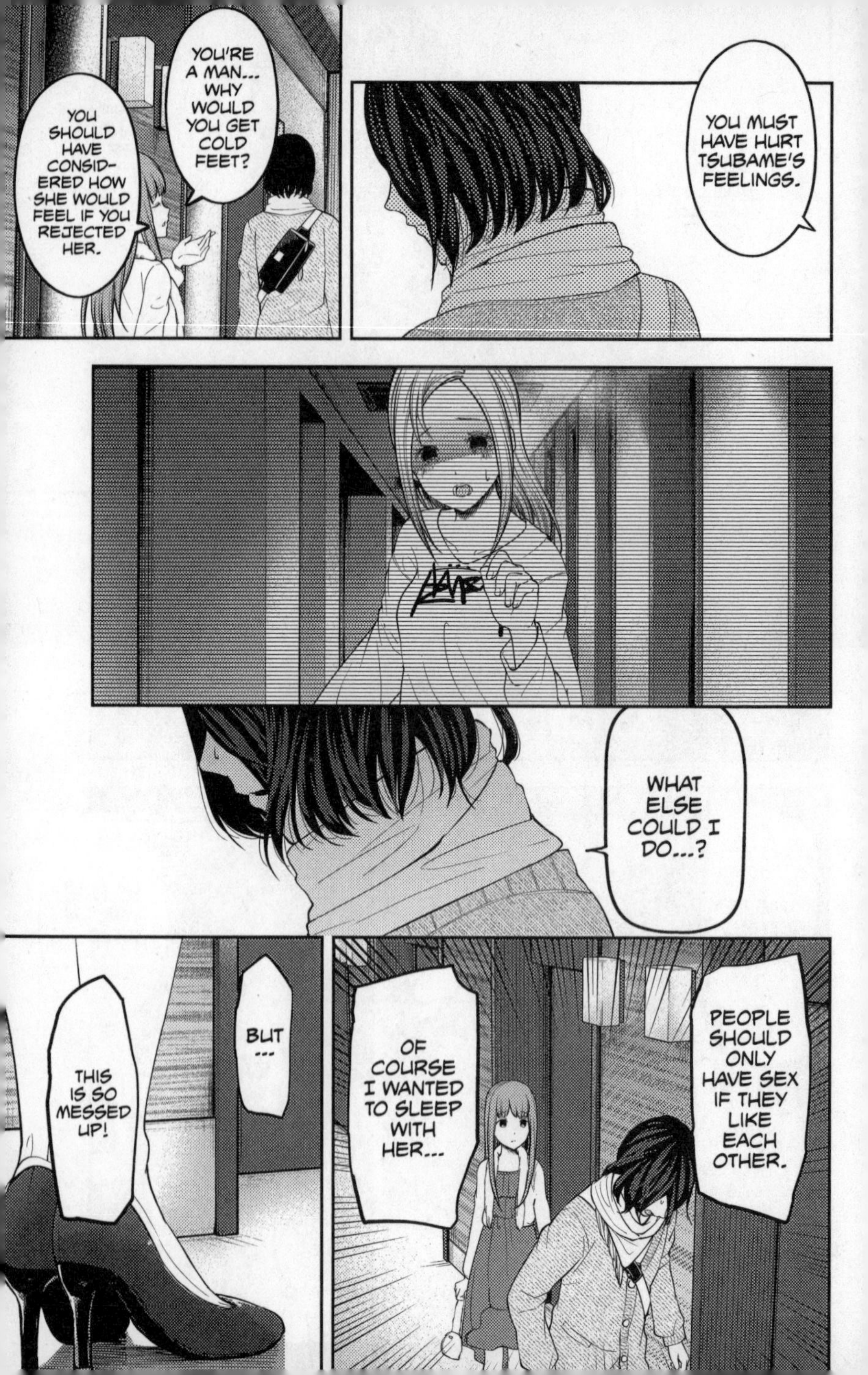
YOU MUST HAVE HURT TSUBAME'S FEELINGS.
YOU'RE A MAN... WHY WOULD YOU GET COLD FEET?
YOU SHOULD HAVE CONSIDERED HOW SHE WOULD FEEL IF YOU REJECTED HER.
WHAT ELSE COULD I DO...?
PEOPLE SHOULD ONLY HAVE SEX IF THEY LIKE EACH OTHER.
OF COURSE I WANTED TO SLEEP WITH HER...
BUT...
THIS IS SO MESSED UP!

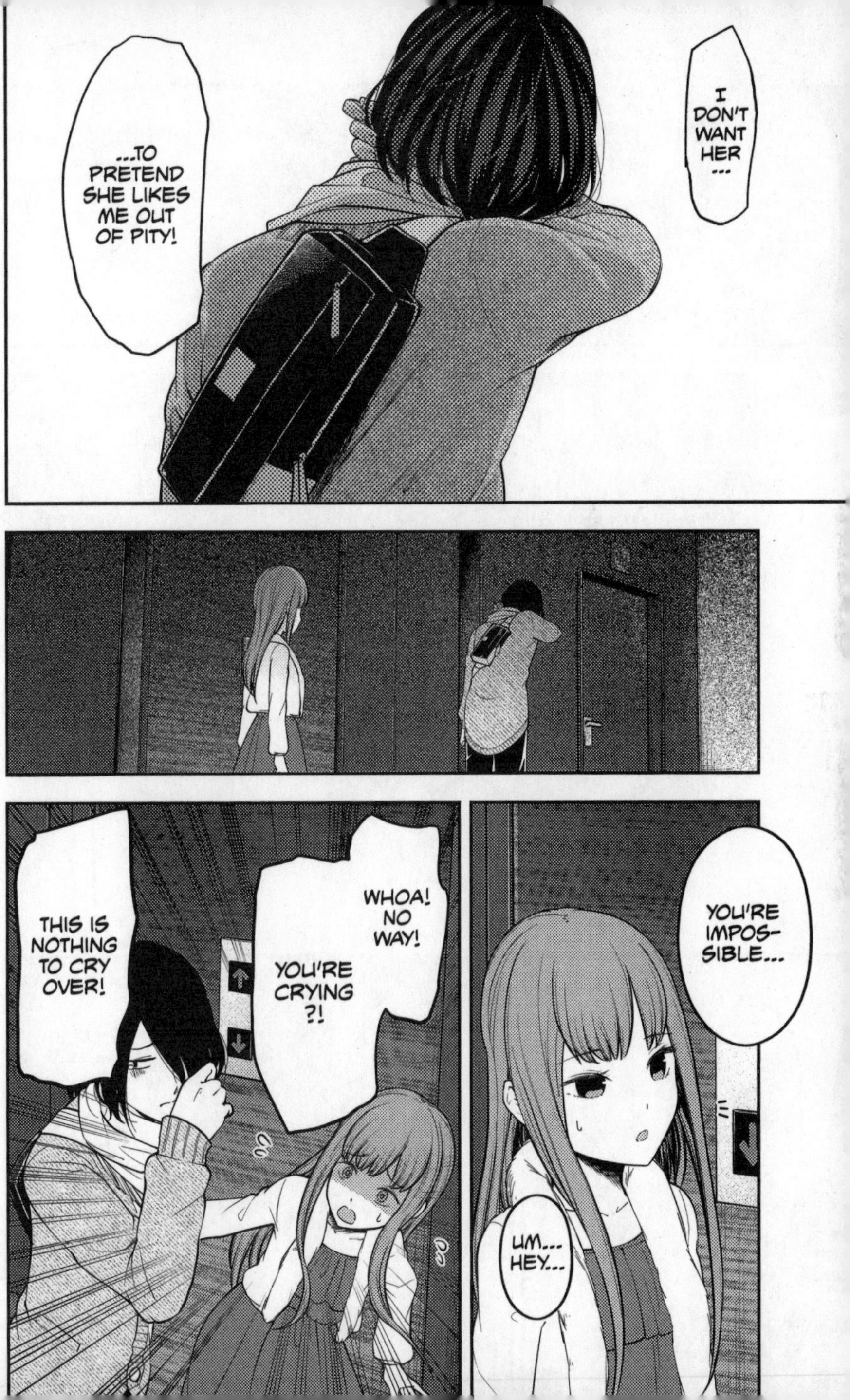
I DON'T WANT HER...
...TO PRETEND SHE LIKES ME OUT OF PITY!
YOU'RE IMPOS-SIBLE...
UM... HEY...
WHOA! NO WAY!
YOU'RE CRYING?!
THIS IS NOTHING TO CRY OVER!

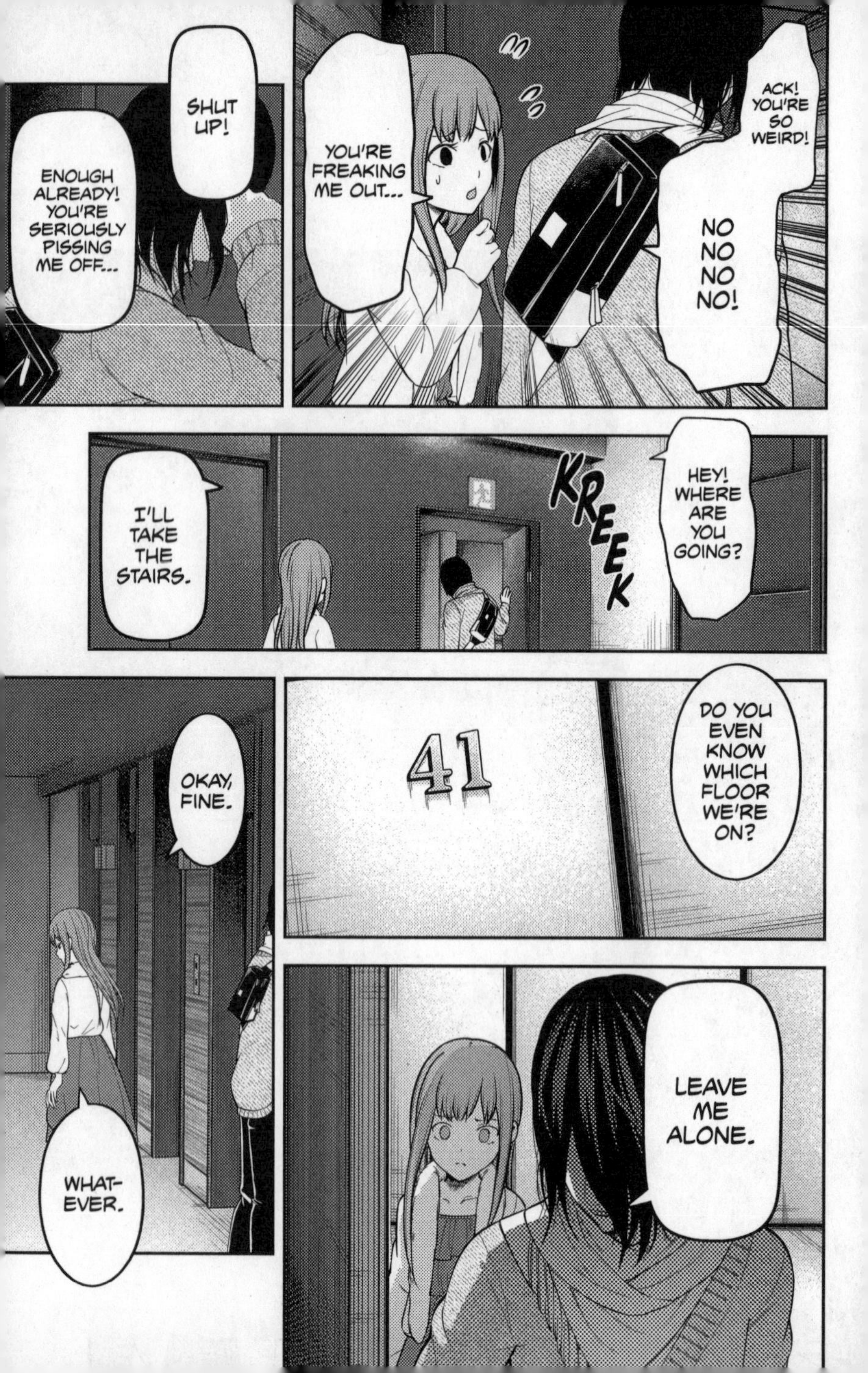
ACK! YOU'RE SO WEIRD!
NO NO NO NO!
YOU'RE FREAKING ME OUT...
SHUT UP!
ENOUGH ALREADY! YOU'RE SERIOUSLY PISSING ME OFF...
HEY! WHERE ARE YOU GOING?
KREEK
I'LL TAKE THE STAIRS.
41
DO YOU EVEN KNOW WHICH FLOOR WE'RE ON?
LEAVE ME ALONE.
OKAY, FINE.
WHAT-EVER.

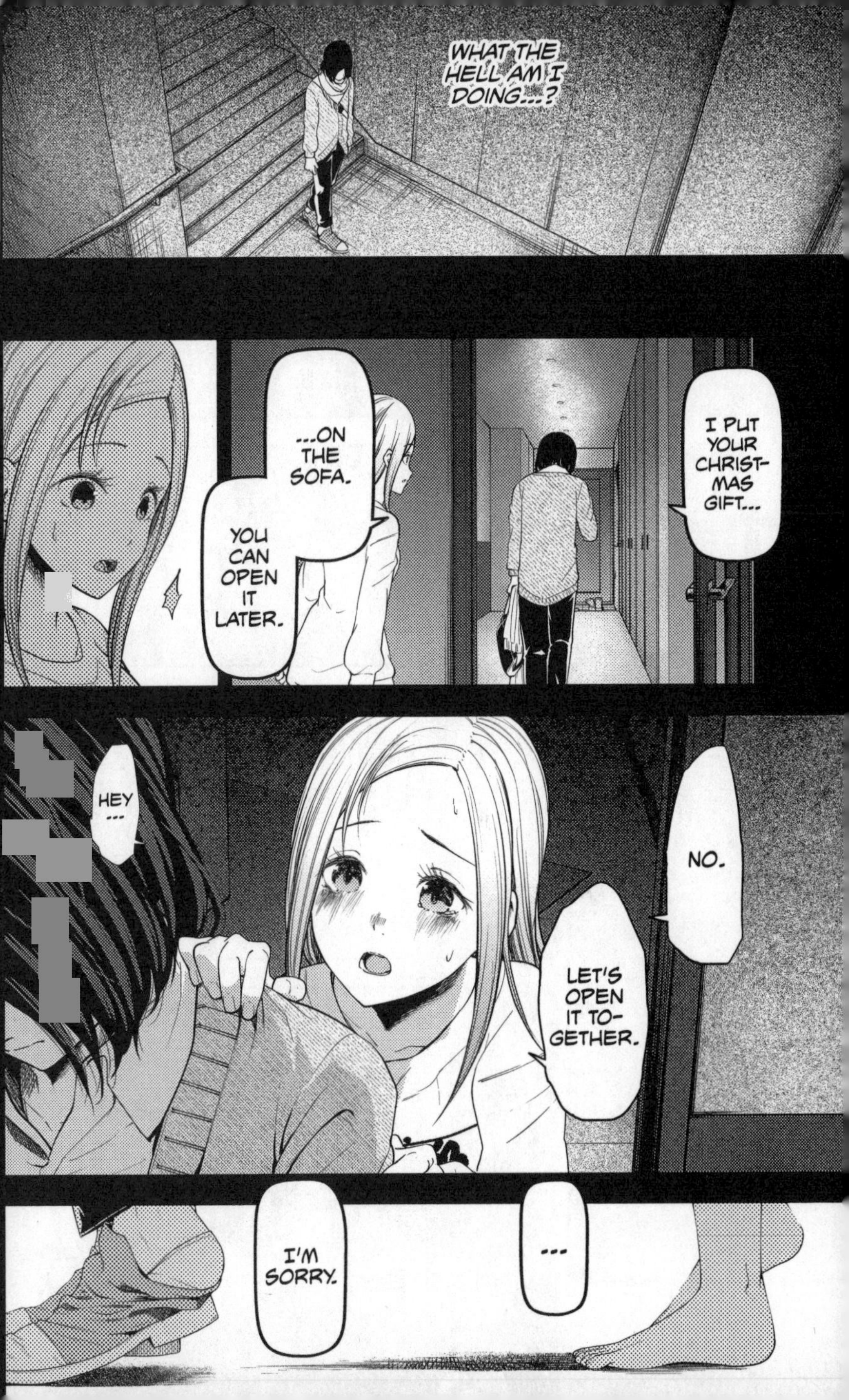
WHAT THE HELL AM I DOING...?
I PUT YOUR CHRIST-MAS GIFT...
...ON THE SOFA.
YOU CAN OPEN IT LATER.
NO.
LET'S OPEN IT TO-GETHER.
HEY...
...
I'M SORRY.

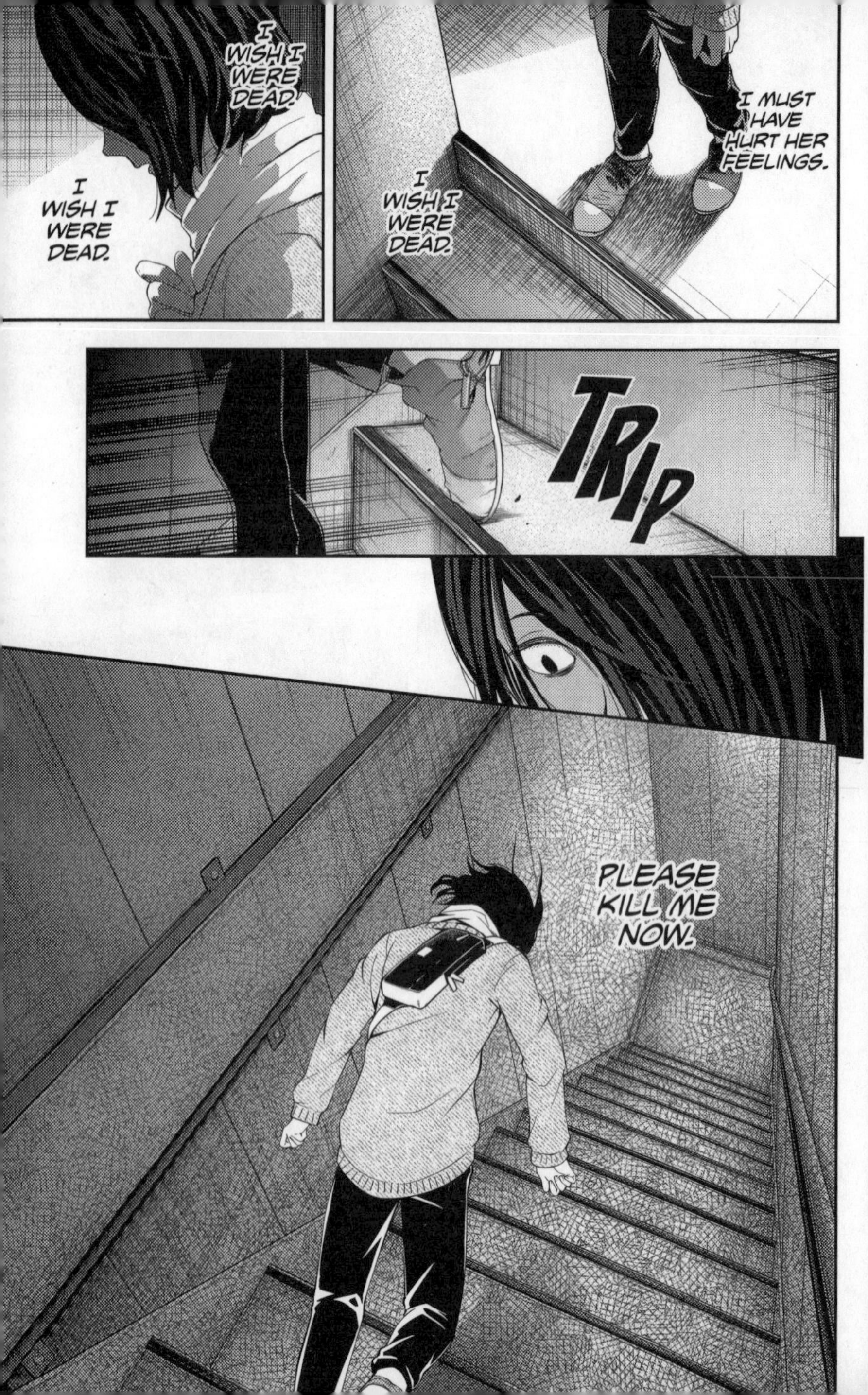
I MUST HAVE HURT HER FEELINGS.
I WISH I WERE DEAD.
I WISH I WERE DEAD.
I WISH I WERE DEAD.
TRIP
PLEASE KILL ME NOW.

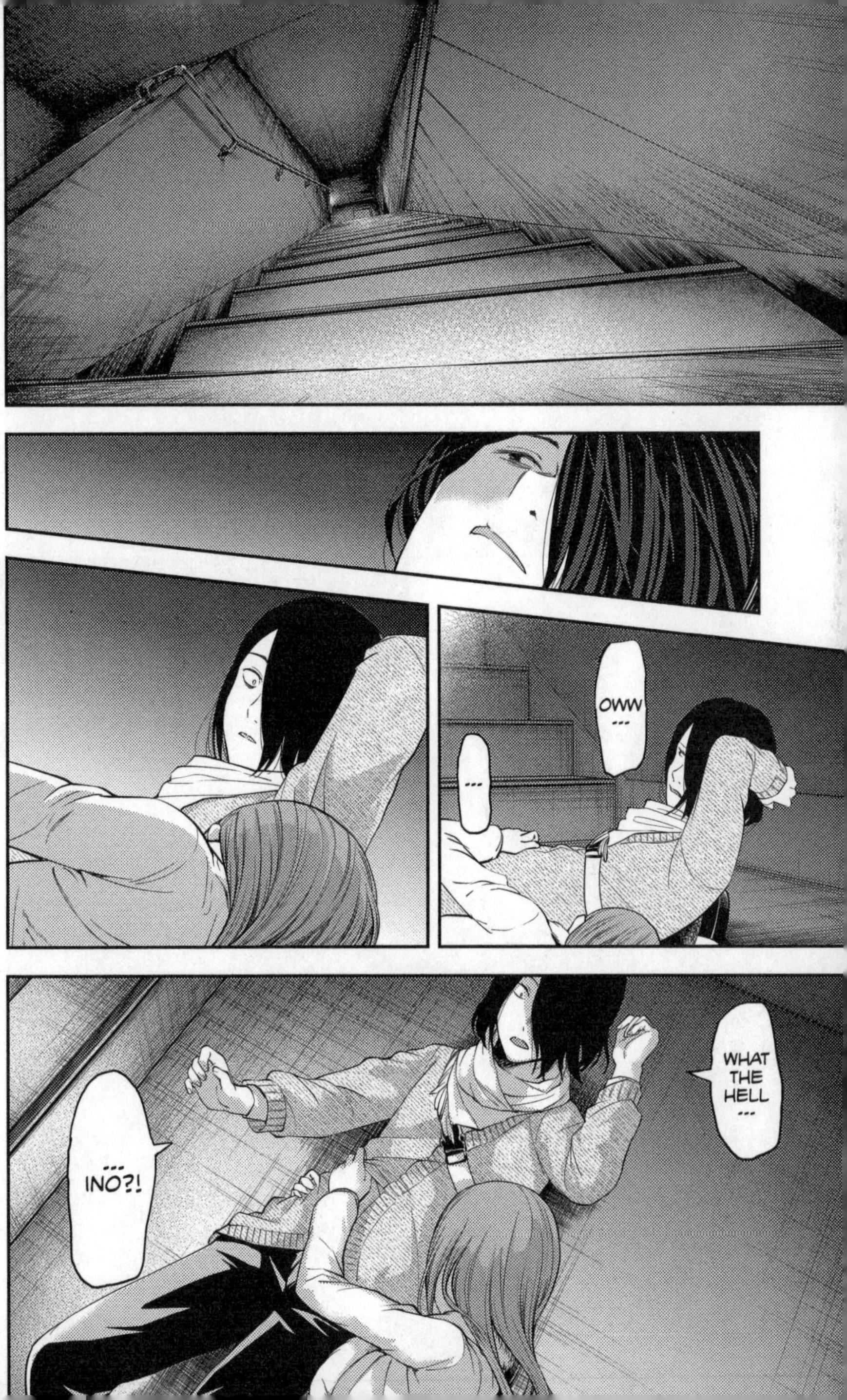
OWW ...
...
WHAT THE HELL ...
... INO?!

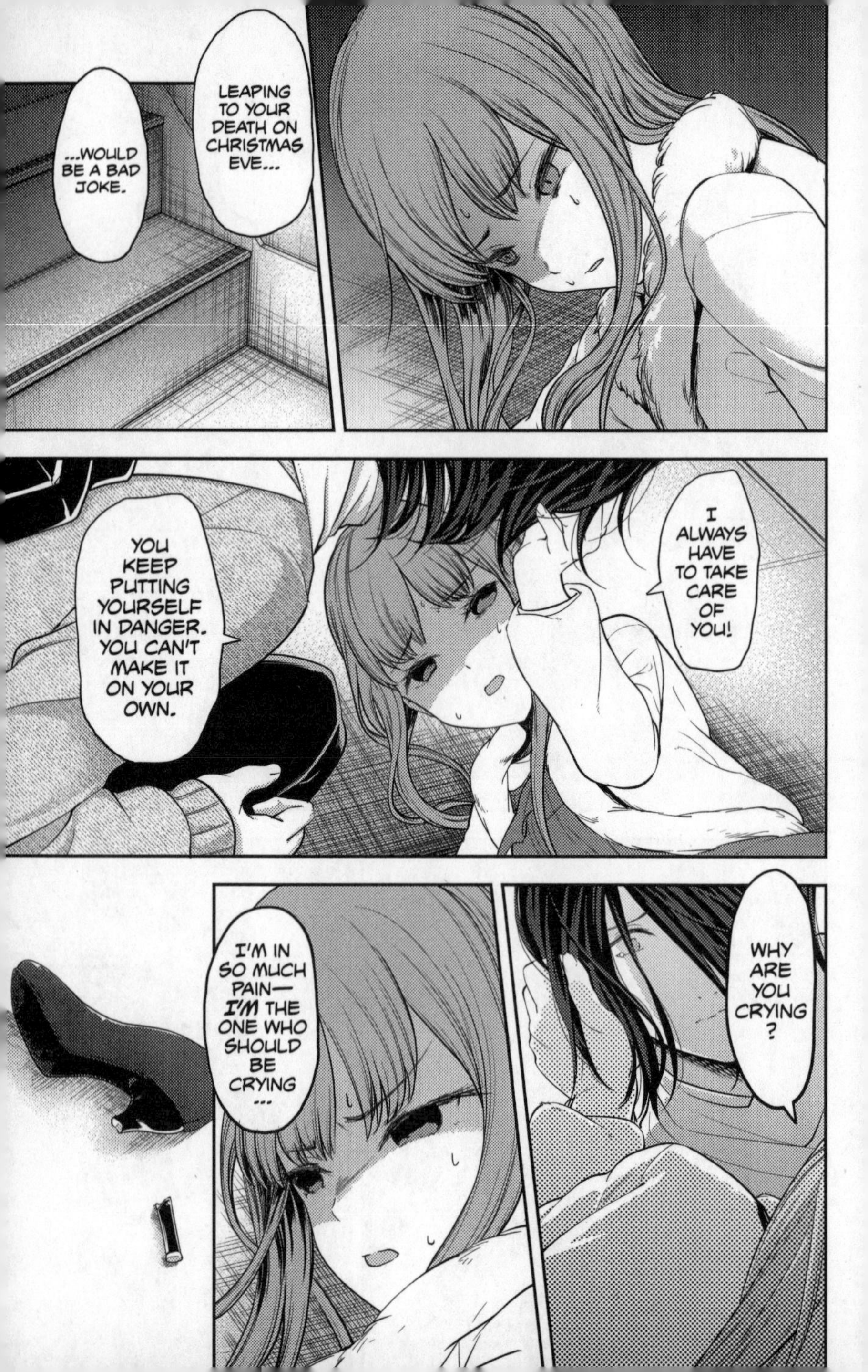
LEAPING TO YOUR DEATH ON CHRISTMAS EVE...
...WOULD BE A BAD JOKE.
I ALWAYS HAVE TO TAKE CARE OF YOU!
YOU KEEP PUTTING YOURSELF IN DANGER. YOU CAN'T MAKE IT ON YOUR OWN.
WHY ARE YOU CRYING?
I'M IN SO MUCH PAIN—*I'M* THE ONE WHO SHOULD BE CRYING...

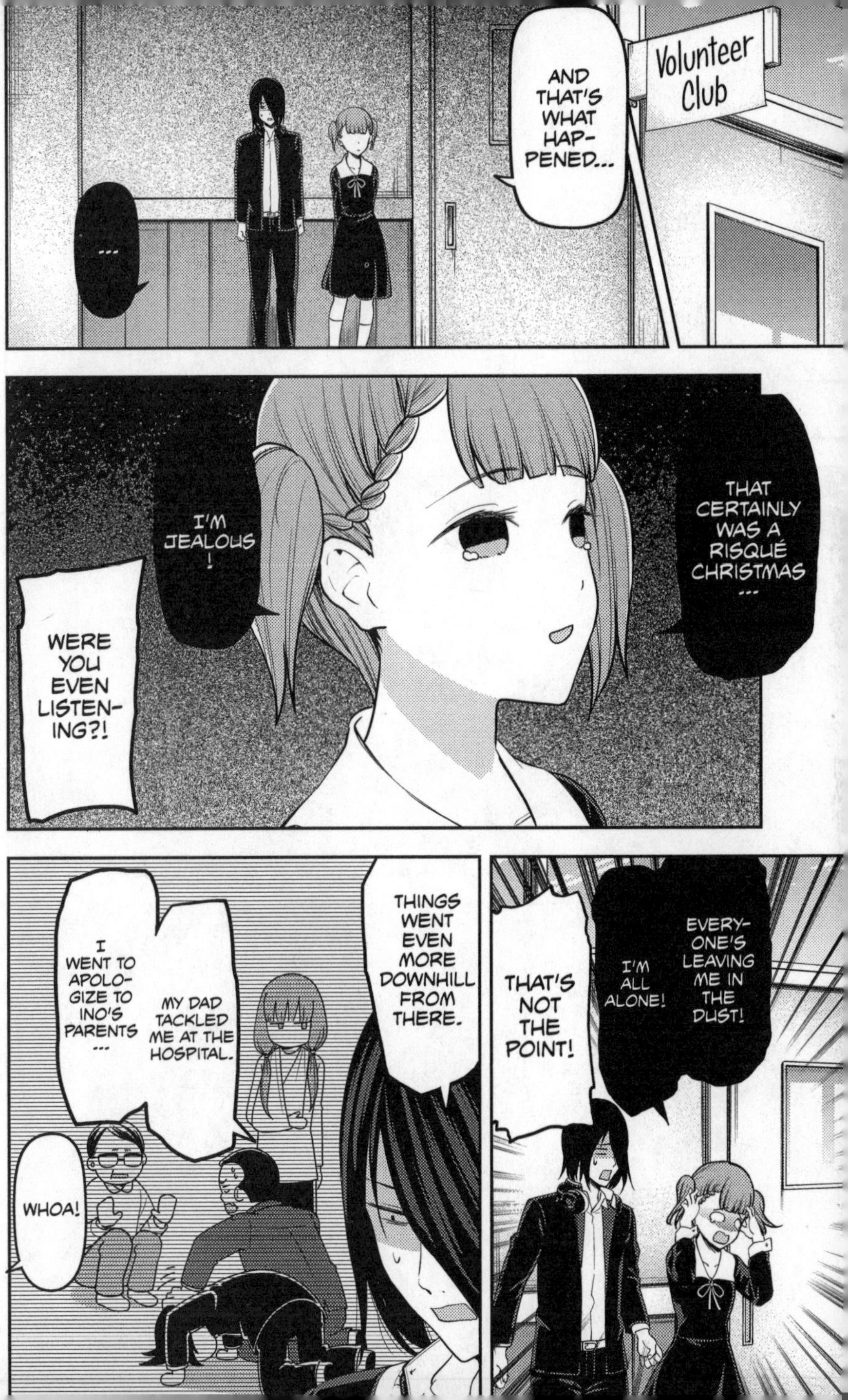
Volunteer Club
AND THAT'S WHAT HAP-PENED...
...
THAT CERTAINLY WAS A RISQUÉ CHRISTMAS...
I'M JEALOUS!
WERE YOU EVEN LISTEN-ING?!
EVERY-ONE'S LEAVING ME IN THE DUST!
I'M ALL ALONE!
THAT'S NOT THE POINT!
THINGS WENT EVEN MORE DOWNHILL FROM THERE.
I WENT TO APOLO-GIZE TO INO'S PARENTS...
MY DAD TACKLED ME AT THE HOSPITAL.
WHOA!

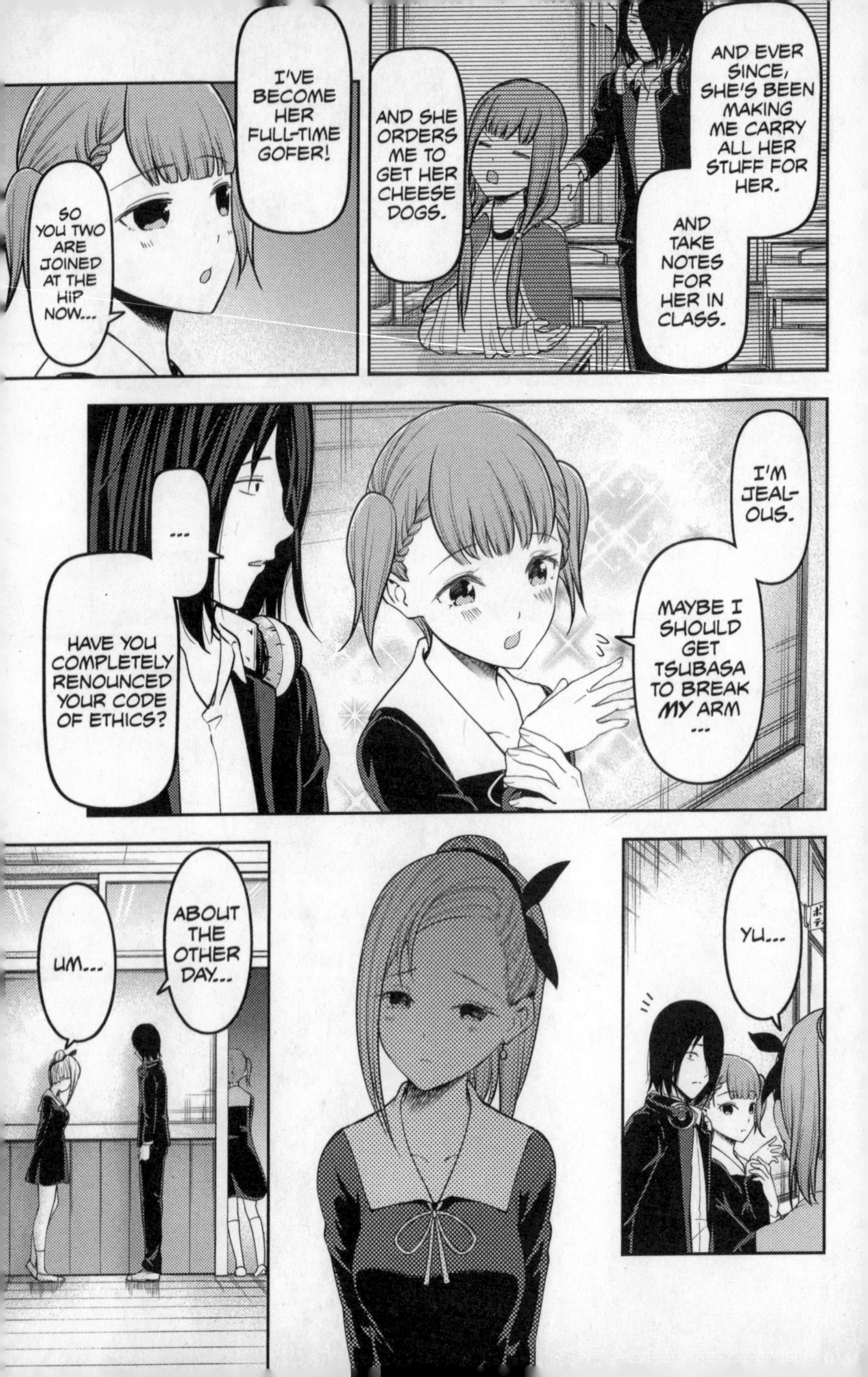
AND EVER SINCE, SHE'S BEEN MAKING ME CARRY ALL HER STUFF FOR HER.
AND TAKE NOTES FOR HER IN CLASS.
AND SHE ORDERS ME TO GET HER CHEESE DOGS.
I'VE BECOME HER FULL-TIME GOFER!
SO YOU TWO ARE JOINED AT THE HIP NOW...
I'M JEAL-OUS.
MAYBE I SHOULD GET TSUBASA TO BREAK MY ARM ...
...
HAVE YOU COMPLETELY RENOUNCED YOUR CODE OF ETHICS?
YU...
ABOUT THE OTHER DAY...
UM...

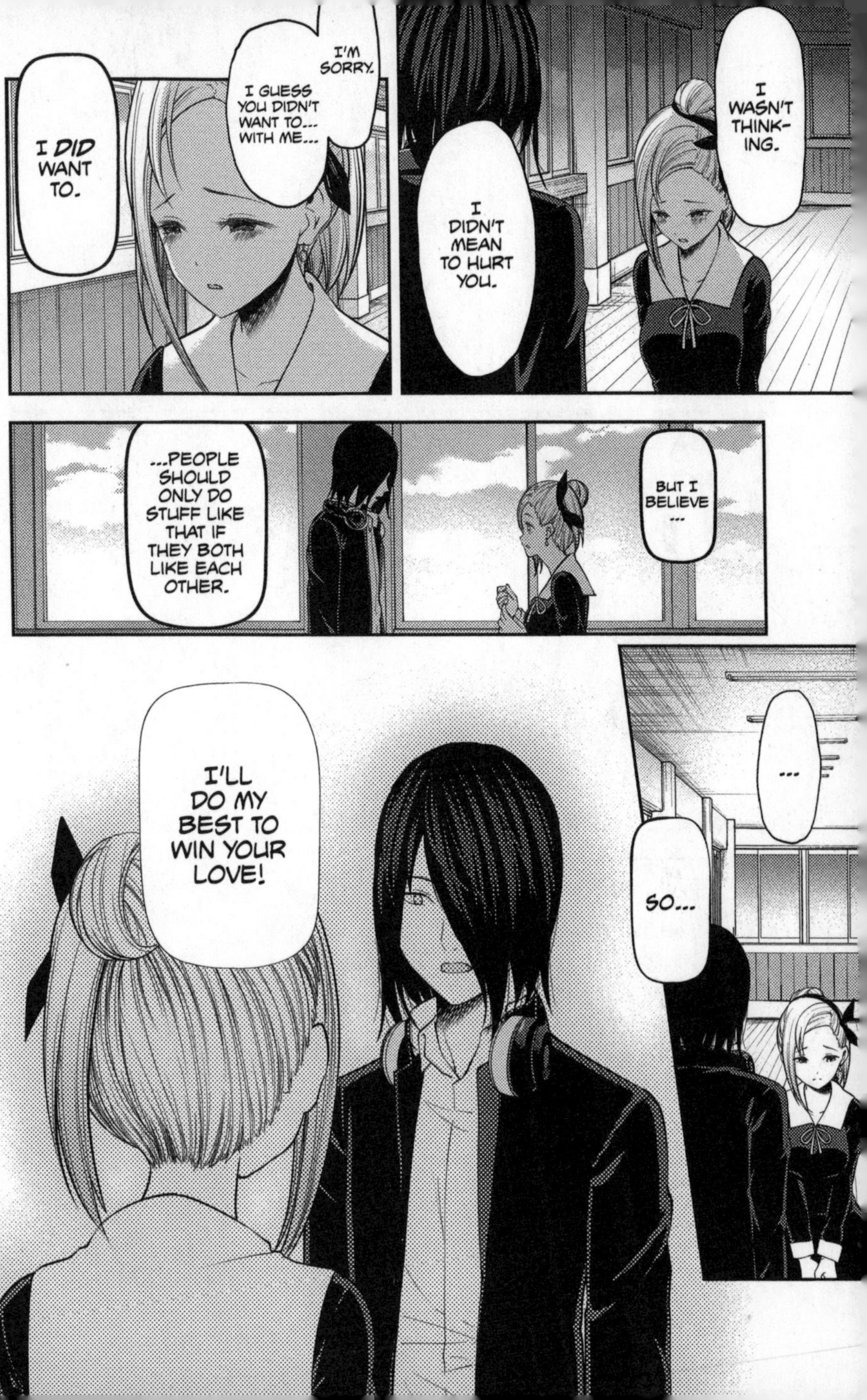
I WASN'T THINKING.
I DIDN'T MEAN TO HURT YOU.
I'M SORRY.
I GUESS YOU DIDN'T WANT TO... WITH ME...
I *DID* WANT TO.
BUT I BELIEVE...
...PEOPLE SHOULD ONLY DO STUFF LIKE THAT IF THEY BOTH LIKE EACH OTHER.
...
SO...
I'LL DO MY BEST TO WIN YOUR LOVE!

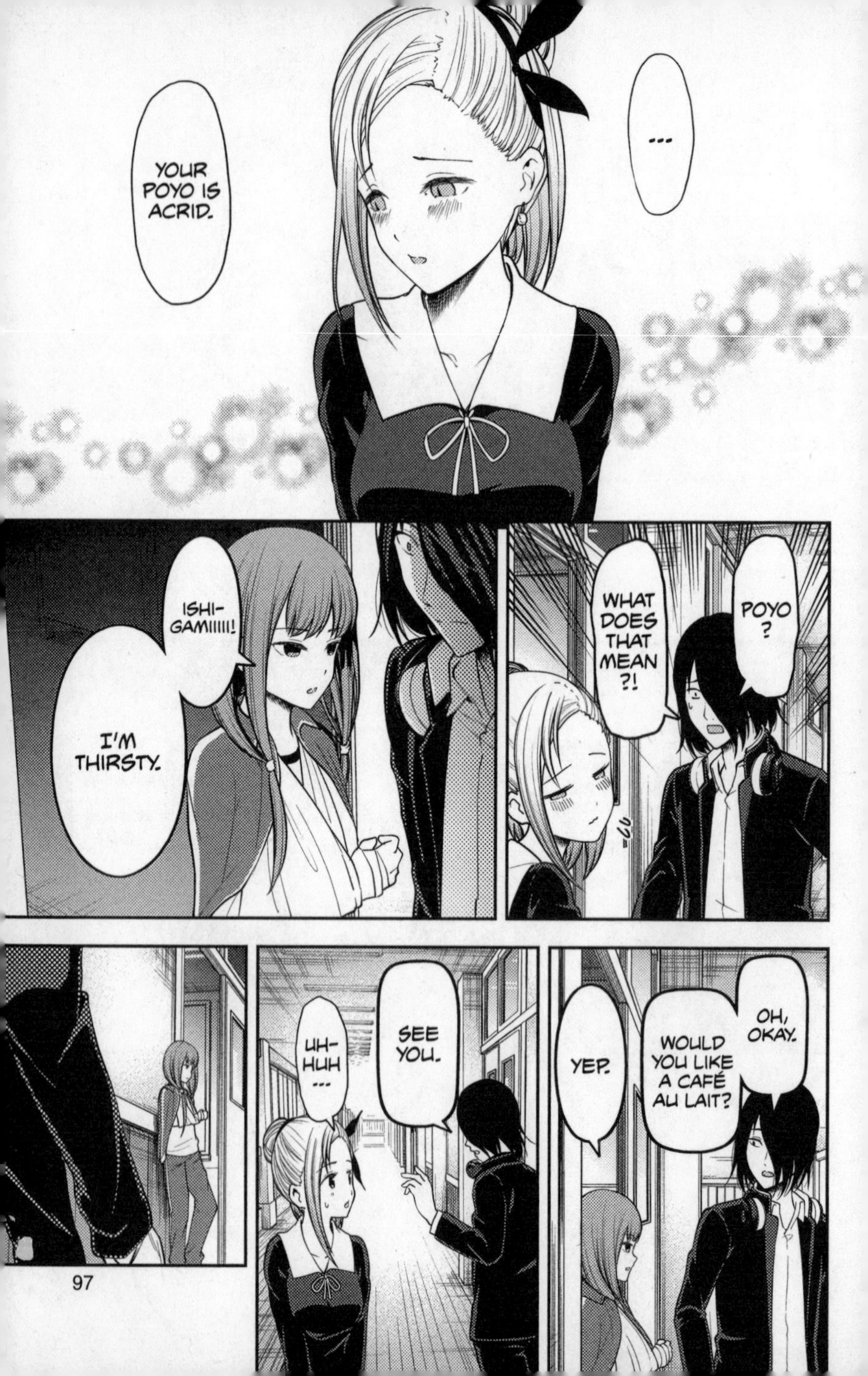
...
YOUR POYO IS ACRID.
POYO?
WHAT DOES THAT MEAN?!
ISHIGAMIIIII!
I'M THIRSTY.
OH, OKAY.
WOULD YOU LIKE A CAFÉ AU LAIT?
YEP.
SEE YOU.
UH-HUH...

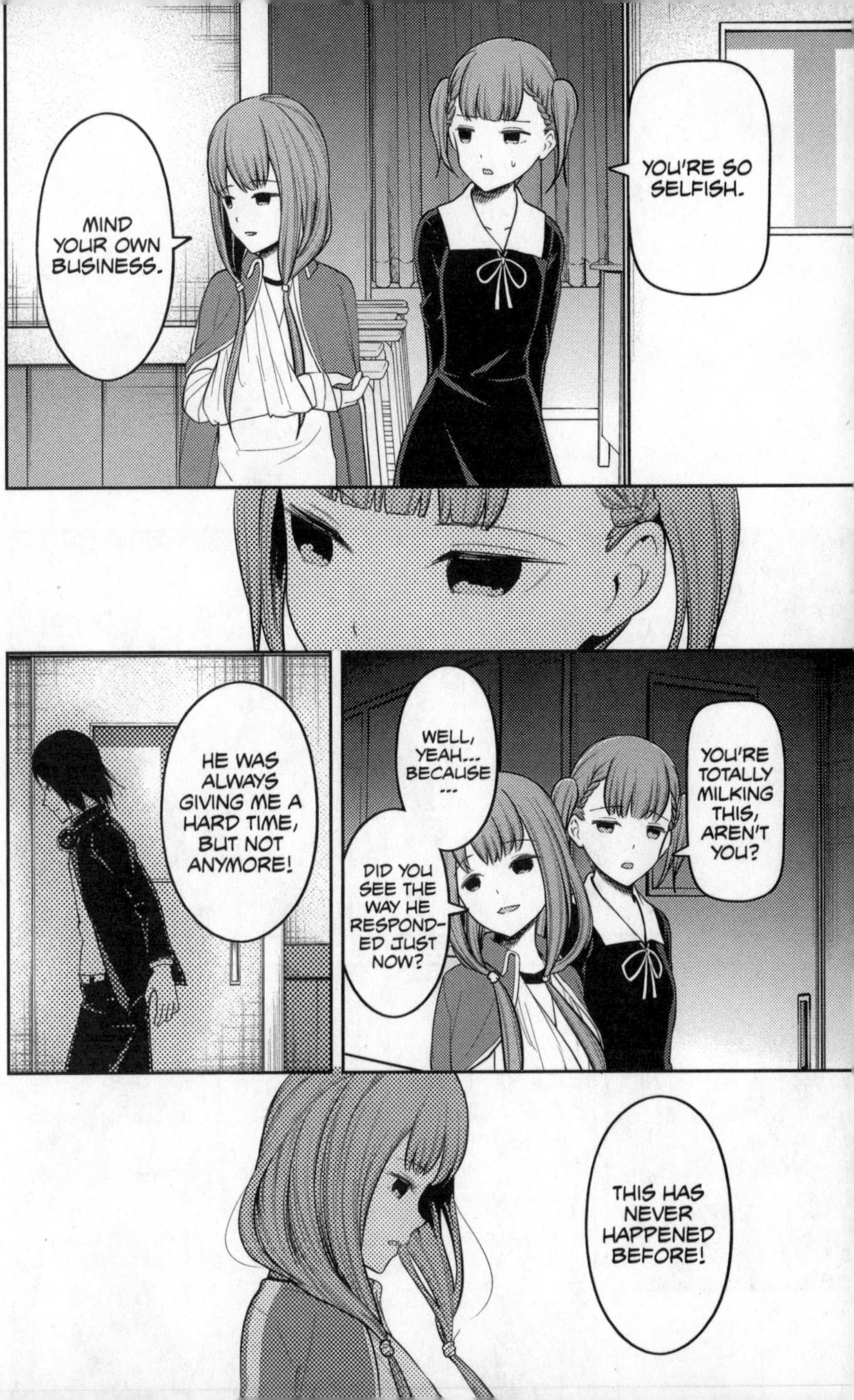
YOU'RE SO SELFISH.
MIND YOUR OWN BUSINESS.
YOU'RE TOTALLY MILKING THIS, AREN'T YOU?
WELL, YEAH... BECAUSE...
DID YOU SEE THE WAY HE RESPOND-ED JUST NOW?
HE WAS ALWAYS GIVING ME A HARD TIME, BUT NOT ANYMORE!
THIS HAS NEVER HAPPENED BEFORE!

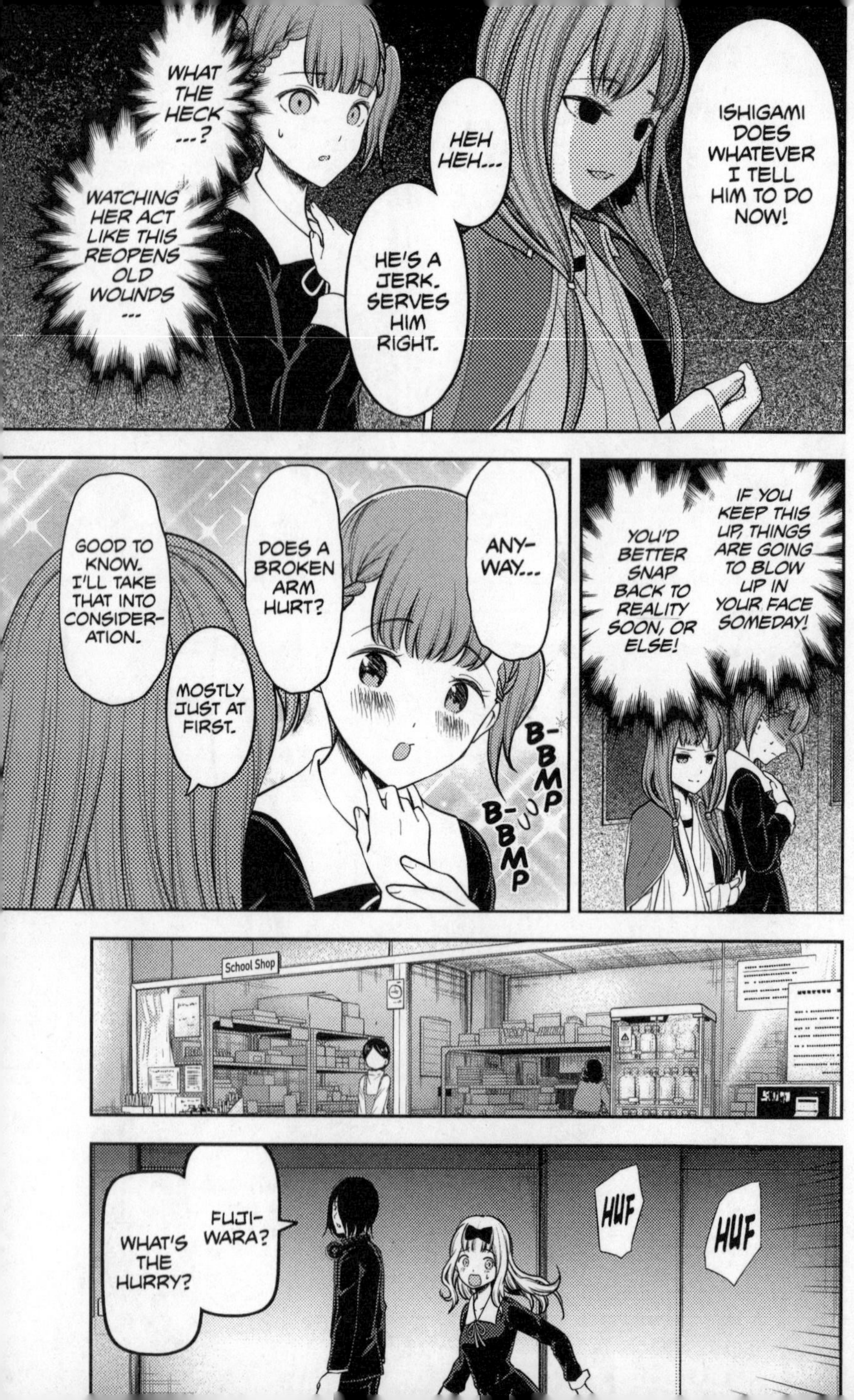
ISHIGAMI DOES WHATEVER I TELL HIM TO DO NOW!
HEH HEH...
HE'S A JERK. SERVES HIM RIGHT.
WHAT THE HECK...?
WATCHING HER ACT LIKE THIS REOPENS OLD WOUNDS...
IF YOU KEEP THIS UP, THINGS ARE GOING TO BLOW UP IN YOUR FACE SOMEDAY!
YOU'D BETTER SNAP BACK TO REALITY SOON, OR ELSE!
ANY-WAY...
DOES A BROKEN ARM HURT?
B-BMP
B-BMP
MOSTLY JUST AT FIRST.
GOOD TO KNOW. I'LL TAKE THAT INTO CONSIDER-ATION.
School Shop
HUF
HUF
FUJI-WARA?
WHAT'S THE HURRY?

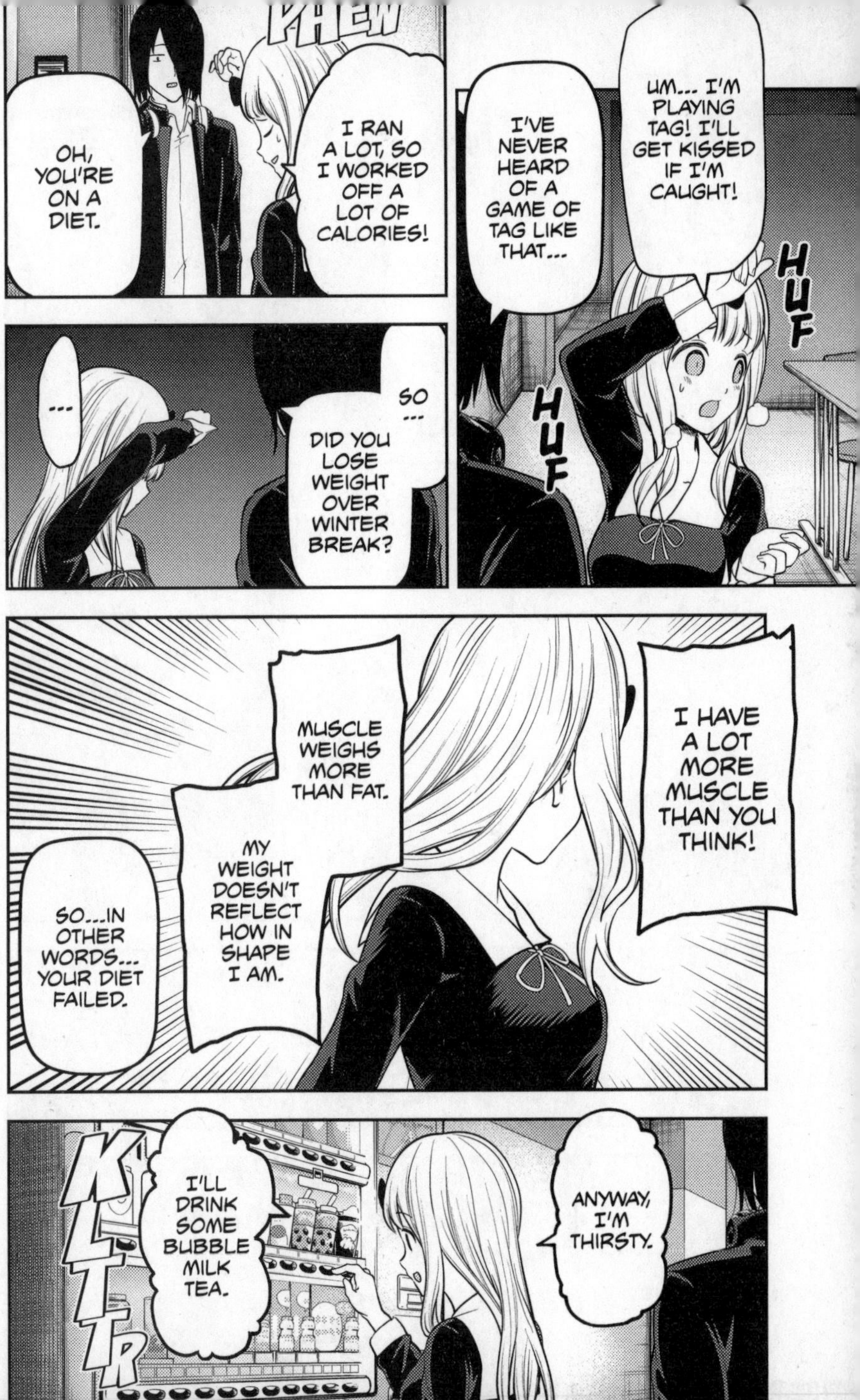
UM... I'M PLAYING TAG! I'LL GET KISSED IF I'M CAUGHT!
I'VE NEVER HEARD OF A GAME OF TAG LIKE THAT...
HUF
HUF
PHEW
I RAN A LOT, SO I WORKED OFF A LOT OF CALORIES!
OH, YOU'RE ON A DIET.
SO...
DID YOU LOSE WEIGHT OVER WINTER BREAK?
...
I HAVE A LOT MORE MUSCLE THAN YOU THINK!
MUSCLE WEIGHS MORE THAN FAT.
MY WEIGHT DOESN'T REFLECT HOW IN SHAPE I AM.
SO...IN OTHER WORDS... YOUR DIET FAILED.
ANYWAY, I'M THIRSTY.
I'LL DRINK SOME BUBBLE MILK TEA.
KLTTR

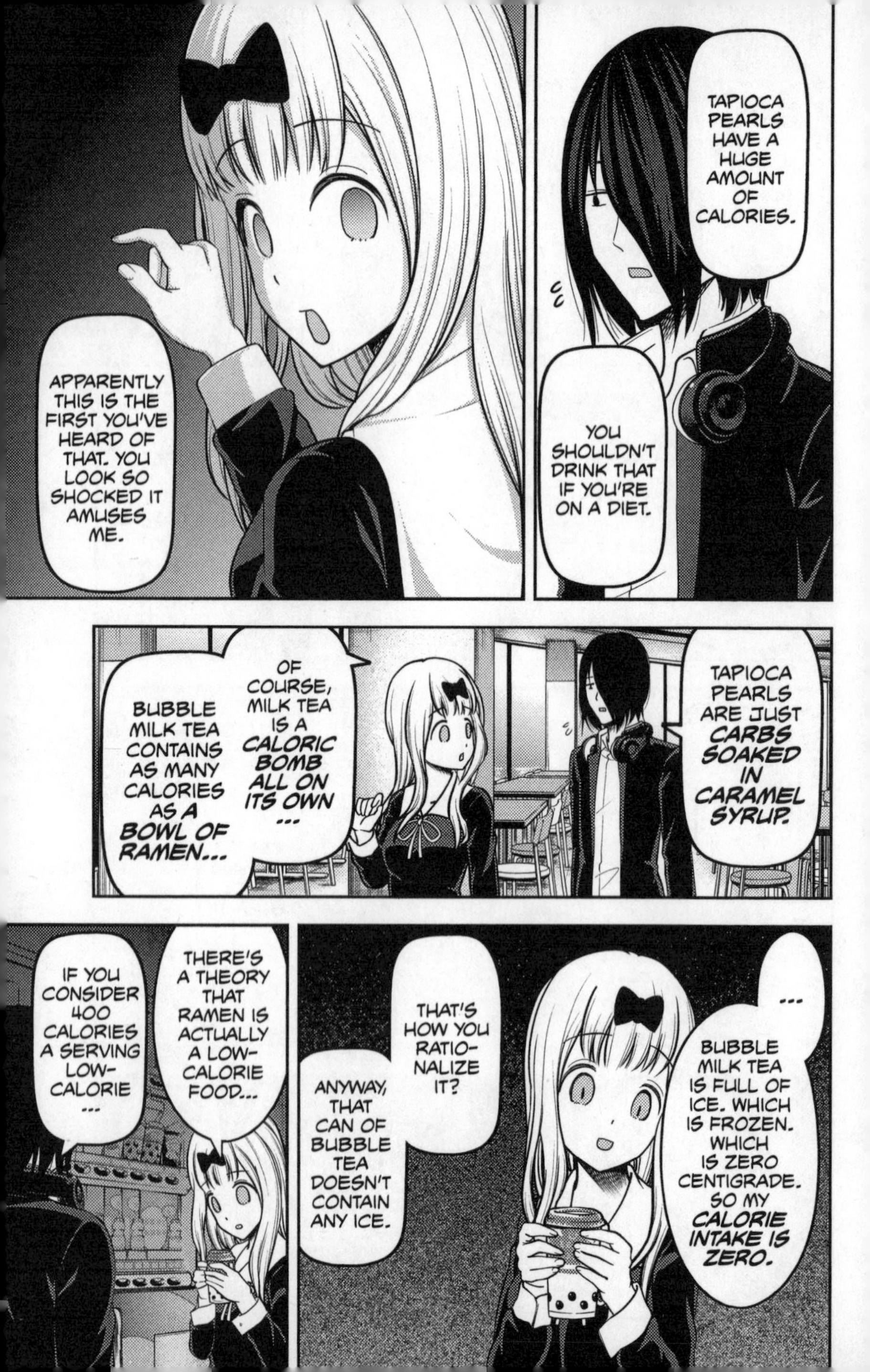
TAPIOCA PEARLS HAVE A HUGE AMOUNT OF CALORIES.
YOU SHOULDN'T DRINK THAT IF YOU'RE ON A DIET.
APPARENTLY THIS IS THE FIRST YOU'VE HEARD OF THAT. YOU LOOK SO SHOCKED IT AMUSES ME.
TAPIOCA PEARLS ARE JUST CARBS SOAKED IN CARAMEL SYRUP.
OF COURSE, MILK TEA IS A CALORIC BOMB ALL ON ITS OWN...
BUBBLE MILK TEA CONTAINS AS MANY CALORIES AS A BOWL OF RAMEN...
...
BUBBLE MILK TEA IS FULL OF ICE. WHICH IS FROZEN. WHICH IS ZERO CENTIGRADE. SO MY CALORIE INTAKE IS ZERO.
THAT'S HOW YOU RATIONALIZE IT?
ANYWAY, THAT CAN OF BUBBLE TEA DOESN'T CONTAIN ANY ICE.
THERE'S A THEORY THAT RAMEN IS ACTUALLY A LOW-CALORIE FOOD...
IF YOU CONSIDER 400 CALORIES A SERVING LOW-CALORIE...

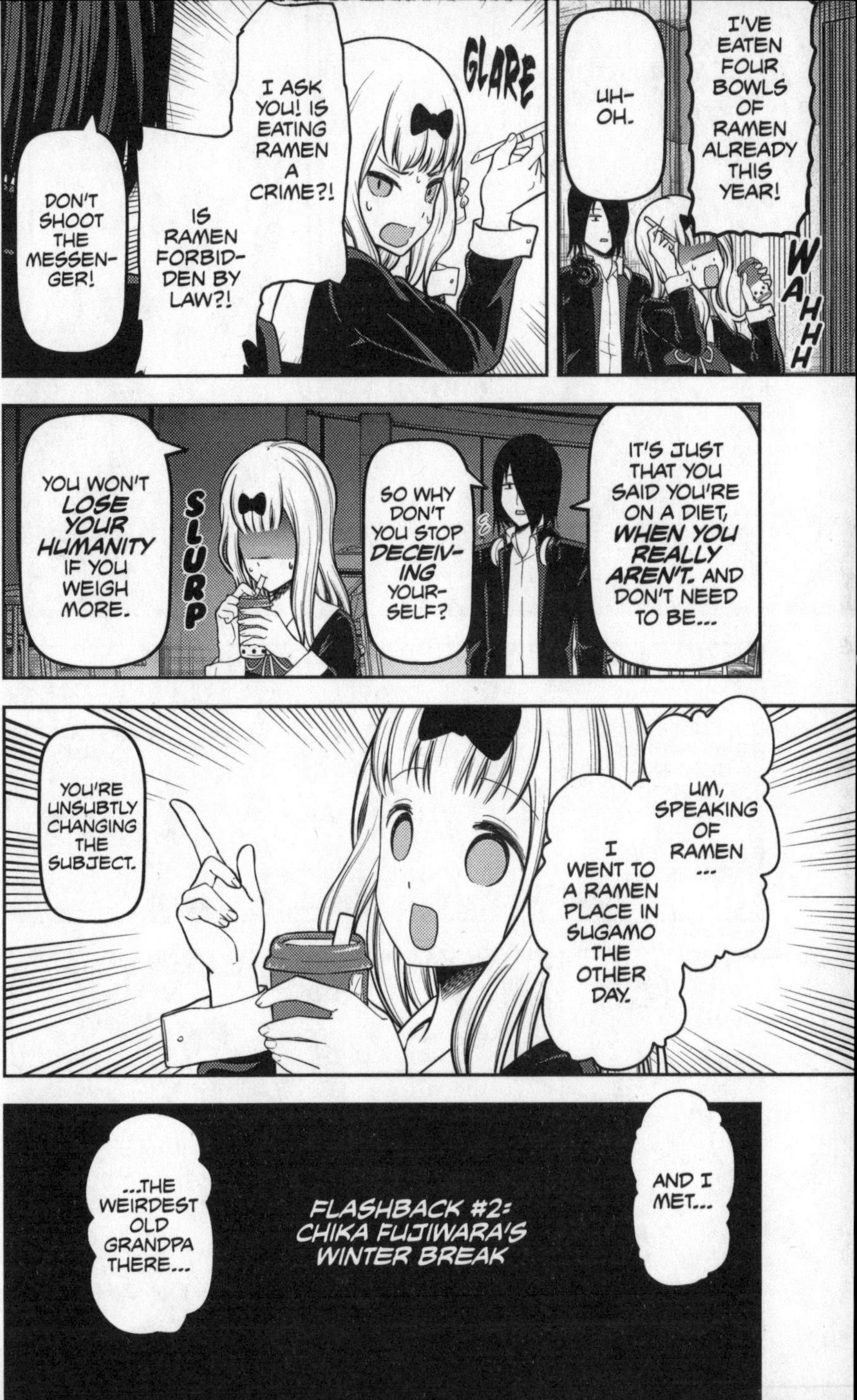
I'VE EATEN FOUR BOWLS OF RAMEN ALREADY THIS YEAR!
UH-OH.
WAHHH
GLARE
I ASK YOU! IS EATING RAMEN A CRIME?!
IS RAMEN FORBIDDEN BY LAW?!
DON'T SHOOT THE MESSENGER!
IT'S JUST THAT YOU SAID YOU'RE ON A DIET, WHEN YOU REALLY AREN'T. AND DON'T NEED TO BE...
SO WHY DON'T YOU STOP DECEIVING YOURSELF?
SLURP
YOU WON'T LOSE YOUR HUMANITY IF YOU WEIGH MORE.
UM, SPEAKING OF RAMEN...
I WENT TO A RAMEN PLACE IN SUGAMO THE OTHER DAY.
YOU'RE UNSUBTLY CHANGING THE SUBJECT.
AND I MET...
FLASHBACK #2: CHIKA FUJIWARA'S WINTER BREAK
...THE WEIRDEST OLD GRANDPA THERE...

INTRODUCTION TO ONE OF THE CHARACTERS IN THE FOLKTALE "PRINCESS KAGUYA"

CHUNAGON ISONOKAMINO MAROTARI

PRINCESS KAGUYA DEMANDED HE BRING HER "A COWRIE SHELL A SWALLOW GAVE BIRTH TO." HE BOASTED THAT HE WOULD BE BACK BEFORE SHE KNEW IT. HE SENT HIS VASSALS TO KEEP WATCH OVER A SWALLOW'S NEST ON THE PEAKED ROOF OF THE OIRYO BUREAU, BUT THEY FAILED TO PROCURE IT. SO HE WENT IN PERSON WHEN THE SWALLOW WAS JUST ABOUT TO LAY AN EGG. SUDDENLY HE SLIPPED AND FELL. ALL HE MANAGED TO GRASP WERE SWALLOW DROPPINGS ON HIS WAY DOWN. AND HE DIED FROM HIS INJURIES.

EVER SINCE, PEOPLE HAVE USED THE EXPRESSION "SWALLOW YOUR PRIDE."

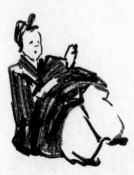

KAGUYA-SAMA

LOVE IS WAR

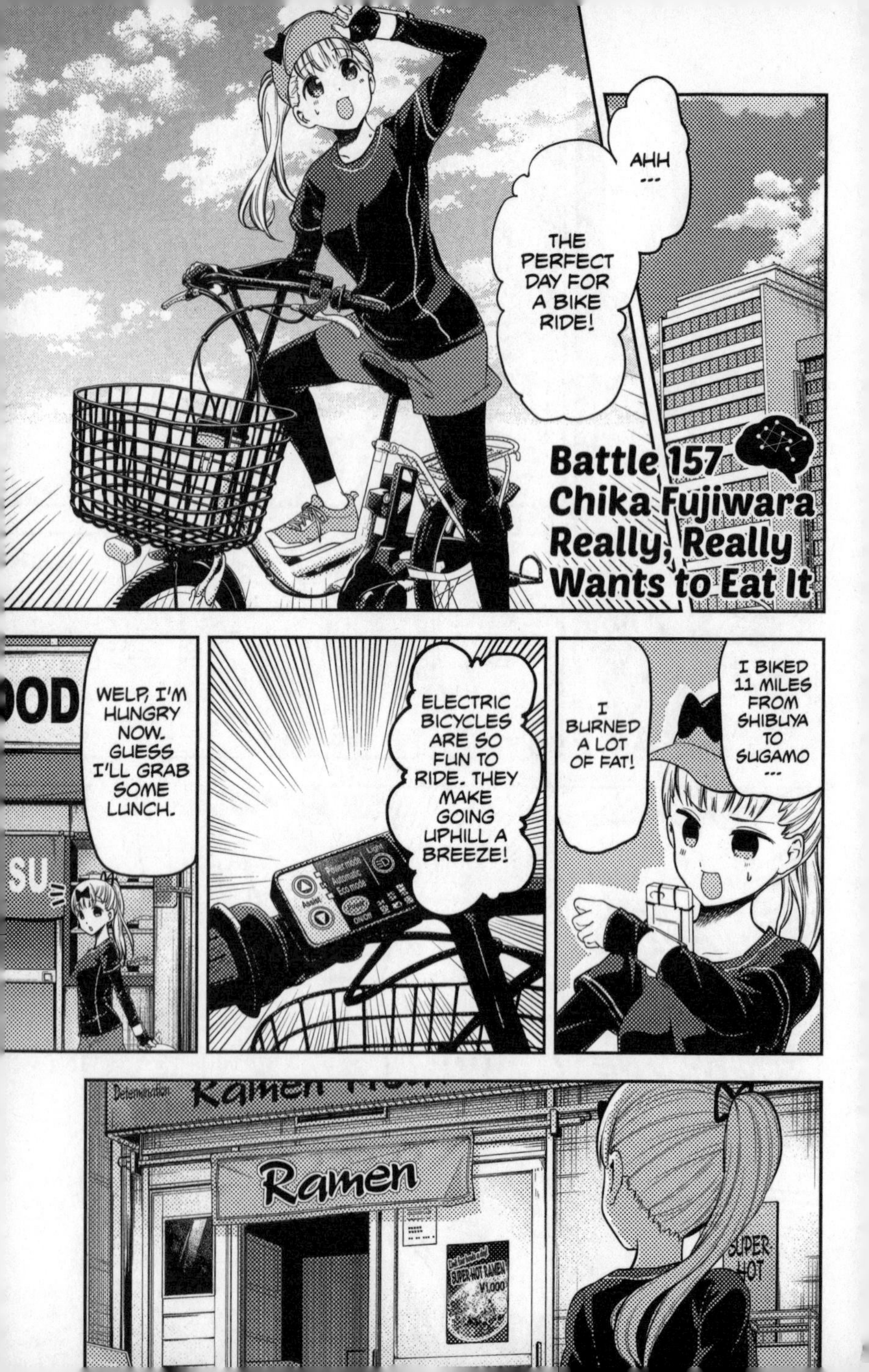
AHH ...
THE PERFECT DAY FOR A BIKE RIDE!
Battle 157 Chika Fujiwara Really, Really Wants to Eat It
I BIKED 11 MILES FROM SHIBUYA TO SUGAMO ...
I BURNED A LOT OF FAT!
ELECTRIC BICYCLES ARE SO FUN TO RIDE. THEY MAKE GOING UPHILL A BREEZE!
Power mode
Automatic
Eco mode
Light
Assist
Power
ON/OFF
WELP, I'M HUNGRY NOW. GUESS I'LL GRAB SOME LUNCH.
Determination
Ramen
SUPER-HOT RAMEN ¥1,000
SUPER HOT

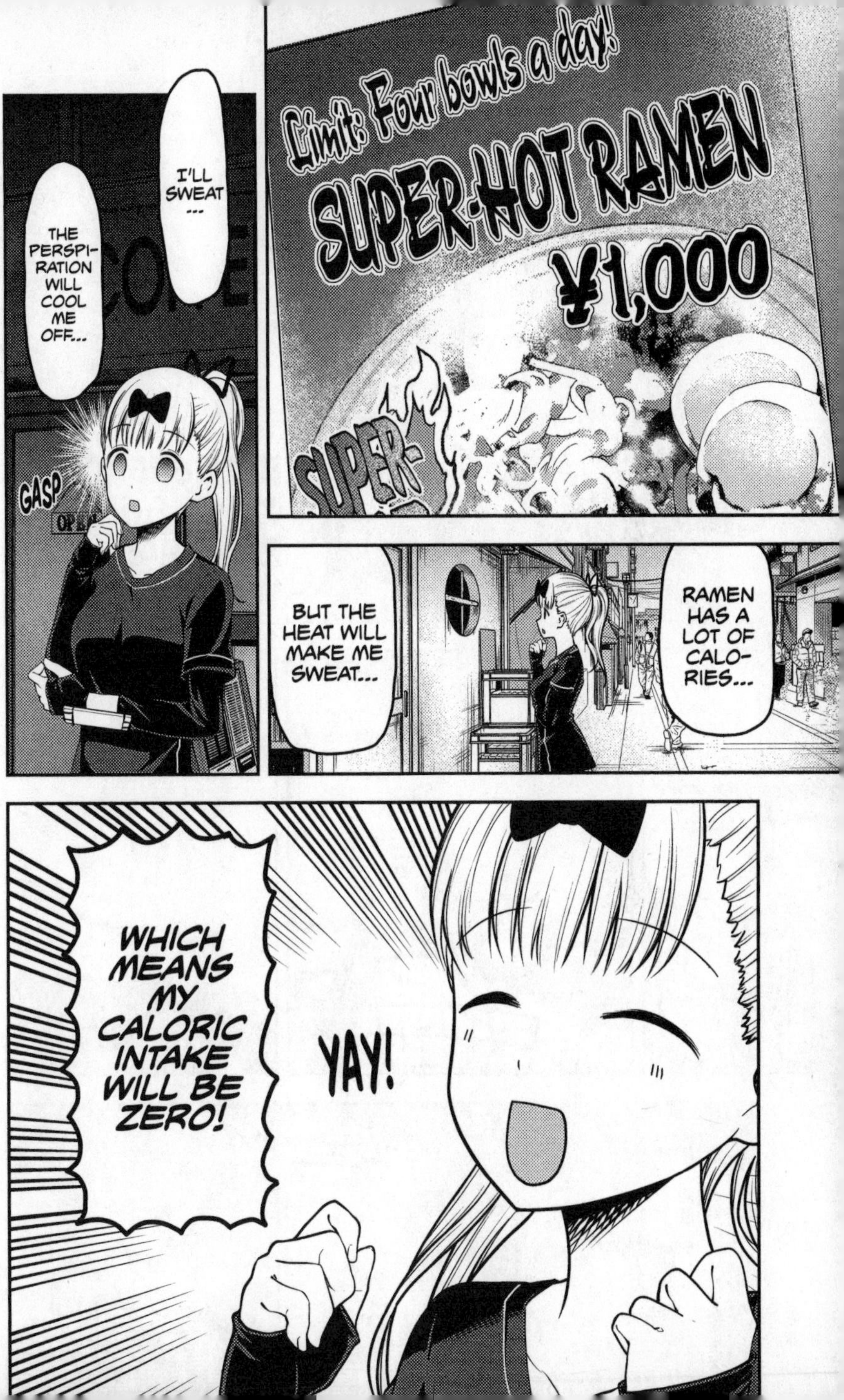
Limit: Four bowls a day!
SUPER-HOT RAMEN
¥1,000
SUPER-
RAMEN HAS A LOT OF CALORIES...
BUT THE HEAT WILL MAKE ME SWEAT...
I'LL SWEAT...
THE PERSPIRATION WILL COOL ME OFF...
GASP
WHICH MEANS MY CALORIC INTAKE WILL BE ZERO!
YAY!

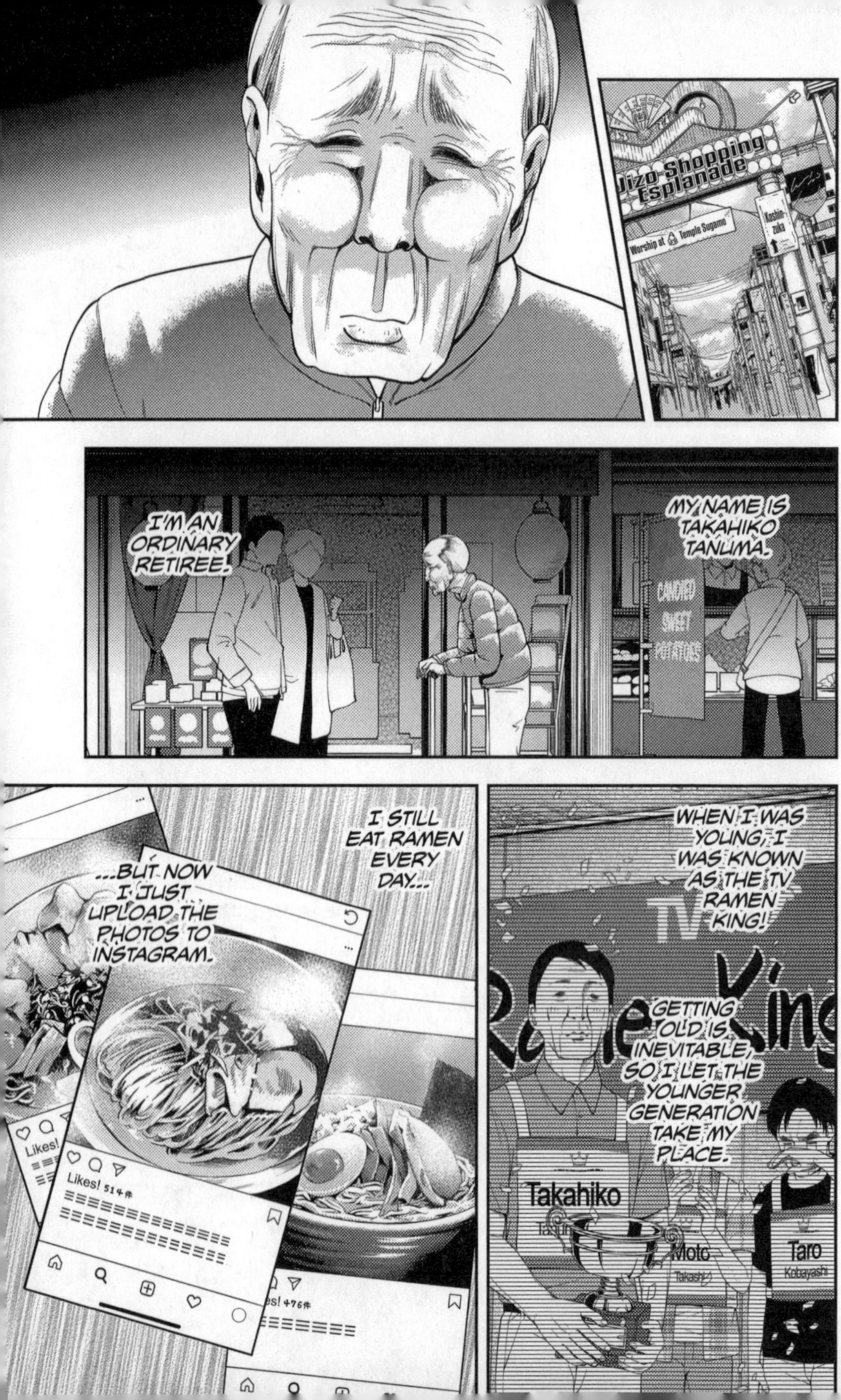
Jizo Shopping Esplanade
Worship at Temple Sugamo
Koshin-zuka
MY NAME IS TAKAHIKO TANUMA.
I'M AN ORDINARY RETIREE.
CANDIED SWEET POTATOES
WHEN I WAS YOUNG, I WAS KNOWN AS THE TV RAMEN KING!
TV
GETTING OLD IS INEVITABLE, SO I LET THE YOUNGER GENERATION TAKE MY PLACE.
Takahiko
Moto
Takashi
Taro
Kobayashi
I STILL EAT RAMEN EVERY DAY...
...BUT NOW I JUST UPLOAD THE PHOTOS TO INSTAGRAM.
Likes! 514件

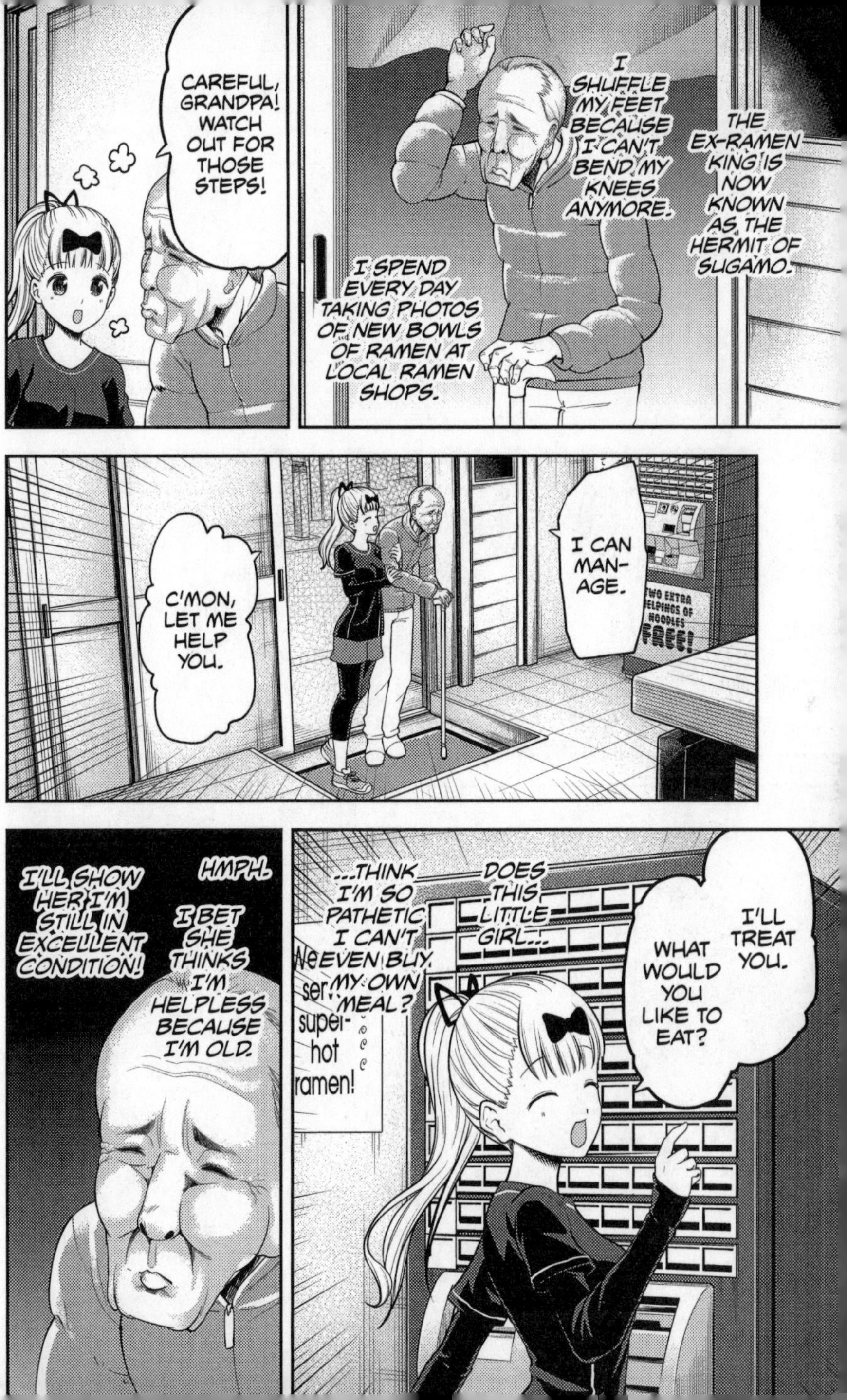
THE EX-RAMEN KING IS NOW KNOWN AS THE HERMIT OF SUGAMO.
I SHUFFLE MY FEET BECAUSE I CAN'T BEND MY KNEES ANYMORE.
I SPEND EVERY DAY TAKING PHOTOS OF NEW BOWLS OF RAMEN AT LOCAL RAMEN SHOPS.
CAREFUL, GRANDPA! WATCH OUT FOR THOSE STEPS!
I CAN MAN-AGE.
TWO EXTRA HELPINGS OF NOODLES FREE!
C'MON, LET ME HELP YOU.
I'LL TREAT YOU.
WHAT WOULD YOU LIKE TO EAT?
DOES THIS LITTLE GIRL...
...THINK I'M SO PATHETIC I CAN'T EVEN BUY MY OWN MEAL?
hot ramen!
HMPH.
I BET SHE THINKS I'M HELPLESS BECAUSE I'M OLD.
I'LL SHOW HER I'M STILL IN EXCELLENT CONDITION!

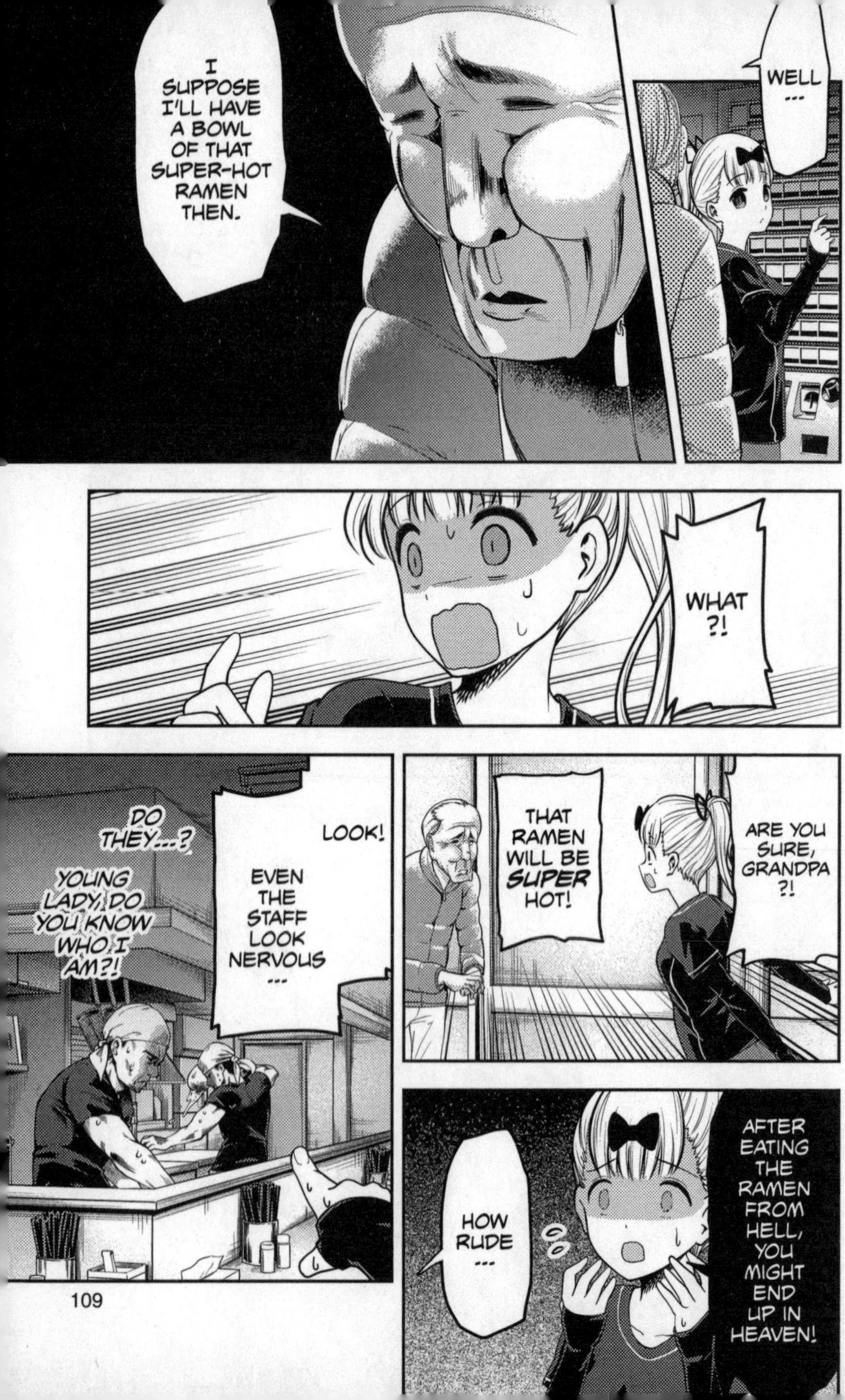
WELL...
I SUPPOSE I'LL HAVE A BOWL OF THAT SUPER-HOT RAMEN THEN.
WHAT?!
ARE YOU SURE, GRANDPA?!
THAT RAMEN WILL BE SUPER HOT!
AFTER EATING THE RAMEN FROM HELL, YOU MIGHT END UP IN HEAVEN!
HOW RUDE...
LOOK!
EVEN THE STAFF LOOK NERVOUS...
DO THEY...?
YOUNG LADY, DO YOU KNOW WHO I AM?!

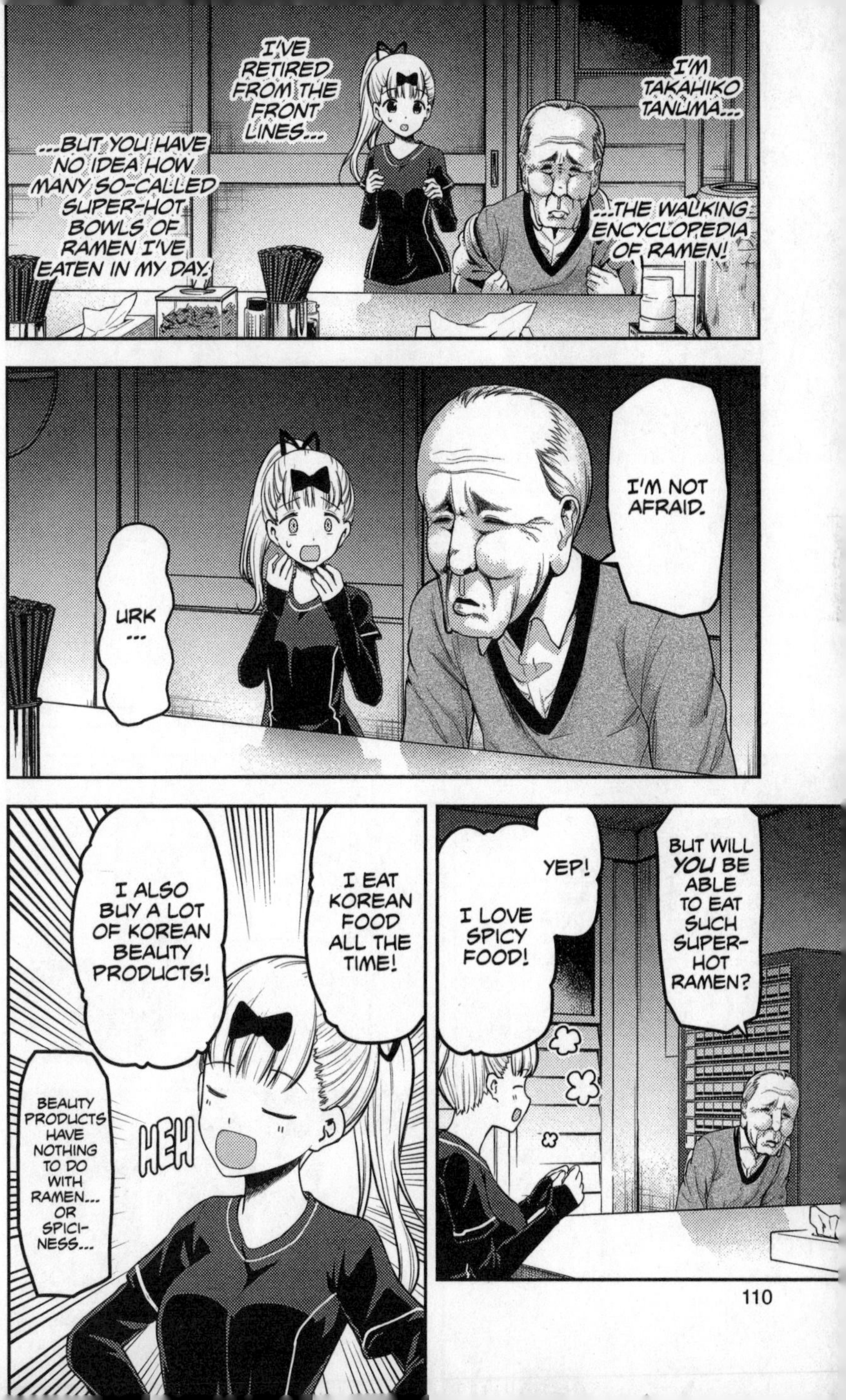
I'M TAKAHIKO TANUMA...
...THE WALKING ENCYCLOPEDIA OF RAMEN!
I'VE RETIRED FROM THE FRONT LINES...
...BUT YOU HAVE NO IDEA HOW MANY SO-CALLED SUPER-HOT BOWLS OF RAMEN I'VE EATEN IN MY DAY.
I'M NOT AFRAID.
URK ...
BUT WILL YOU BE ABLE TO EAT SUCH SUPER-HOT RAMEN?
YEP!
I LOVE SPICY FOOD!
I EAT KOREAN FOOD ALL THE TIME!
I ALSO BUY A LOT OF KOREAN BEAUTY PRODUCTS!
HEH
BEAUTY PRODUCTS HAVE NOTHING TO DO WITH RAMEN... OR SPICI-NESS...

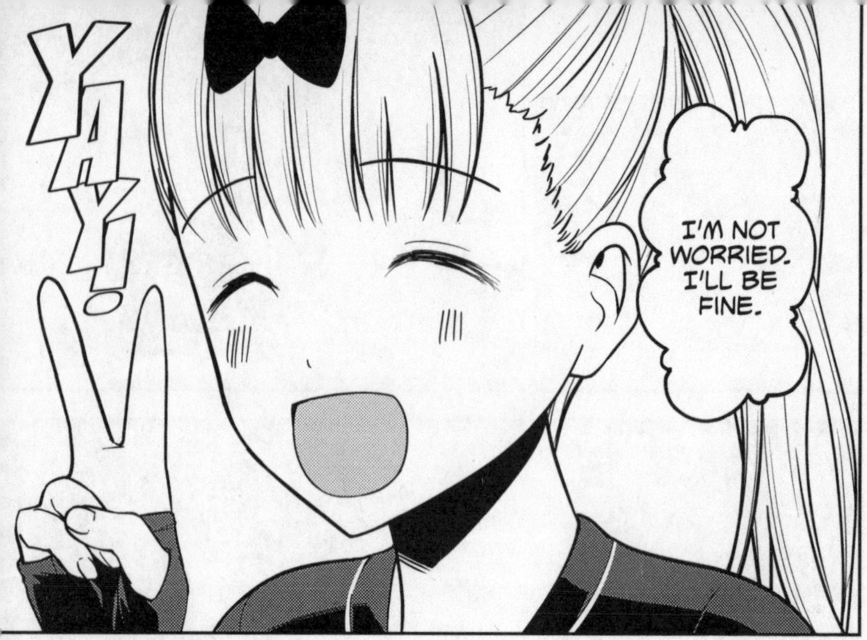
I'M NOT WORRIED. I'LL BE FINE.
YAY!

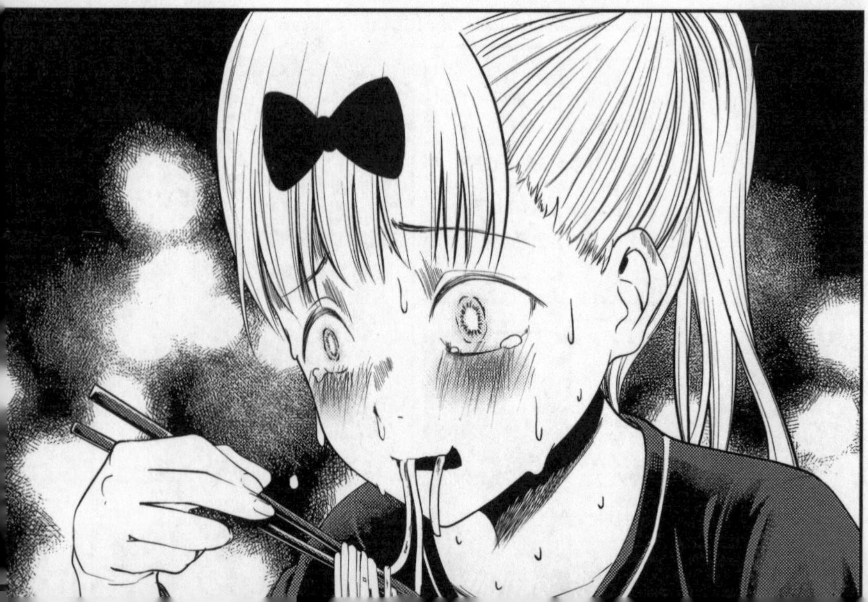

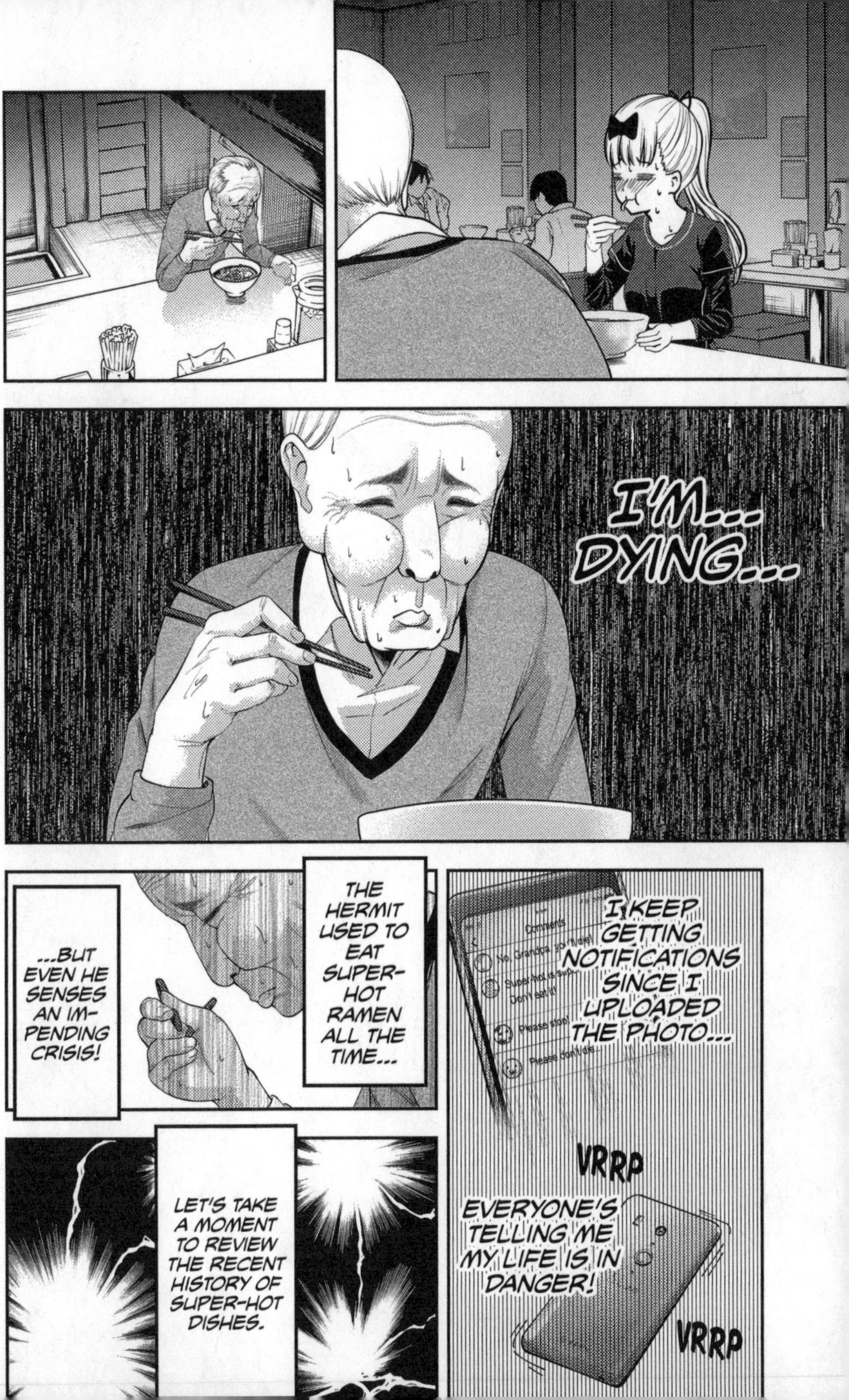
I'M... DYING...
I KEEP GETTING NOTIFICATIONS SINCE I UPLOADED THE PHOTO...
VRRP
EVERYONE'S TELLING ME MY LIFE IS IN DANGER!
VRRP
THE HERMIT USED TO EAT SUPER-HOT RAMEN ALL THE TIME...
...BUT EVEN HE SENSES AN IMPENDING CRISIS!
LET'S TAKE A MOMENT TO REVIEW THE RECENT HISTORY OF SUPER-HOT DISHES.

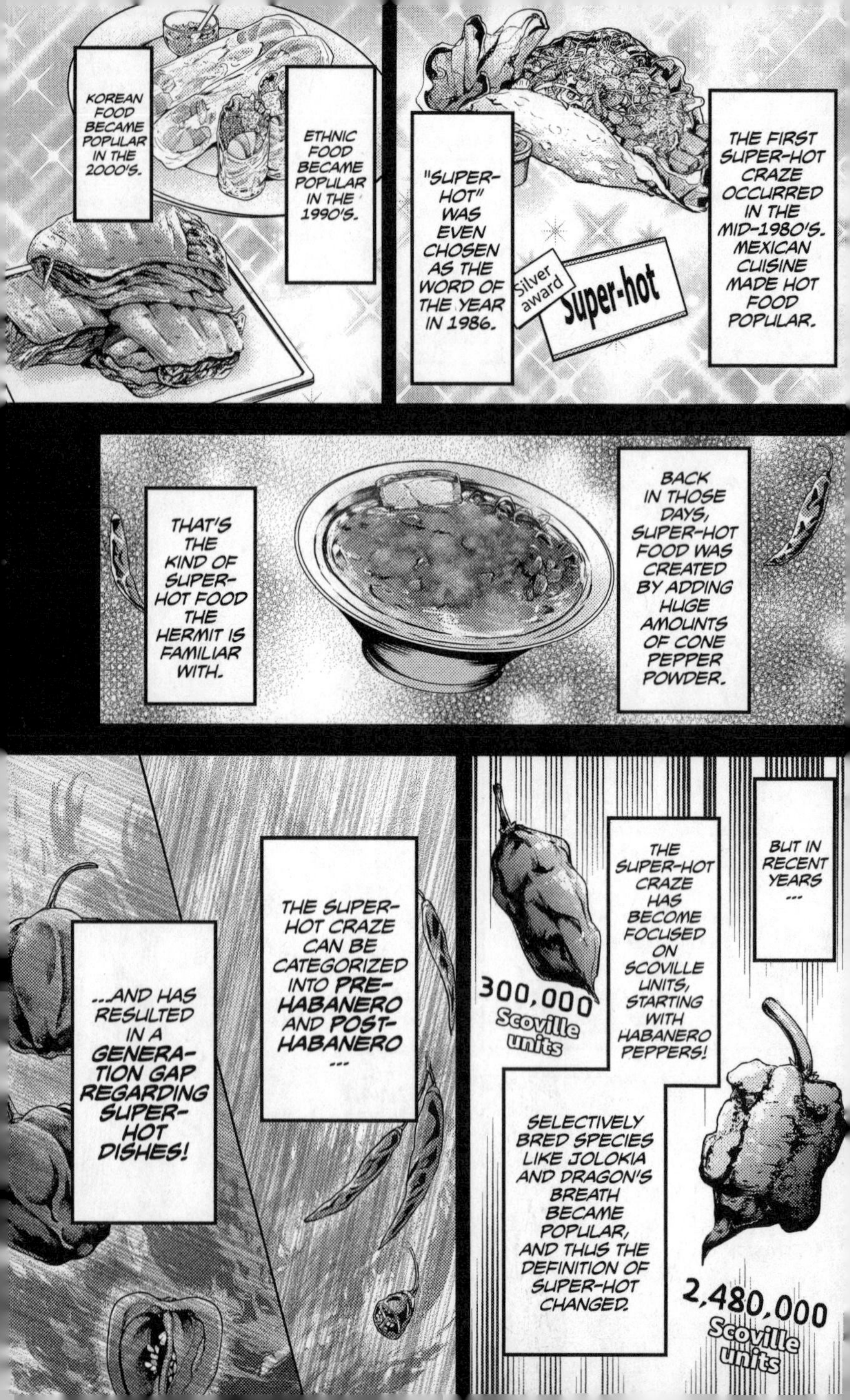
THE FIRST SUPER-HOT CRAZE OCCURRED IN THE MID-1980'S. MEXICAN CUISINE MADE HOT FOOD POPULAR.
"SUPER-HOT" WAS EVEN CHOSEN AS THE WORD OF THE YEAR IN 1986.
Silver award
Super-hot
ETHNIC FOOD BECAME POPULAR IN THE 1990'S.
KOREAN FOOD BECAME POPULAR IN THE 2000'S.
BACK IN THOSE DAYS, SUPER-HOT FOOD WAS CREATED BY ADDING HUGE AMOUNTS OF CONE PEPPER POWDER.
THAT'S THE KIND OF SUPER-HOT FOOD THE HERMIT IS FAMILIAR WITH.
BUT IN RECENT YEARS...
THE SUPER-HOT CRAZE HAS BECOME FOCUSED ON SCOVILLE UNITS, STARTING WITH HABANERO PEPPERS!
300,000 Scoville units
SELECTIVELY BRED SPECIES LIKE JOLOKIA AND DRAGON'S BREATH BECAME POPULAR, AND THUS THE DEFINITION OF SUPER-HOT CHANGED.
2,480,000 Scoville units
THE SUPER-HOT CRAZE CAN BE CATEGORIZED INTO PRE-HABANERO AND POST-HABANERO...
...AND HAS RESULTED IN A GENERATION GAP REGARDING SUPER-HOT DISHES!

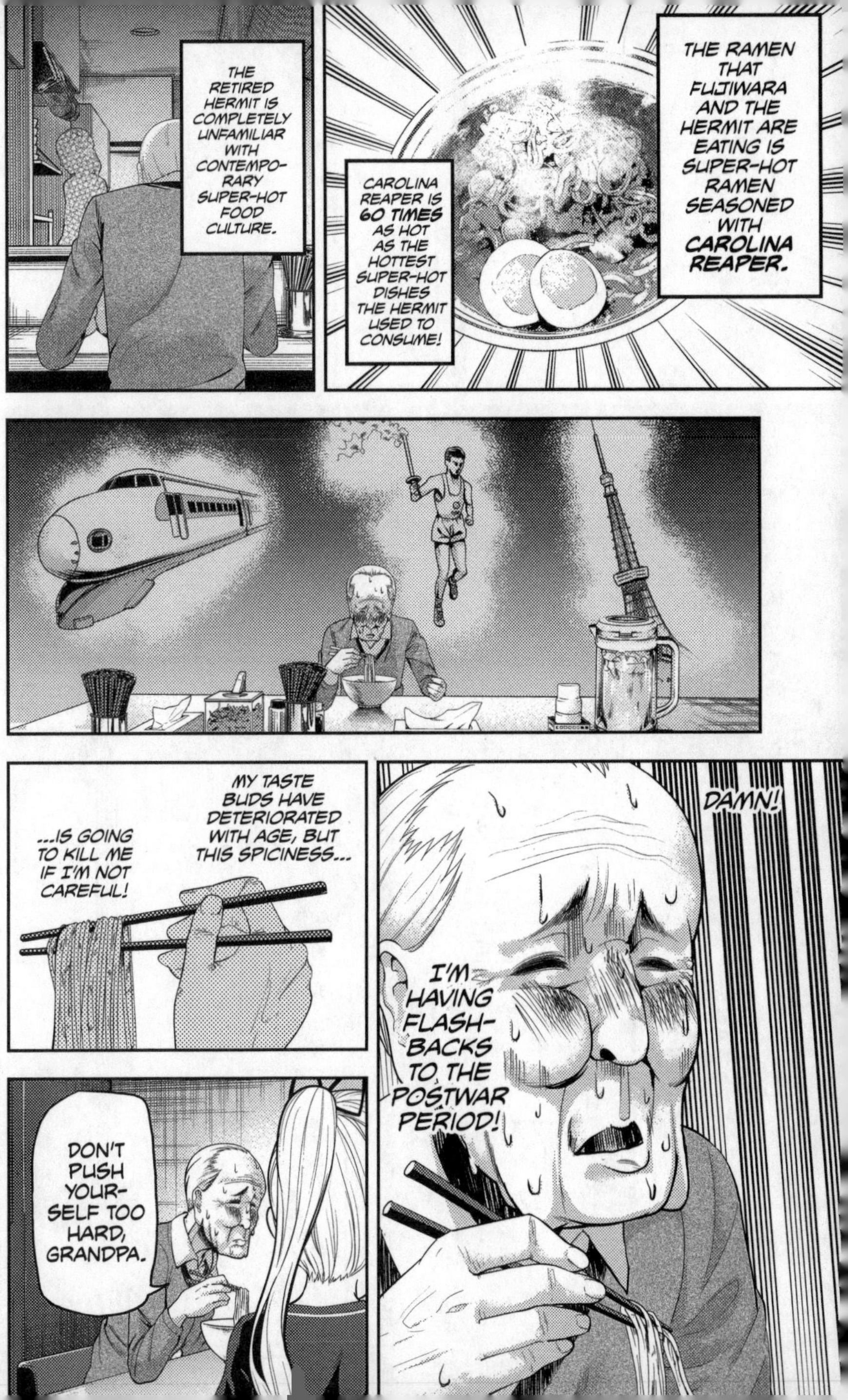
THE RAMEN THAT FUJIWARA AND THE HERMIT ARE EATING IS SUPER-HOT RAMEN SEASONED WITH CAROLINA REAPER.
CAROLINA REAPER IS 60 TIMES AS HOT AS THE HOTTEST SUPER-HOT DISHES THE HERMIT USED TO CONSUME!
THE RETIRED HERMIT IS COMPLETELY UNFAMILIAR WITH CONTEMPORARY SUPER-HOT FOOD CULTURE.
DAMN!
I'M HAVING FLASHBACKS TO THE POSTWAR PERIOD!
MY TASTE BUDS HAVE DETERIORATED WITH AGE, BUT THIS SPICINESS...
...IS GOING TO KILL ME IF I'M NOT CAREFUL!
DON'T PUSH YOURSELF TOO HARD, GRANDPA.

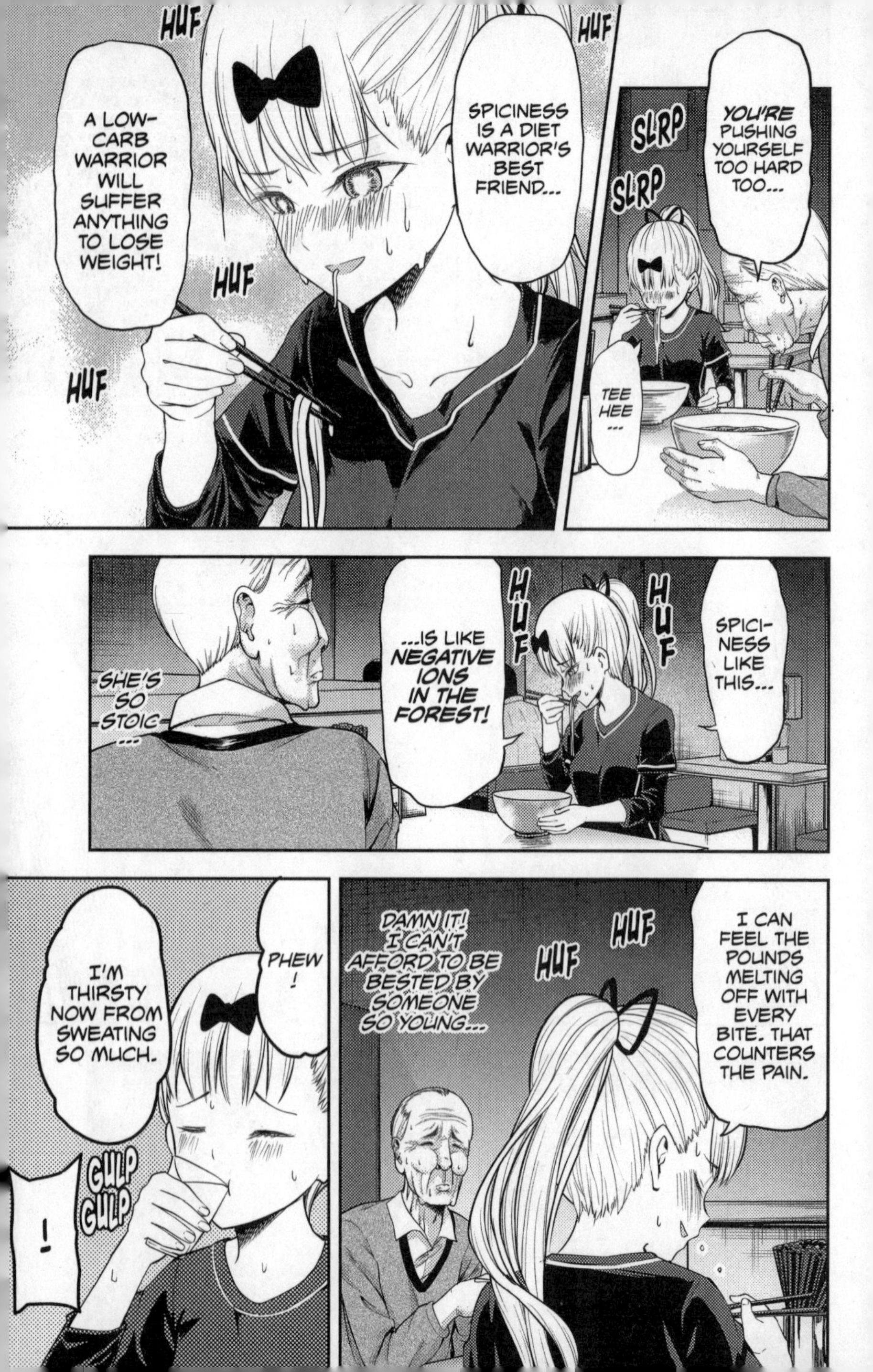
YOU'RE PUSHING YOURSELF TOO HARD TOO...
SLRP
SLRP
TEE HEE...
HUF
SPICINESS IS A DIET WARRIOR'S BEST FRIEND...
HUF
A LOW-CARB WARRIOR WILL SUFFER ANYTHING TO LOSE WEIGHT!
HUF
HUF
SPICINESS LIKE THIS...
HUF
HUF
...IS LIKE NEGATIVE IONS IN THE FOREST!
SHE'S SO STOIC...
I CAN FEEL THE POUNDS MELTING OFF WITH EVERY BITE. THAT COUNTERS THE PAIN.
HUF
HUF
DAMN IT! I CAN'T AFFORD TO BE BESTED BY SOMEONE SO YOUNG...
PHEW!
I'M THIRSTY NOW FROM SWEATING SO MUCH.
GULP GULP
!

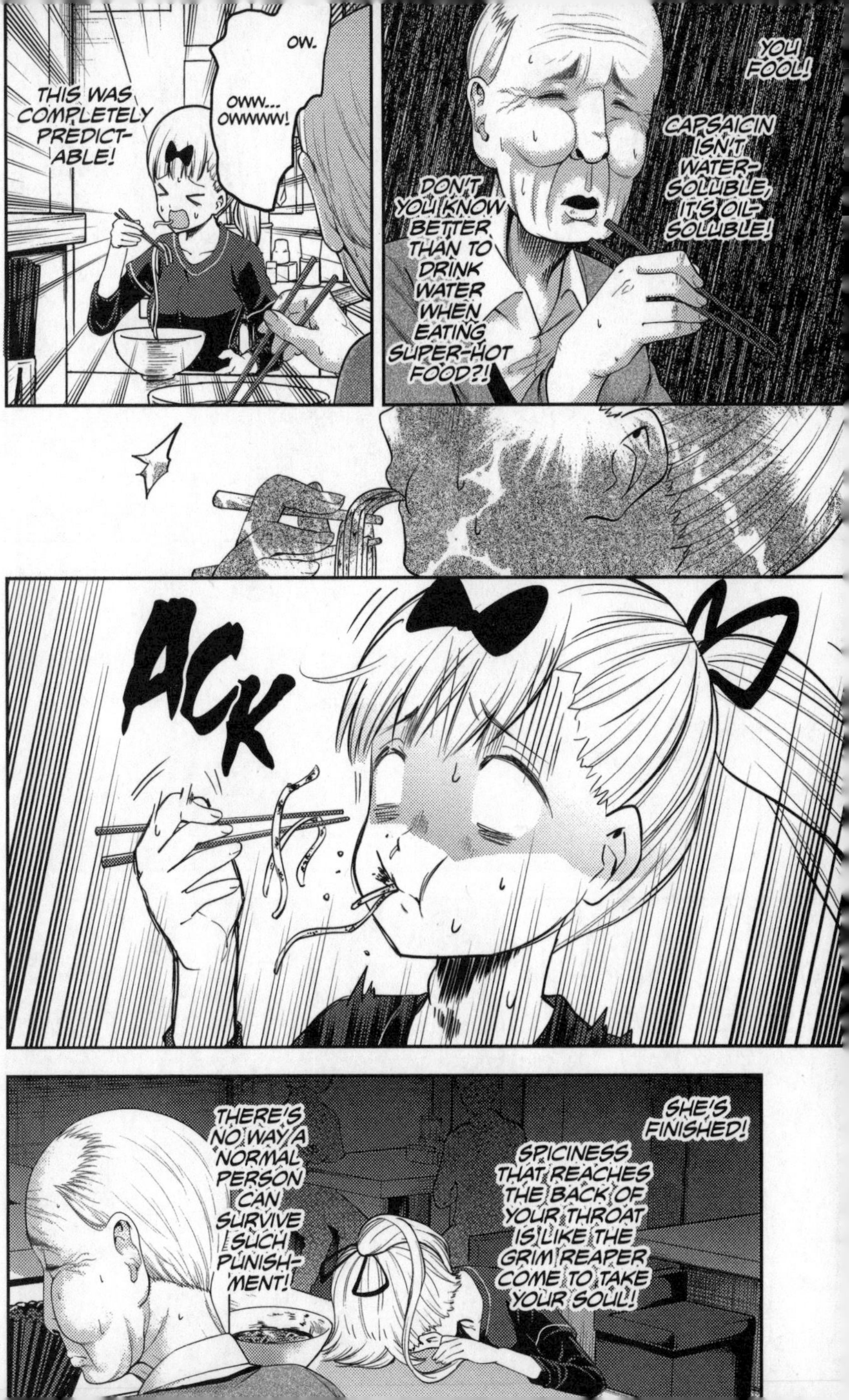
YOU FOOL!
CAPSAICIN ISN'T WATER-SOLUBLE, IT'S OIL-SOLUBLE!
DON'T YOU KNOW BETTER THAN TO DRINK WATER WHEN EATING SUPER-HOT FOOD?!
OW.
OWW... OWWWW!
THIS WAS COMPLETELY PREDICT-ABLE!
ACK
SHE'S FINISHED!
SPICINESS THAT REACHES THE BACK OF YOUR THROAT IS LIKE THE GRIM REAPER COME TO TAKE YOUR SOUL!
THERE'S NO WAY A NORMAL PERSON CAN SURVIVE SUCH PUNISH-MENT!

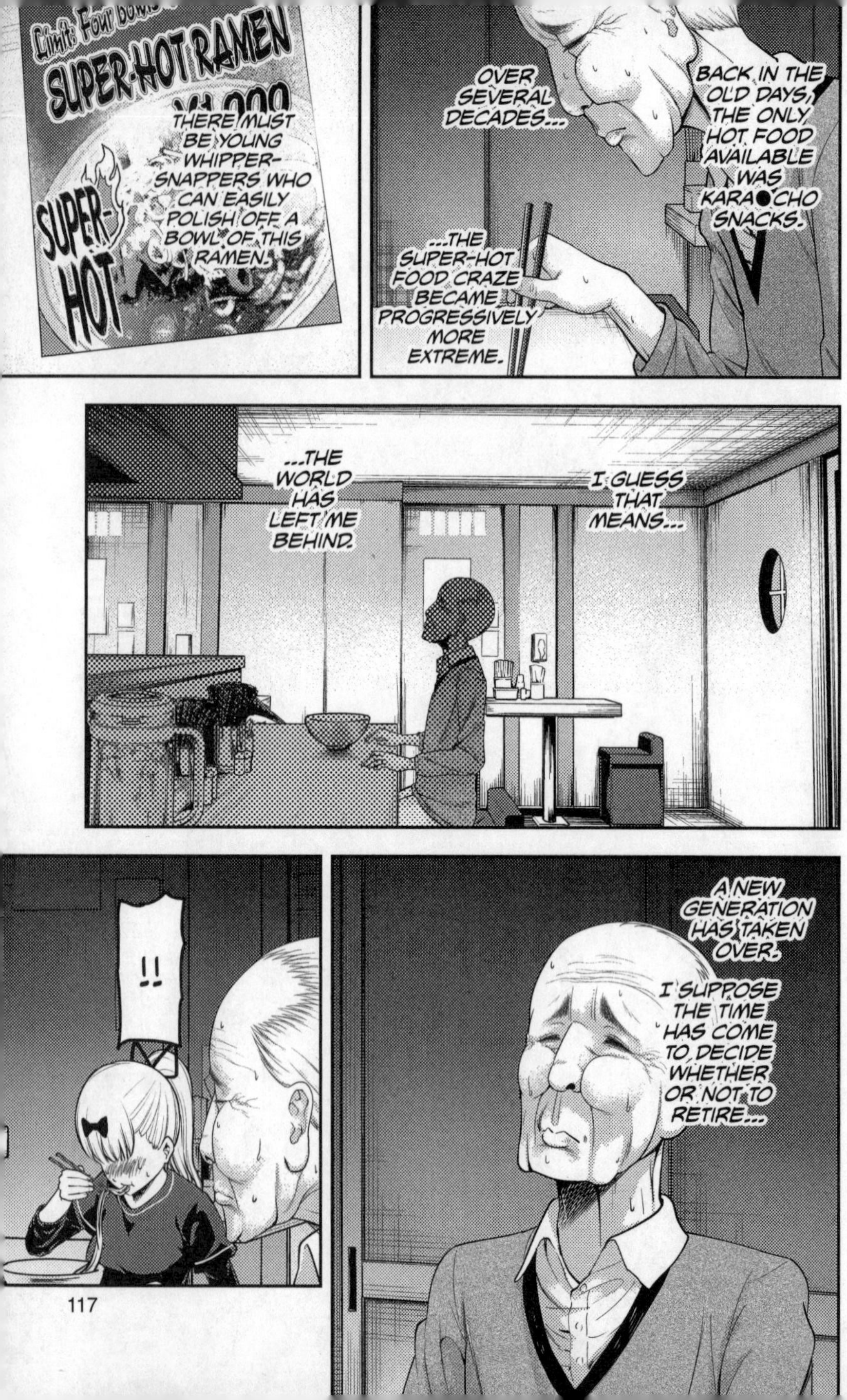
BACK IN THE OLD DAYS, THE ONLY HOT FOOD AVAILABLE WAS KARA●CHO SNACKS.
OVER SEVERAL DECADES...
...THE SUPER-HOT FOOD CRAZE BECAME PROGRESSIVELY MORE EXTREME.
SUPER-HOT RAMEN
THERE MUST BE YOUNG WHIPPER-SNAPPERS WHO CAN EASILY POLISH OFF A BOWL OF THIS RAMEN.
SUPER-HOT
I GUESS THAT MEANS...
...THE WORLD HAS LEFT ME BEHIND.
A NEW GENERATION HAS TAKEN OVER.
I SUPPOSE THE TIME HAS COME TO DECIDE WHETHER OR NOT TO RETIRE...
!!

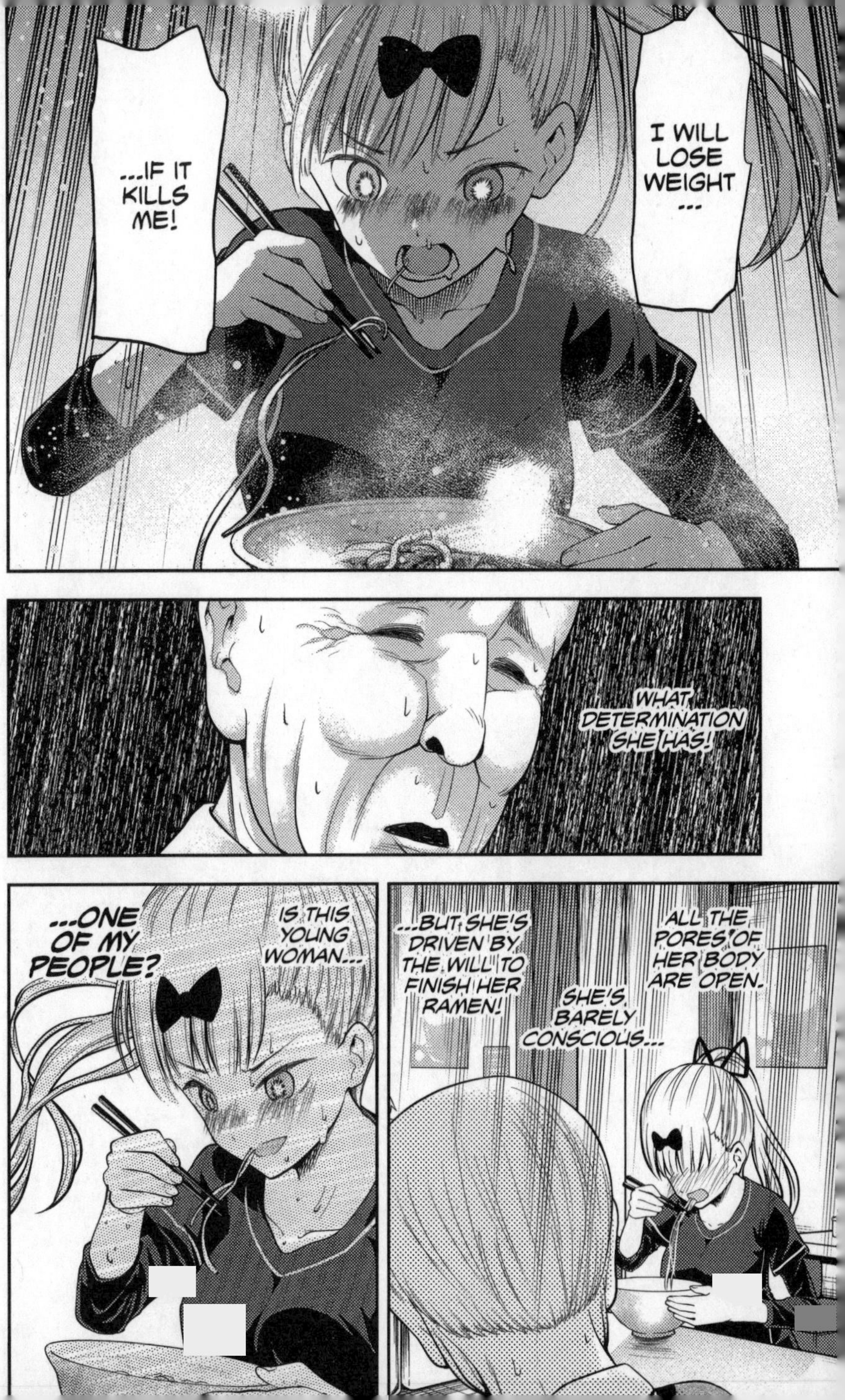
I WILL LOSE WEIGHT ...
...IF IT KILLS ME!
WHAT DETERMINATION SHE HAS!
ALL THE PORES OF HER BODY ARE OPEN.
SHE'S BARELY CONSCIOUS...
...BUT SHE'S DRIVEN BY THE WILL TO FINISH HER RAMEN!
IS THIS YOUNG WOMAN...
...ONE OF MY PEOPLE?

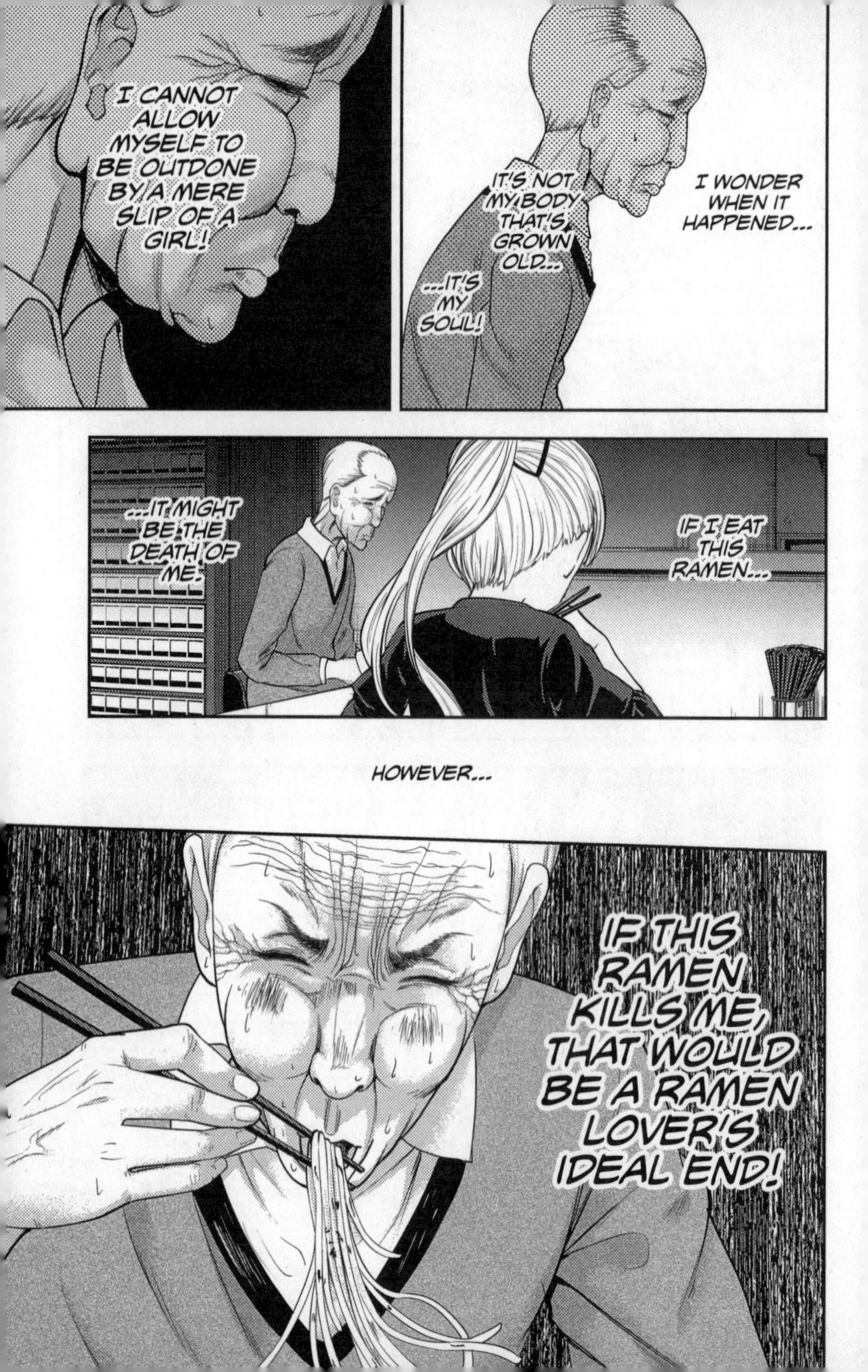
I WONDER WHEN IT HAPPENED...
IT'S NOT MY BODY THAT'S GROWN OLD...
...IT'S MY SOUL!
I CANNOT ALLOW MYSELF TO BE OUTDONE BY A MERE SLIP OF A GIRL!
IF I EAT THIS RAMEN...
...IT MIGHT BE THE DEATH OF ME.
HOWEVER...
IF THIS RAMEN KILLS ME, THAT WOULD BE A RAMEN LOVER'S IDEAL END!

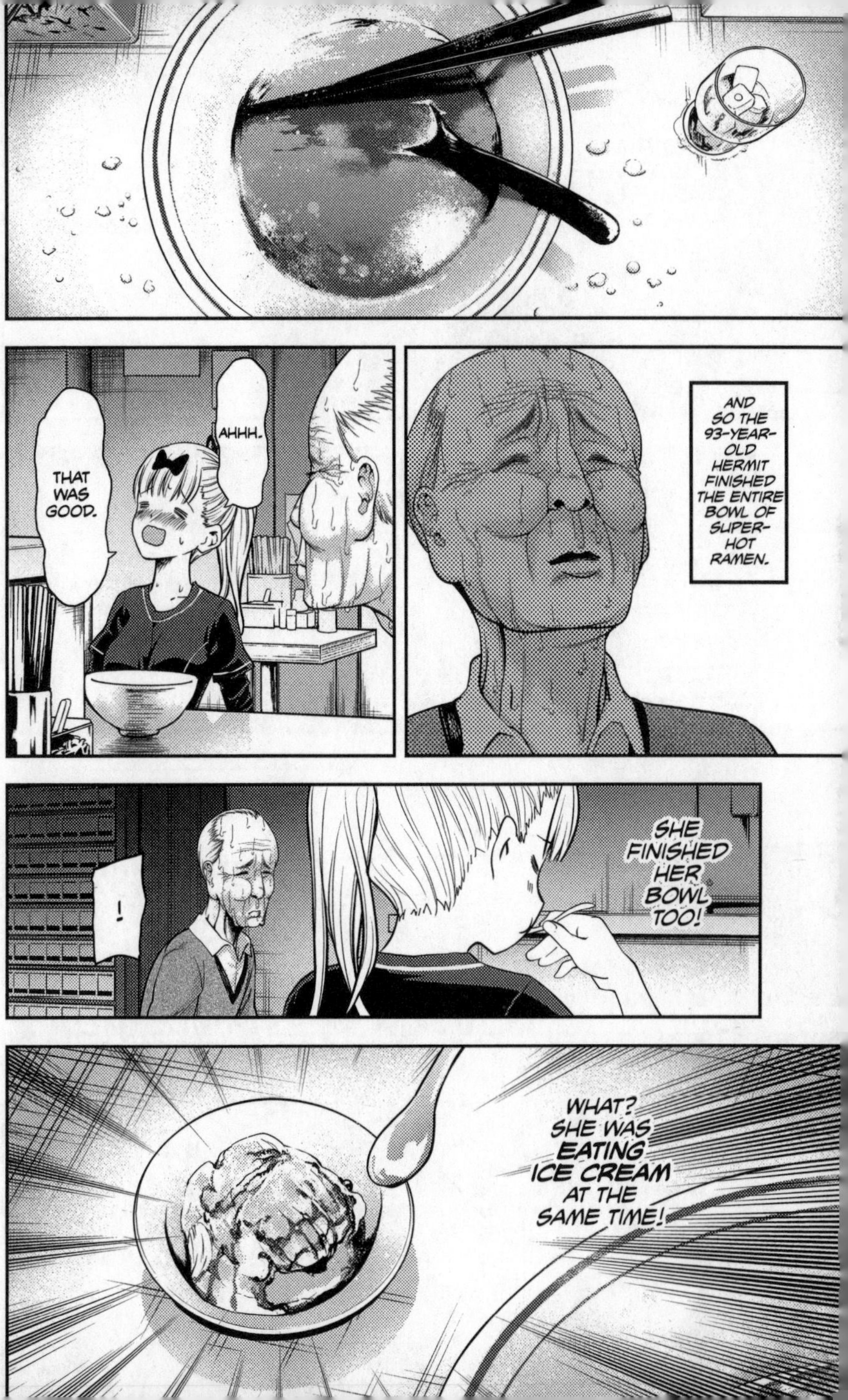
AND SO THE 93-YEAR-OLD HERMIT FINISHED THE ENTIRE BOWL OF SUPER-HOT RAMEN.
AHHH.
THAT WAS GOOD.
SHE FINISHED HER BOWL TOO!
!
WHAT? SHE WAS EATING ICE CREAM AT THE SAME TIME!

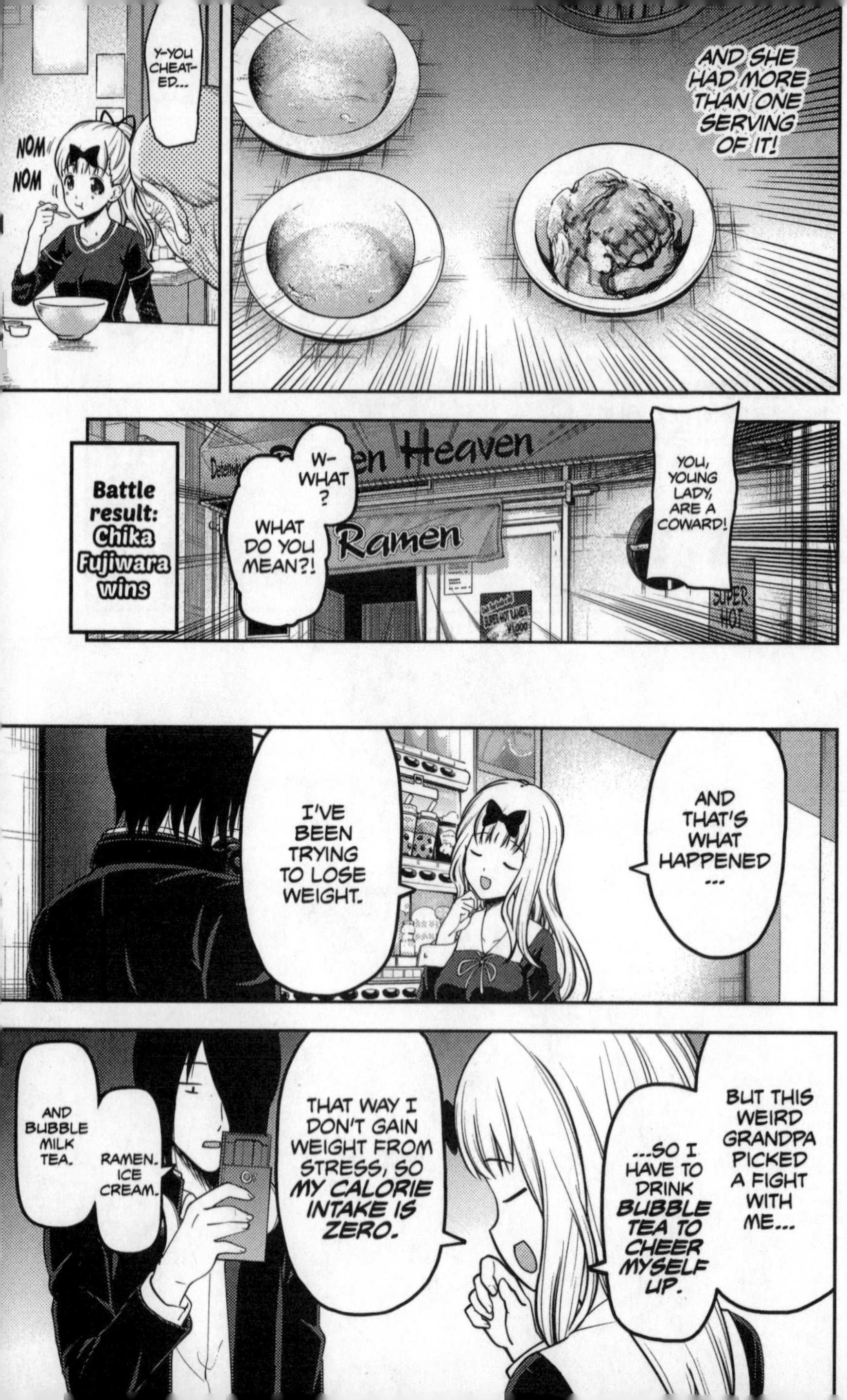
AND SHE HAD MORE THAN ONE SERVING OF IT!
Y-YOU CHEAT-ED...
NOM NOM
YOU, YOUNG LADY, ARE A COWARD!
W-WHAT? WHAT DO YOU MEAN?!
Ramen
SUPER HOT
Battle result: Chika Fujiwara wins
AND THAT'S WHAT HAPPENED...
I'VE BEEN TRYING TO LOSE WEIGHT.
BUT THIS WEIRD GRANDPA PICKED A FIGHT WITH ME...
...SO I HAVE TO DRINK *BUBBLE TEA TO CHEER MYSELF UP*.
THAT WAY I DON'T GAIN WEIGHT FROM STRESS, SO *MY CALORIE INTAKE IS ZERO*.
RAMEN. ICE CREAM.
AND BUBBLE MILK TEA.

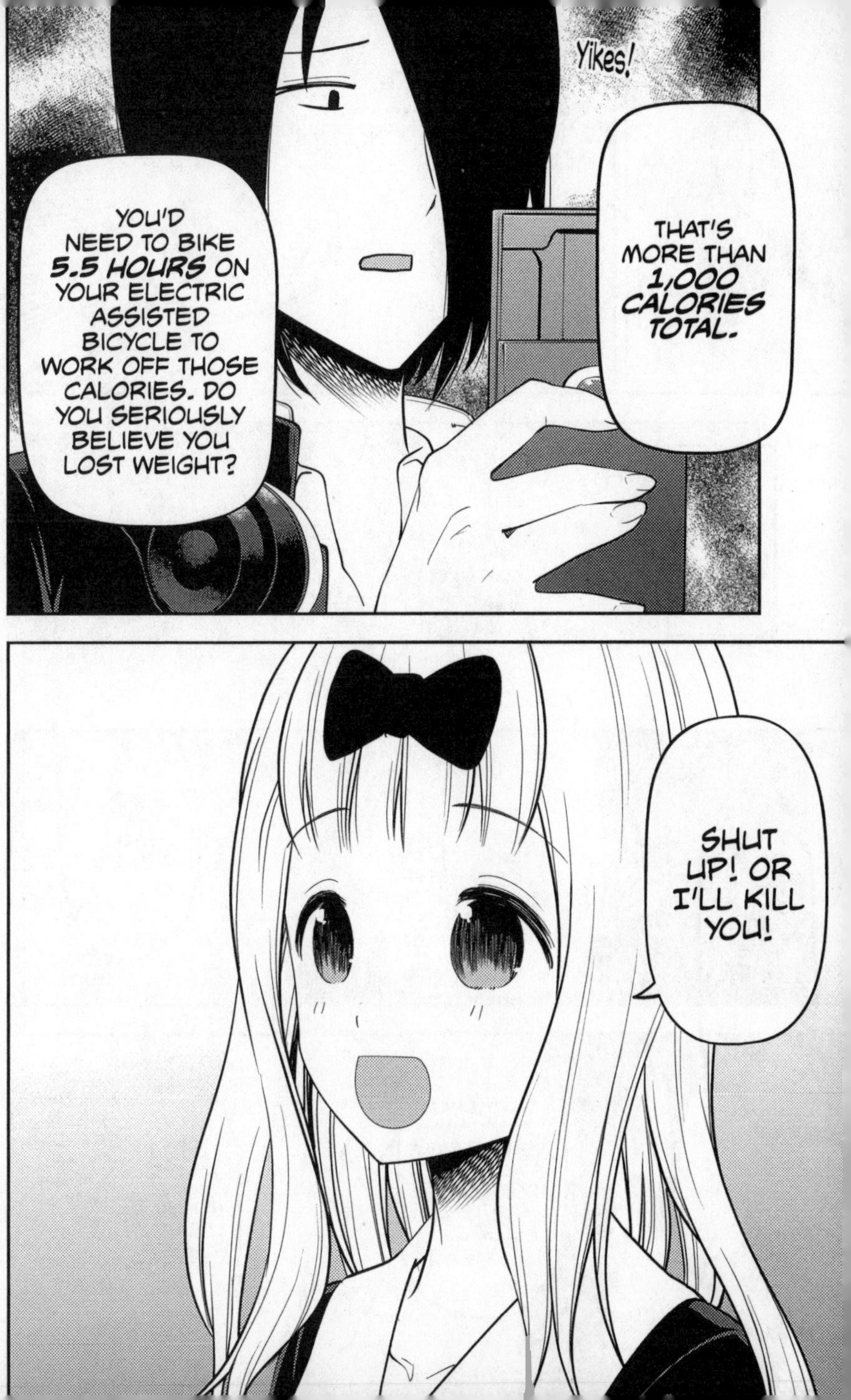
Yikes!
THAT'S MORE THAN 1,000 CALORIES TOTAL.
YOU'D NEED TO BIKE 5.5 HOURS ON YOUR ELECTRIC ASSISTED BICYCLE TO WORK OFF THOSE CALORIES. DO YOU SERIOUSLY BELIEVE YOU LOST WEIGHT?
SHUT UP! OR I'LL KILL YOU!

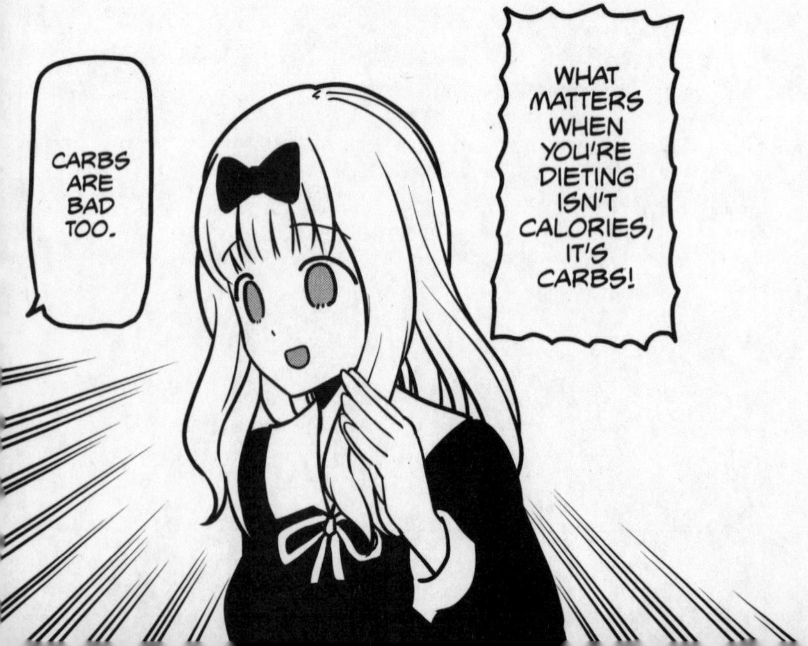
WHAT MATTERS WHEN YOU'RE DIETING ISN'T CALORIES, IT'S CARBS!
CARBS ARE BAD TOO.

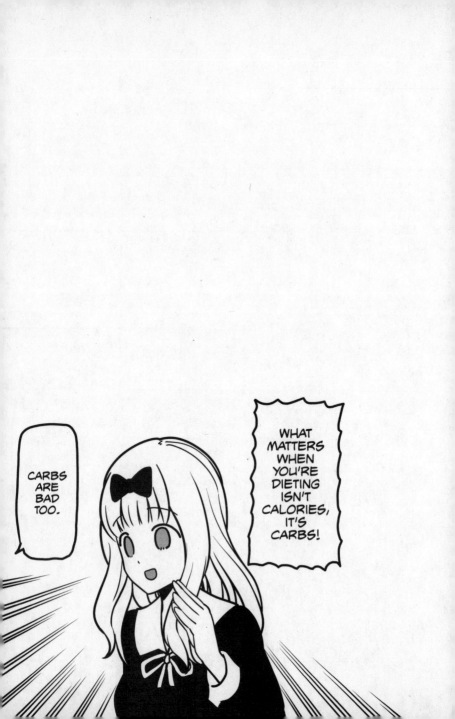

KAGUYA-SAMA
LOVE IS WAR

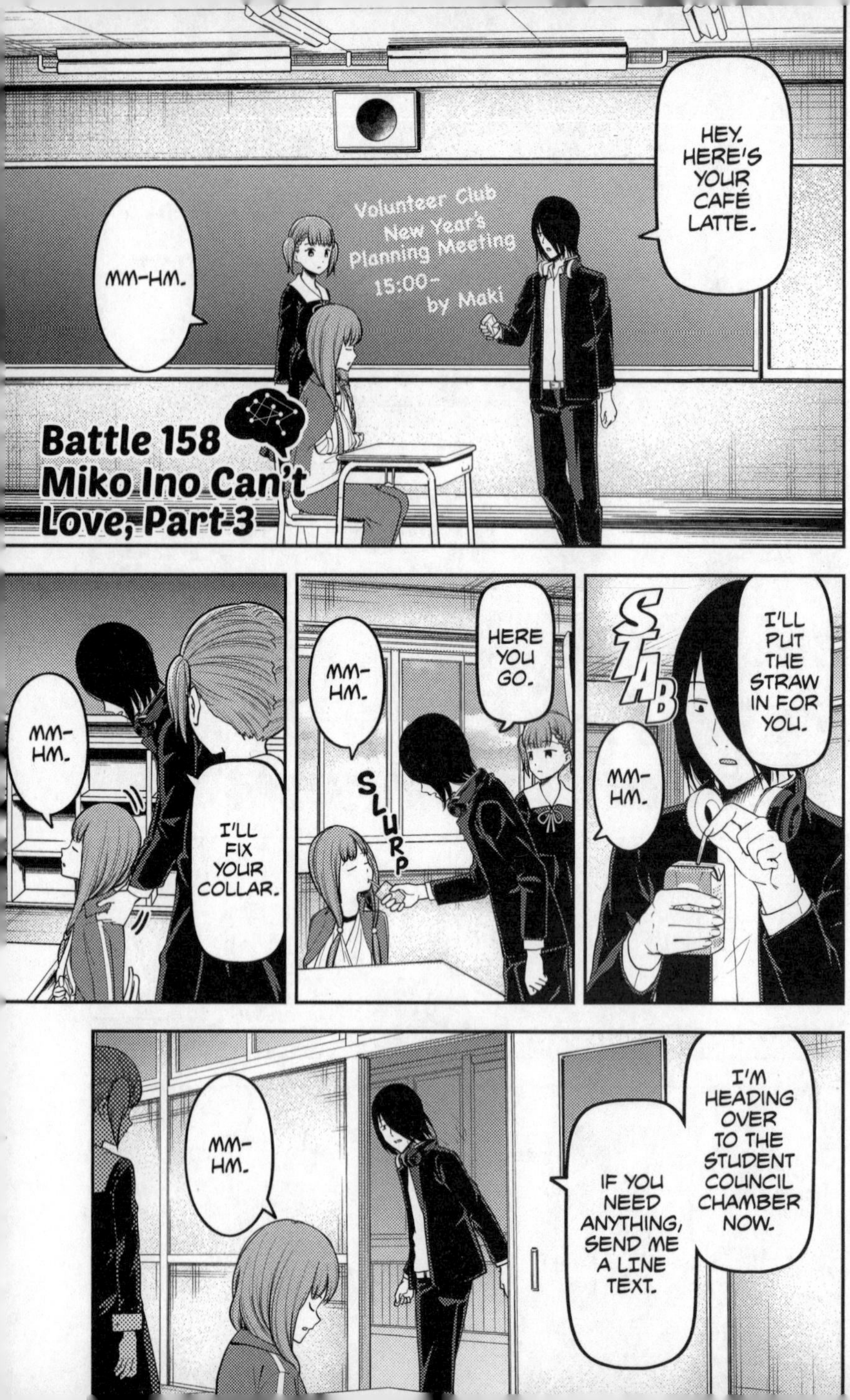
HEY. HERE'S YOUR CAFÉ LATTE.
Volunteer Club New Year's Planning Meeting 15:00- by Maki
MM-HM.
Battle 158 Miko Ino Can't Love, Part 3
I'LL PUT THE STRAW IN FOR YOU.
STAB
MM-HM.
HERE YOU GO.
MM-HM.
SLURP
I'LL FIX YOUR COLLAR.
MM-HM.
I'M HEADING OVER TO THE STUDENT COUNCIL CHAMBER NOW.
IF YOU NEED ANYTHING, SEND ME A LINE TEXT.
MM-HM.

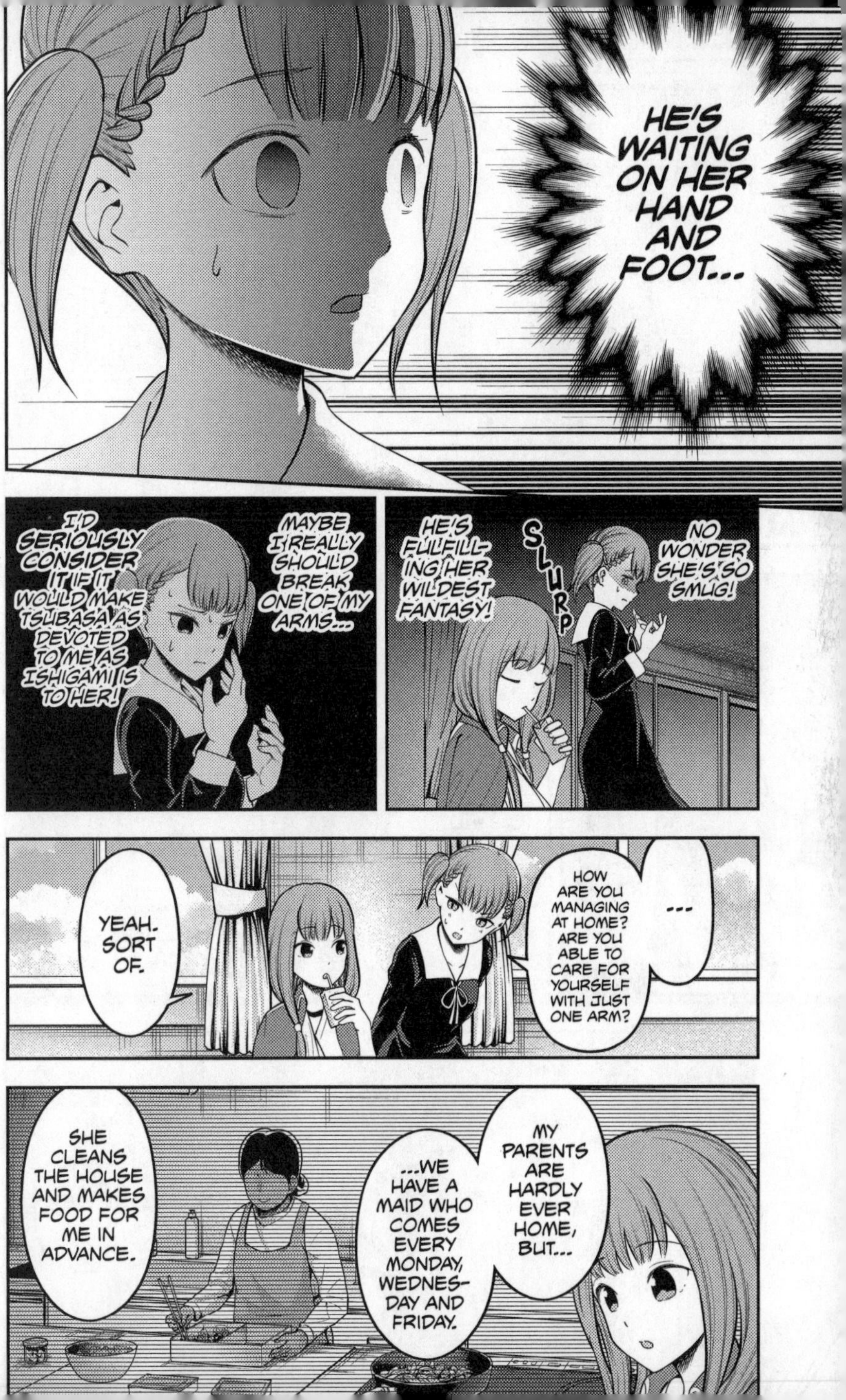
HE'S WAITING ON HER HAND AND FOOT...
NO WONDER SHE'S SO SMUG!
SLURP
HE'S FULFILLING HER WILDEST FANTASY!
MAYBE I REALLY SHOULD BREAK ONE OF MY ARMS...
I'D SERIOUSLY CONSIDER IT IF IT WOULD MAKE TSUBASA AS DEVOTED TO ME AS ISHIGAMI IS TO HER!
...
HOW ARE YOU MANAGING AT HOME? ARE YOU ABLE TO CARE FOR YOURSELF WITH JUST ONE ARM?
YEAH. SORT OF.
MY PARENTS ARE HARDLY EVER HOME, BUT...
...WE HAVE A MAID WHO COMES EVERY MONDAY, WEDNESDAY AND FRIDAY.
SHE CLEANS THE HOUSE AND MAKES FOOD FOR ME IN ADVANCE.

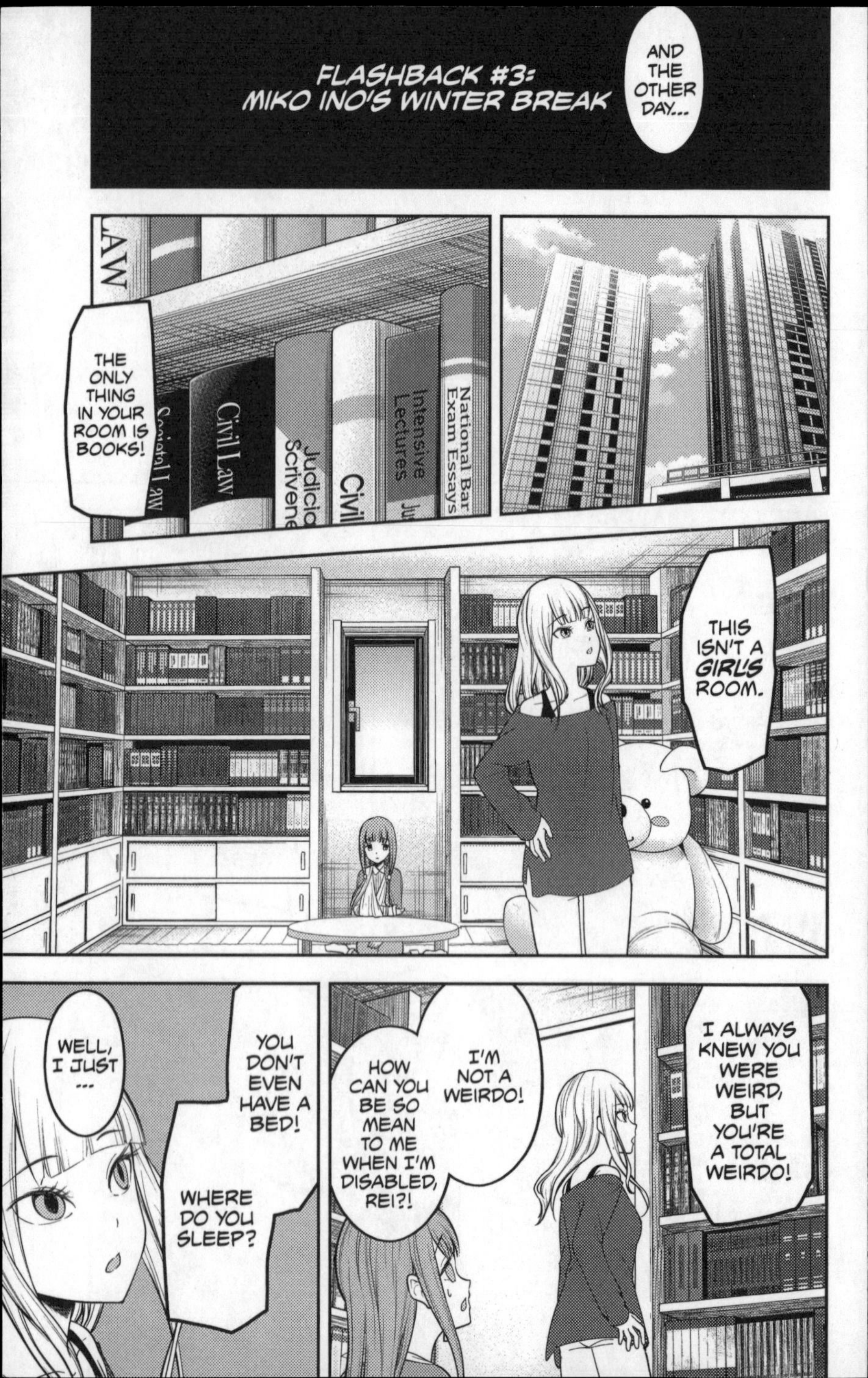
AND THE OTHER DAY...
FLASHBACK #3: MIKO INO'S WINTER BREAK
THE ONLY THING IN YOUR ROOM IS BOOKS!
National Bar Exam Essays
Intensive Lectures
Civil Law
THIS ISN'T A GIRL'S ROOM.
I ALWAYS KNEW YOU WERE WEIRD, BUT YOU'RE A TOTAL WEIRDO!
I'M NOT A WEIRDO!
HOW CAN YOU BE SO MEAN TO ME WHEN I'M DISABLED, REI?!
YOU DON'T EVEN HAVE A BED!
WHERE DO YOU SLEEP?
WELL, I JUST...

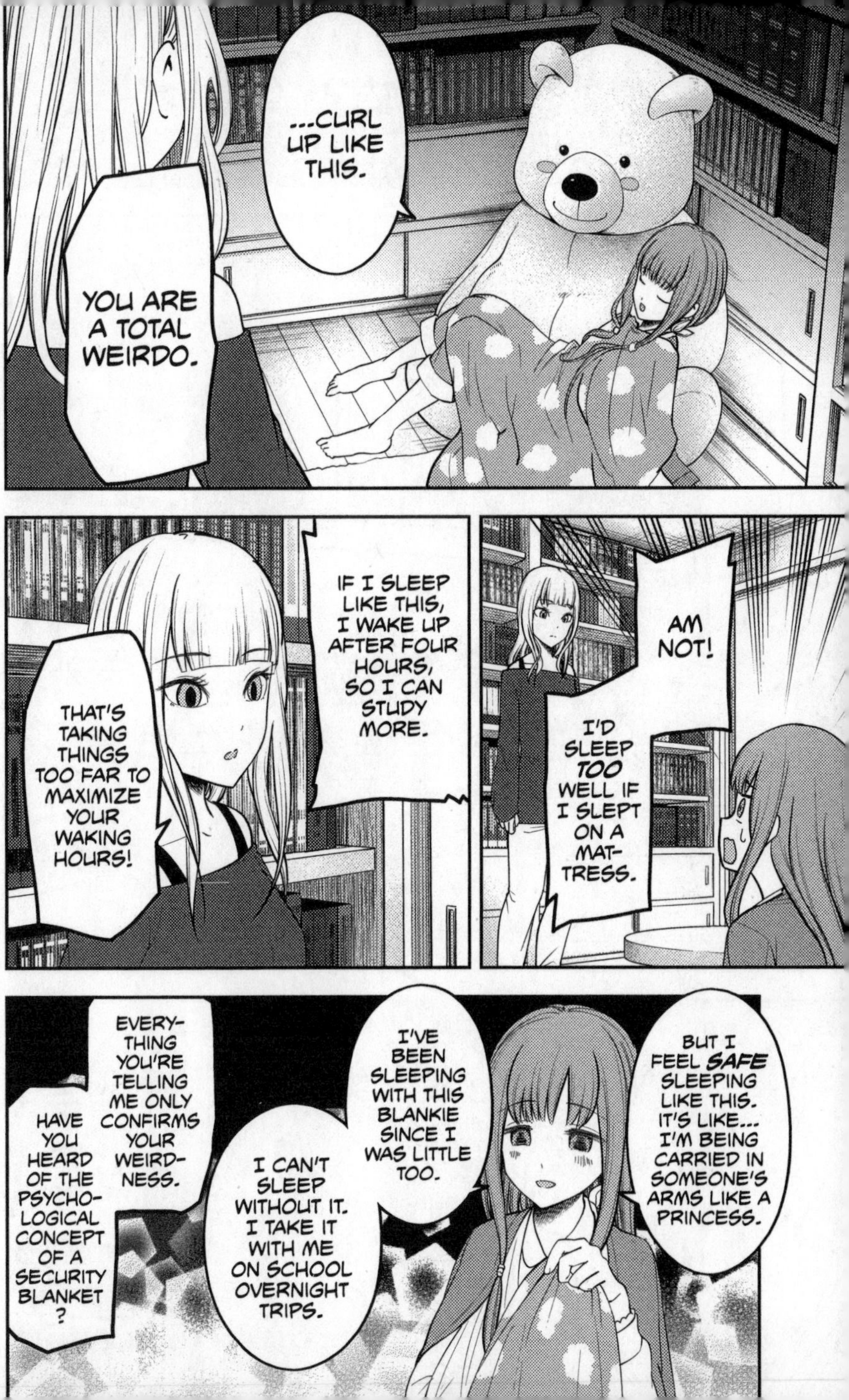
...CURL UP LIKE THIS.
YOU ARE A TOTAL WEIRDO.
AM NOT!
I'D SLEEP *TOO* WELL IF I SLEPT ON A MAT-TRESS.
IF I SLEEP LIKE THIS, I WAKE UP AFTER FOUR HOURS, SO I CAN STUDY MORE.
THAT'S TAKING THINGS TOO FAR TO MAXIMIZE YOUR WAKING HOURS!
BUT I FEEL *SAFE* SLEEPING LIKE THIS. IT'S LIKE... I'M BEING CARRIED IN SOMEONE'S ARMS LIKE A PRINCESS.
I'VE BEEN SLEEPING WITH THIS BLANKIE SINCE I WAS LITTLE TOO.
I CAN'T SLEEP WITHOUT IT. I TAKE IT WITH ME ON SCHOOL OVERNIGHT TRIPS.
EVERY-THING YOU'RE TELLING ME ONLY CONFIRMS YOUR WEIRD-NESS.
HAVE YOU HEARD OF THE PSYCHO-LOGICAL CONCEPT OF A SECURITY BLANKET?

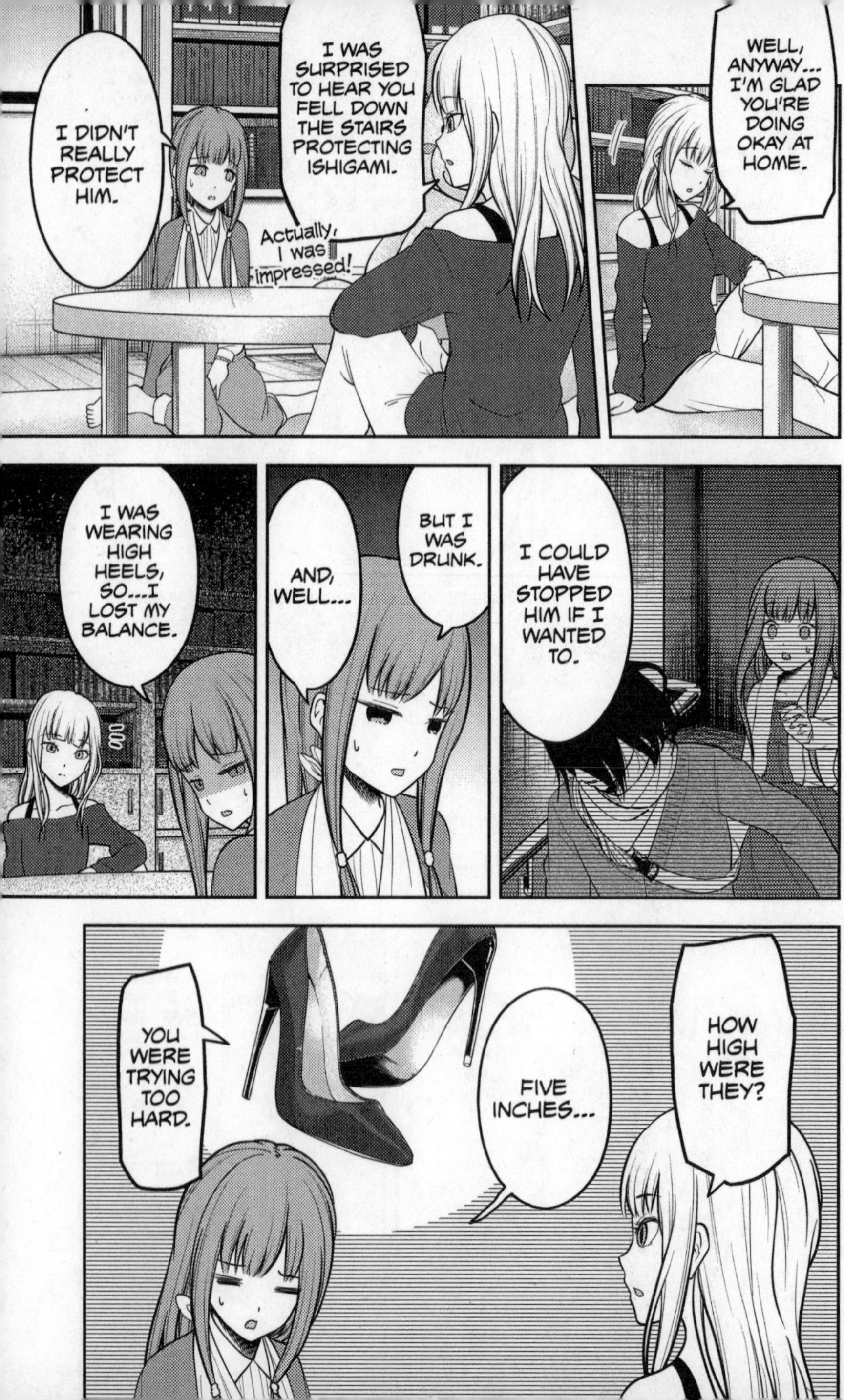
WELL, ANYWAY... I'M GLAD YOU'RE DOING OKAY AT HOME.
I WAS SURPRISED TO HEAR YOU FELL DOWN THE STAIRS PROTECTING ISHIGAMI.
Actually, I was impressed!
I DIDN'T REALLY PROTECT HIM.
I COULD HAVE STOPPED HIM IF I WANTED TO.
BUT I WAS DRUNK.
AND, WELL...
I WAS WEARING HIGH HEELS, SO...I LOST MY BALANCE.
HOW HIGH WERE THEY?
FIVE INCHES...
YOU WERE TRYING TOO HARD.

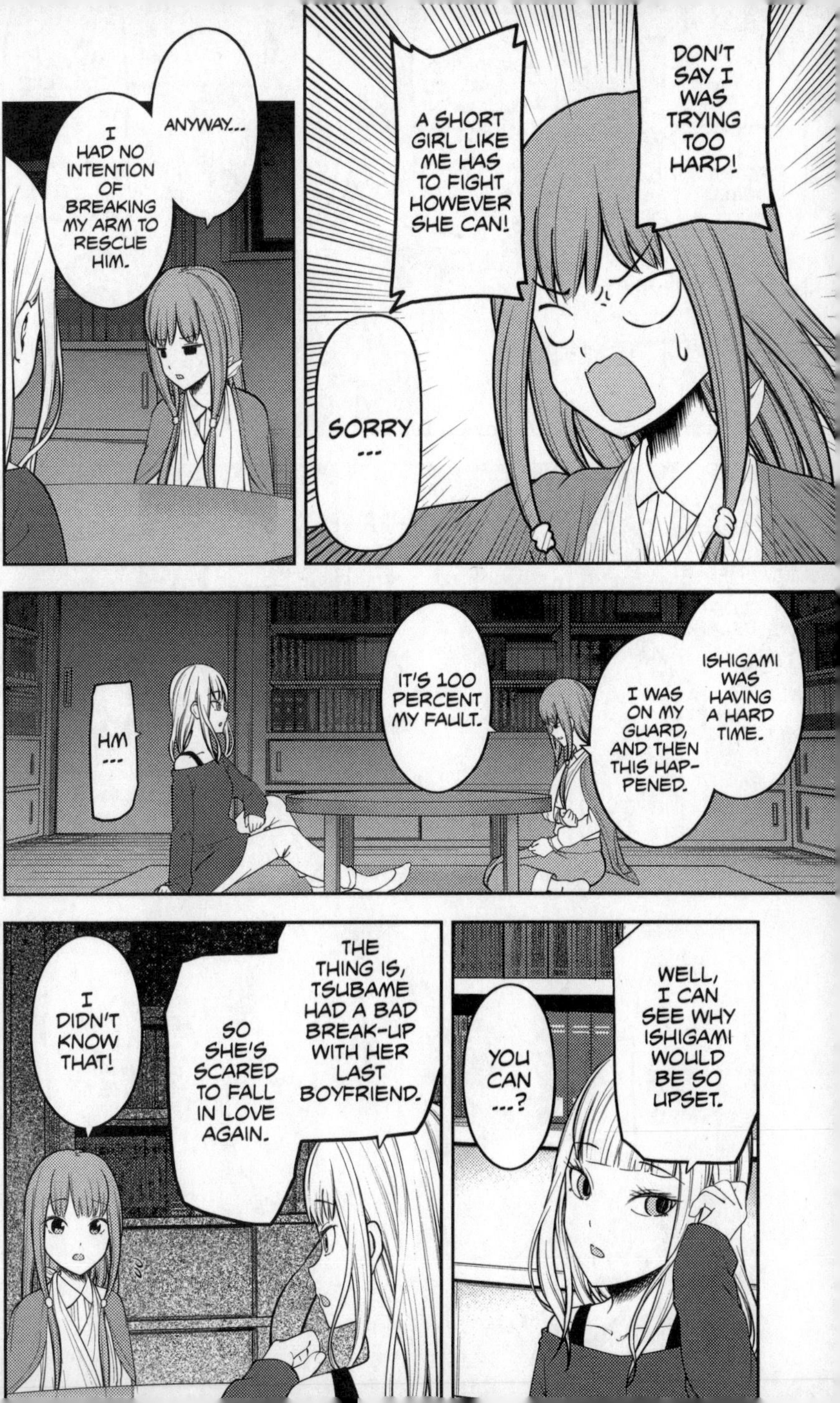
DON'T SAY I WAS TRYING TOO HARD!
A SHORT GIRL LIKE ME HAS TO FIGHT HOWEVER SHE CAN!
SORRY ---
ANYWAY...
I HAD NO INTENTION OF BREAKING MY ARM TO RESCUE HIM.
ISHIGAMI WAS HAVING A HARD TIME.
I WAS ON MY GUARD, AND THEN THIS HAP-PENED.
IT'S 100 PERCENT MY FAULT.
HM ---
WELL, I CAN SEE WHY ISHIGAMI WOULD BE SO UPSET.
YOU CAN ---?
THE THING IS, TSUBAME HAD A BAD BREAK-UP WITH HER LAST BOYFRIEND.
SO SHE'S SCARED TO FALL IN LOVE AGAIN.
I DIDN'T KNOW THAT!

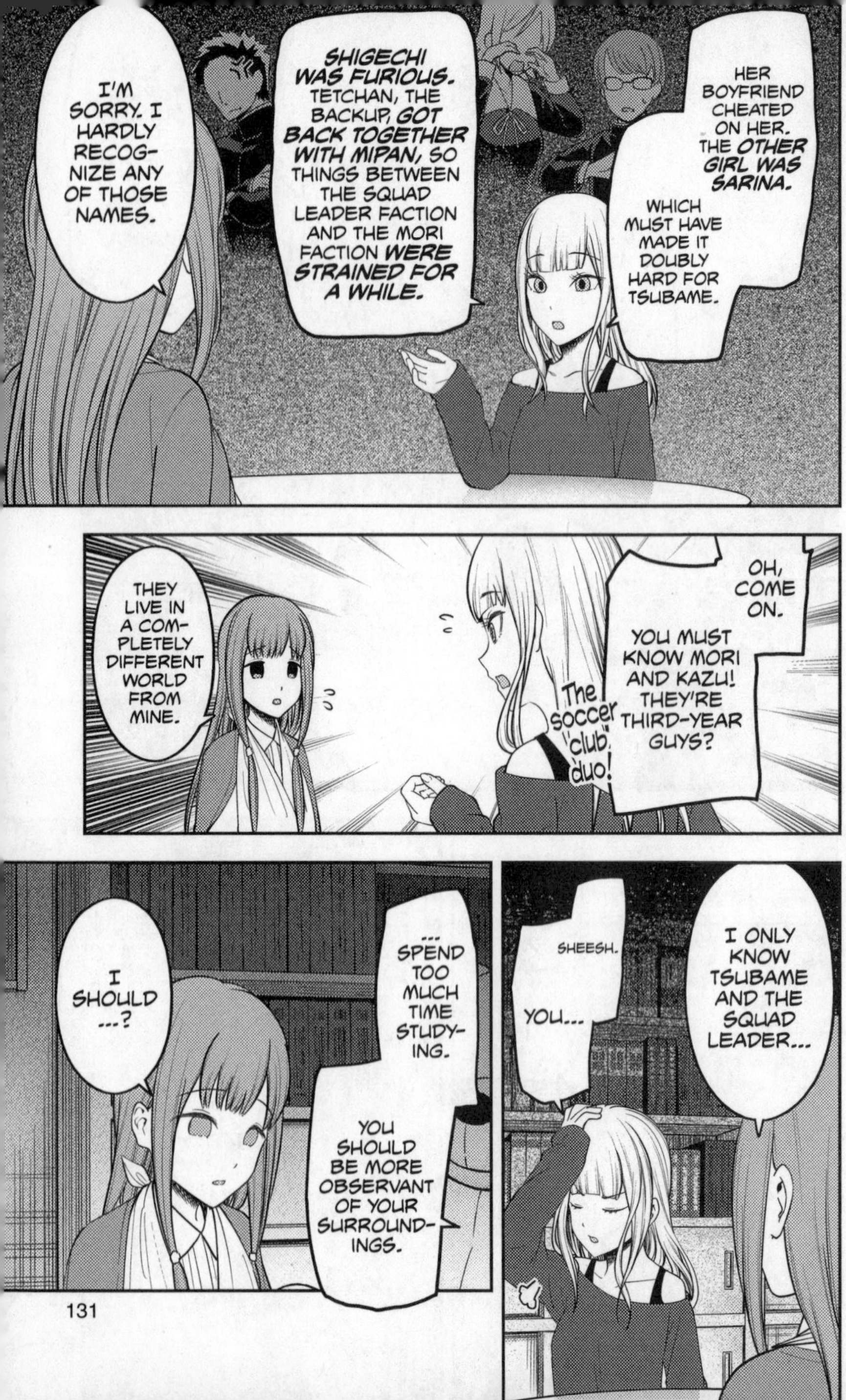

HER BOYFRIEND CHEATED ON HER. THE OTHER GIRL WAS SARINA.
WHICH MUST HAVE MADE IT DOUBLY HARD FOR TSUBAME.
SHIGECHI WAS FURIOUS. TETCHAN, THE BACKUP, GOT BACK TOGETHER WITH MIPAN, SO THINGS BETWEEN THE SQUAD LEADER FACTION AND THE MORI FACTION WERE STRAINED FOR A WHILE.
I'M SORRY. I HARDLY RECOG-NIZE ANY OF THOSE NAMES.
OH, COME ON.
YOU MUST KNOW MORI AND KAZU! THEY'RE THIRD-YEAR GUYS?
The soccer "club" duo!
THEY LIVE IN A COM-PLETELY DIFFERENT WORLD FROM MINE.
I ONLY KNOW TSUBAME AND THE SQUAD LEADER...
SHEESH.
YOU...
...SPEND TOO MUCH TIME STUDY-ING.
YOU SHOULD BE MORE OBSERVANT OF YOUR SURROUND-INGS.
I SHOULD...?

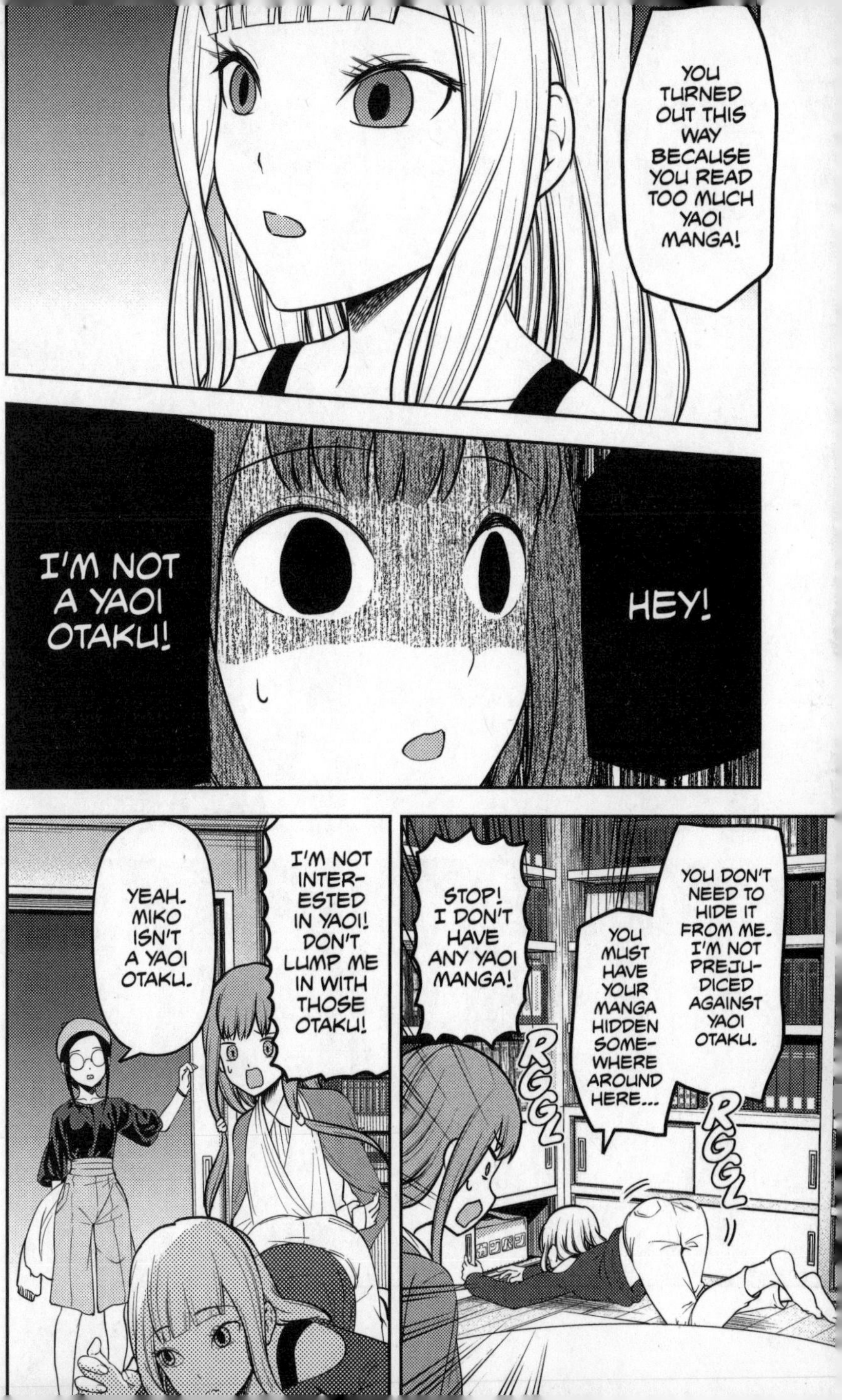
YOU TURNED OUT THIS WAY BECAUSE YOU READ TOO MUCH YAOI MANGA!
HEY!
I'M NOT A YAOI OTAKU!
YOU DON'T NEED TO HIDE IT FROM ME. I'M NOT PREJU-DICED AGAINST YAOI OTAKU.
YOU MUST HAVE YOUR MANGA HIDDEN SOME-WHERE AROUND HERE...
RGGL
RGGL
STOP! I DON'T HAVE ANY YAOI MANGA!
I'M NOT INTER-ESTED IN YAOI! DON'T LUMP ME IN WITH THOSE OTAKU!
YEAH. MIKO ISN'T A YAOI OTAKU.

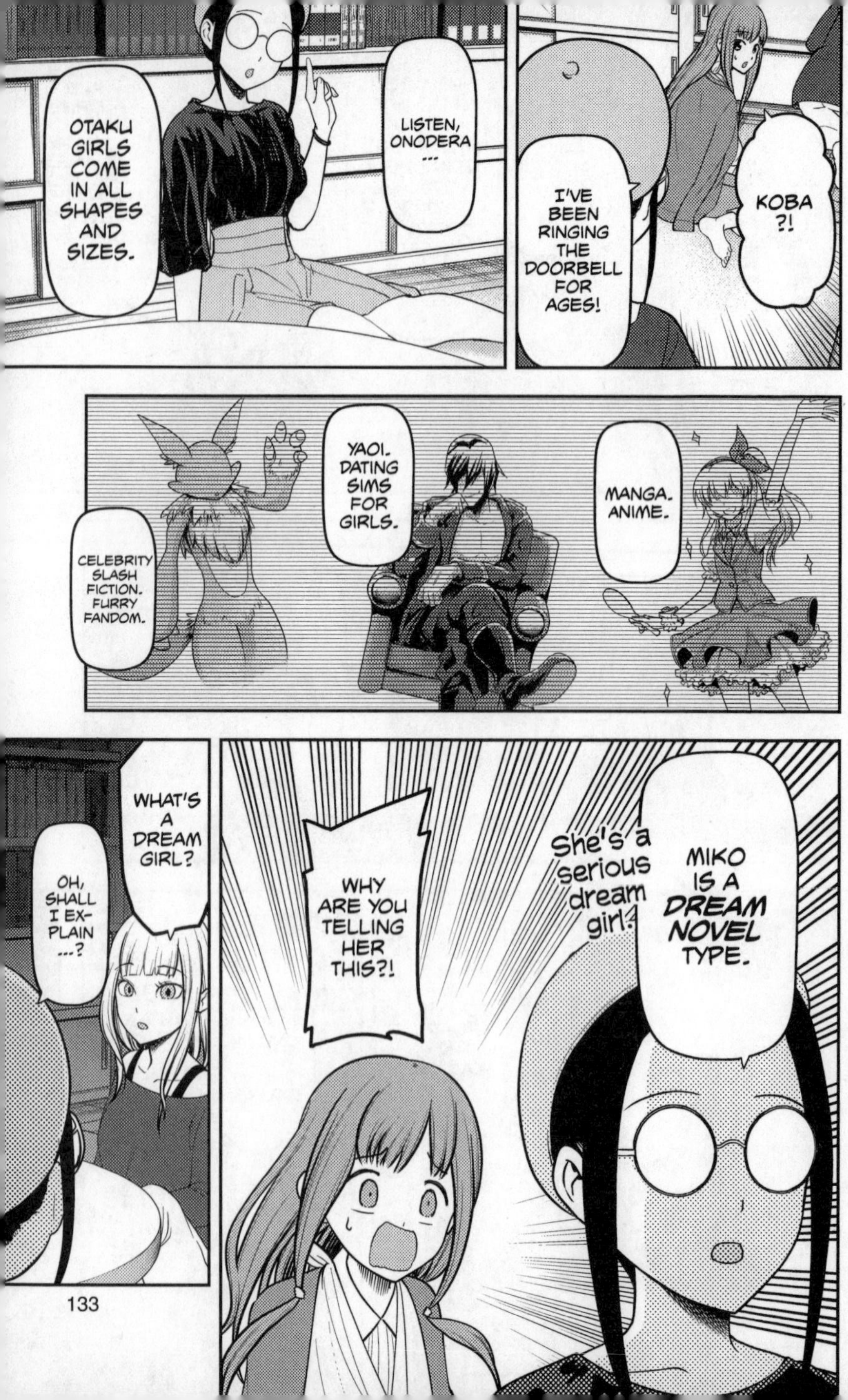
KOBA?!
I'VE BEEN RINGING THE DOORBELL FOR AGES!
LISTEN, ONODERA...
OTAKU GIRLS COME IN ALL SHAPES AND SIZES.
MANGA. ANIME.
YAOI. DATING SIMS FOR GIRLS.
CELEBRITY SLASH FICTION. FURRY FANDOM.
MIKO IS A ***DREAM NOVEL*** TYPE.
She's a serious dream girl.
WHY ARE YOU TELLING HER THIS?!
WHAT'S A DREAM GIRL?
OH, SHALL I EX-PLAIN...?

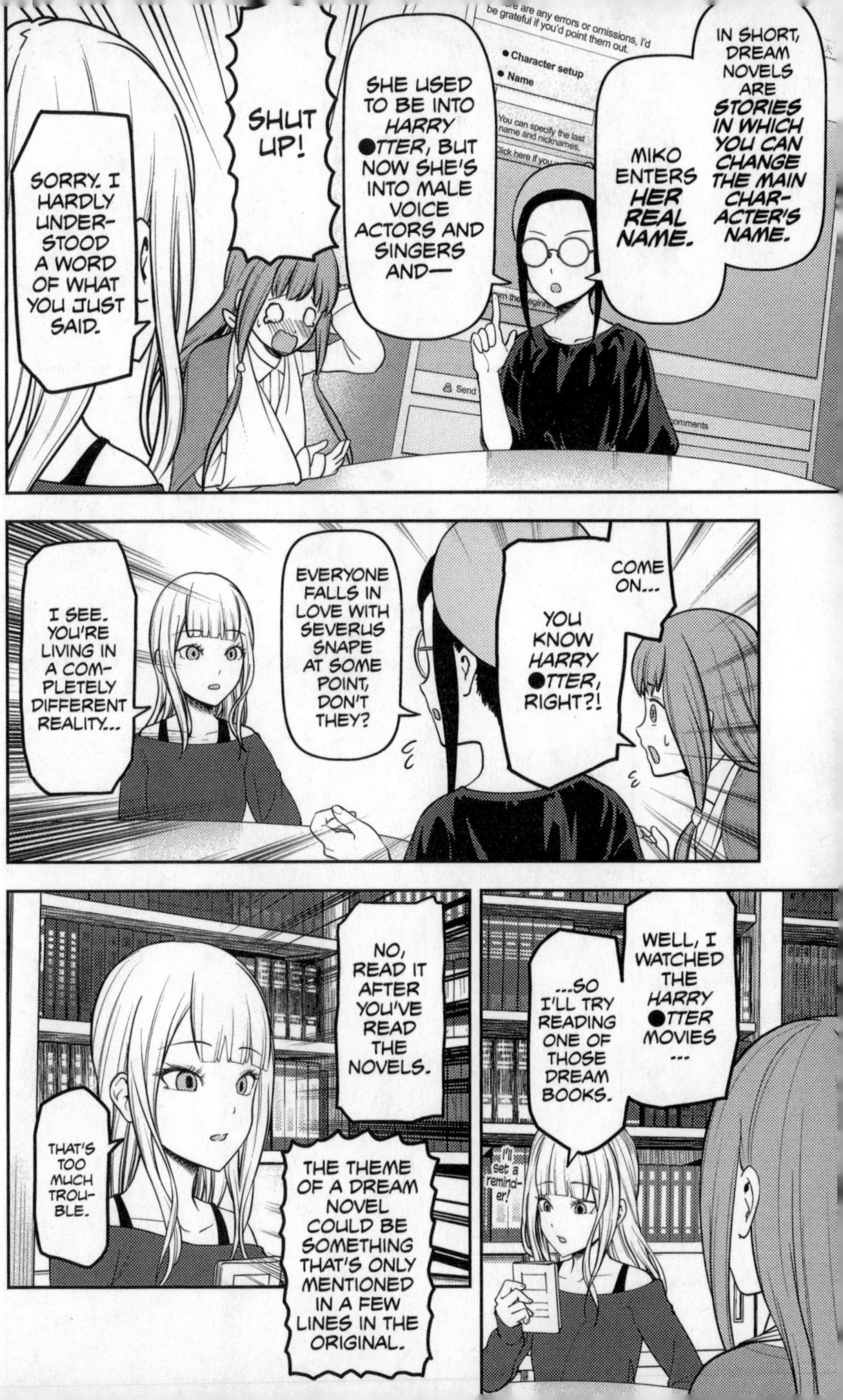
be grateful if you'd point them out.
Character setup
Name
You can specify the last name and nicknames.
Send
IN SHORT, DREAM NOVELS ARE STORIES IN WHICH YOU CAN CHANGE THE MAIN CHARACTER'S NAME.
MIKO ENTERS HER REAL NAME.
SHE USED TO BE INTO HARRY ●TTER, BUT NOW SHE'S INTO MALE VOICE ACTORS AND SINGERS AND—
SHUT UP!
SORRY. I HARDLY UNDERSTOOD A WORD OF WHAT YOU JUST SAID.
COME ON...
YOU KNOW HARRY ●TTER, RIGHT?!
EVERYONE FALLS IN LOVE WITH SEVERUS SNAPE AT SOME POINT, DON'T THEY?
I SEE. YOU'RE LIVING IN A COMPLETELY DIFFERENT REALITY...
WELL, I WATCHED THE HARRY ●TTER MOVIES...
...SO I'LL TRY READING ONE OF THOSE DREAM BOOKS.
I'll set a reminder!
NO, READ IT AFTER YOU'VE READ THE NOVELS.
THE THEME OF A DREAM NOVEL COULD BE SOMETHING THAT'S ONLY MENTIONED IN A FEW LINES IN THE ORIGINAL.
THAT'S TOO MUCH TROUBLE.

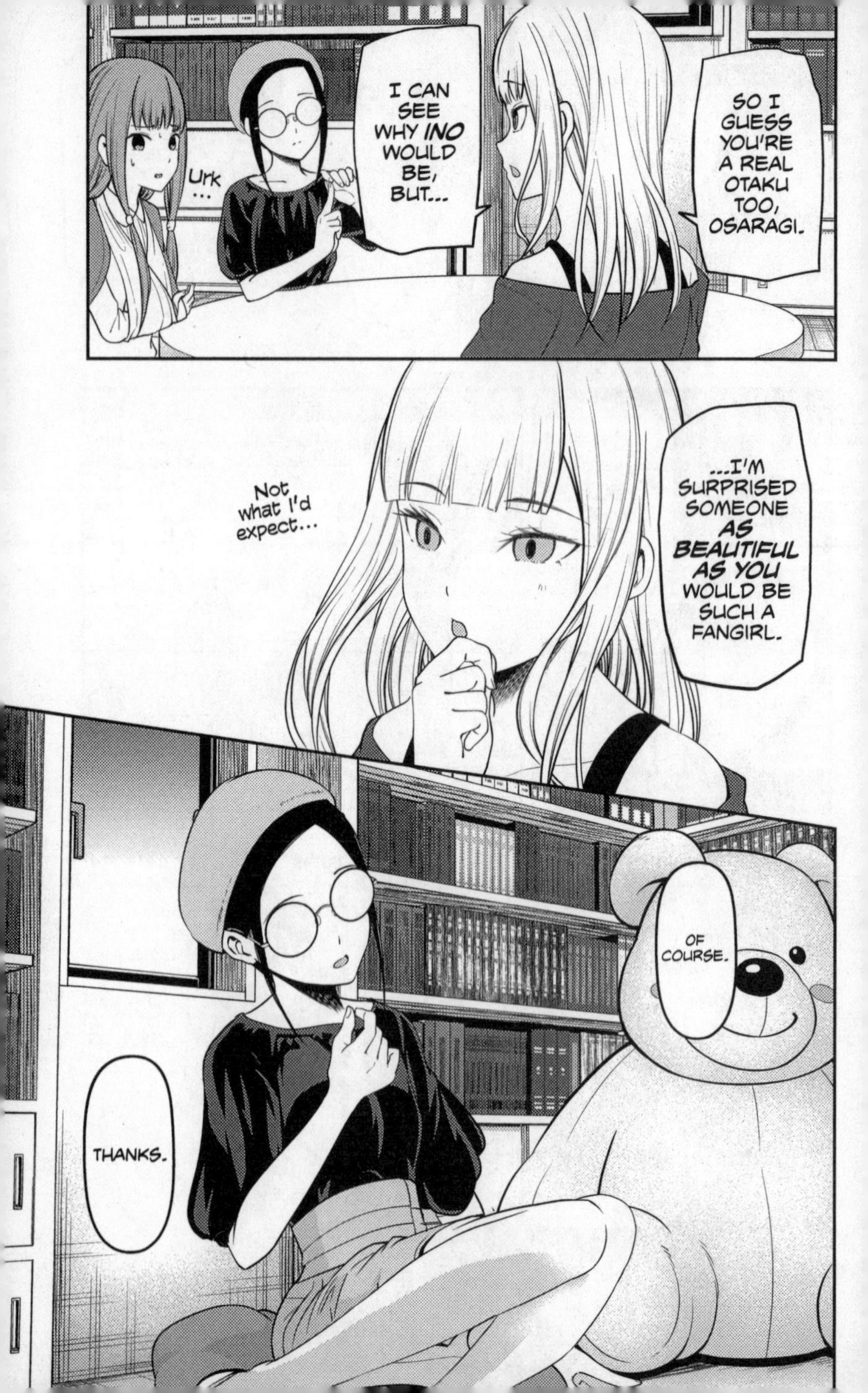
SO I GUESS YOU'RE A REAL OTAKU TOO, OSARAGI.
I CAN SEE WHY INO WOULD BE, BUT...
Urk ...
...I'M SURPRISED SOMEONE AS BEAUTIFUL AS YOU WOULD BE SUCH A FANGIRL.
Not what I'd expect...
OF COURSE.
THANKS.

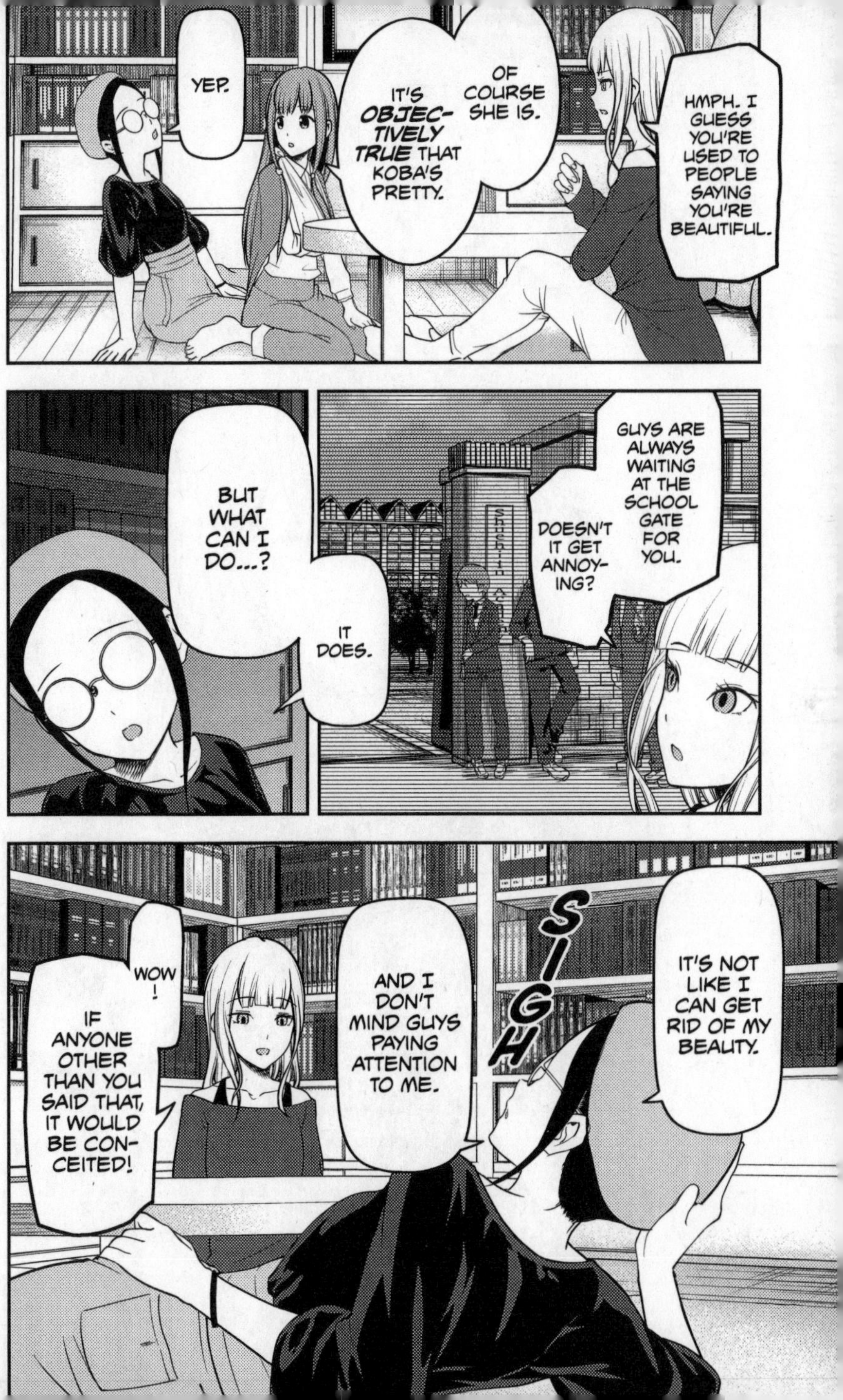
HMPH. I GUESS YOU'RE USED TO PEOPLE SAYING YOU'RE BEAUTIFUL.
OF COURSE SHE IS.
IT'S OBJECTIVELY TRUE THAT KOBA'S PRETTY.
YEP.
GUYS ARE ALWAYS WAITING AT THE SCHOOL GATE FOR YOU.
DOESN'T IT GET ANNOYING?
IT DOES.
BUT WHAT CAN I DO...?
IT'S NOT LIKE I CAN GET RID OF MY BEAUTY.
SIGH
AND I DON'T MIND GUYS PAYING ATTENTION TO ME.
WOW!
IF ANYONE OTHER THAN YOU SAID THAT, IT WOULD BE CONCEITED!

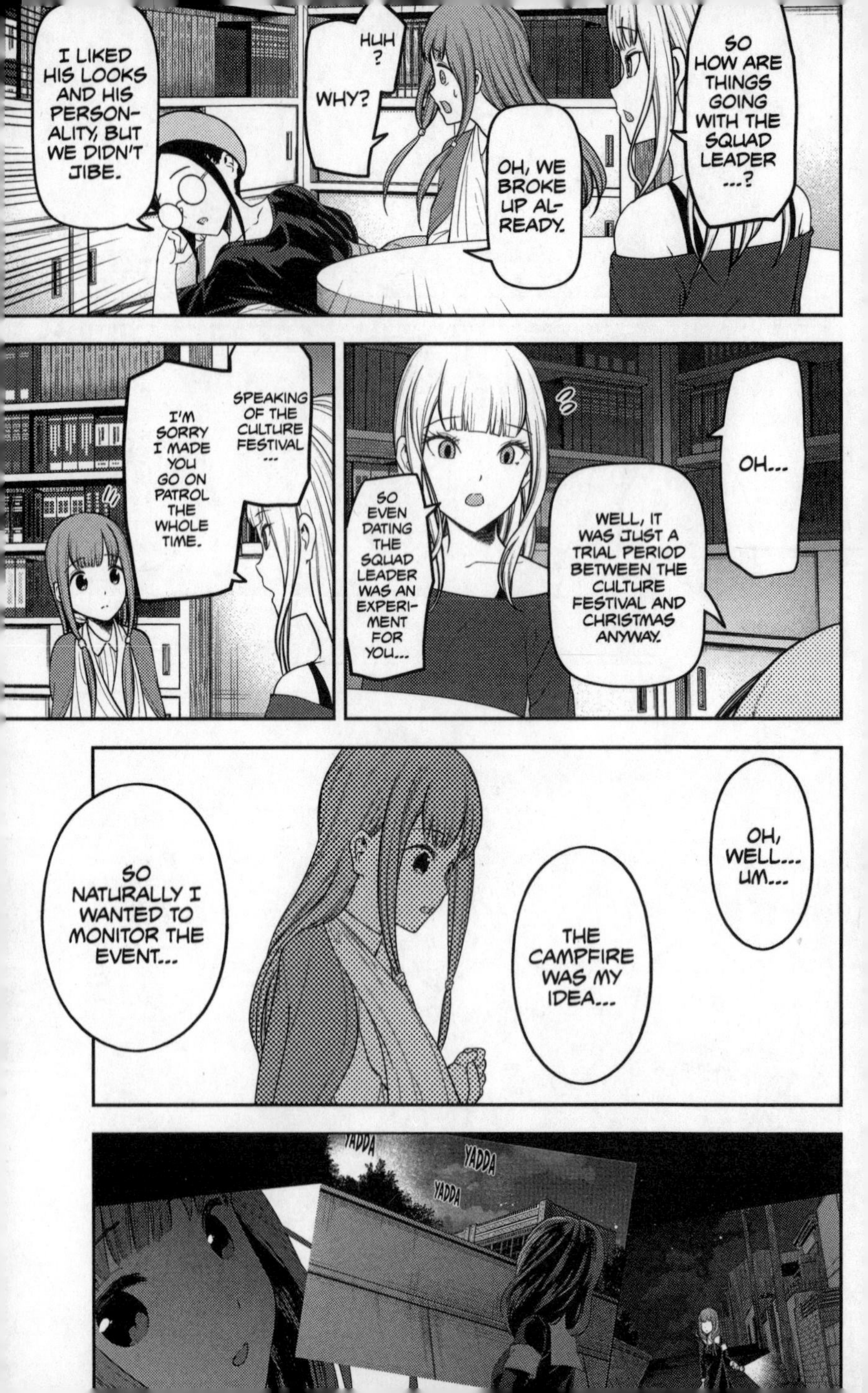
SO HOW ARE THINGS GOING WITH THE SQUAD LEADER ...?
OH, WE BROKE UP AL-READY.
HUH? WHY?
I LIKED HIS LOOKS AND HIS PERSON-ALITY, BUT WE DIDN'T JIBE.
OH...
WELL, IT WAS JUST A TRIAL PERIOD BETWEEN THE CULTURE FESTIVAL AND CHRISTMAS ANYWAY.
SO EVEN DATING THE SQUAD LEADER WAS AN EXPERI-MENT FOR YOU...
SPEAKING OF THE CULTURE FESTIVAL ...
I'M SORRY I MADE YOU GO ON PATROL THE WHOLE TIME.
OH, WELL... UM...
THE CAMPFIRE WAS MY IDEA...
SO NATURALLY I WANTED TO MONITOR THE EVENT...
YADDA
YADDA
YADDA

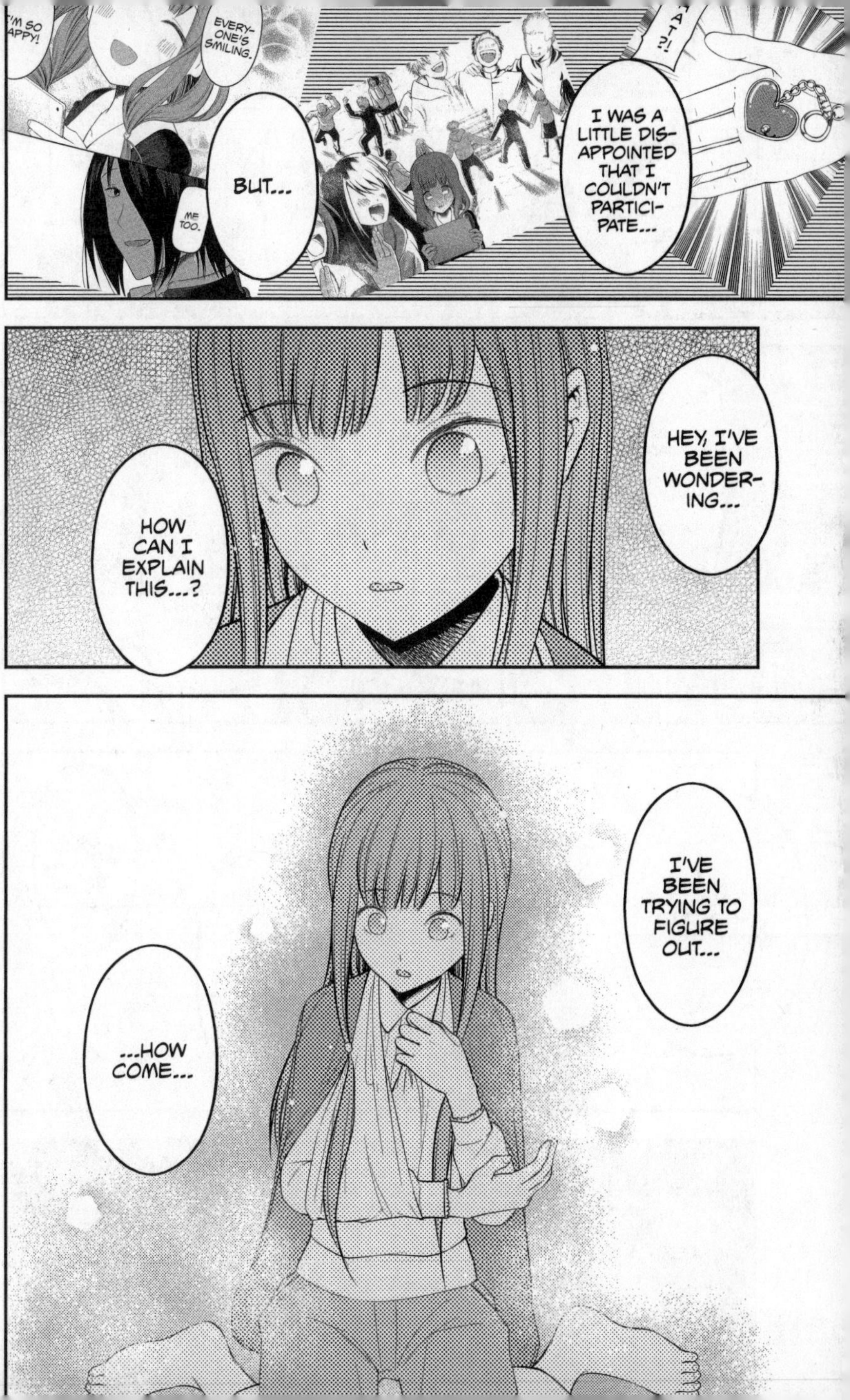

AT?!
I WAS A LITTLE DIS-APPOINTED THAT I COULDN'T PARTICI-PATE...
BUT...
EVERY-ONE'S SMILING.
I'M SO APPY!
ME TOO.
HEY, I'VE BEEN WONDER-ING...
HOW CAN I EXPLAIN THIS...?
I'VE BEEN TRYING TO FIGURE OUT...
...HOW COME...

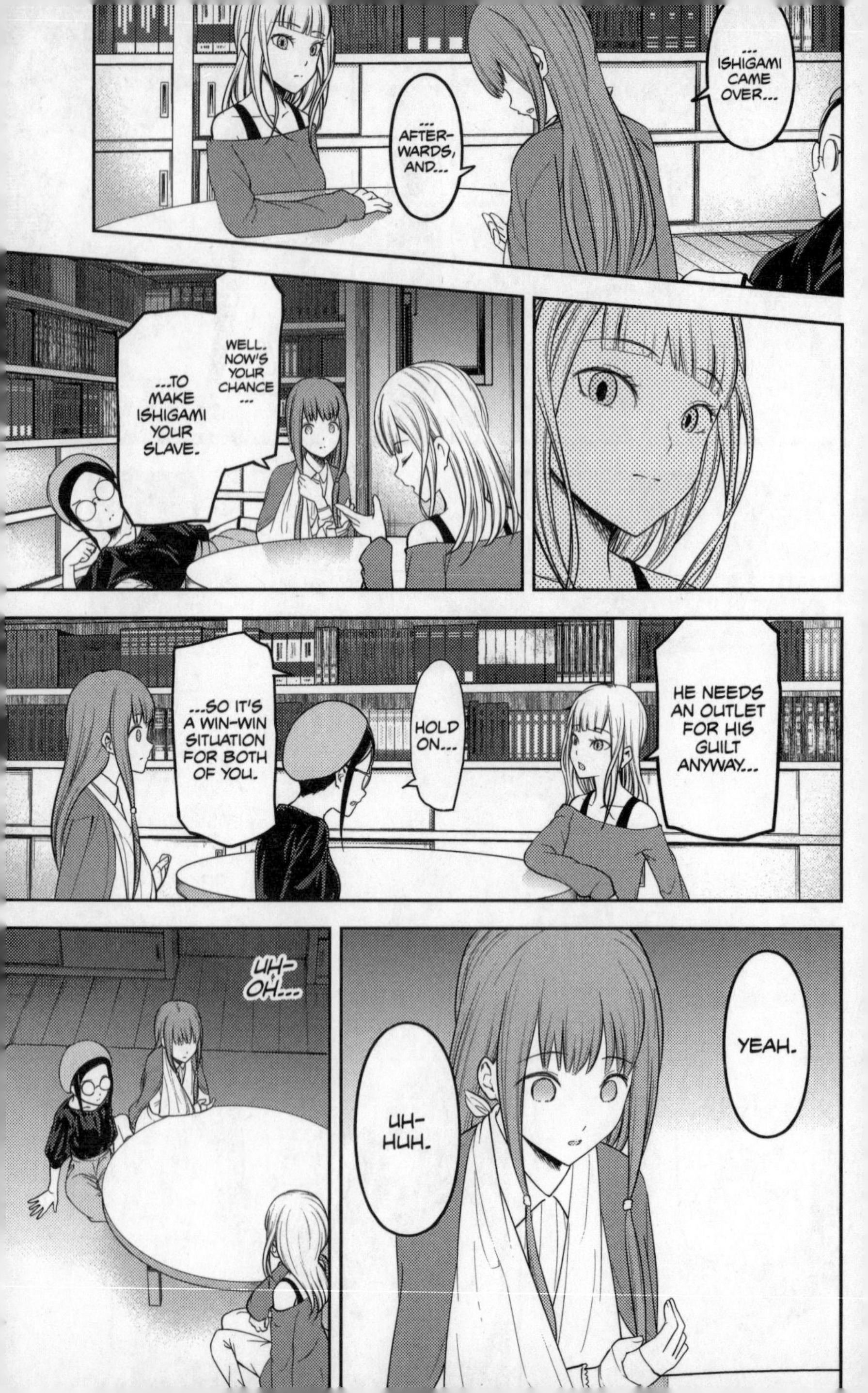

...ISHIGAMI CAME OVER...
...AFTER-WARDS, AND...
WELL. NOW'S YOUR CHANCE...
...TO MAKE ISHIGAMI YOUR SLAVE.
HE NEEDS AN OUTLET FOR HIS GUILT ANYWAY...
HOLD ON...
...SO IT'S A WIN-WIN SITUATION FOR BOTH OF YOU.
YEAH.
UH-HUH.
UH-OH...

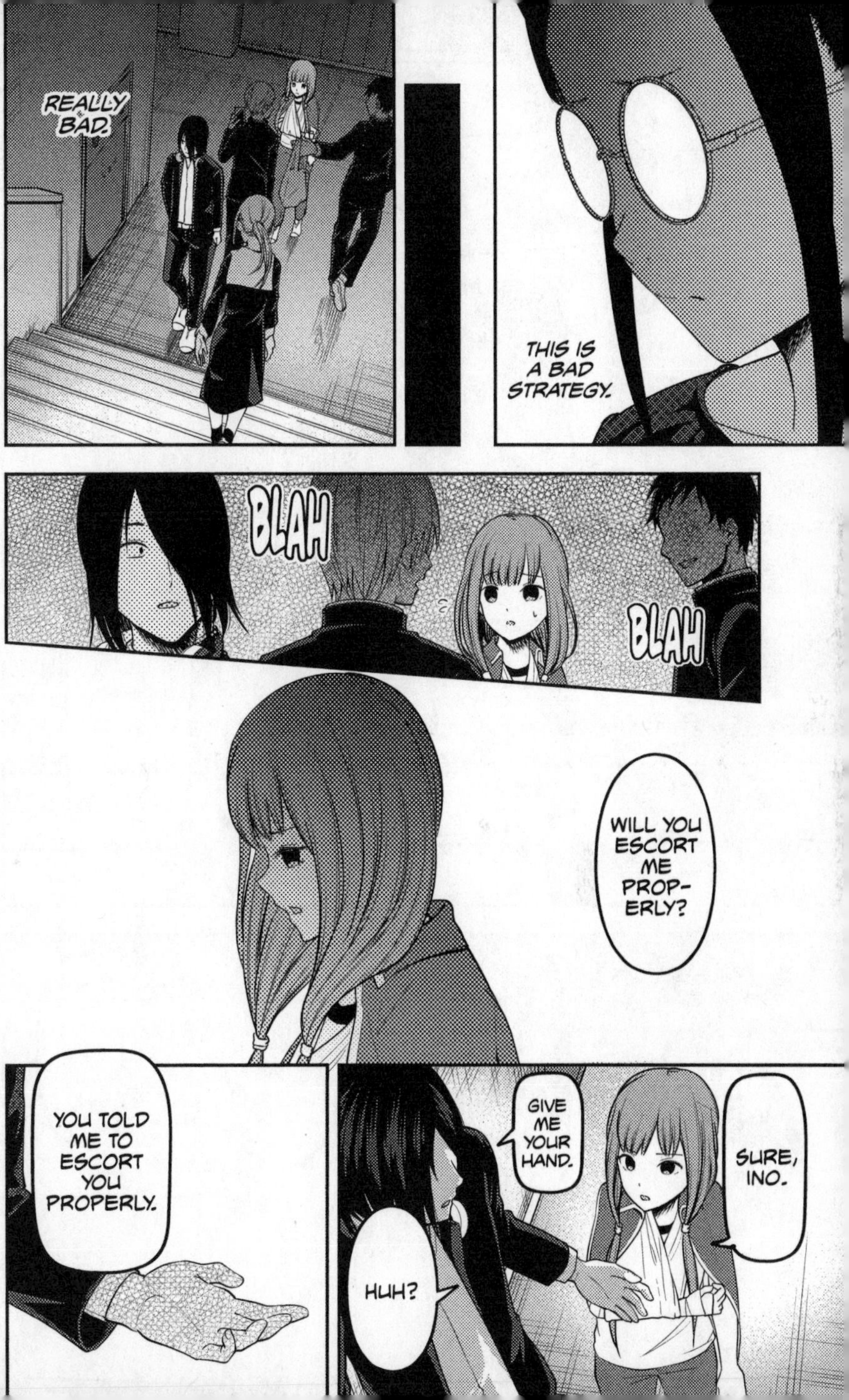
THIS IS A BAD STRATEGY.
REALLY BAD.
BLAH
BLAH
WILL YOU ESCORT ME PROPERLY?
SURE, INO.
GIVE ME YOUR HAND.
HUH?
YOU TOLD ME TO ESCORT YOU PROPERLY.

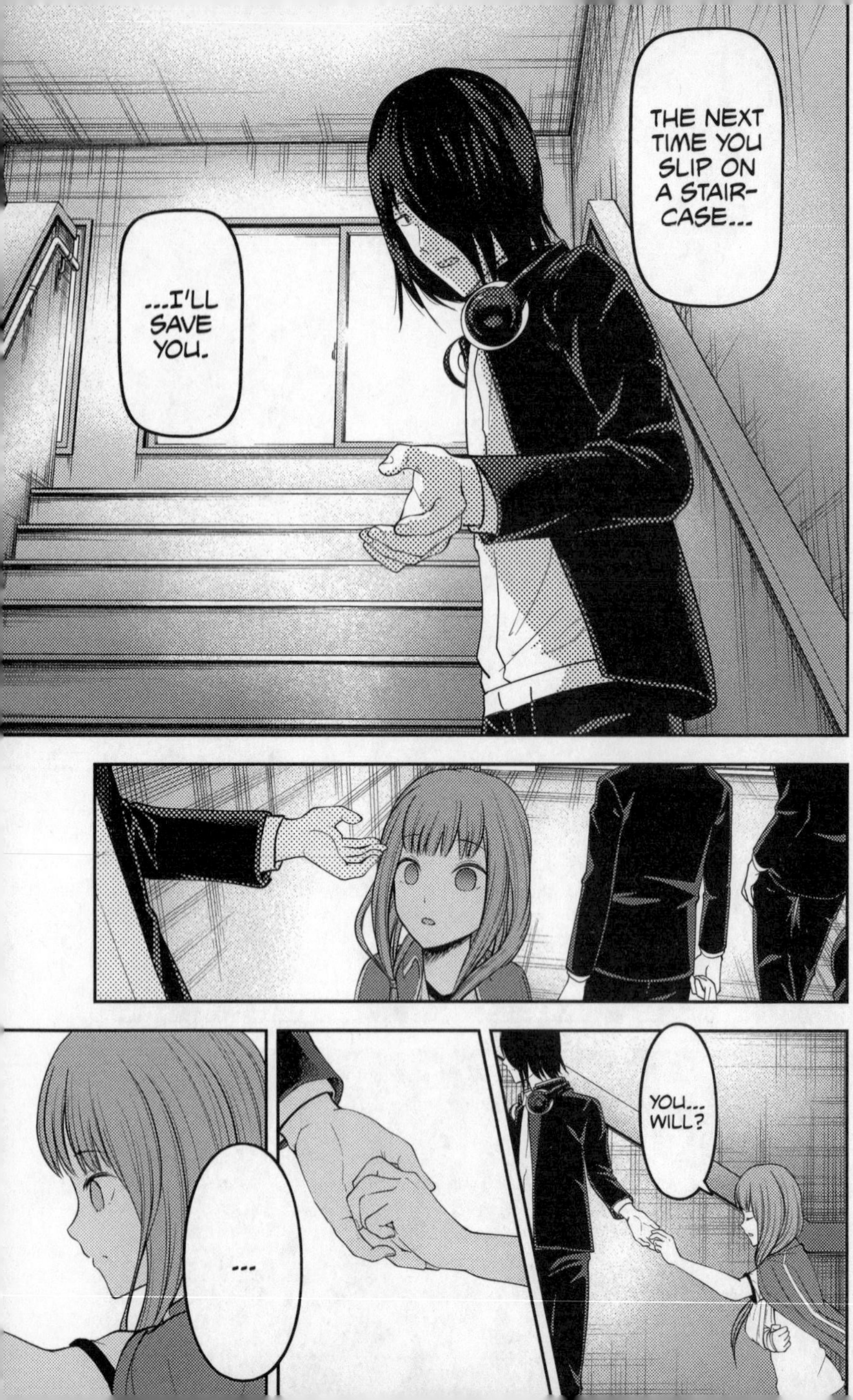
THE NEXT TIME YOU SLIP ON A STAIR-CASE...
...I'LL SAVE YOU.
YOU... WILL?
...

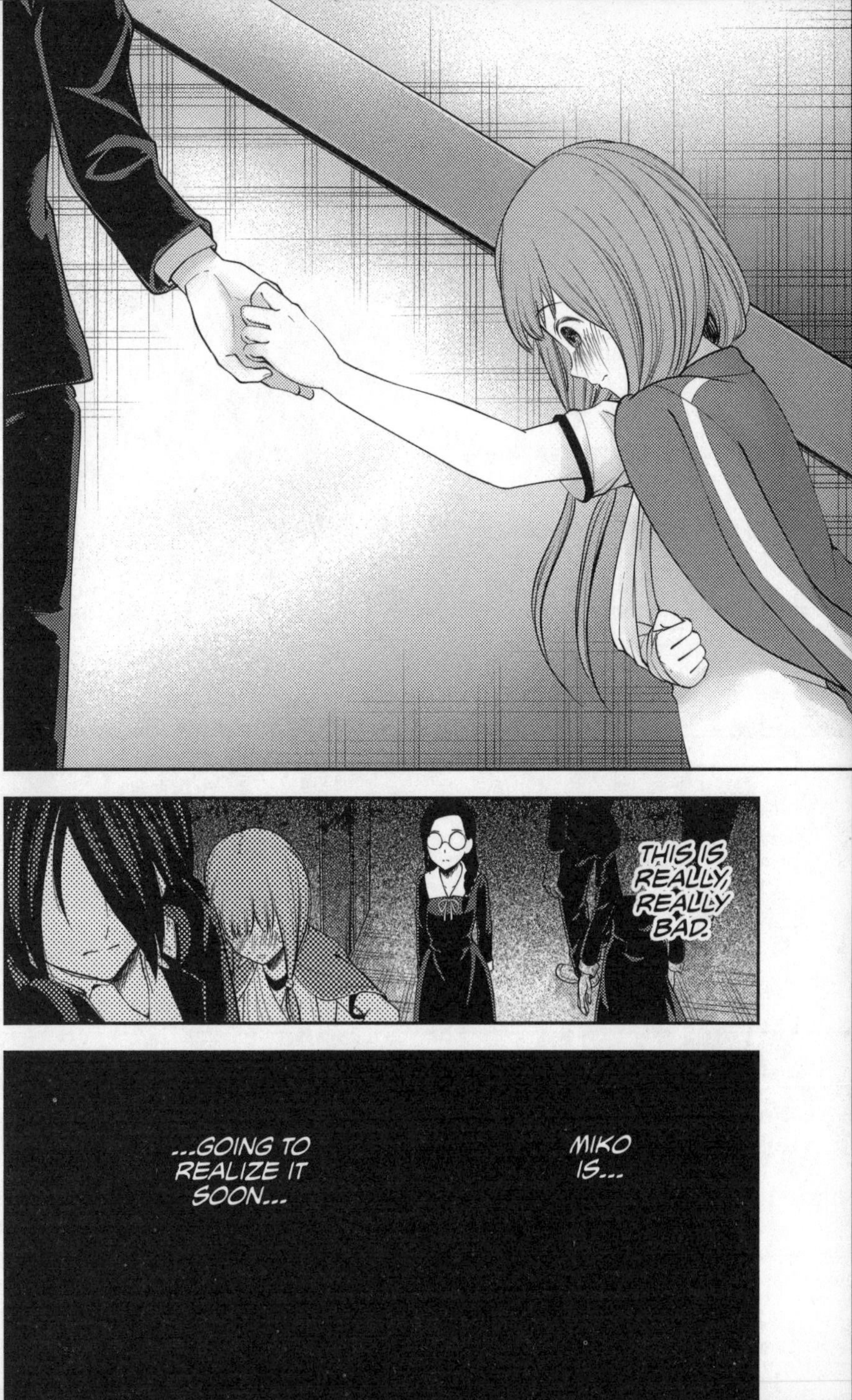
THIS IS REALLY, REALLY BAD.
MIKO IS...
...GOING TO REALIZE IT SOON...

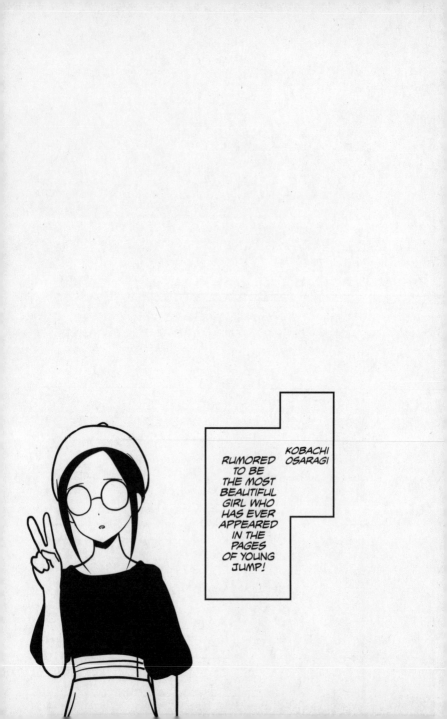

KOBACHI OSARAGI
RUMORED TO BE THE MOST BEAUTIFUL GIRL WHO HAS EVER APPEARED IN THE PAGES OF YOUNG JUMP!

KAGUYA-SAMA

LOVE IS WAR

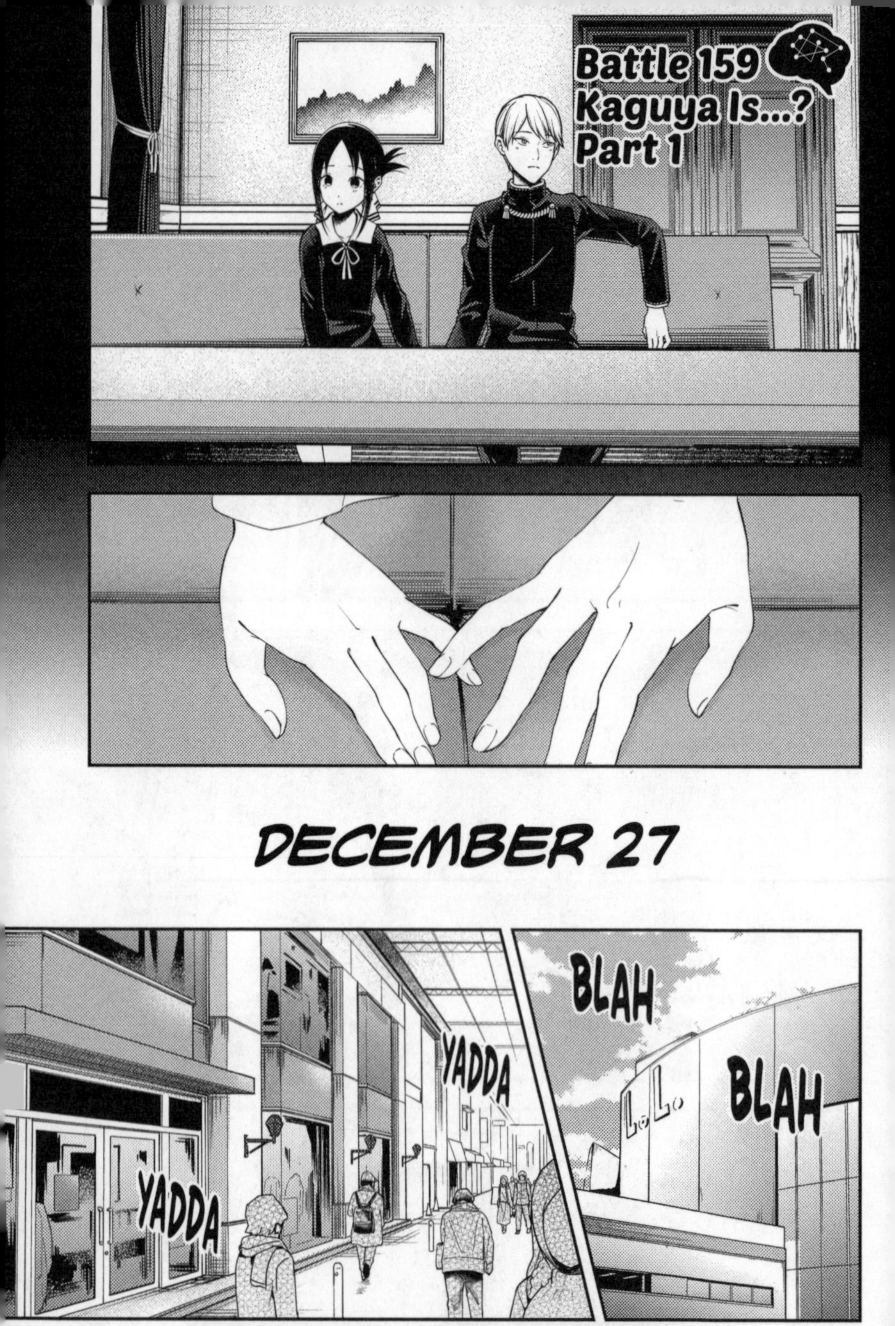
Battle 159
Kaguya Is...?
Part 1
DECEMBER 27
BLAH
BLAH
YADDA
YADDA
FLASHBACK #4: MIYUKI SHIROGANE AND
KAGUYA SHINOMIYA'S WINTER BREAK

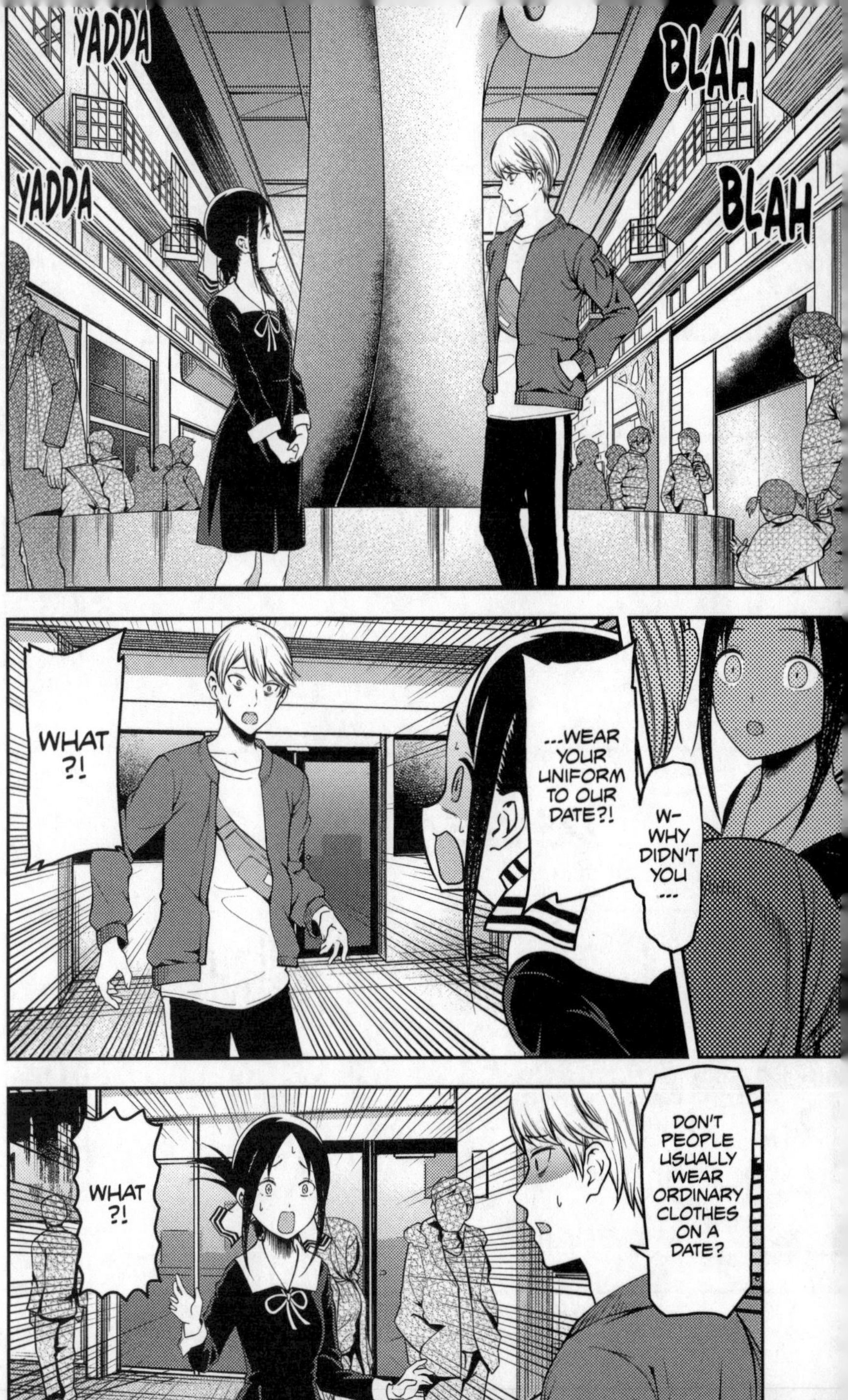
BLAH BLAH
YADDA YADDA
W-WHY DIDN'T YOU ...
...WEAR YOUR UNIFORM TO OUR DATE?!
WHAT?!
DON'T PEOPLE USUALLY WEAR ORDINARY CLOTHES ON A DATE?
WHAT?!

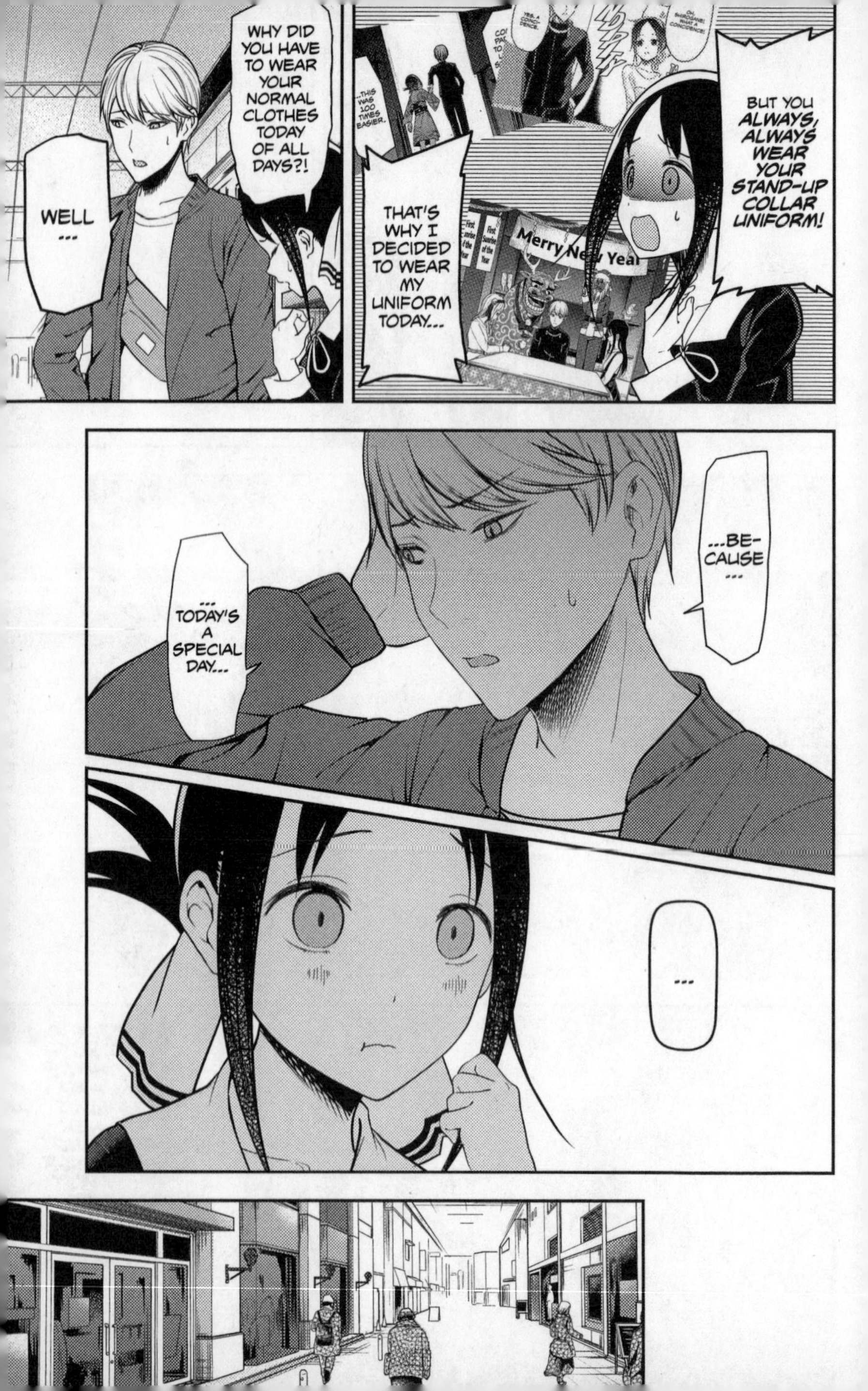
BUT YOU ALWAYS, ALWAYS WEAR YOUR STAND-UP COLLAR UNIFORM!
OH, SHIROGANE! WHAT A COINCIDENCE!
YES, A COINCIDENCE.
...THIS WAS 100 TIMES EASIER.
THAT'S WHY I DECIDED TO WEAR MY UNIFORM TODAY...
WHY DID YOU HAVE TO WEAR YOUR NORMAL CLOTHES TODAY OF ALL DAYS?!
WELL...
...BE-CAUSE...
...TODAY'S A SPECIAL DAY...
...

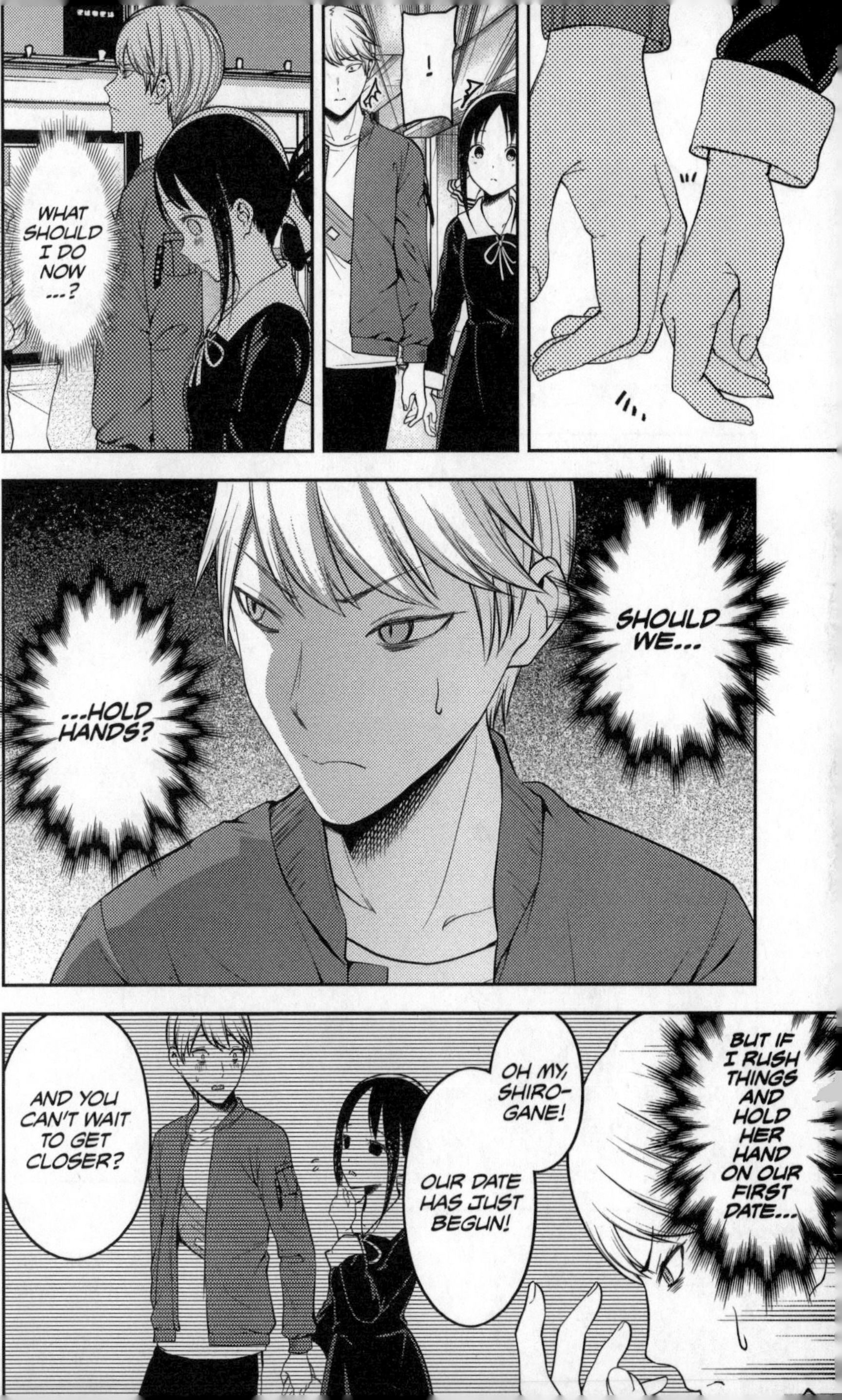
!
WHAT SHOULD I DO NOW ...?
SHOULD WE...
...HOLD HANDS?
BUT IF I RUSH THINGS AND HOLD HER HAND ON OUR FIRST DATE...
OH MY, SHIRO-GANE!
OUR DATE HAS JUST BEGUN!
AND YOU CAN'T WAIT TO GET CLOSER?

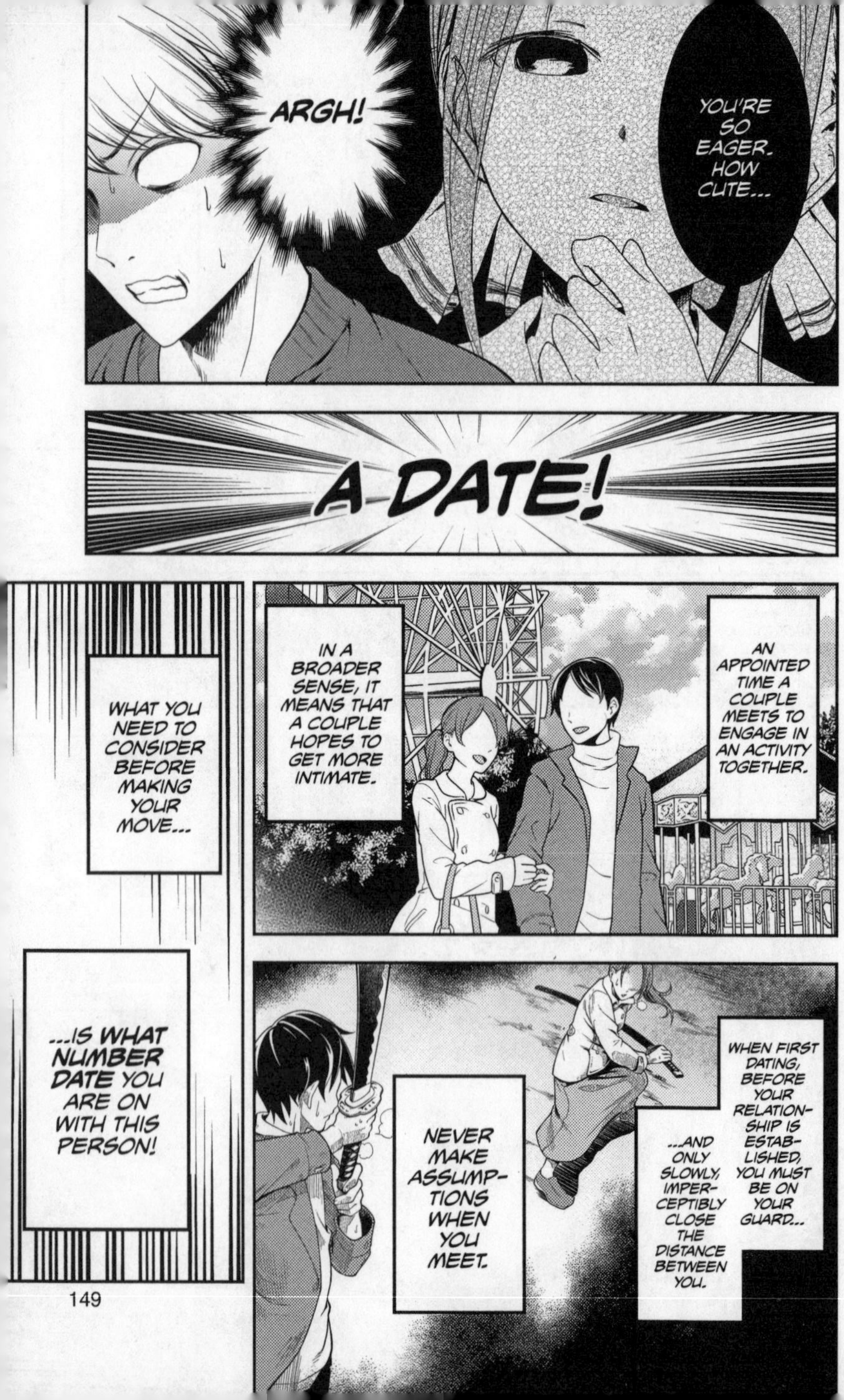
YOU'RE SO EAGER. HOW CUTE...
ARGH!
A DATE!
AN APPOINTED TIME A COUPLE MEETS TO ENGAGE IN AN ACTIVITY TOGETHER.
IN A BROADER SENSE, IT MEANS THAT A COUPLE HOPES TO GET MORE INTIMATE.
WHEN FIRST DATING, BEFORE YOUR RELATIONSHIP IS ESTABLISHED, YOU MUST BE ON YOUR GUARD...
...AND ONLY SLOWLY, IMPERCEPTIBLY CLOSE THE DISTANCE BETWEEN YOU.
NEVER MAKE ASSUMPTIONS WHEN YOU MEET.
WHAT YOU NEED TO CONSIDER BEFORE MAKING YOUR MOVE...
...IS WHAT NUMBER DATE YOU ARE ON WITH THIS PERSON!

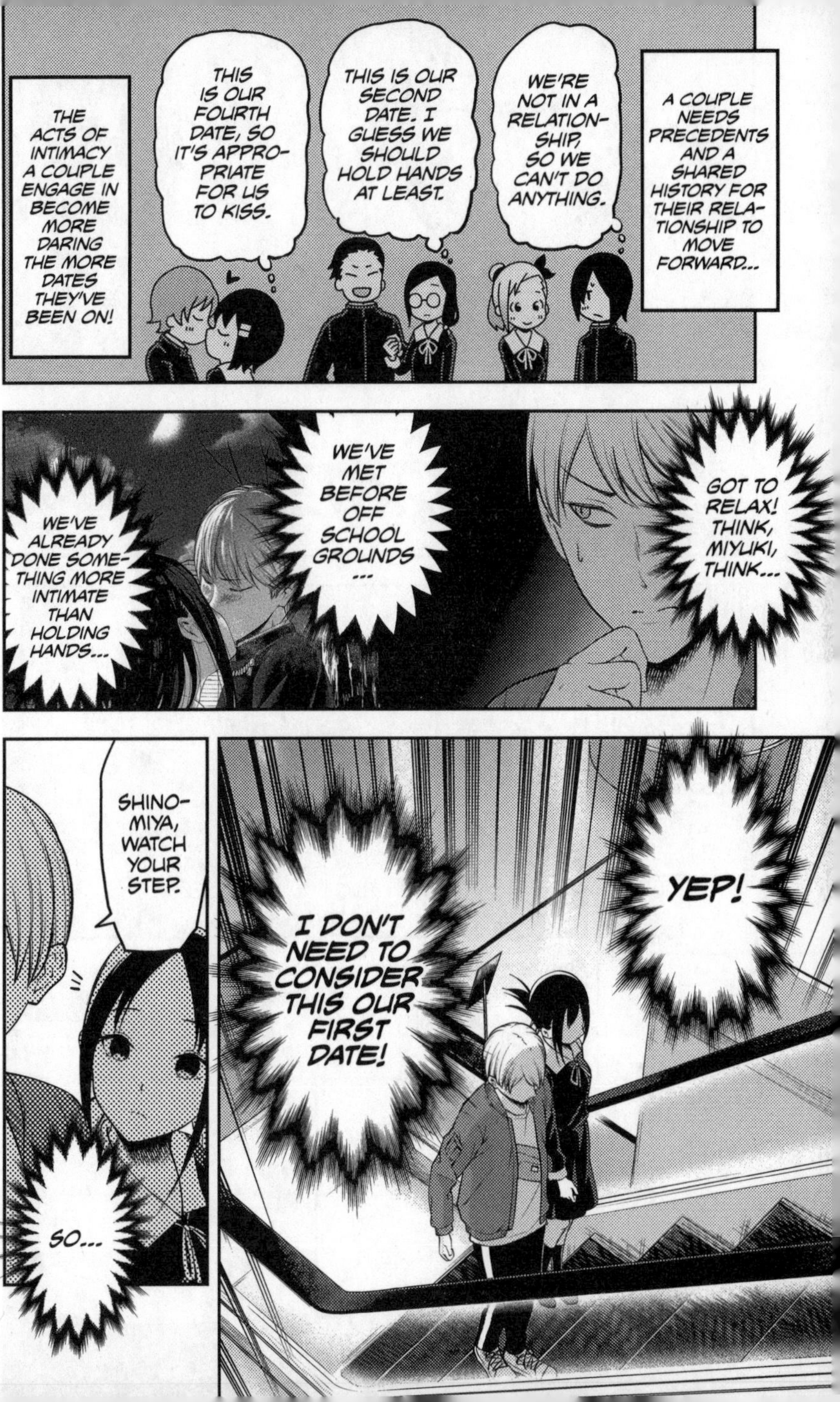
A COUPLE NEEDS PRECEDENTS AND A SHARED HISTORY FOR THEIR RELATIONSHIP TO MOVE FORWARD...
WE'RE NOT IN A RELATIONSHIP, SO WE CAN'T DO ANYTHING.
THIS IS OUR SECOND DATE. I GUESS WE SHOULD HOLD HANDS AT LEAST.
THIS IS OUR FOURTH DATE, SO IT'S APPROPRIATE FOR US TO KISS.
THE ACTS OF INTIMACY A COUPLE ENGAGE IN BECOME MORE DARING THE MORE DATES THEY'VE BEEN ON!
GOT TO RELAX! THINK, MIYUKI, THINK...
WE'VE MET BEFORE OFF SCHOOL GROUNDS...
WE'VE ALREADY DONE SOMETHING MORE INTIMATE THAN HOLDING HANDS...
YEP!
I DON'T NEED TO CONSIDER THIS OUR FIRST DATE!
SHINOMIYA, WATCH YOUR STEP.
SO...

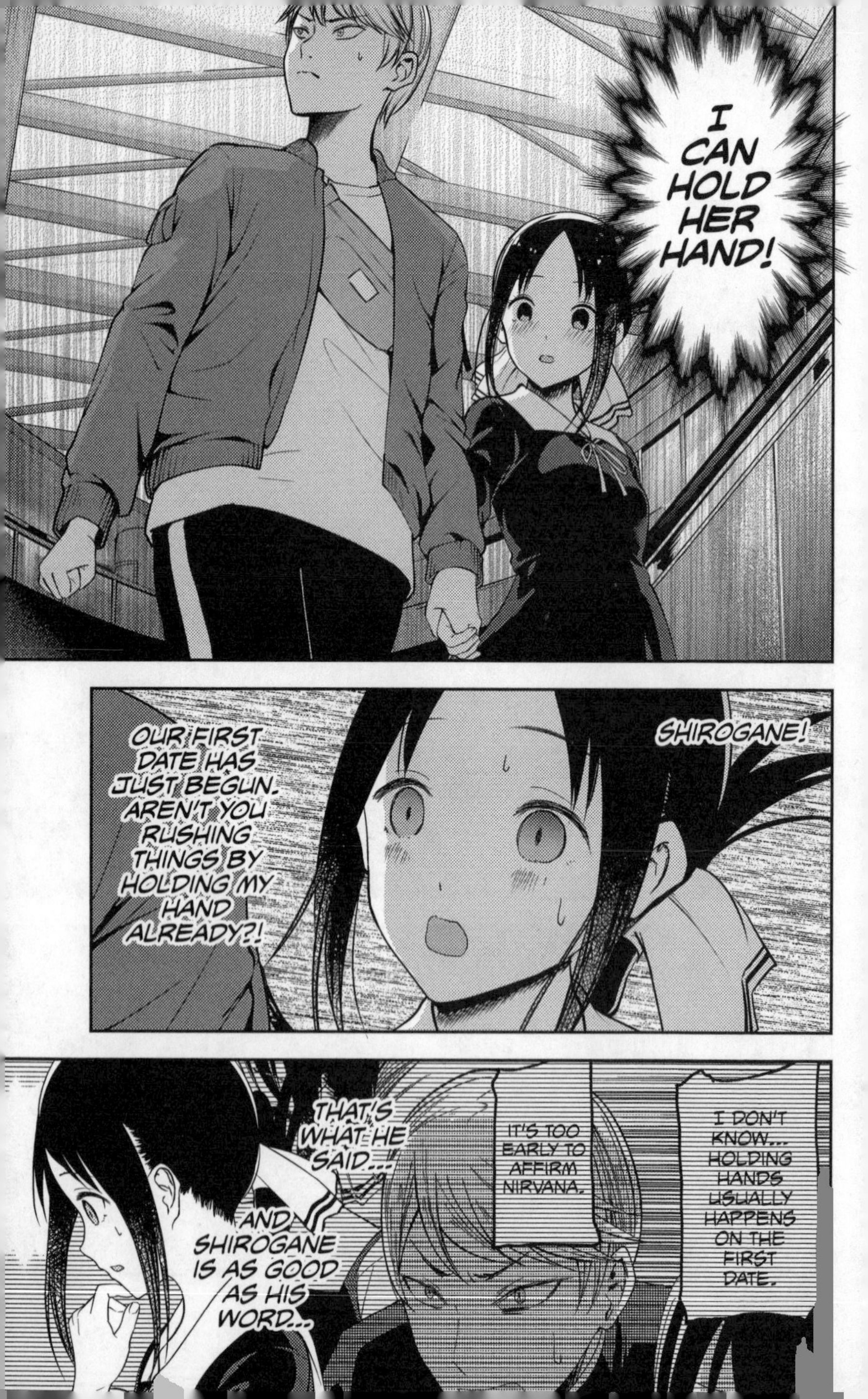
I CAN HOLD HER HAND!
SHIROGANE!
OUR FIRST DATE HAS JUST BEGUN. AREN'T YOU RUSHING THINGS BY HOLDING MY HAND ALREADY?!
I DON'T KNOW... HOLDING HANDS USUALLY HAPPENS ON THE FIRST DATE.
IT'S TOO EARLY TO AFFIRM NIRVANA.
THAT'S WHAT HE SAID...
AND SHIROGANE IS AS GOOD AS HIS WORD...

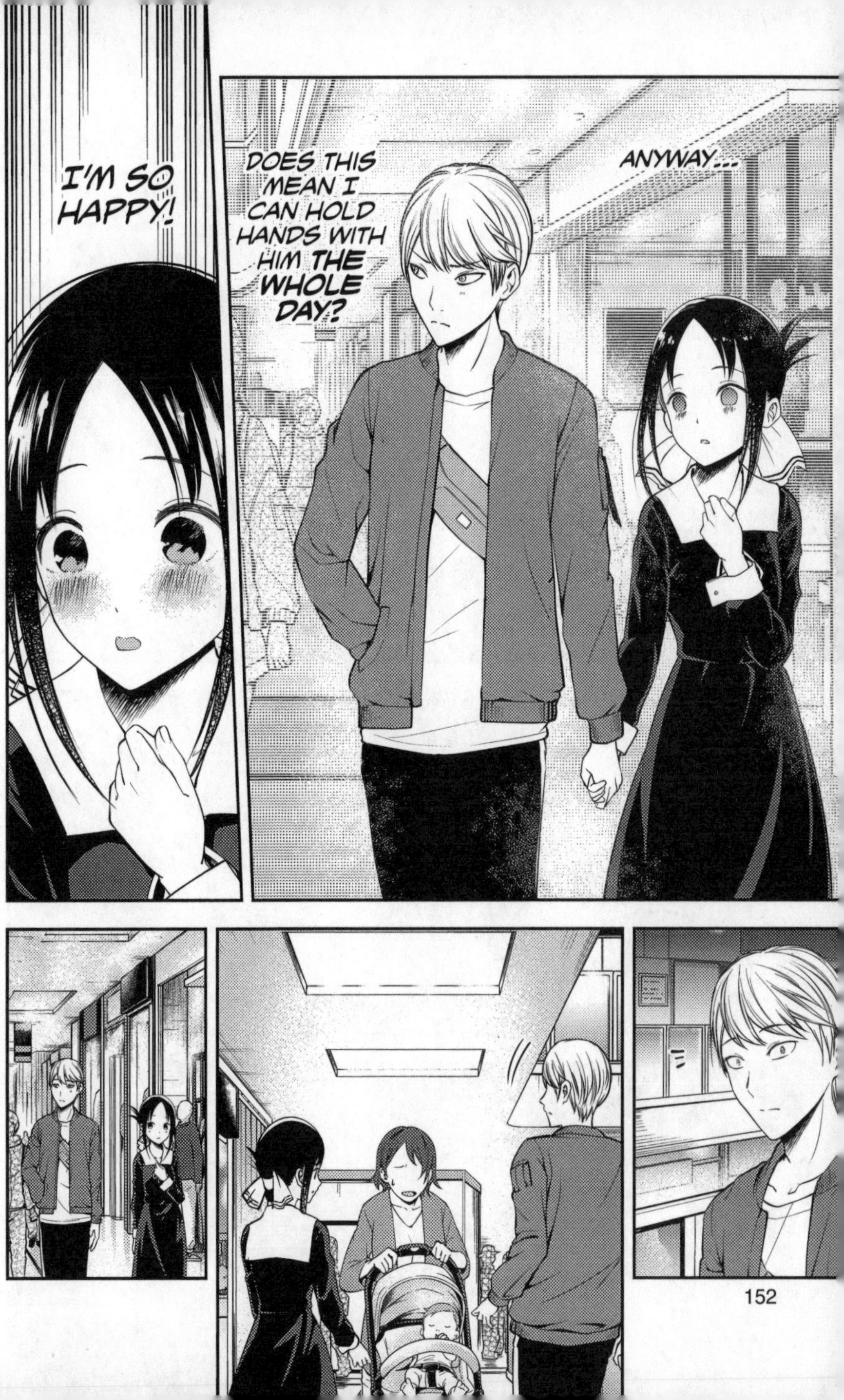
ANYWAY...
DOES THIS MEAN I CAN HOLD HANDS WITH HIM THE WHOLE DAY?
I'M SO HAPPY!

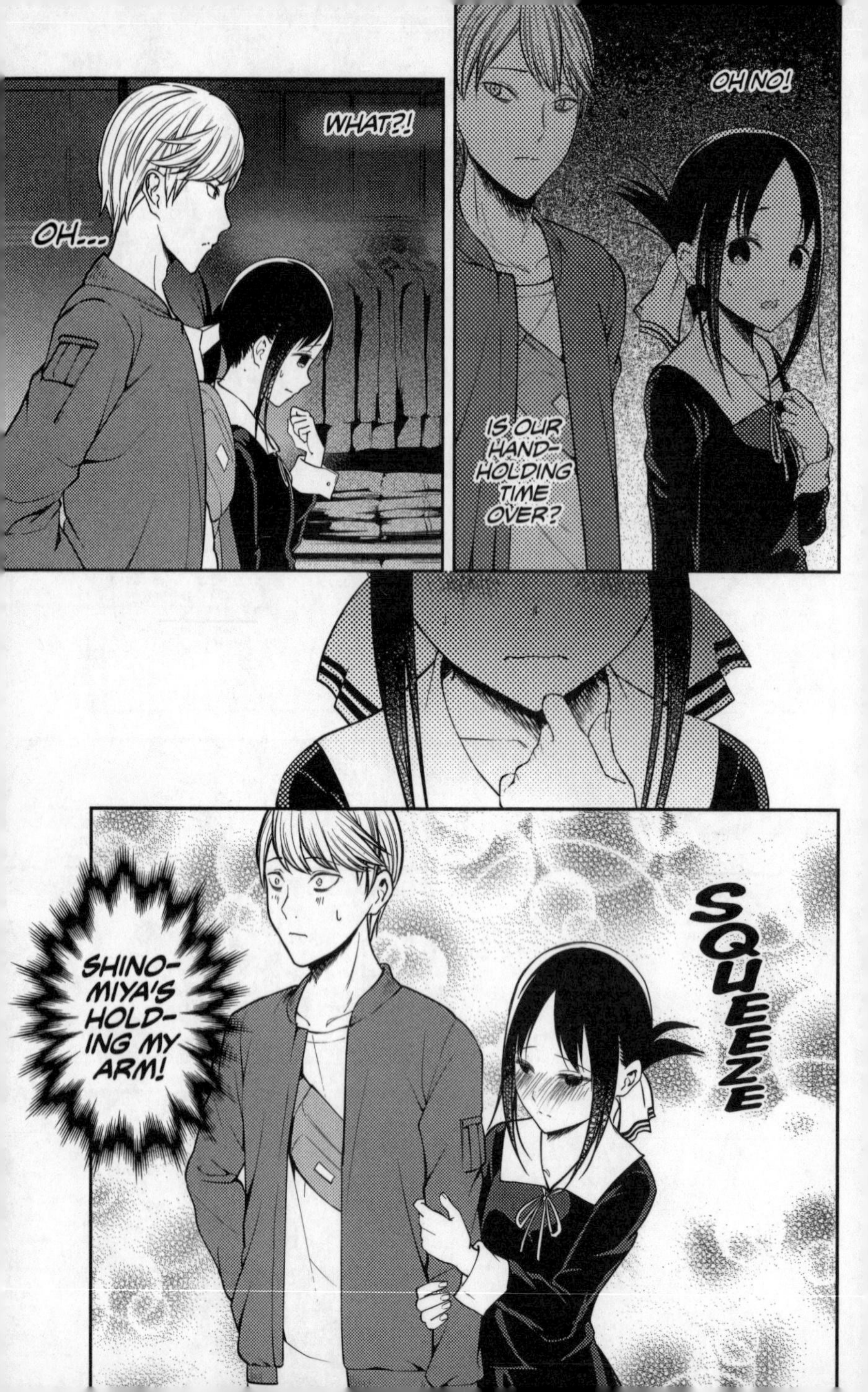
OH NO!
IS OUR HAND-HOLDING TIME OVER?
WHAT?!
OH...
SQUEEZE
SHINOMIYA'S HOLDING MY ARM!

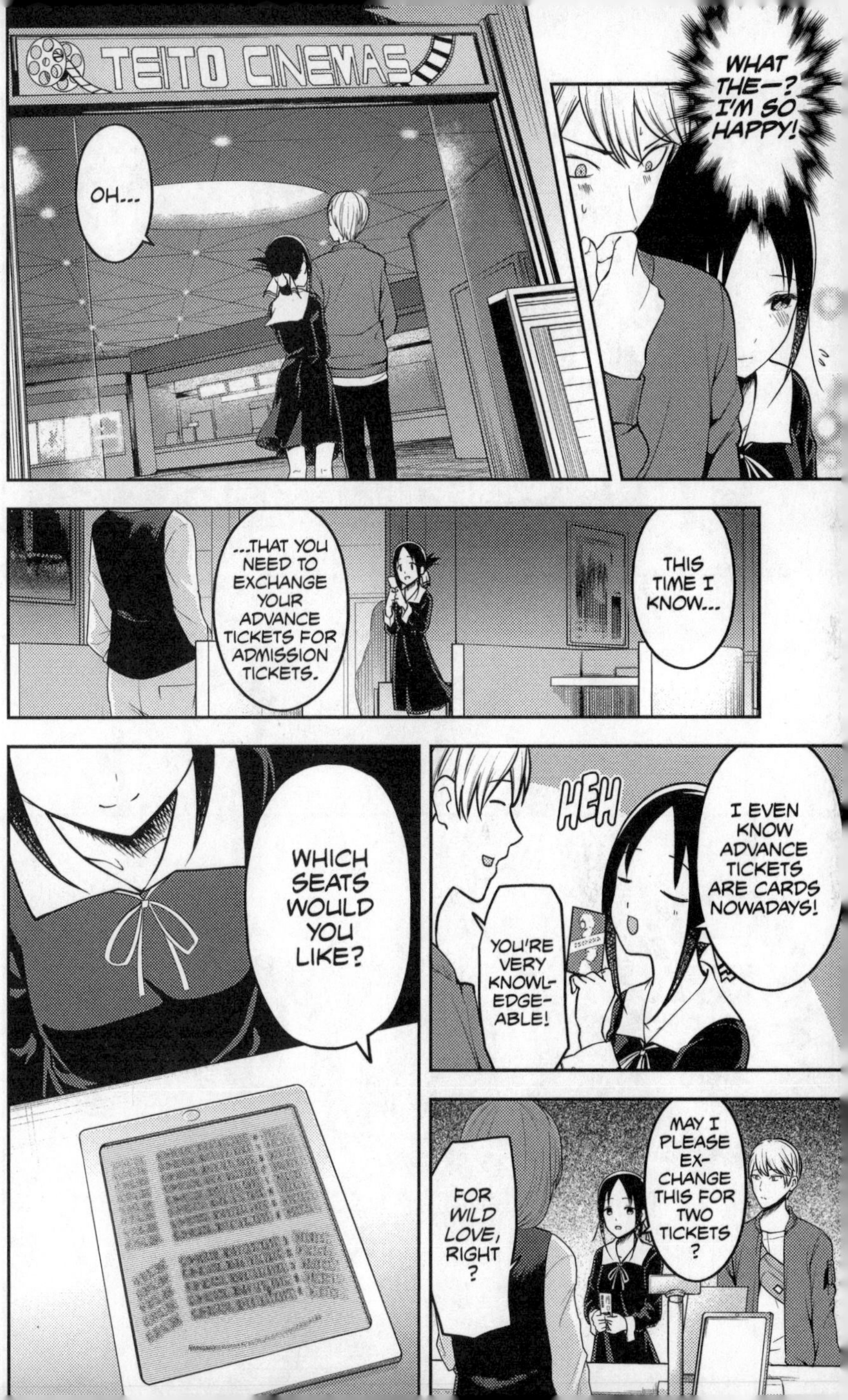
WHAT THE—? I'M SO HAPPY!
TEITO CINEMAS
OH...
THIS TIME I KNOW...
...THAT YOU NEED TO EXCHANGE YOUR ADVANCE TICKETS FOR ADMISSION TICKETS.
HEH
I EVEN KNOW ADVANCE TICKETS ARE CARDS NOWADAYS!
YOU'RE VERY KNOWL-EDGE-ABLE!
MAY I PLEASE EX-CHANGE THIS FOR TWO TICKETS?
FOR WILD LOVE, RIGHT?
WHICH SEATS WOULD YOU LIKE?

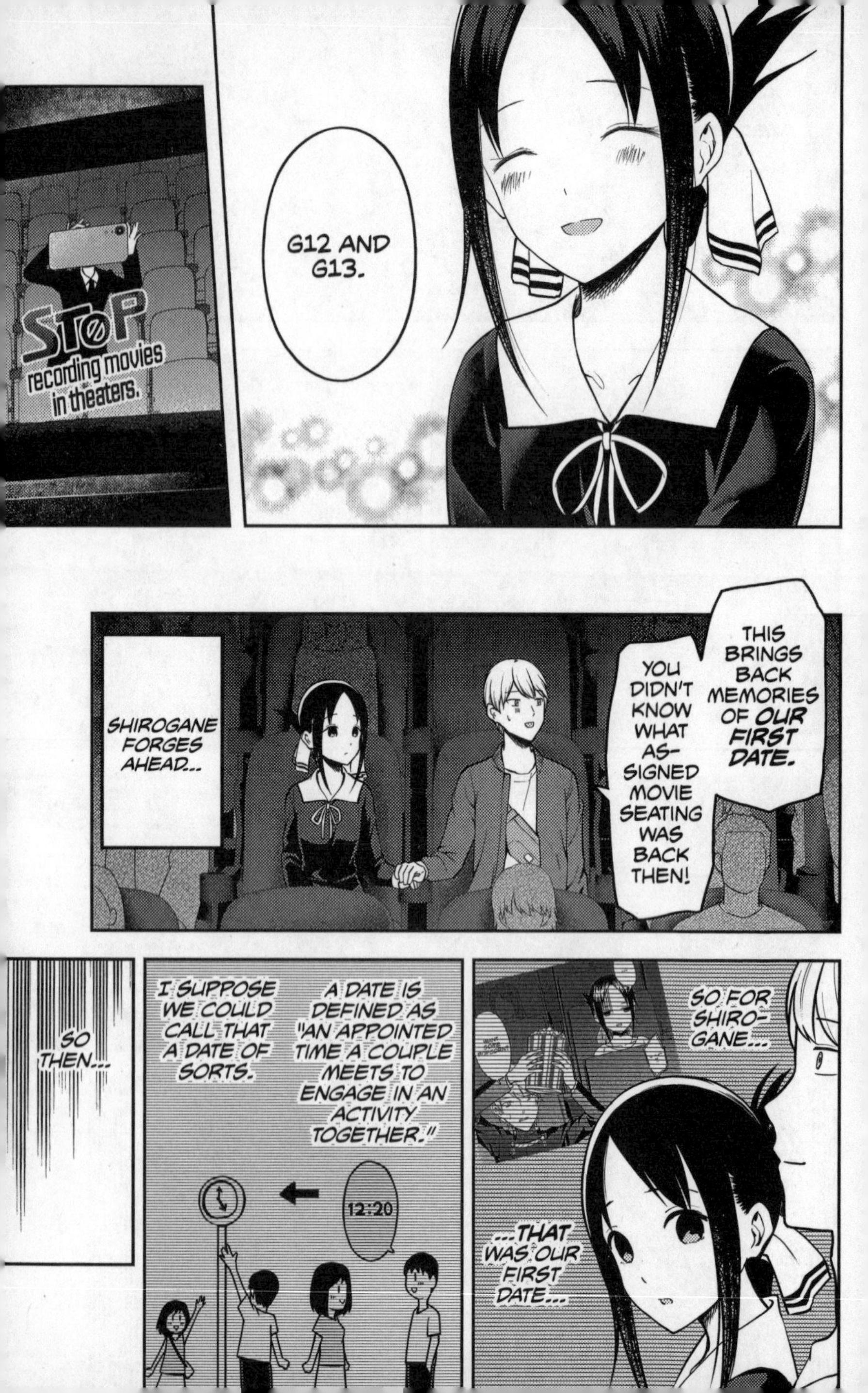
G12 AND G13.
STOP recording movies in theaters.
THIS BRINGS BACK MEMORIES OF OUR FIRST DATE.
YOU DIDN'T KNOW WHAT AS-SIGNED MOVIE SEATING WAS BACK THEN!
SHIROGANE FORGES AHEAD...
SO FOR SHIRO-GANE...
...THAT WAS OUR FIRST DATE...
A DATE IS DEFINED AS "AN APPOINTED TIME A COUPLE MEETS TO ENGAGE IN AN ACTIVITY TOGETHER."
I SUPPOSE WE COULD CALL THAT A DATE OF SORTS.
12:20
SO THEN...

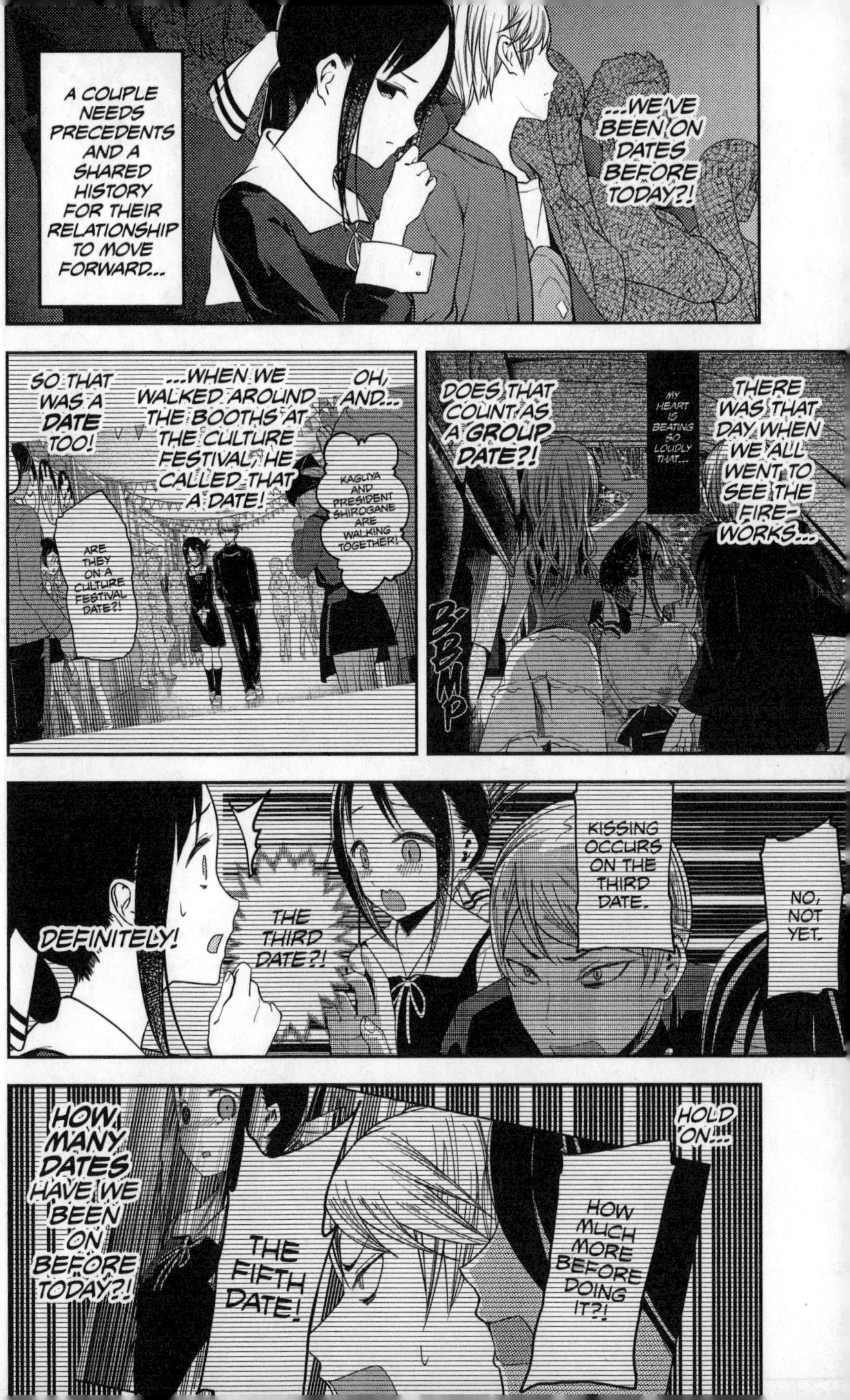
...WE'VE BEEN ON DATES BEFORE TODAY?!
A COUPLE NEEDS PRECEDENTS AND A SHARED HISTORY FOR THEIR RELATIONSHIP TO MOVE FORWARD...
THERE WAS THAT DAY WHEN WE ALL WENT TO SEE THE FIRE-WORKS...
MY HEART IS BEATING SO LOUDLY THAT...
DOES THAT COUNT AS A GROUP DATE?!
BA-BUMP
OH, AND...
...WHEN WE WALKED AROUND THE BOOTHS AT THE CULTURE FESTIVAL, HE CALLED THAT A DATE!
KAGUYA AND PRESIDENT SHIROGANE ARE WALKING TOGETHER!
SO THAT WAS A DATE TOO!
ARE THEY ON A CULTURE FESTIVAL DATE?!
NO, NOT YET.
KISSING OCCURS ON THE THIRD DATE.
THE THIRD DATE?!
DEFINITELY!
HOLD ON...
HOW MUCH MORE BEFORE DOING IT?!
THE FIFTH DATE!
HOW MANY DATES HAVE WE BEEN ON BEFORE TODAY?!

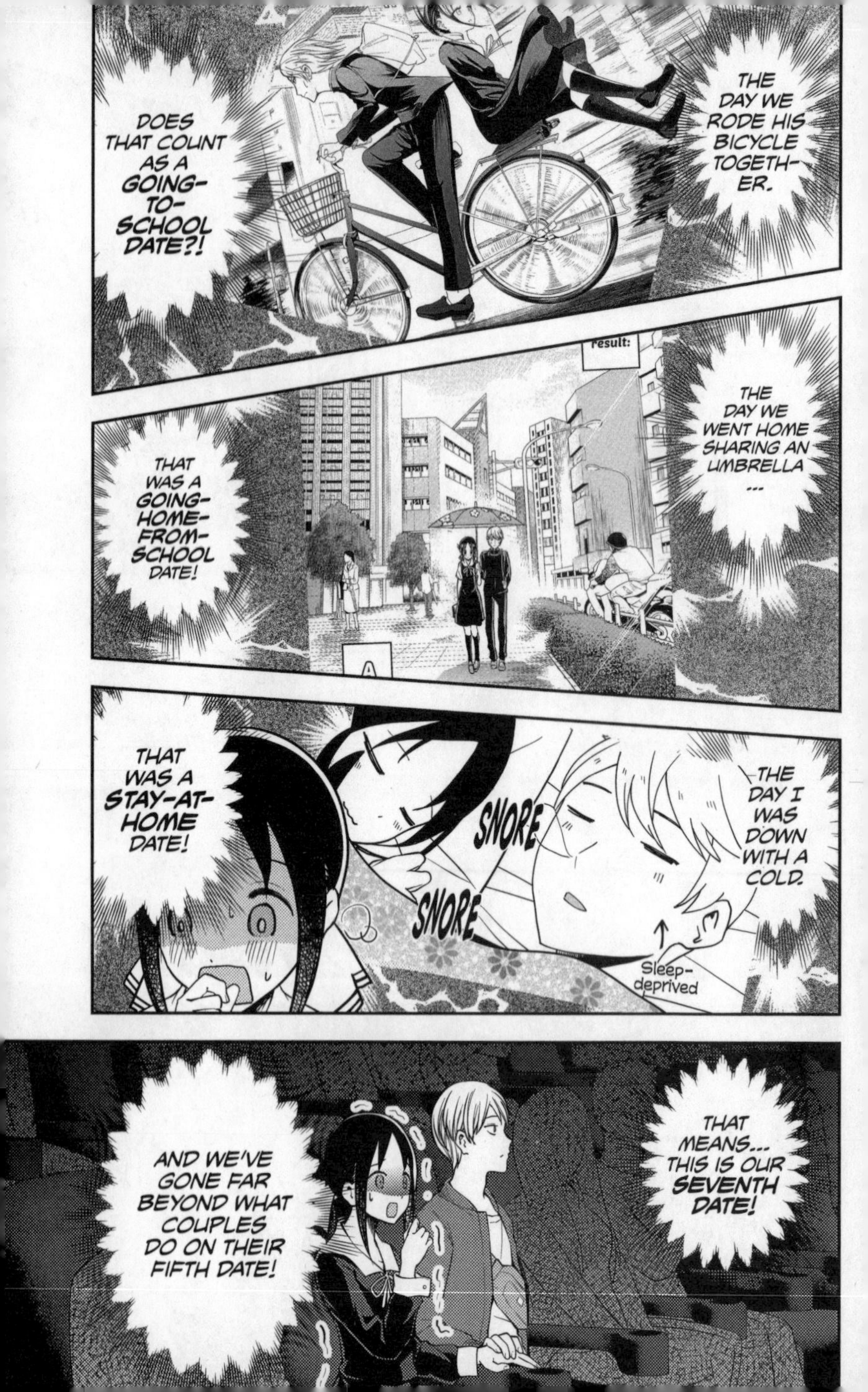
THE DAY WE RODE HIS BICYCLE TOGETHER.
DOES THAT COUNT AS A GOING-TO-SCHOOL DATE?!
THE DAY WE WENT HOME SHARING AN UMBRELLA...
result:
THAT WAS A GOING-HOME-FROM-SCHOOL DATE!
A
THE DAY I WAS DOWN WITH A COLD.
SNORE
SNORE
Sleep-deprived
THAT WAS A STAY-AT-HOME DATE!
THAT MEANS... THIS IS OUR SEVENTH DATE!
AND WE'VE GONE FAR BEYOND WHAT COUPLES DO ON THEIR FIFTH DATE!

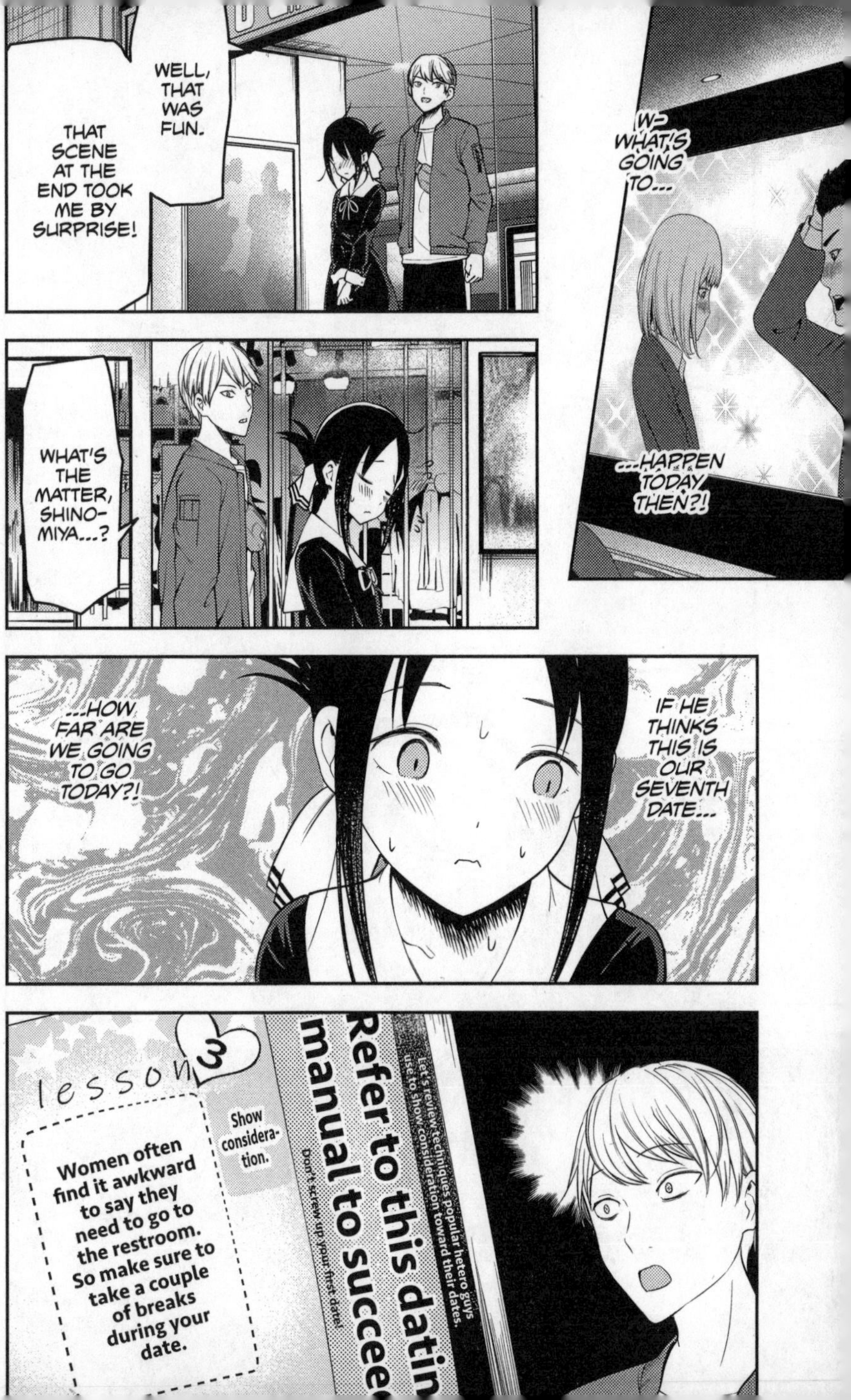
W-WHAT'S GOING TO...
---HAPPEN TODAY THEN?!
WELL, THAT WAS FUN.
THAT SCENE AT THE END TOOK ME BY SURPRISE!
WHAT'S THE MATTER, SHINO-MIYA...?
IF HE THINKS THIS IS OUR SEVENTH DATE...
...HOW FAR ARE WE GOING TO GO TODAY?!
Refer to this datin
manual to succee
Let's review techniques popular hetero guys use to show consideration toward their dates.
Don't screw up your first date!
lesson 3
Show considera-tion.
Women often find it awkward to say they need to go to the restroom. So make sure to take a couple of breaks during your date.

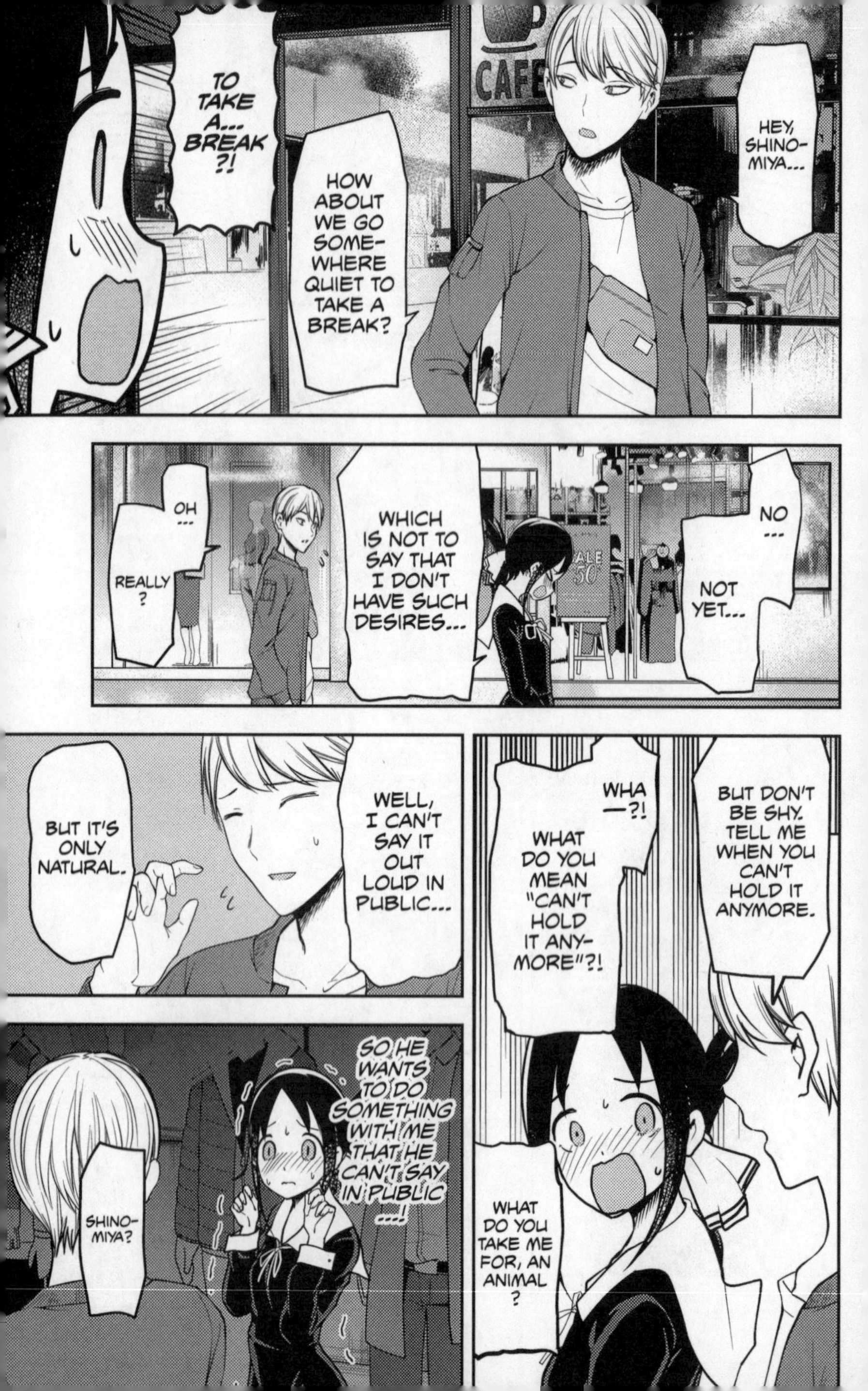
HEY, SHINO-MIYA...
HOW ABOUT WE GO SOME-WHERE QUIET TO TAKE A BREAK?
TO TAKE A... BREAK ?!
NO... NOT YET...
WHICH IS NOT TO SAY THAT I DON'T HAVE SUCH DESIRES...
OH... REALLY?
BUT DON'T BE SHY. TELL ME WHEN YOU CAN'T HOLD IT ANYMORE.
WHA—?!
WHAT DO YOU MEAN "CAN'T HOLD IT ANY-MORE"?!
WHAT DO YOU TAKE ME FOR, AN ANIMAL?
WELL, I CAN'T SAY IT OUT LOUD IN PUBLIC...
BUT IT'S ONLY NATURAL.
SO HE WANTS TO DO SOMETHING WITH ME THAT HE CAN'T SAY IN PUBLIC...!
SHINO-MIYA?

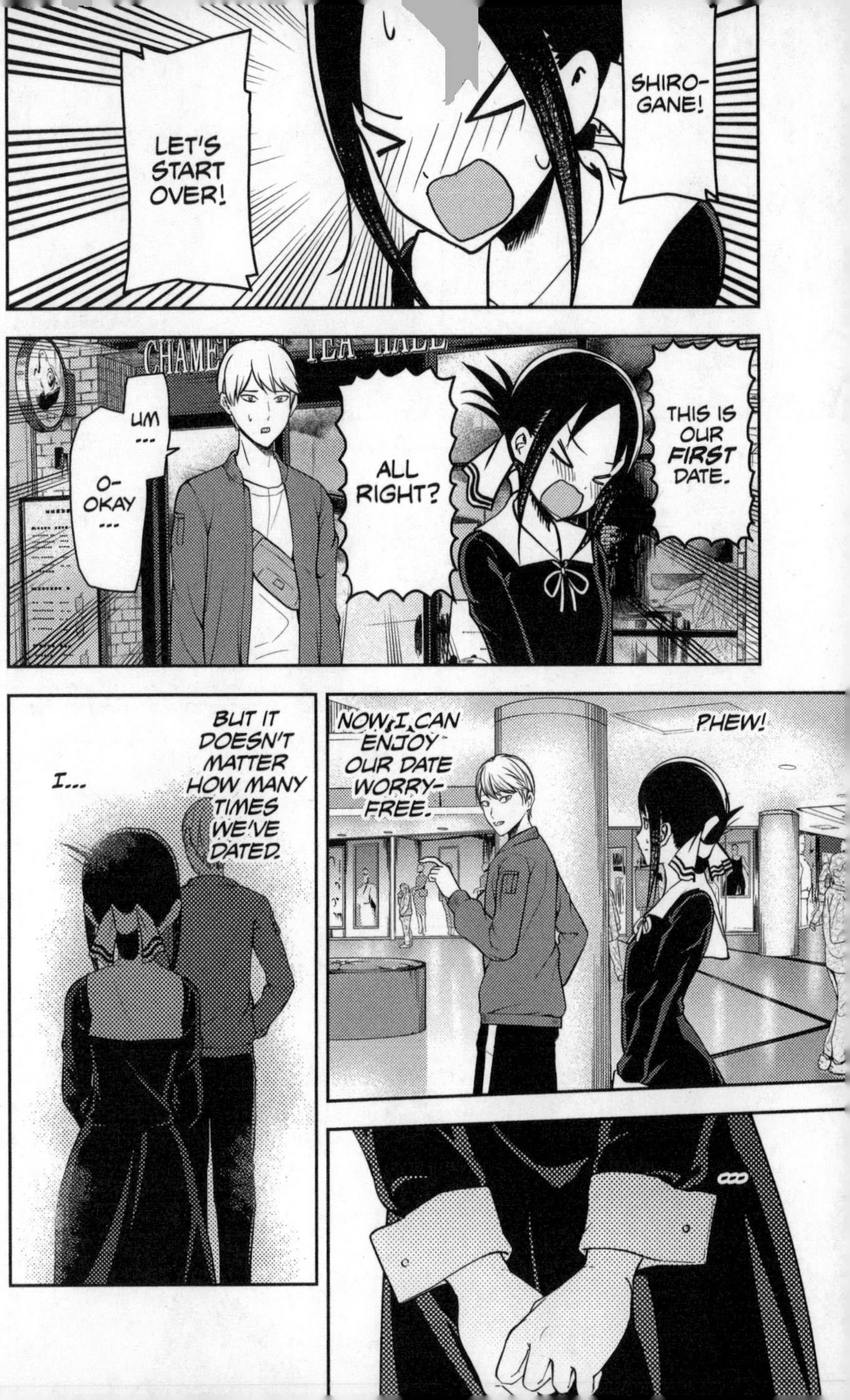
SHIRO-GANE!
LET'S START OVER!
THIS IS OUR FIRST DATE.
ALL RIGHT?
UM...
O-OKAY...
PHEW!
NOW I CAN ENJOY OUR DATE WORRY-FREE.
BUT IT DOESN'T MATTER HOW MANY TIMES WE'VE DATED.
I...

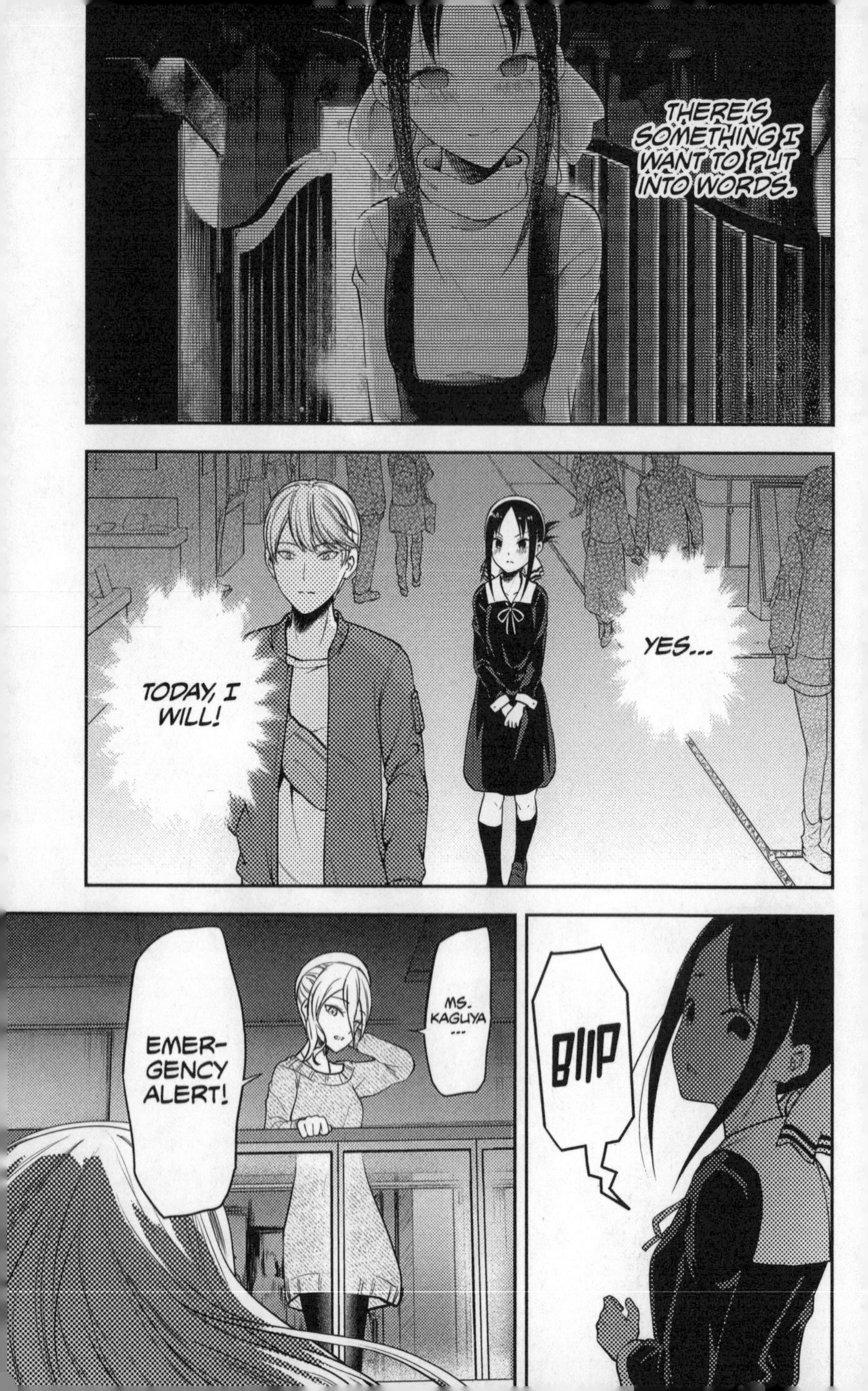
THERE IS SOMETHING I WANT TO PUT INTO WORDS.
YES...
TODAY, I WILL!
BIIP
MS. KAGUYA ...
EMERGENCY ALERT!

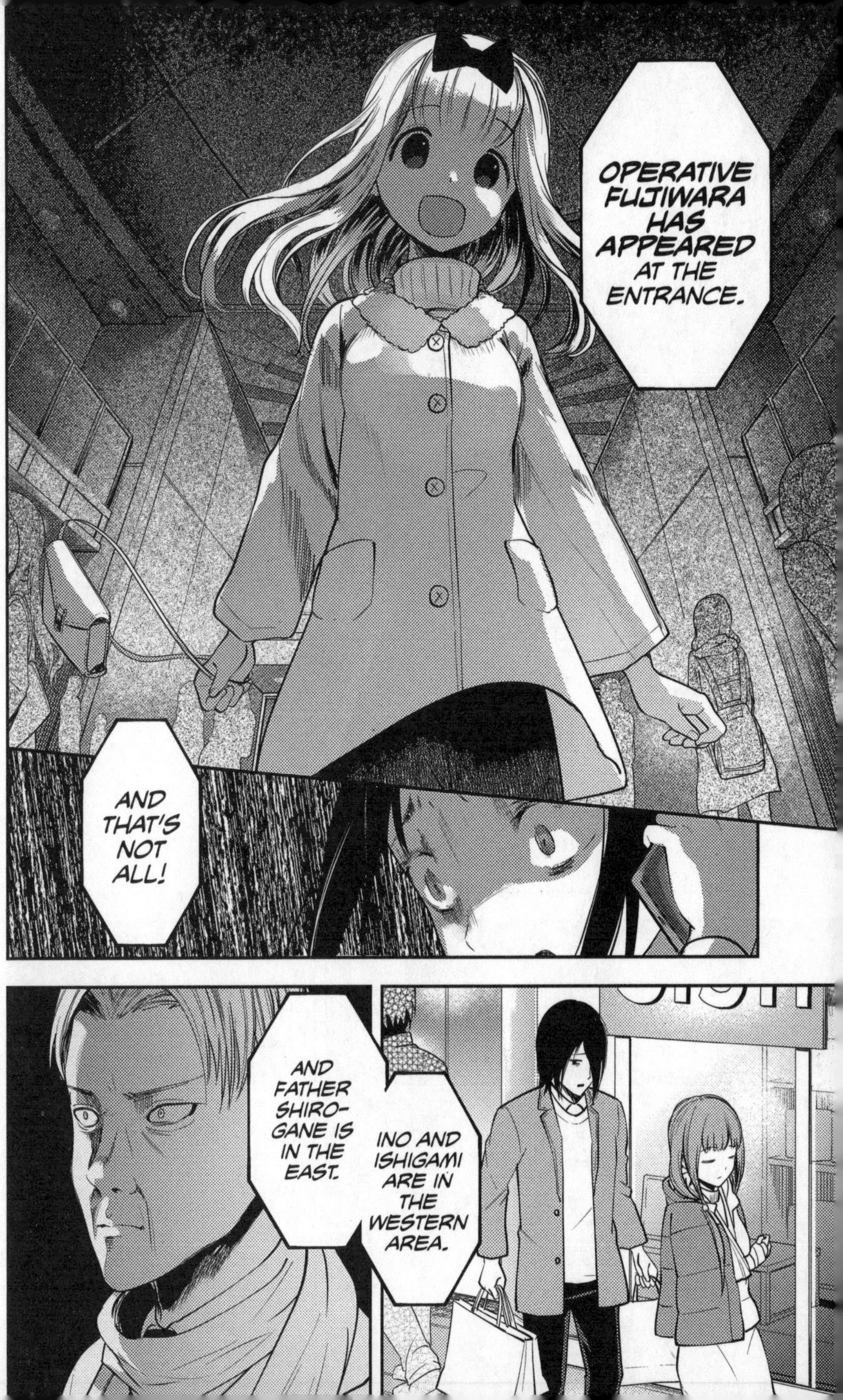
OPERATIVE FUJIWARA HAS APPEARED AT THE ENTRANCE.
AND THAT'S NOT ALL!
AND FATHER SHIROGANE IS IN THE EAST.
INO AND ISHIGAMI ARE IN THE WESTERN AREA.

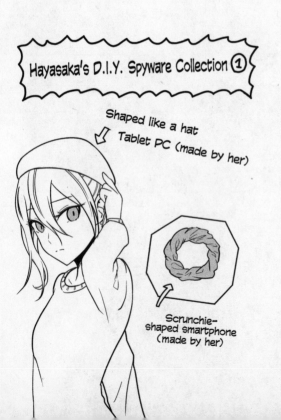

Hayasaka's D.I.Y. Spyware Collection ①

Shaped like a hat
⇩ Tablet PC (made by her)

Scrunchie-
shaped smartphone
(made by her)

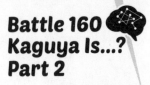

Battle 160
Kaguya Is...?
Part 2

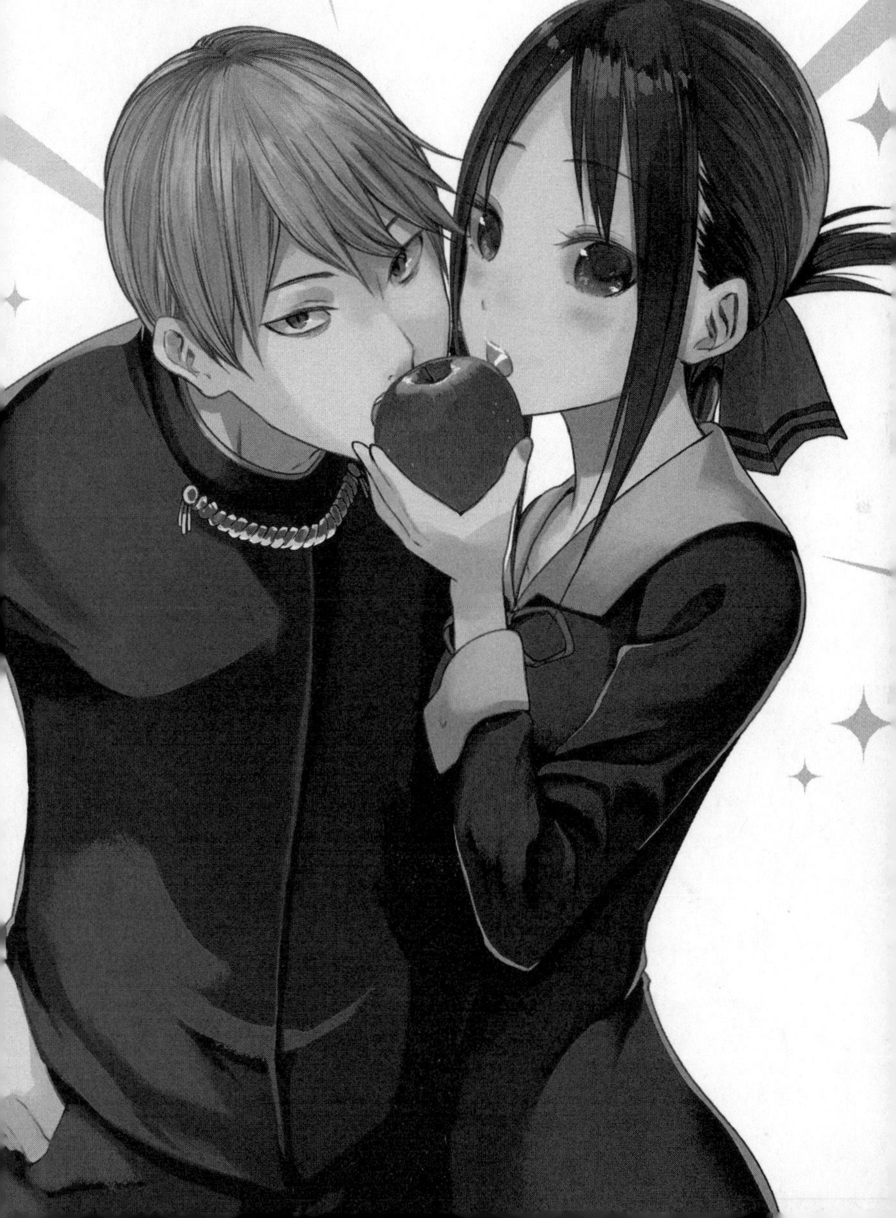

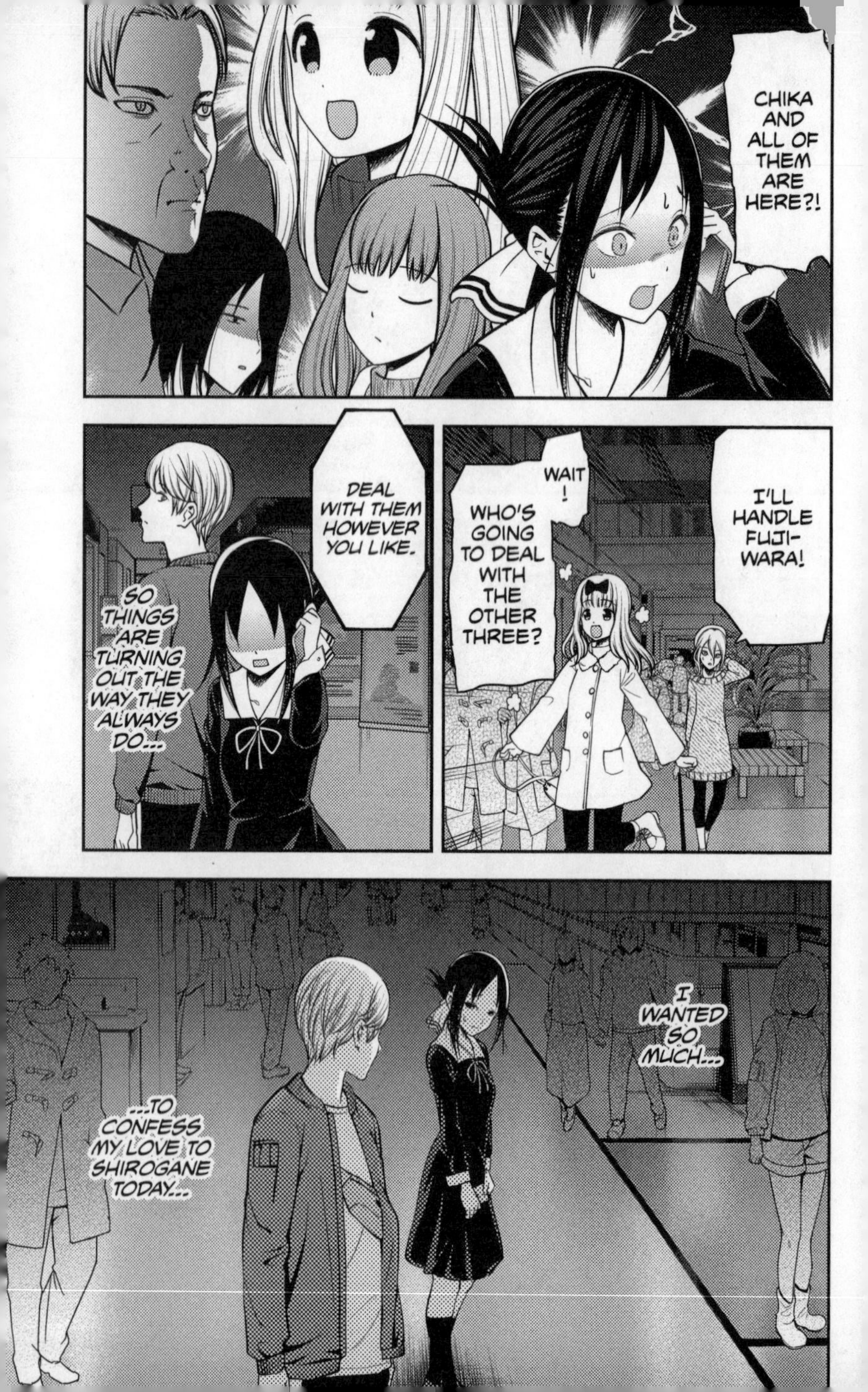
CHIKA AND ALL OF THEM ARE HERE?!
I'LL HANDLE FUJI-WARA!
WAIT!
WHO'S GOING TO DEAL WITH THE OTHER THREE?
DEAL WITH THEM HOWEVER YOU LIKE.
SO THINGS ARE TURNING OUT THE WAY THEY ALWAYS DO...
I WANTED SO MUCH...
...TO CONFESS MY LOVE TO SHIROGANE TODAY...

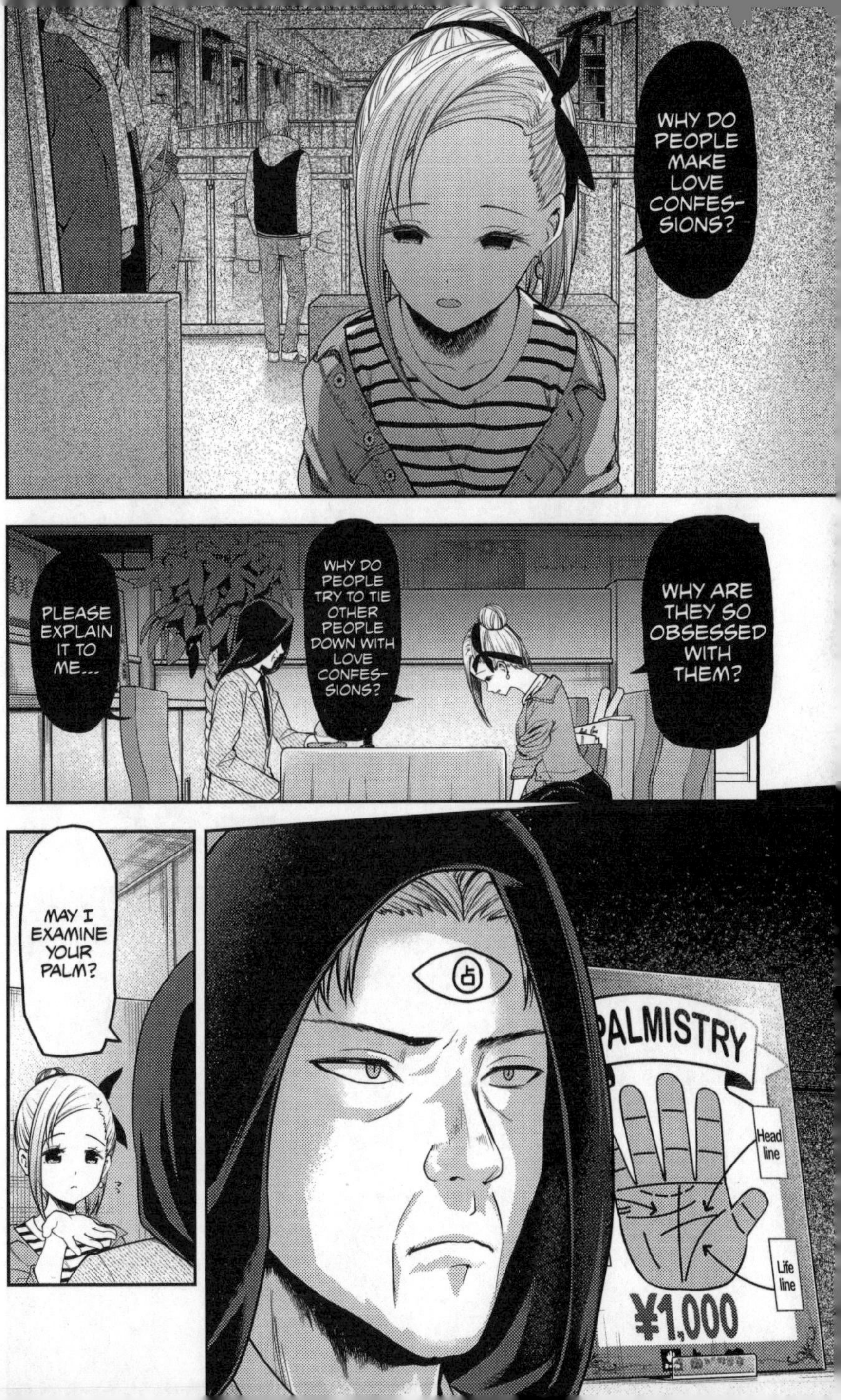
WHY DO PEOPLE MAKE LOVE CONFES-SIONS?
WHY ARE THEY SO OBSESSED WITH THEM?
WHY DO PEOPLE TRY TO TIE OTHER PEOPLE DOWN WITH LOVE CONFES-SIONS?
PLEASE EXPLAIN IT TO ME...
PALMISTRY
Head line
Life line
¥1,000
MAY I EXAMINE YOUR PALM?

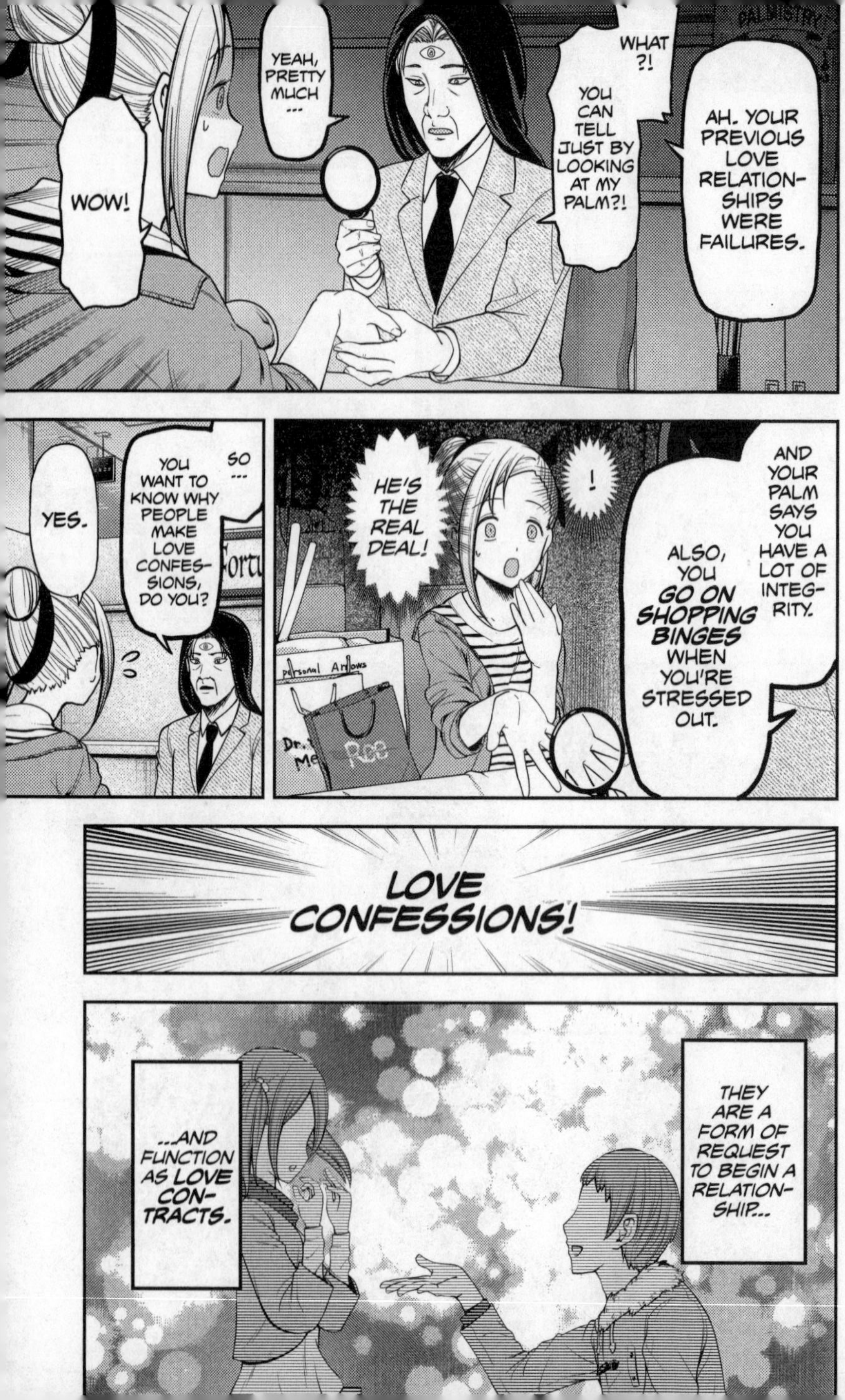
PALMISTRY
AH. YOUR PREVIOUS LOVE RELATIONSHIPS WERE FAILURES.
WHAT?!
YOU CAN TELL JUST BY LOOKING AT MY PALM?!
YEAH, PRETTY MUCH...
WOW!
AND YOUR PALM SAYS YOU HAVE A LOT OF INTEGRITY.
ALSO, YOU GO ON SHOPPING BINGES WHEN YOU'RE STRESSED OUT.
!
HE'S THE REAL DEAL!
SO...
YOU WANT TO KNOW WHY PEOPLE MAKE LOVE CONFESSIONS, DO YOU?
YES.
LOVE CONFESSIONS!
THEY ARE A FORM OF REQUEST TO BEGIN A RELATIONSHIP...
...AND FUNCTION AS LOVE CONTRACTS.

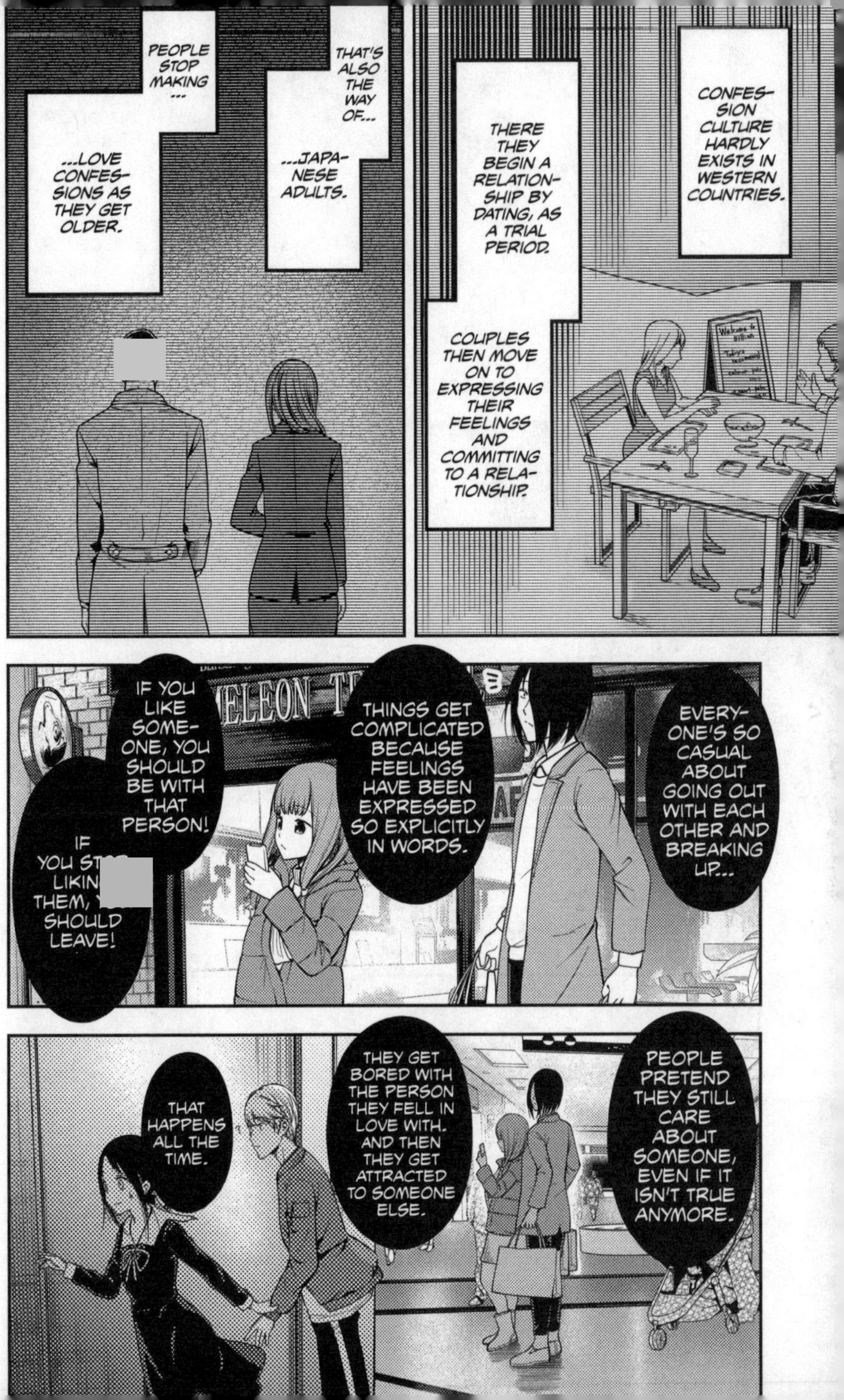
CONFESSION CULTURE HARDLY EXISTS IN WESTERN COUNTRIES.
THERE THEY BEGIN A RELATIONSHIP BY DATING, AS A TRIAL PERIOD.
COUPLES THEN MOVE ON TO EXPRESSING THEIR FEELINGS AND COMMITTING TO A RELATIONSHIP.
PEOPLE STOP MAKING...
...LOVE CONFESSIONS AS THEY GET OLDER.
THAT'S ALSO THE WAY OF...
...JAPANESE ADULTS.
EVERYONE'S SO CASUAL ABOUT GOING OUT WITH EACH OTHER AND BREAKING UP...
THINGS GET COMPLICATED BECAUSE FEELINGS HAVE BEEN EXPRESSED SO EXPLICITLY IN WORDS.
IF YOU LIKE SOMEONE, YOU SHOULD BE WITH THAT PERSON!
IF YOU ST[redacted] LIKIN[redacted] THEM, Y[redacted] SHOULD LEAVE!
PEOPLE PRETEND THEY STILL CARE ABOUT SOMEONE, EVEN IF IT ISN'T TRUE ANYMORE.
THEY GET BORED WITH THE PERSON THEY FELL IN LOVE WITH. AND THEN THEY GET ATTRACTED TO SOMEONE ELSE.
THAT HAPPENS ALL THE TIME.

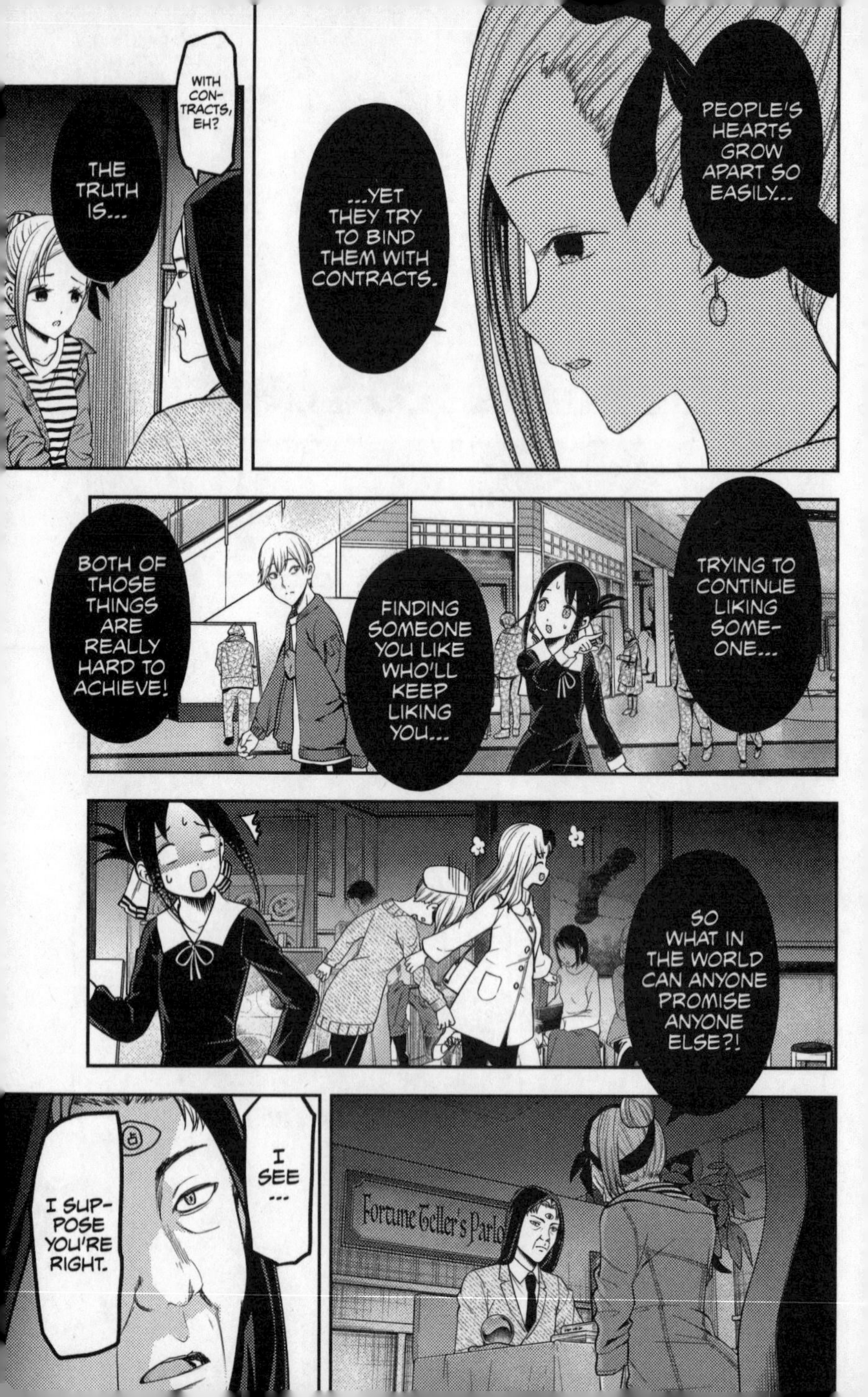
PEOPLE'S HEARTS GROW APART SO EASILY...
...YET THEY TRY TO BIND THEM WITH CONTRACTS.
WITH CONTRACTS, EH?
THE TRUTH IS...
TRYING TO CONTINUE LIKING SOMEONE...
FINDING SOMEONE YOU LIKE WHO'LL KEEP LIKING YOU...
BOTH OF THOSE THINGS ARE REALLY HARD TO ACHIEVE!
SO WHAT IN THE WORLD CAN ANYONE PROMISE ANYONE ELSE?!
Fortune Teller's Parlo
I SEE...
I SUPPOSE YOU'RE RIGHT.

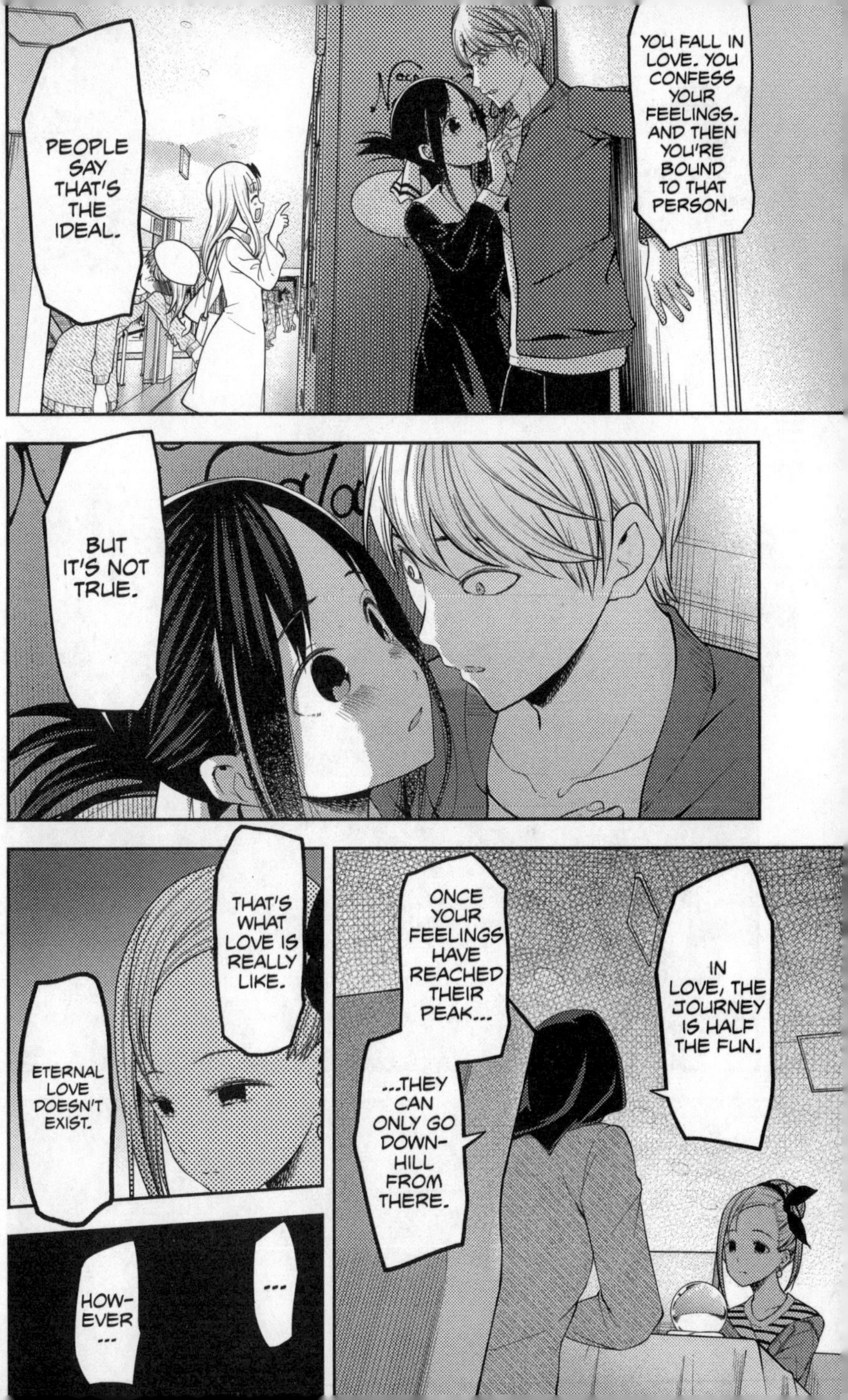
YOU FALL IN LOVE. YOU CONFESS YOUR FEELINGS. AND THEN YOU'RE BOUND TO THAT PERSON.
PEOPLE SAY THAT'S THE IDEAL.
BUT IT'S NOT TRUE.
IN LOVE, THE JOURNEY IS HALF THE FUN.
ONCE YOUR FEELINGS HAVE REACHED THEIR PEAK...
...THEY CAN ONLY GO DOWN-HILL FROM THERE.
THAT'S WHAT LOVE IS REALLY LIKE.
ETERNAL LOVE DOESN'T EXIST.
...
HOW-EVER...

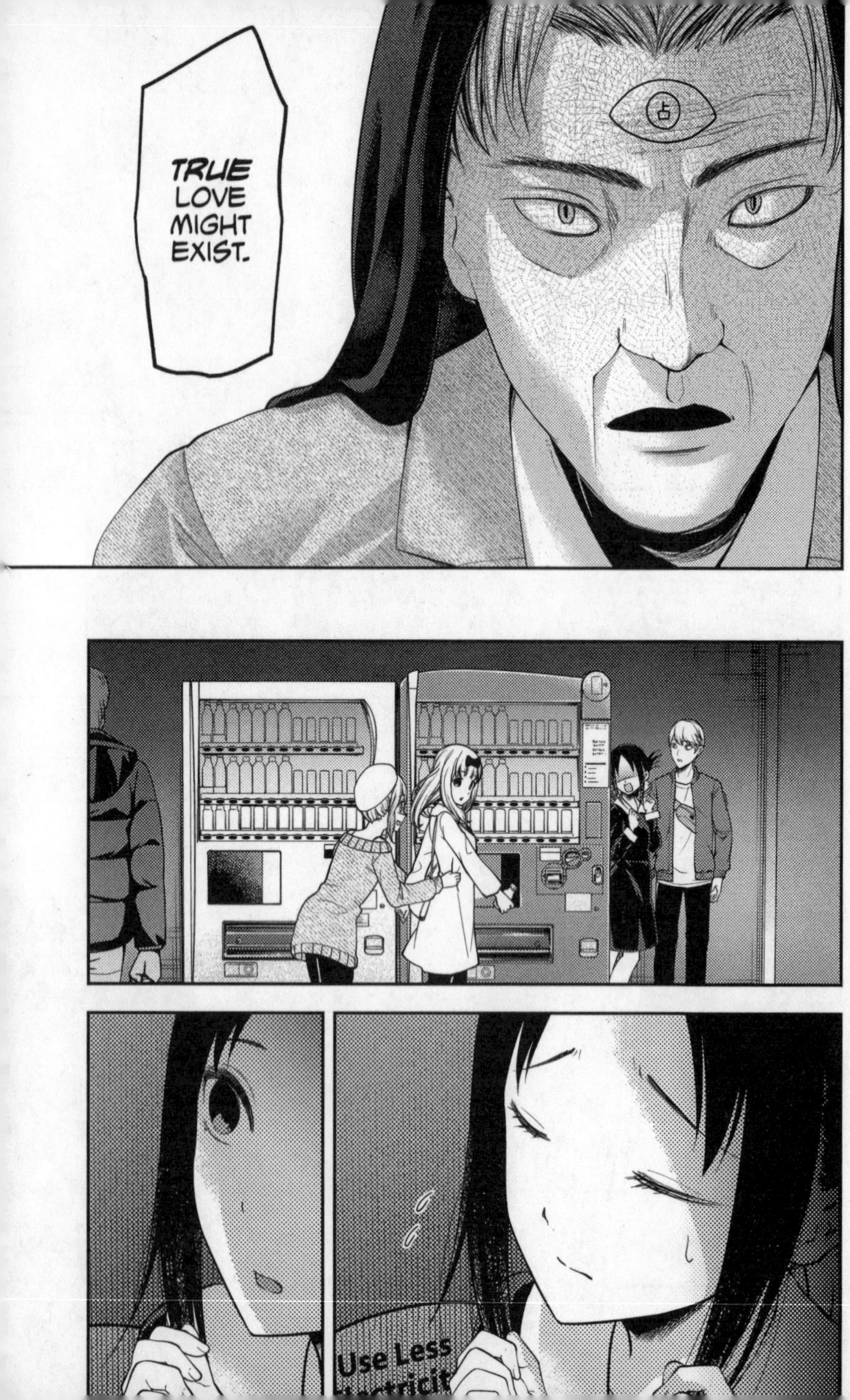
TRUE LOVE MIGHT EXIST.
Use Less

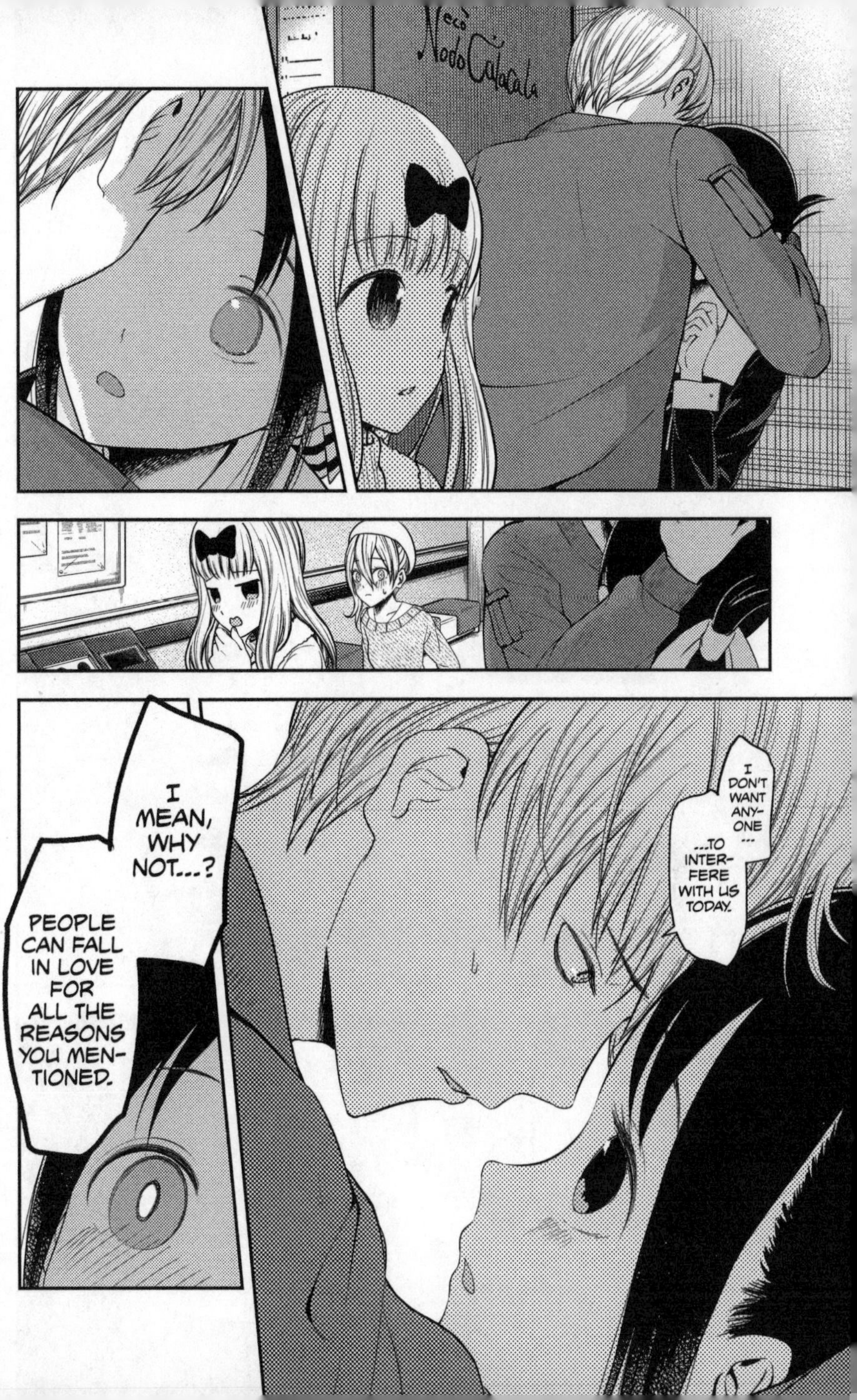
I DON'T WANT ANYONE...
...TO INTERFERE WITH US TODAY.
I MEAN, WHY NOT...?
PEOPLE CAN FALL IN LOVE FOR ALL THE REASONS YOU MENTIONED.

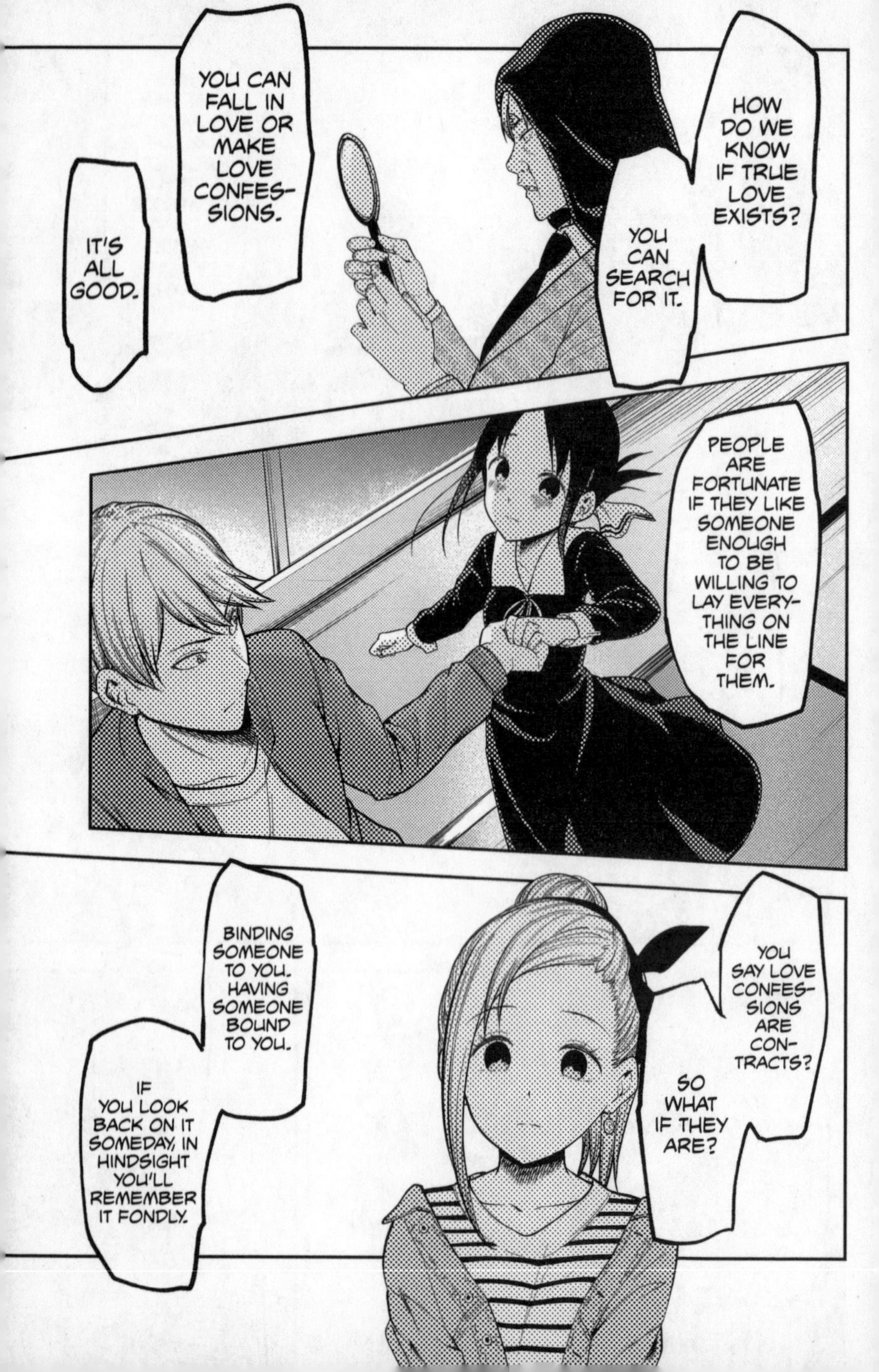
HOW DO WE KNOW IF TRUE LOVE EXISTS?
YOU CAN SEARCH FOR IT.
YOU CAN FALL IN LOVE OR MAKE LOVE CONFESSIONS.
IT'S ALL GOOD.
PEOPLE ARE FORTUNATE IF THEY LIKE SOMEONE ENOUGH TO BE WILLING TO LAY EVERYTHING ON THE LINE FOR THEM.
YOU SAY LOVE CONFESSIONS ARE CONTRACTS?
SO WHAT IF THEY ARE?
BINDING SOMEONE TO YOU. HAVING SOMEONE BOUND TO YOU.
IF YOU LOOK BACK ON IT SOMEDAY, IN HINDSIGHT YOU'LL REMEMBER IT FONDLY.

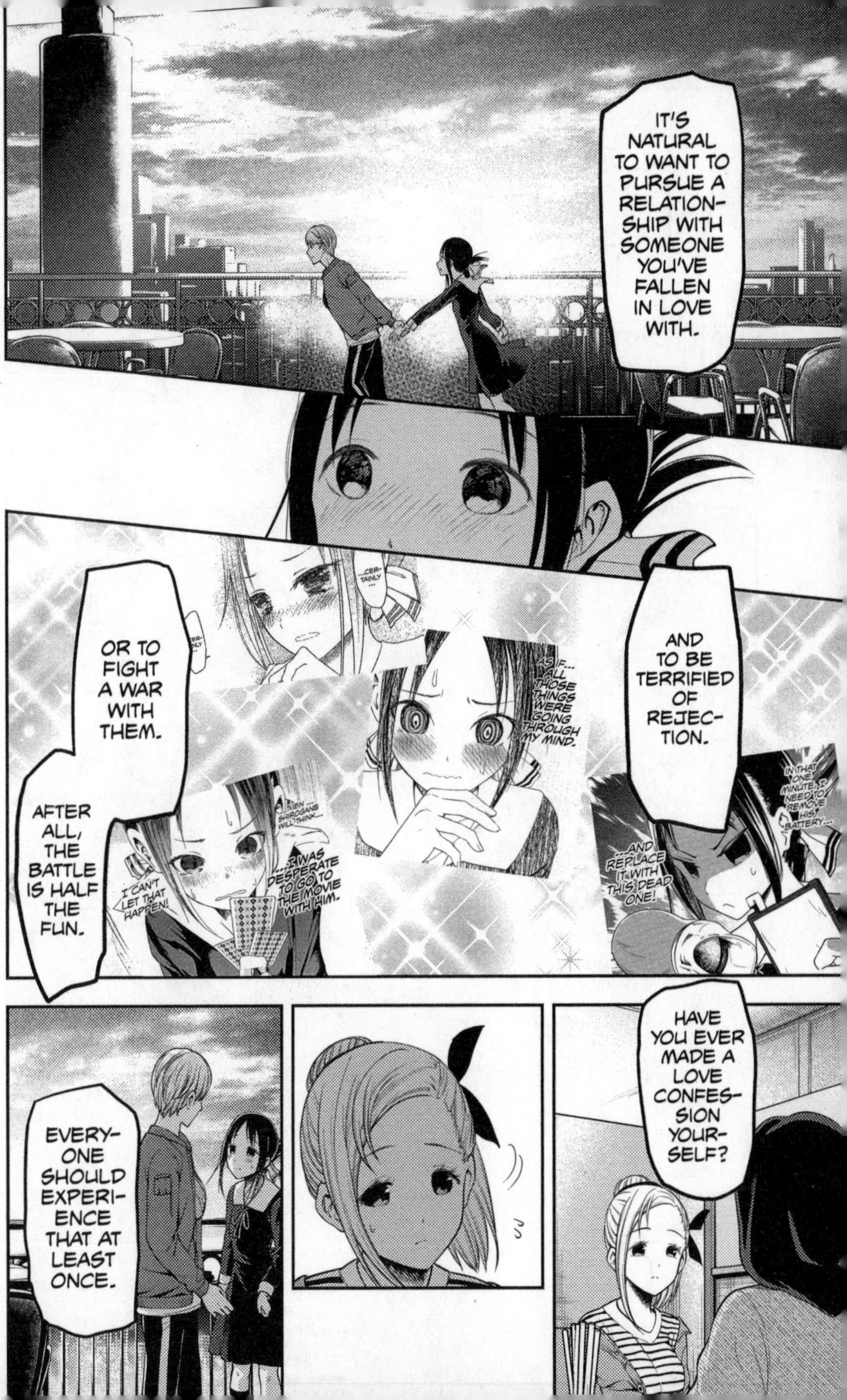
IT'S NATURAL TO WANT TO PURSUE A RELATIONSHIP WITH SOMEONE YOU'VE FALLEN IN LOVE WITH.
AND TO BE TERRIFIED OF REJECTION.
IN THAT ONE MINUTE, I NEED TO REMOVE HIS BATTERY...
...AND REPLACE IT WITH THIS DEAD ONE!
AS IF... ALL THOSE THINGS WERE GOING THROUGH MY MIND.
...CERTAINLY...
OR TO FIGHT A WAR WITH THEM.
...THEN ... SHIROGANE WILL THINK...
...I WAS DESPERATE TO GO TO THE MOVIE WITH HIM.
I CAN'T LET THAT HAPPEN!
AFTER ALL, THE BATTLE IS HALF THE FUN.
HAVE YOU EVER MADE A LOVE CONFESSION YOURSELF?
EVERYONE SHOULD EXPERIENCE THAT AT LEAST ONCE.

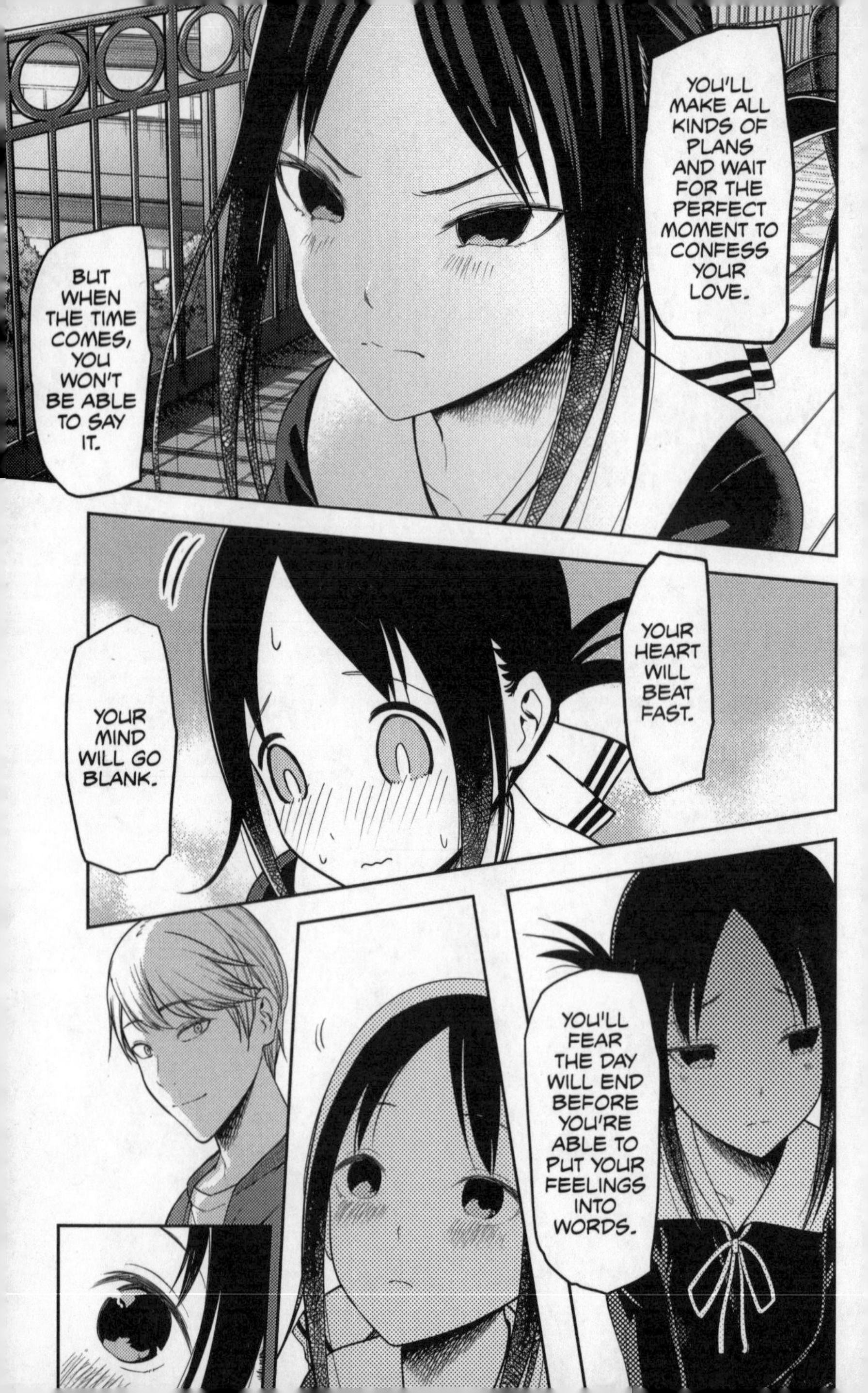
YOU'LL MAKE ALL KINDS OF PLANS AND WAIT FOR THE PERFECT MOMENT TO CONFESS YOUR LOVE.
BUT WHEN THE TIME COMES, YOU WON'T BE ABLE TO SAY IT.
YOUR HEART WILL BEAT FAST.
YOUR MIND WILL GO BLANK.
YOU'LL FEAR THE DAY WILL END BEFORE YOU'RE ABLE TO PUT YOUR FEELINGS INTO WORDS.

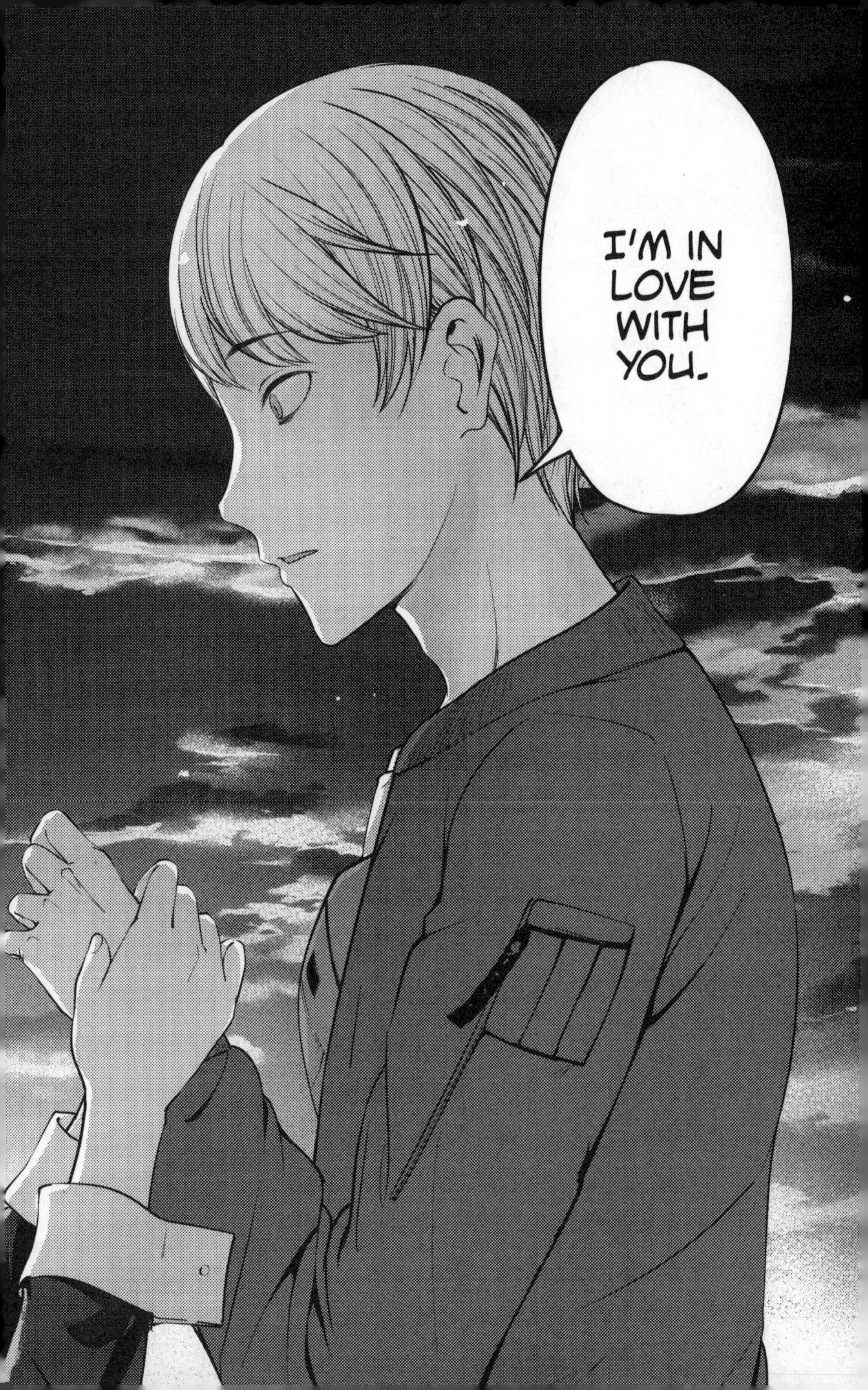
I'M IN LOVE WITH YOU.

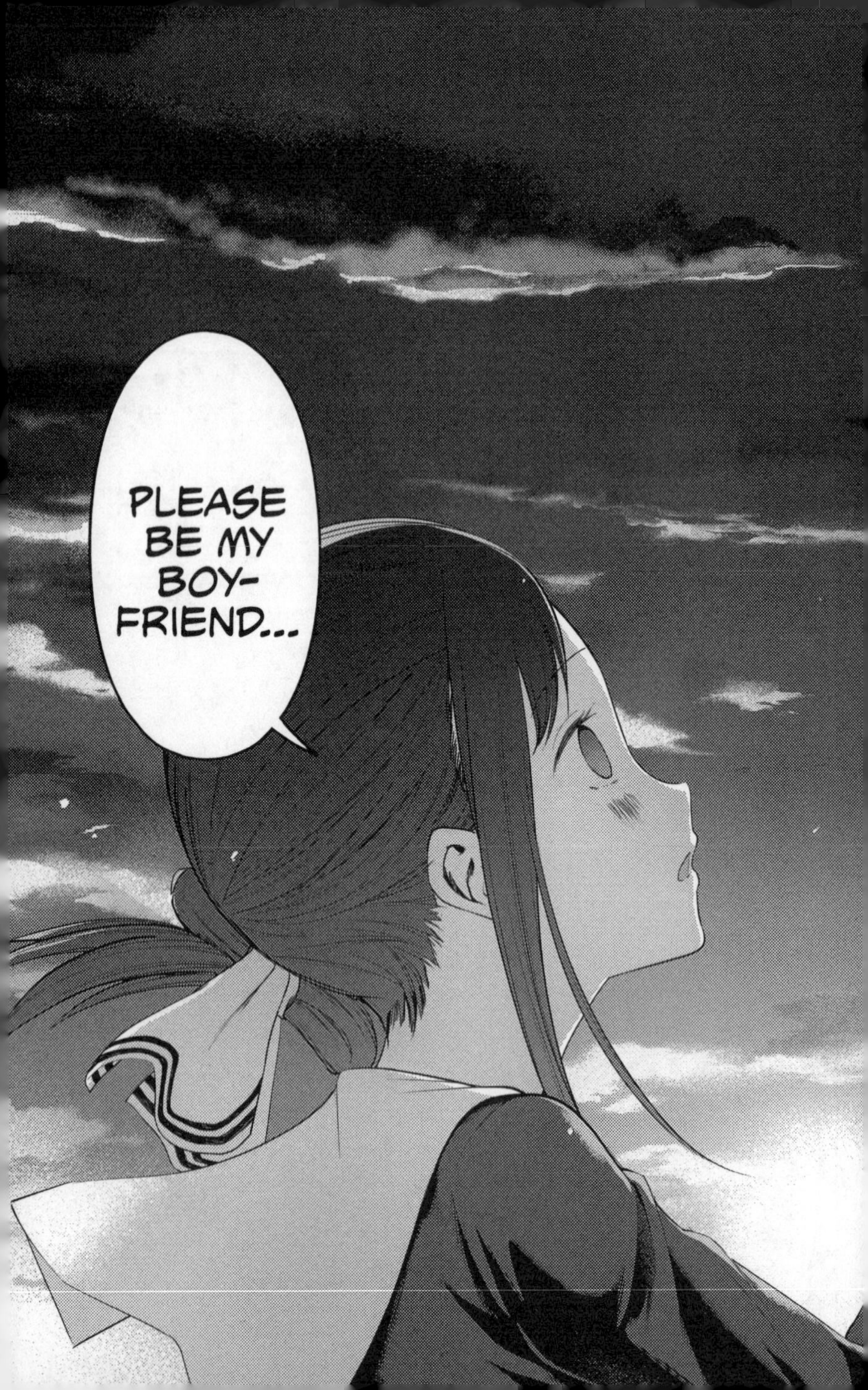
PLEASE BE MY BOY-FRIEND...

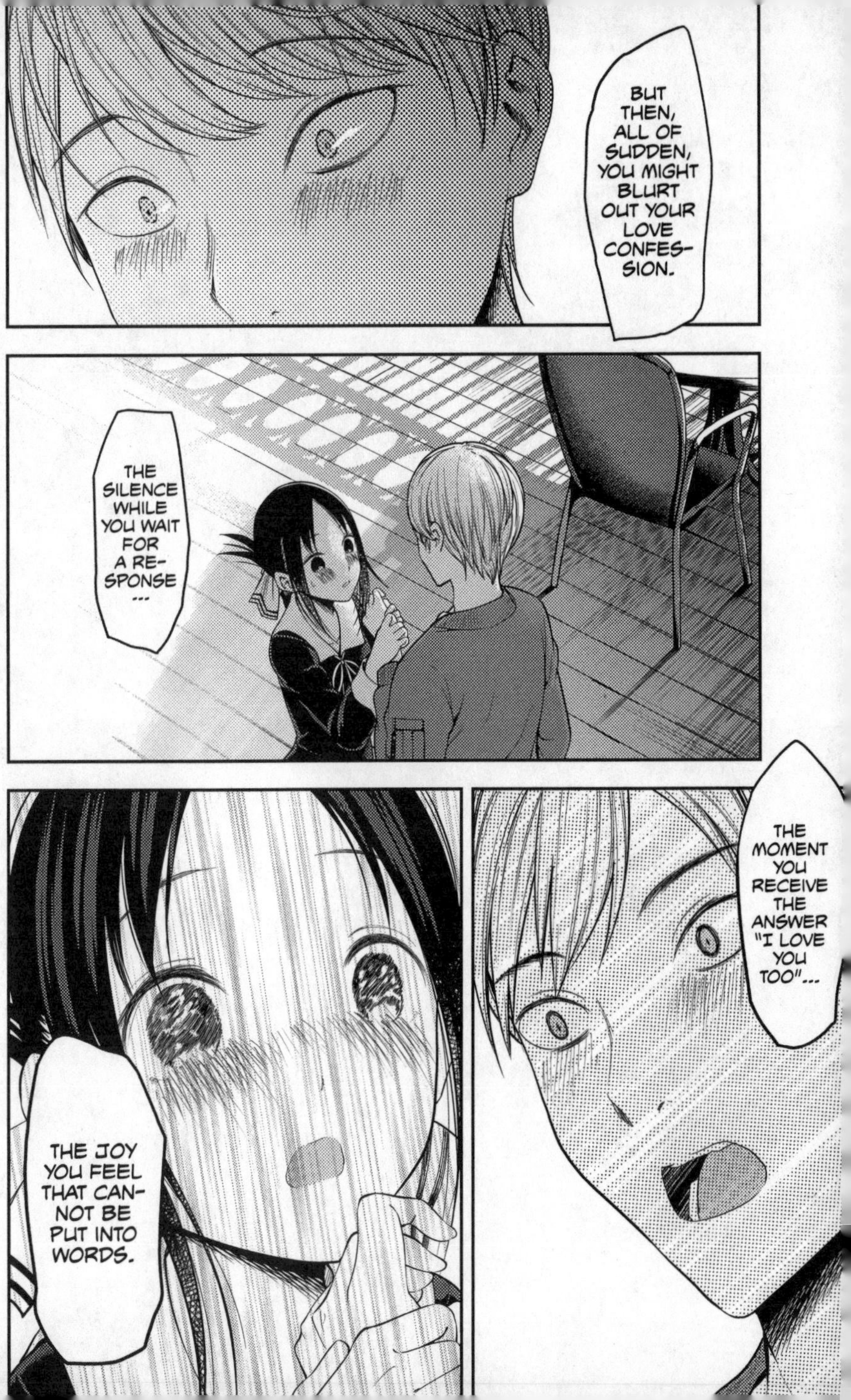
BUT THEN, ALL OF SUDDEN, YOU MIGHT BLURT OUT YOUR LOVE CONFES-SION.
THE SILENCE WHILE YOU WAIT FOR A RE-SPONSE ...
THE MOMENT YOU RECEIVE THE ANSWER "I LOVE YOU TOO"...
THE JOY YOU FEEL THAT CAN-NOT BE PUT INTO WORDS.

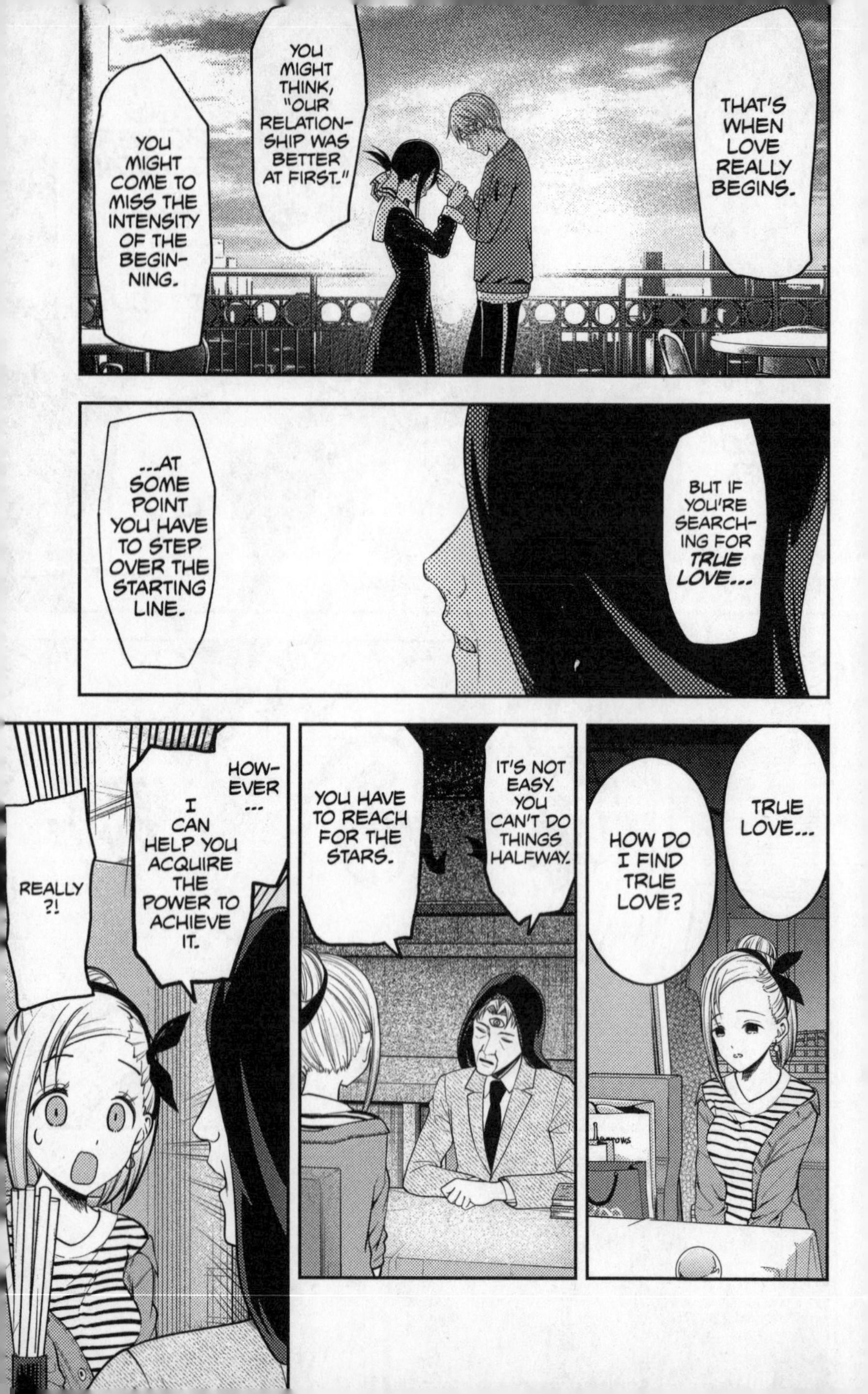
THAT'S WHEN LOVE REALLY BEGINS.
YOU MIGHT THINK, "OUR RELATIONSHIP WAS BETTER AT FIRST."
YOU MIGHT COME TO MISS THE INTENSITY OF THE BEGINNING.
BUT IF YOU'RE SEARCHING FOR TRUE LOVE...
...AT SOME POINT YOU HAVE TO STEP OVER THE STARTING LINE.
TRUE LOVE...
HOW DO I FIND TRUE LOVE?
IT'S NOT EASY. YOU CAN'T DO THINGS HALFWAY.
YOU HAVE TO REACH FOR THE STARS.
HOWEVER...
I CAN HELP YOU ACQUIRE THE POWER TO ACHIEVE IT.
REALLY?!

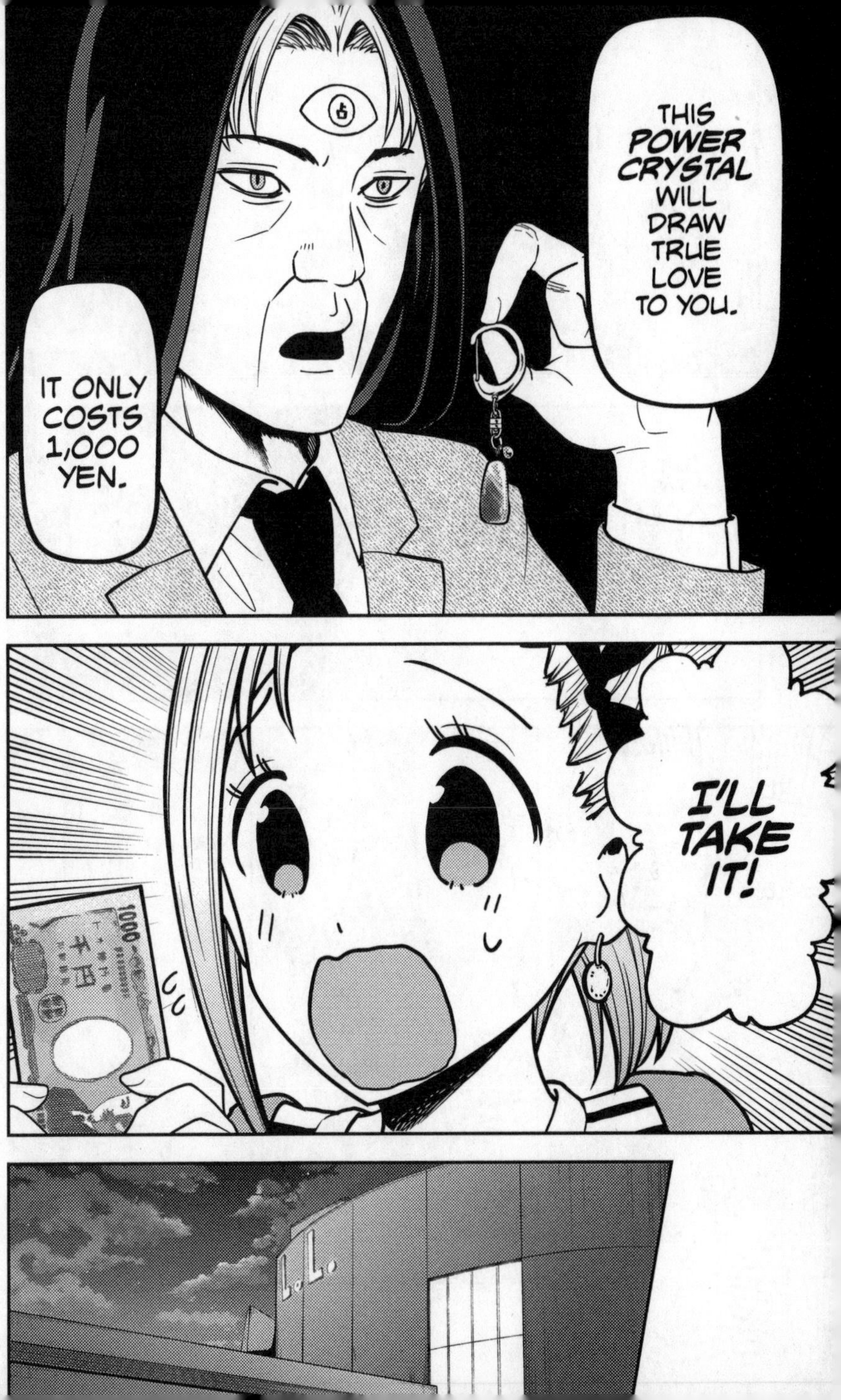
THIS POWER CRYSTAL WILL DRAW TRUE LOVE TO YOU.
IT ONLY COSTS 1,000 YEN.
I'LL TAKE IT!
L.L.

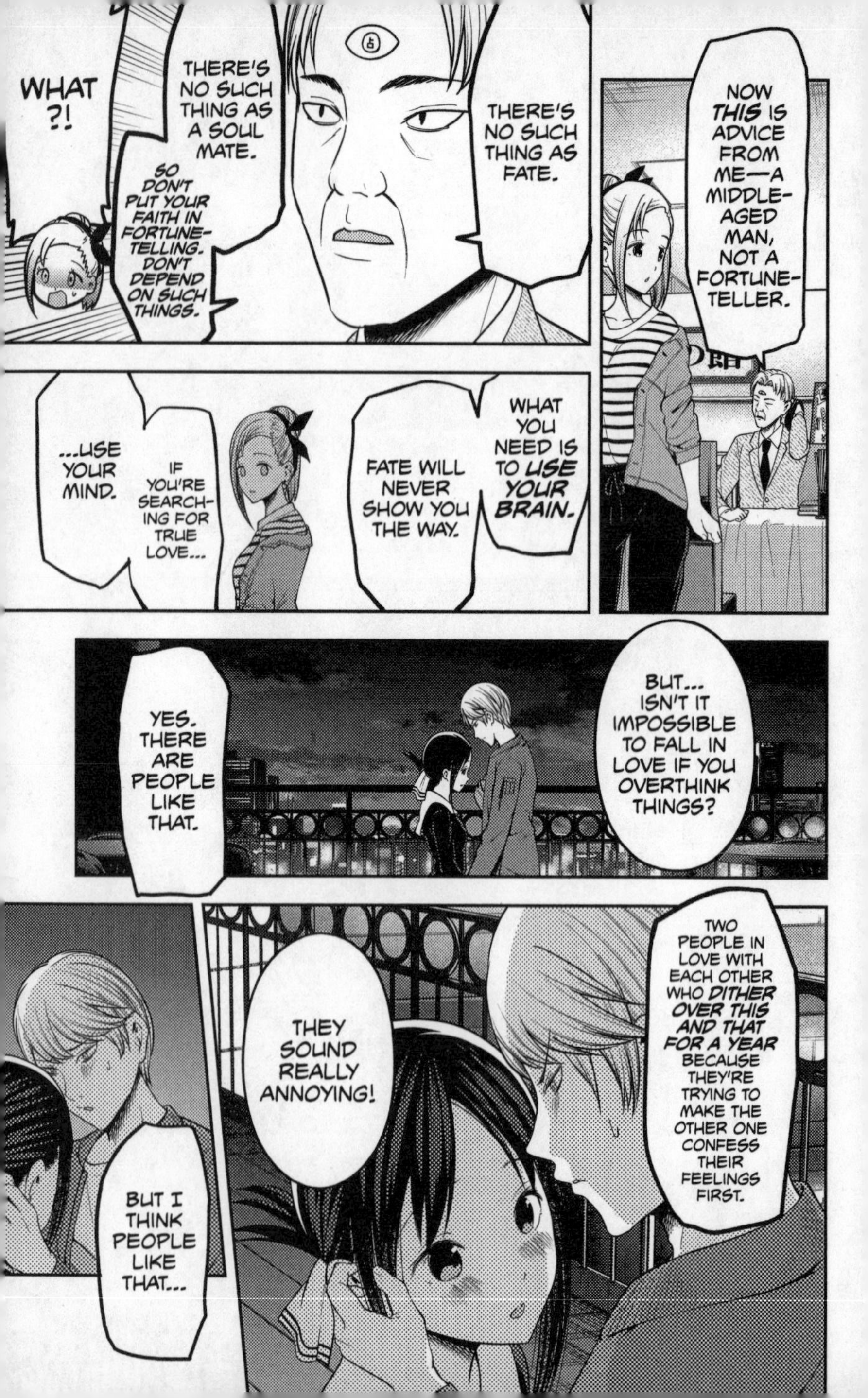
NOW *THIS* IS ADVICE FROM ME—A MIDDLE-AGED MAN, NOT A FORTUNE-TELLER.
THERE'S NO SUCH THING AS FATE.
THERE'S NO SUCH THING AS A SOUL MATE.
SO DON'T PUT YOUR FAITH IN FORTUNE-TELLING. DON'T DEPEND ON SUCH THINGS.
WHAT ?!
WHAT YOU NEED IS TO *USE YOUR BRAIN*.
FATE WILL NEVER SHOW YOU THE WAY.
IF YOU'RE SEARCHING FOR TRUE LOVE...
...USE YOUR MIND.
BUT... ISN'T IT IMPOSSIBLE TO FALL IN LOVE IF YOU OVERTHINK THINGS?
YES. THERE ARE PEOPLE LIKE THAT.
TWO PEOPLE IN LOVE WITH EACH OTHER WHO *DITHER OVER THIS AND THAT FOR A YEAR* BECAUSE THEY'RE TRYING TO MAKE THE OTHER ONE CONFESS THEIR FEELINGS FIRST.
THEY SOUND REALLY ANNOYING!
BUT I THINK PEOPLE LIKE THAT...

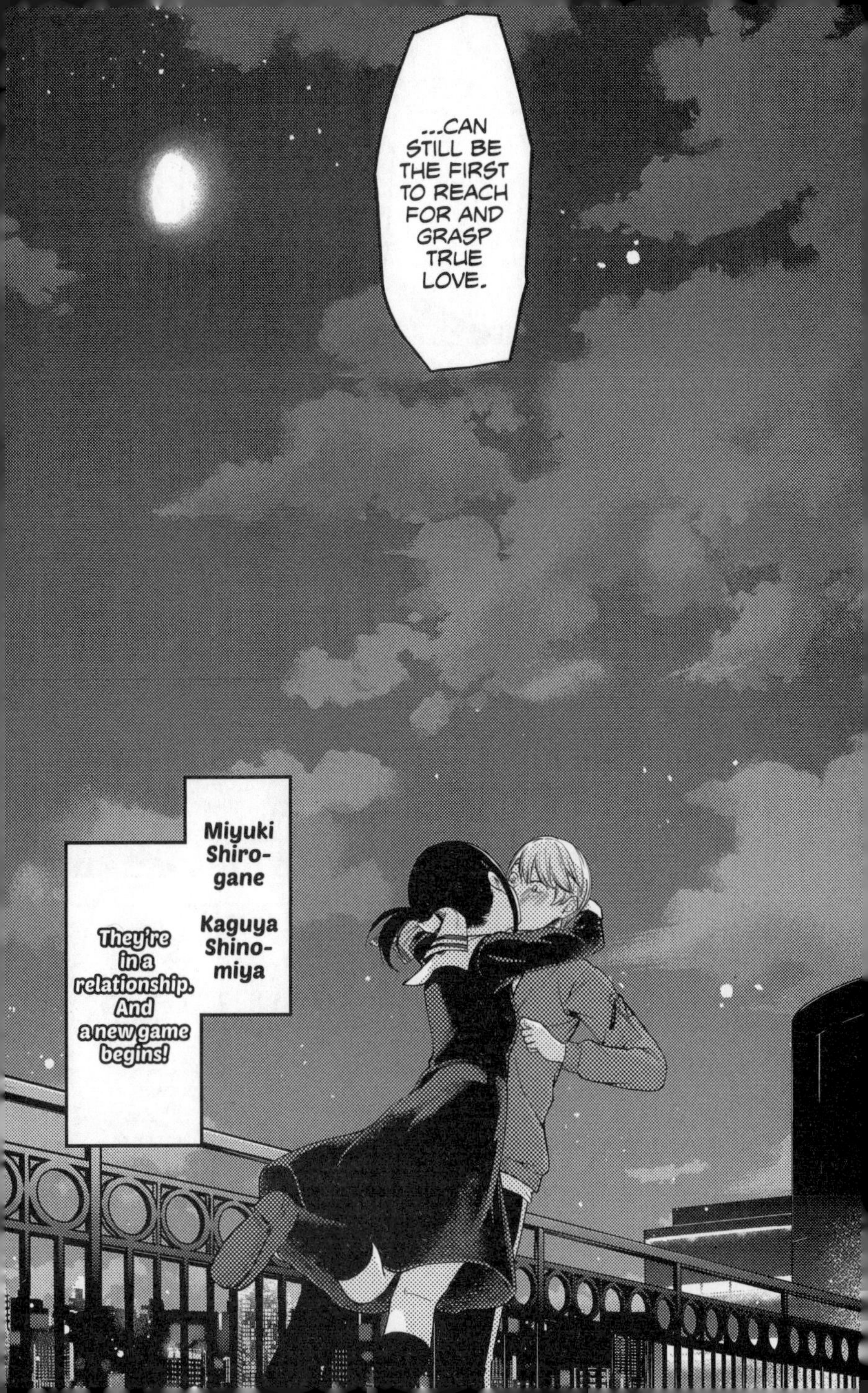
...CAN STILL BE THE FIRST TO REACH FOR AND GRASP TRUE LOVE.
Miyuki Shirogane
Kaguya Shinomiya
They're in a relationship. And a new game begins!

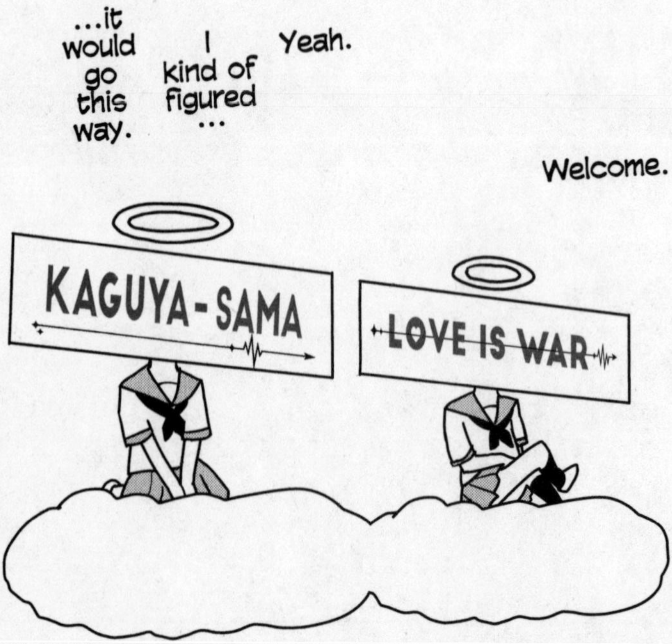
Welcome.
Yeah.
I kind of figured...
...it would go this way.
KAGUYA-SAMA
LOVE IS WAR

KAGUYA-SAMA
LOVE IS WAR

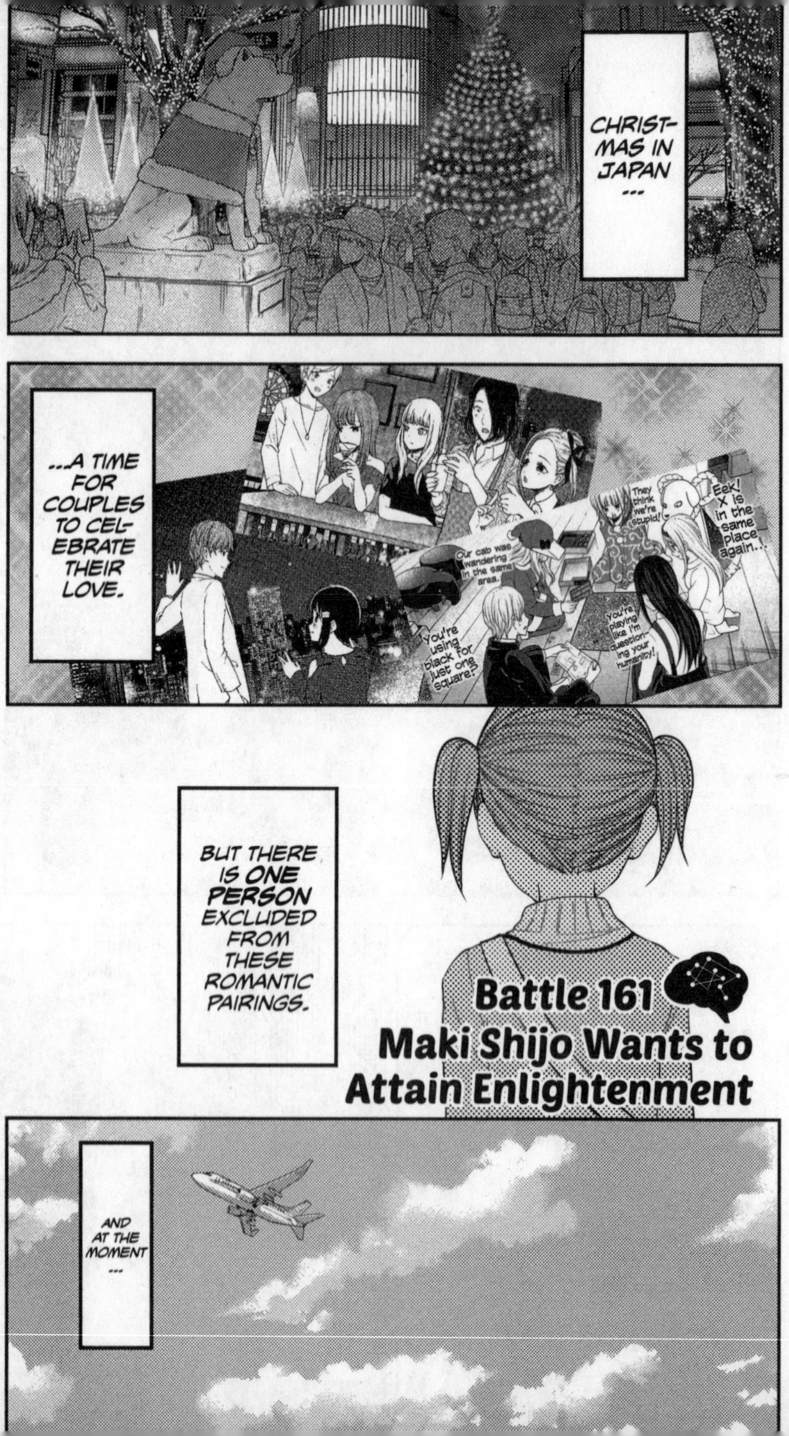
CHRIST-MAS IN JAPAN...
...A TIME FOR COUPLES TO CEL-EBRATE THEIR LOVE.
Eek! X is in the same place again...
They think we're stupid!
Our cab was wandering in the same area.
You're playing like I'm question-ing your humanity!
You're using black for just one square?
BUT THERE IS ONE PERSON EXCLUDED FROM THESE ROMANTIC PAIRINGS.
Battle 161
Maki Shijo Wants to Attain Enlightenment
AND AT THE MOMENT...

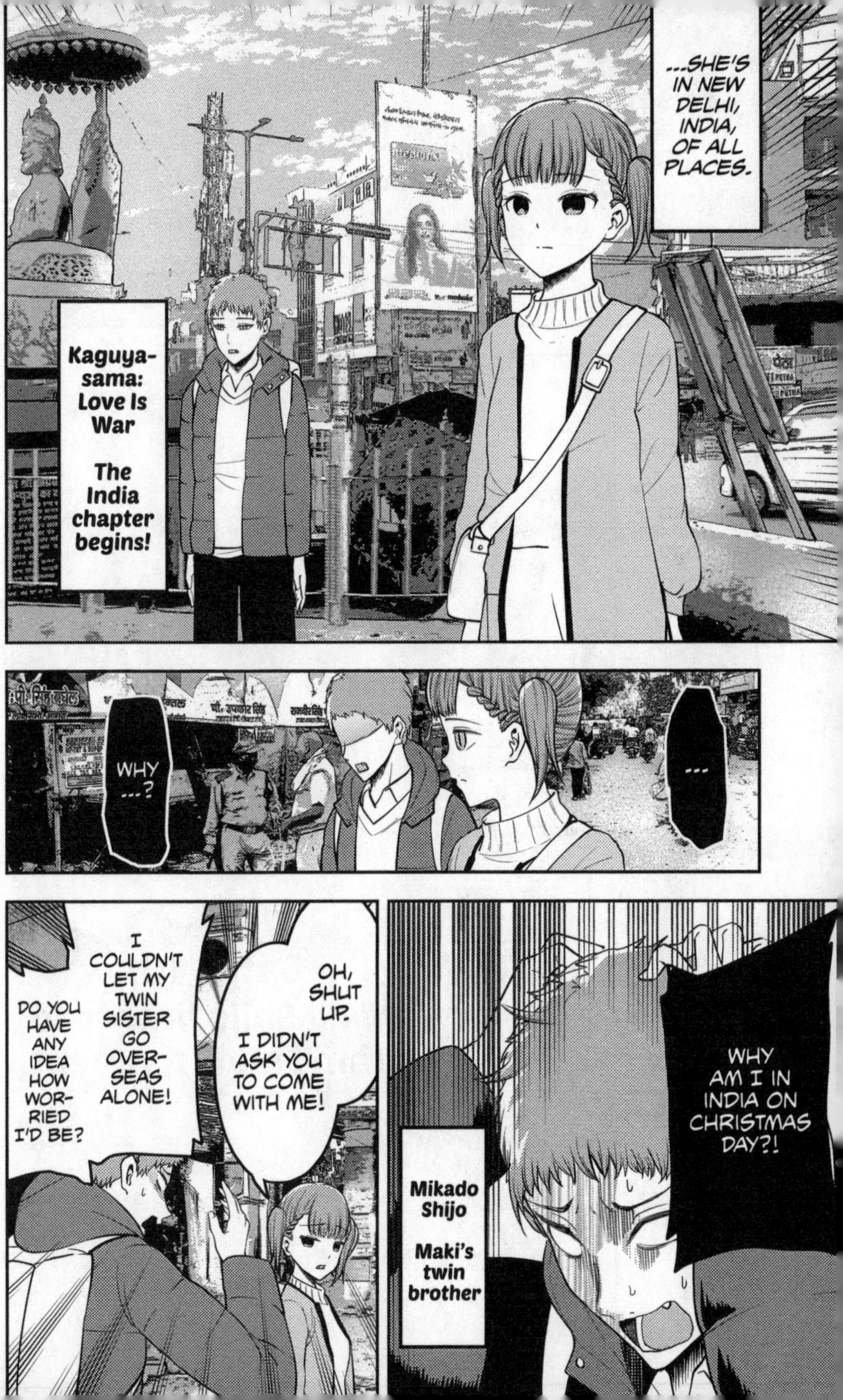
...SHE'S IN NEW DELHI, INDIA, OF ALL PLACES.
Kaguya-sama: Love Is War
The India chapter begins!
...
WHY ...?
WHY AM I IN INDIA ON CHRISTMAS DAY?!
Mikado Shijo
Maki's twin brother
OH, SHUT UP.
I DIDN'T ASK YOU TO COME WITH ME!
I COULDN'T LET MY TWIN SISTER GO OVER-SEAS ALONE!
DO YOU HAVE ANY IDEA HOW WOR-RIED I'D BE?

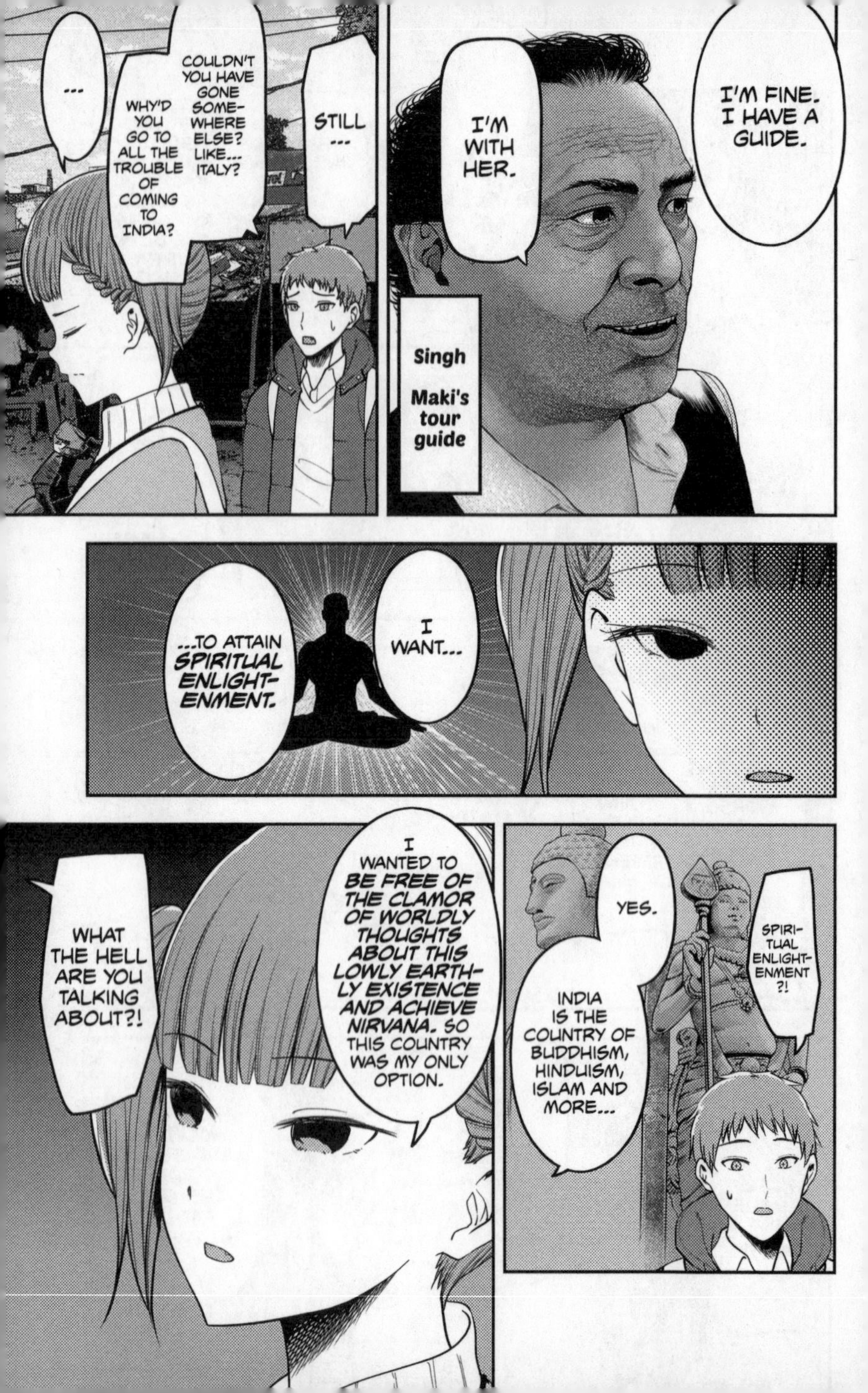

I'M FINE. I HAVE A GUIDE.
I'M WITH HER.
Singh
Maki's tour guide
STILL...
COULDN'T YOU HAVE GONE SOME-WHERE ELSE? LIKE... ITALY?
WHY'D YOU GO TO ALL THE TROUBLE OF COMING TO INDIA?
...
I WANT...
...TO ATTAIN SPIRITUAL ENLIGHT-ENMENT.
SPIRI-TUAL ENLIGHT-ENMENT?!
YES.
INDIA IS THE COUNTRY OF BUDDHISM, HINDUISM, ISLAM AND MORE...
I WANTED TO BE FREE OF THE CLAMOR OF WORLDLY THOUGHTS ABOUT THIS LOWLY EARTH-LY EXISTENCE AND ACHIEVE NIRVANA. SO THIS COUNTRY WAS MY ONLY OPTION.
WHAT THE HELL ARE YOU TALKING ABOUT?!

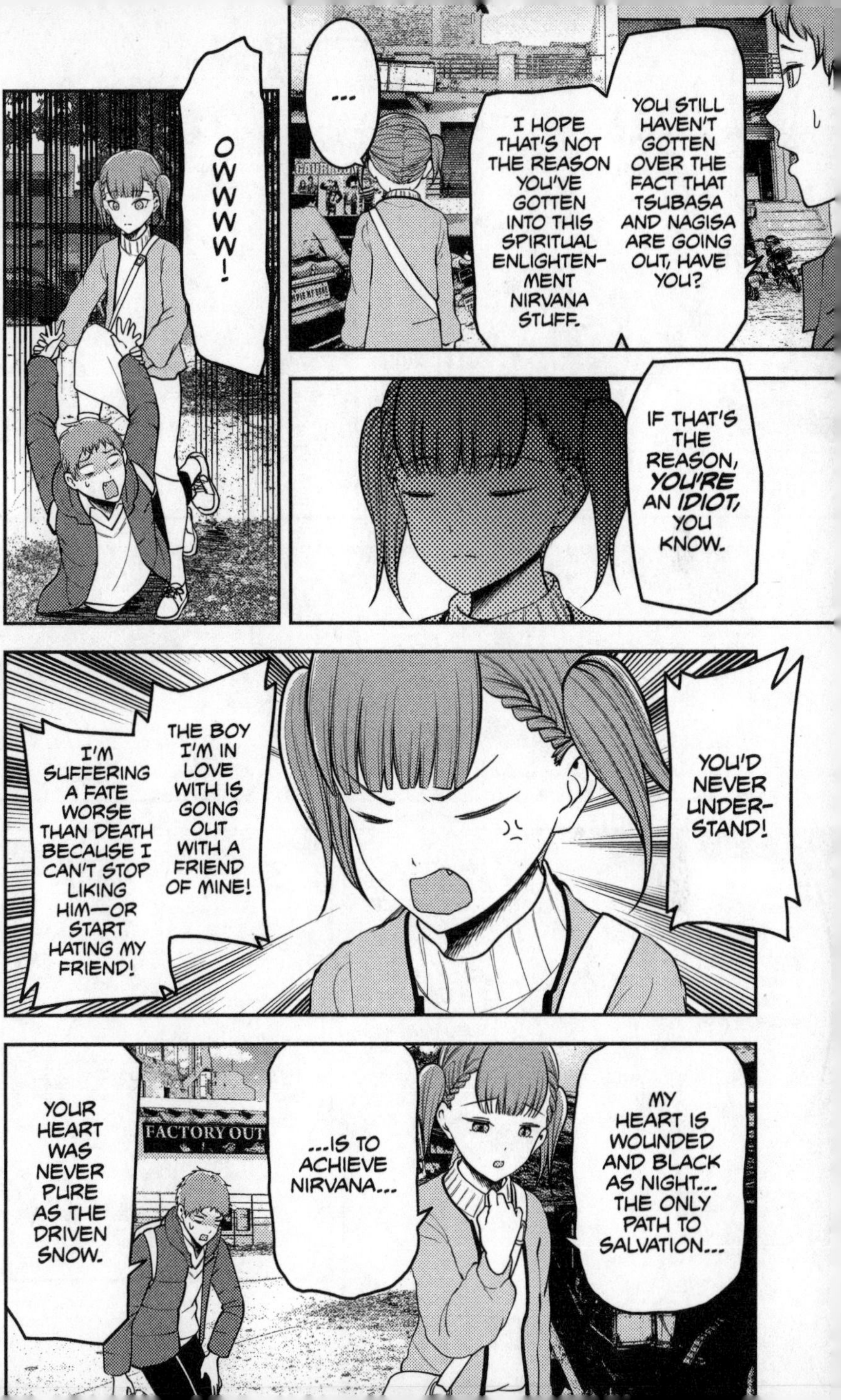
YOU STILL HAVEN'T GOTTEN OVER THE FACT THAT TSUBASA AND NAGISA ARE GOING OUT, HAVE YOU?
I HOPE THAT'S NOT THE REASON YOU'VE GOTTEN INTO THIS SPIRITUAL ENLIGHTENMENT NIRVANA STUFF.
...
IF THAT'S THE REASON, *YOU'RE* AN *IDIOT,* YOU KNOW.
OWWWWW!
YOU'D NEVER UNDERSTAND!
THE BOY I'M IN LOVE WITH IS GOING OUT WITH A FRIEND OF MINE!
I'M SUFFERING A FATE WORSE THAN DEATH BECAUSE I CAN'T STOP LIKING HIM—OR START HATING MY FRIEND!
MY HEART IS WOUNDED AND BLACK AS NIGHT... THE ONLY PATH TO SALVATION...
...IS TO ACHIEVE NIRVANA...
FACTORY OUT
YOUR HEART WAS NEVER PURE AS THE DRIVEN SNOW.

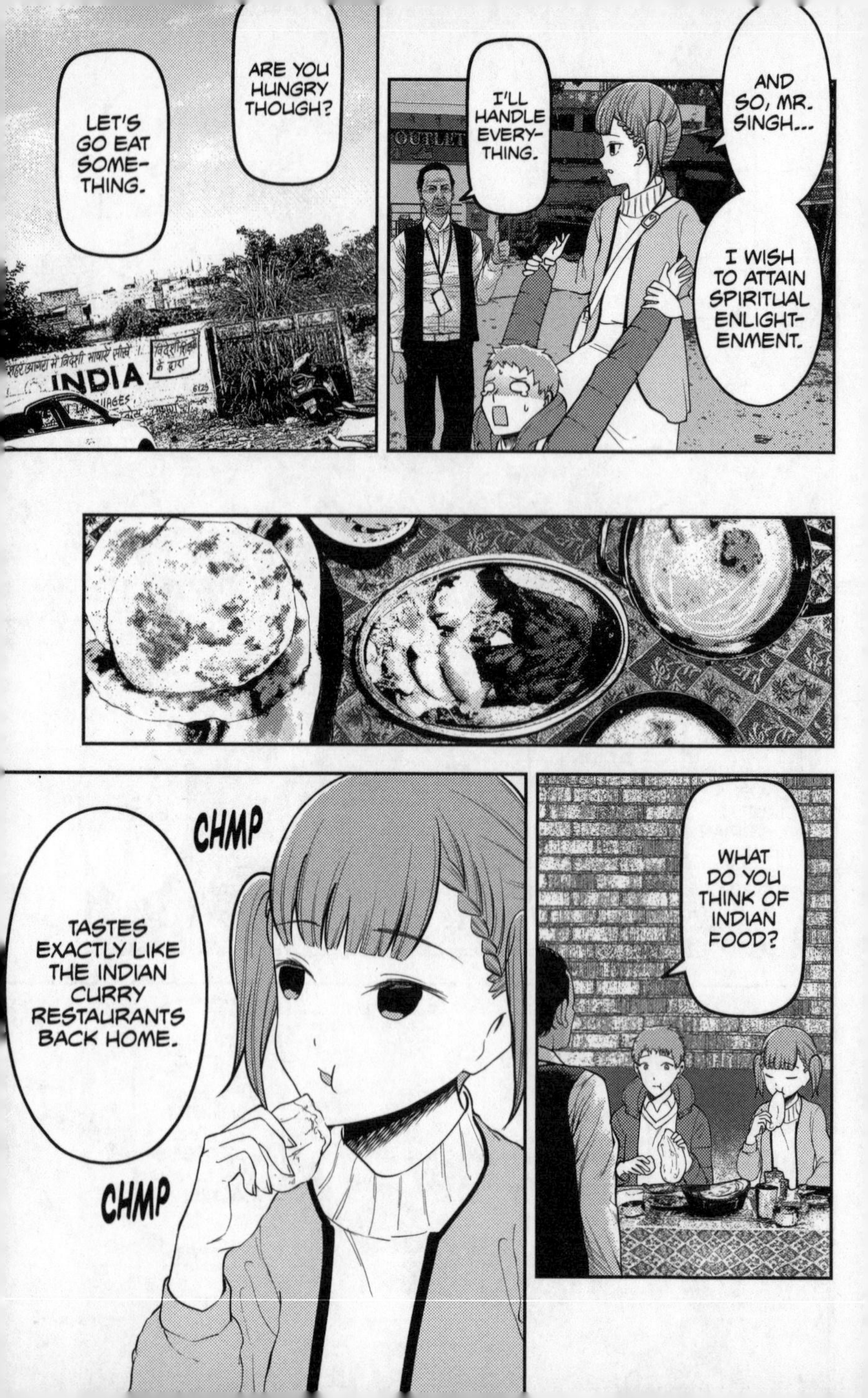
AND SO, MR. SINGH...
I WISH TO ATTAIN SPIRITUAL ENLIGHTENMENT.
I'LL HANDLE EVERYTHING.
ARE YOU HUNGRY THOUGH?
LET'S GO EAT SOMETHING.
INDIA
WHAT DO YOU THINK OF INDIAN FOOD?
CHMP
TASTES EXACTLY LIKE THE INDIAN CURRY RESTAURANTS BACK HOME.
CHMP

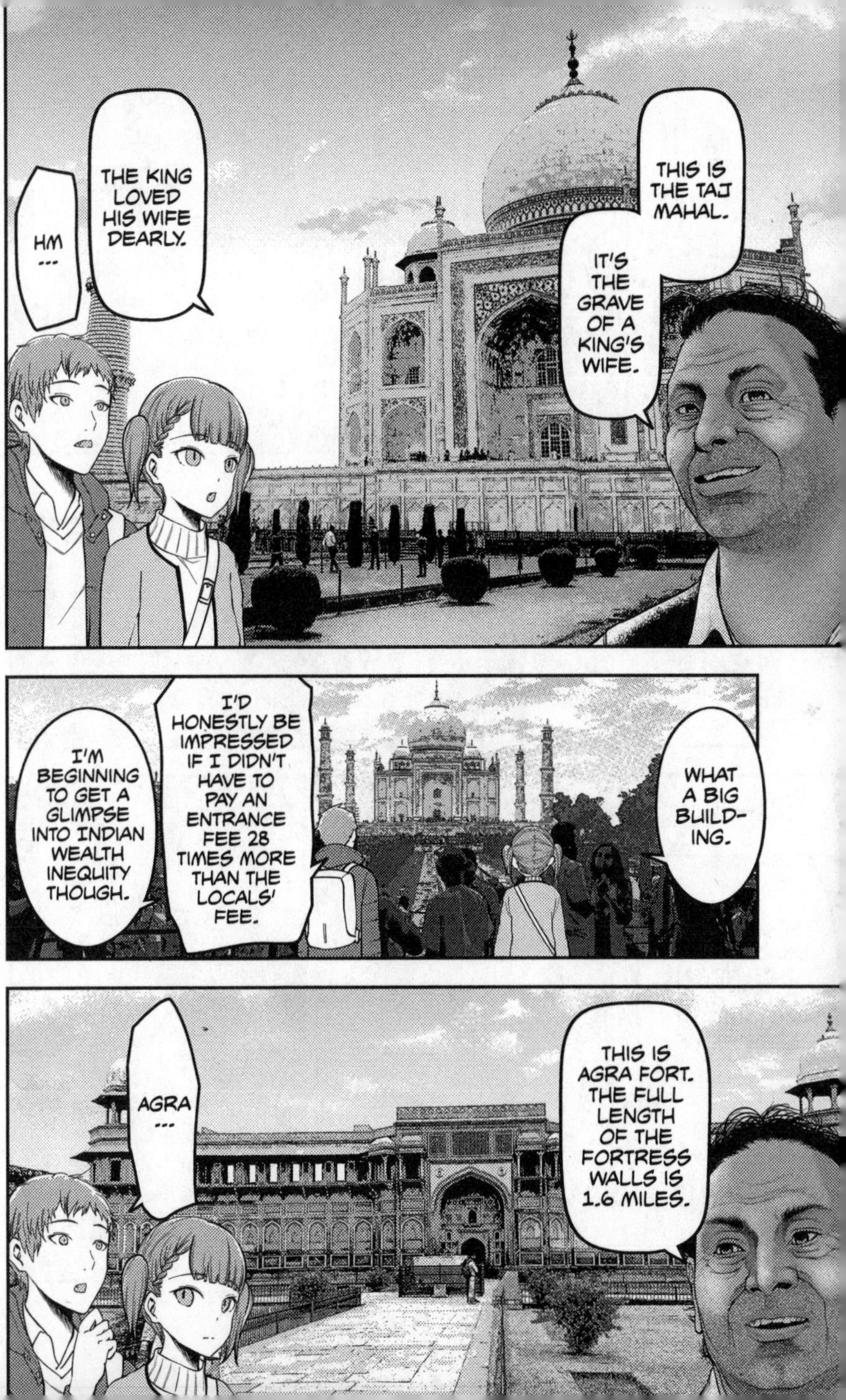
THIS IS THE TAJ MAHAL.
IT'S THE GRAVE OF A KING'S WIFE.
THE KING LOVED HIS WIFE DEARLY.
HM ...
WHAT A BIG BUILD-ING.
I'D HONESTLY BE IMPRESSED IF I DIDN'T HAVE TO PAY AN ENTRANCE FEE 28 TIMES MORE THAN THE LOCALS' FEE.
I'M BEGINNING TO GET A GLIMPSE INTO INDIAN WEALTH INEQUITY THOUGH.
THIS IS AGRA FORT. THE FULL LENGTH OF THE FORTRESS WALLS IS 1.6 MILES.
AGRA ...

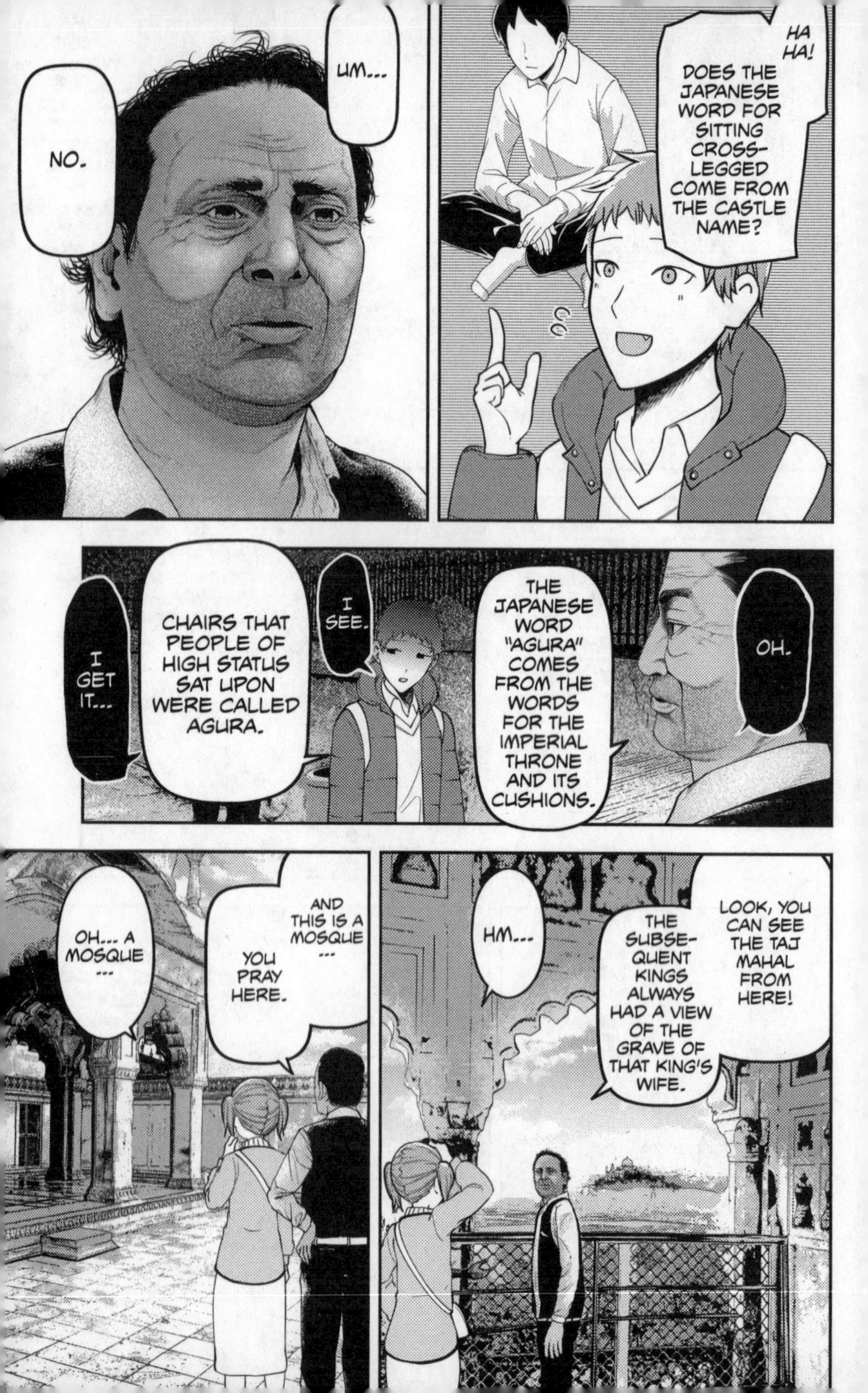
HA HA! DOES THE JAPANESE WORD FOR SITTING CROSS-LEGGED COME FROM THE CASTLE NAME?
UM...
NO.
OH.
THE JAPANESE WORD "AGURA" COMES FROM THE WORDS FOR THE IMPERIAL THRONE AND ITS CUSHIONS.
I SEE.
CHAIRS THAT PEOPLE OF HIGH STATUS SAT UPON WERE CALLED AGURA.
I GET IT...
LOOK, YOU CAN SEE THE TAJ MAHAL FROM HERE!
THE SUBSEQUENT KINGS ALWAYS HAD A VIEW OF THE GRAVE OF THAT KING'S WIFE.
HM...
AND THIS IS A MOSQUE ...
YOU PRAY HERE.
OH... A MOSQUE ...

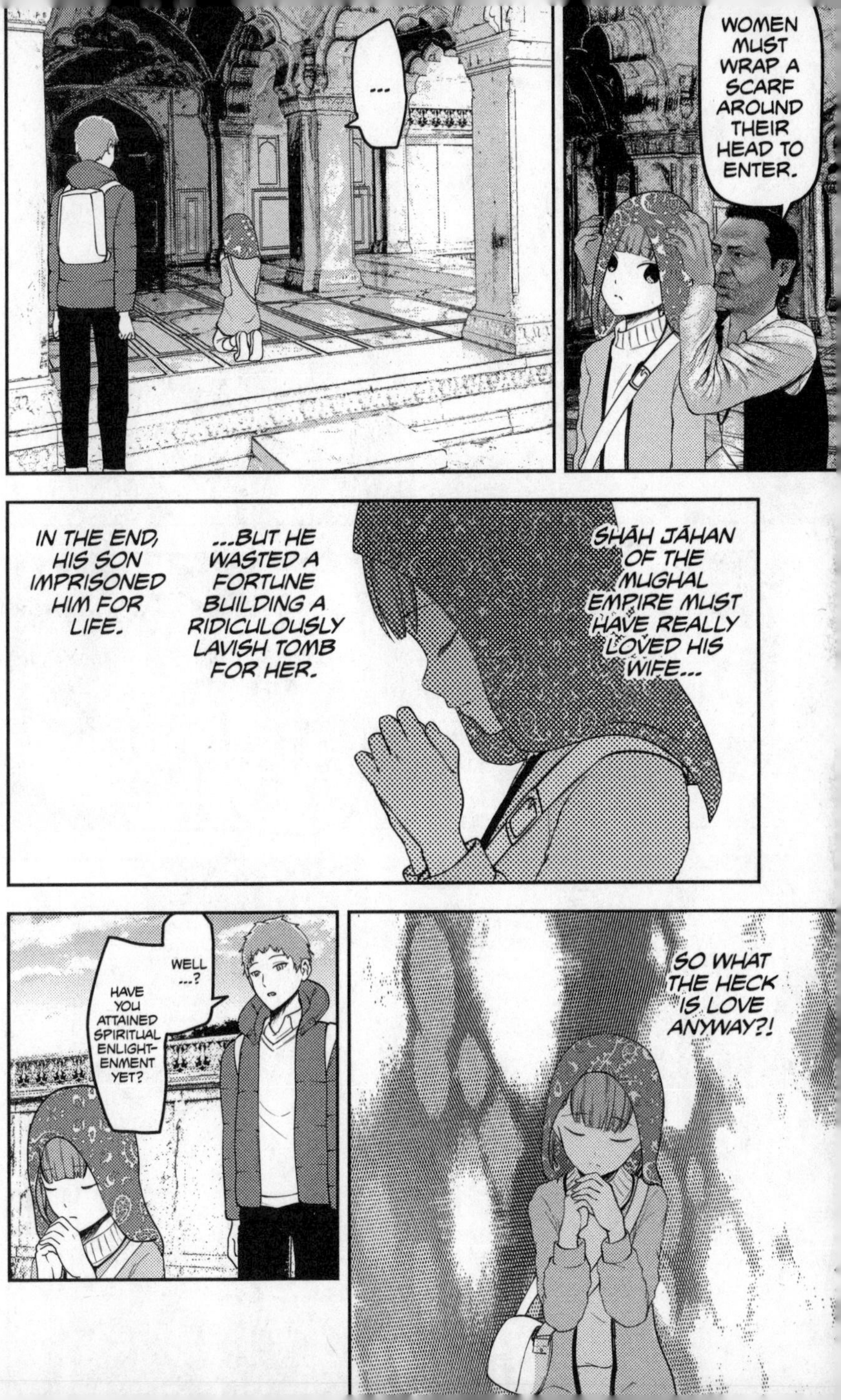
WOMEN MUST WRAP A SCARF AROUND THEIR HEAD TO ENTER.
...
SHĀH JĀHAN OF THE MUGHAL EMPIRE MUST HAVE REALLY LOVED HIS WIFE...
...BUT HE WASTED A FORTUNE BUILDING A RIDICULOUSLY LAVISH TOMB FOR HER.
IN THE END, HIS SON IMPRISONED HIM FOR LIFE.
SO WHAT THE HECK IS LOVE ANYWAY?!
WELL...? HAVE YOU ATTAINED SPIRITUAL ENLIGHTENMENT YET?

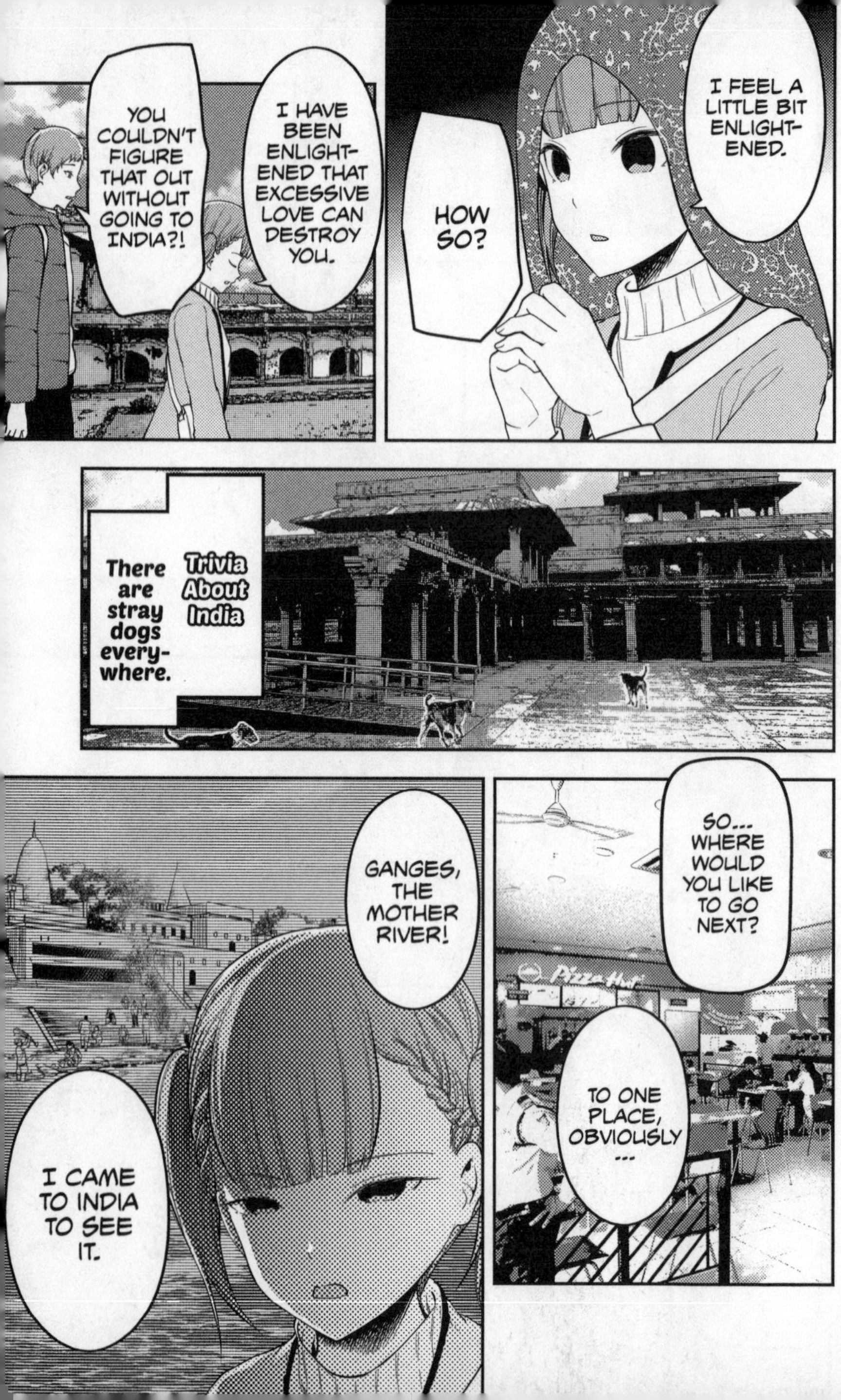
I FEEL A LITTLE BIT ENLIGHTENED.
HOW SO?
I HAVE BEEN ENLIGHTENED THAT EXCESSIVE LOVE CAN DESTROY YOU.
YOU COULDN'T FIGURE THAT OUT WITHOUT GOING TO INDIA?!
Trivia About India
There are stray dogs everywhere.
SO... WHERE WOULD YOU LIKE TO GO NEXT?
Pizza Hut
TO ONE PLACE, OBVIOUSLY...
GANGES, THE MOTHER RIVER!
I CAME TO INDIA TO SEE IT.

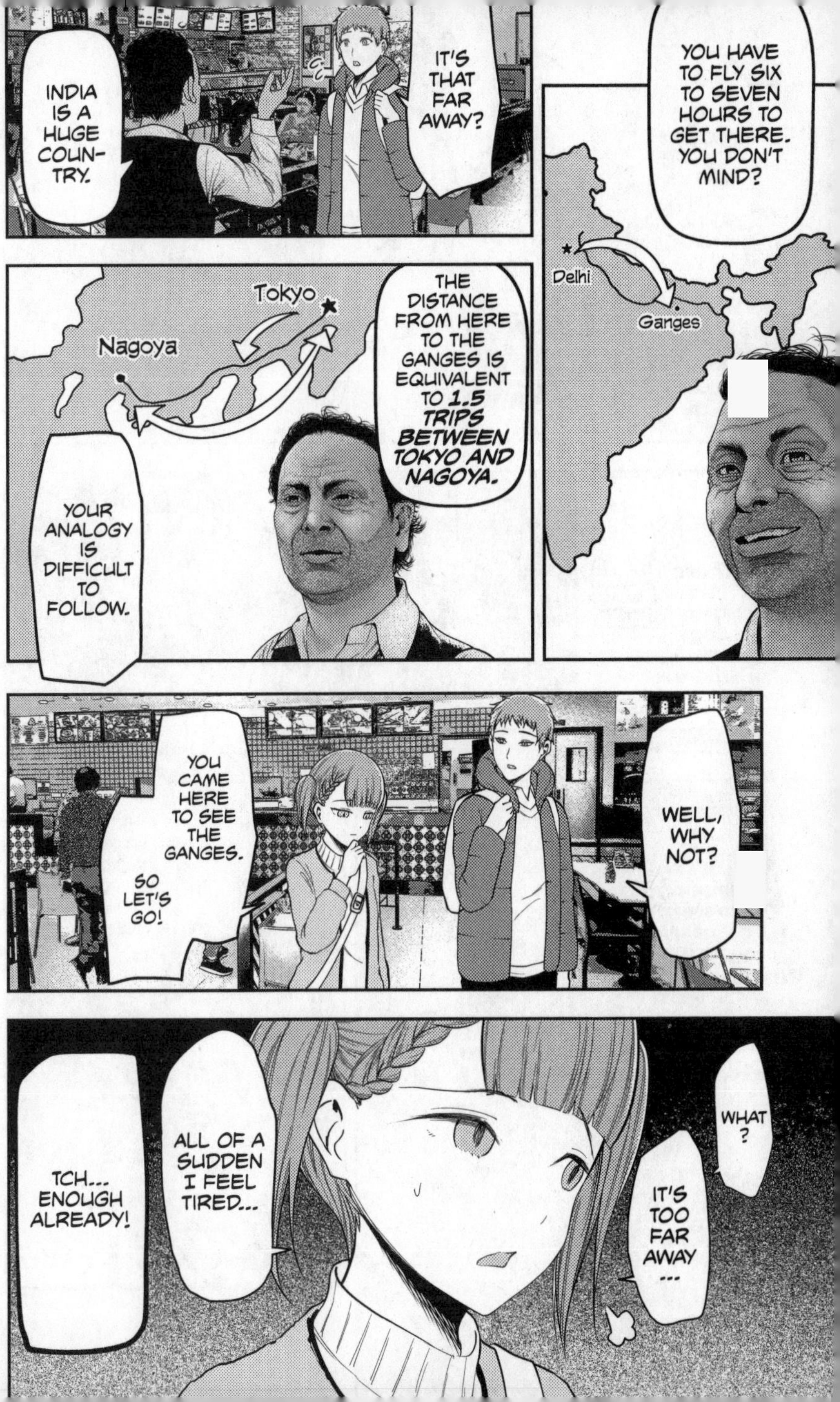
YOU HAVE TO FLY SIX TO SEVEN HOURS TO GET THERE. YOU DON'T MIND?
Delhi
Ganges
IT'S THAT FAR AWAY?
INDIA IS A HUGE COUNTRY.
THE DISTANCE FROM HERE TO THE GANGES IS EQUIVALENT TO 1.5 TRIPS BETWEEN TOKYO AND NAGOYA.
Tokyo
Nagoya
YOUR ANALOGY IS DIFFICULT TO FOLLOW.
WELL, WHY NOT?
YOU CAME HERE TO SEE THE GANGES.
SO LET'S GO!
WHAT?
IT'S TOO FAR AWAY...
ALL OF A SUDDEN I FEEL TIRED...
TCH... ENOUGH ALREADY!

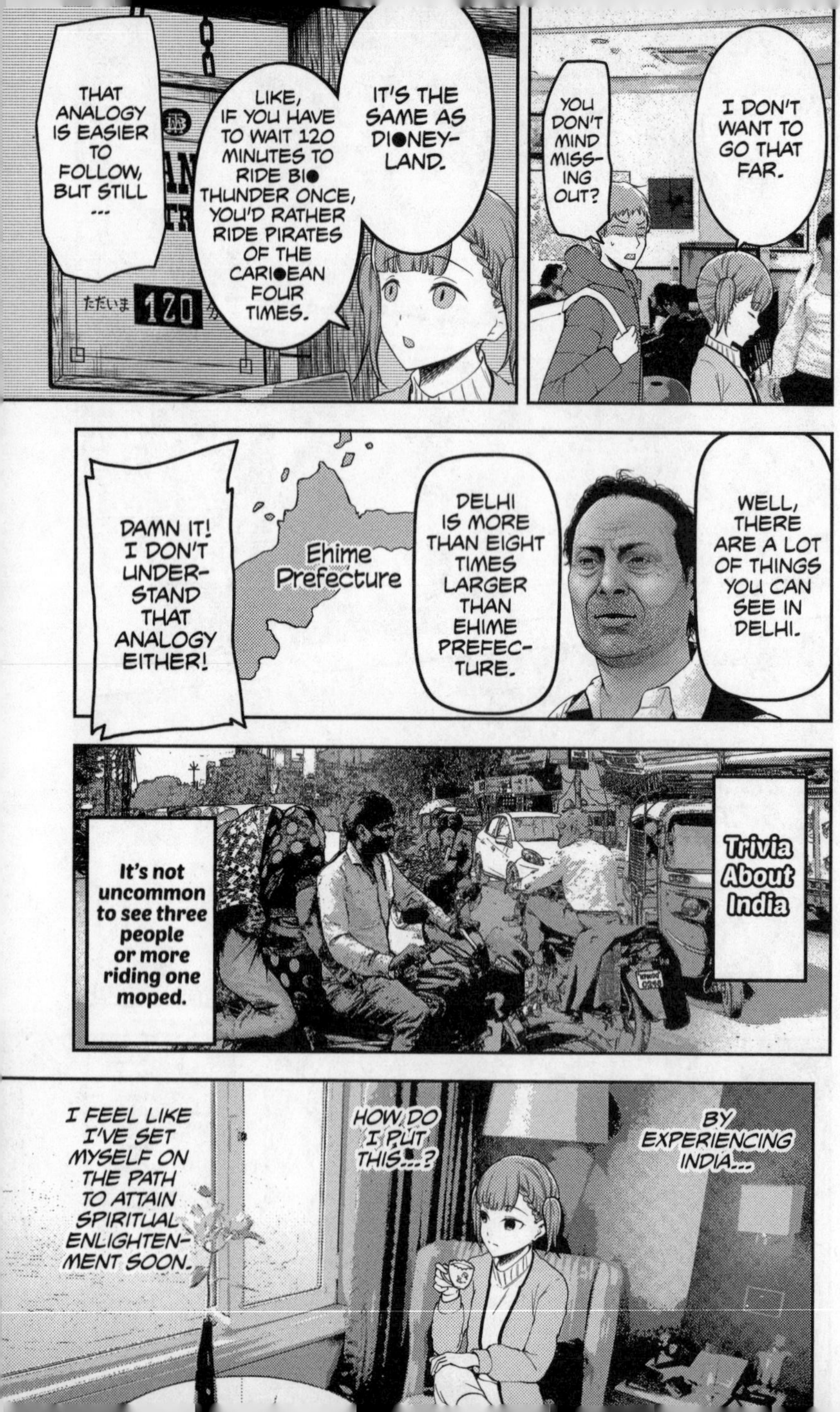

I DON'T WANT TO GO THAT FAR.
YOU DON'T MIND MISSING OUT?
IT'S THE SAME AS DI●NEYLAND.
LIKE, IF YOU HAVE TO WAIT 120 MINUTES TO RIDE BI● THUNDER ONCE, YOU'D RATHER RIDE PIRATES OF THE CARI●EAN FOUR TIMES.
ただいま 120
THAT ANALOGY IS EASIER TO FOLLOW, BUT STILL...
WELL, THERE ARE A LOT OF THINGS YOU CAN SEE IN DELHI.
DELHI IS MORE THAN EIGHT TIMES LARGER THAN EHIME PREFECTURE.
Ehime Prefecture
DAMN IT! I DON'T UNDERSTAND THAT ANALOGY EITHER!
Trivia About India
It's not uncommon to see three people or more riding one moped.
BY EXPERIENCING INDIA...
HOW DO I PUT THIS...?
I FEEL LIKE I'VE SET MYSELF ON THE PATH TO ATTAIN SPIRITUAL ENLIGHTENMENT SOON.

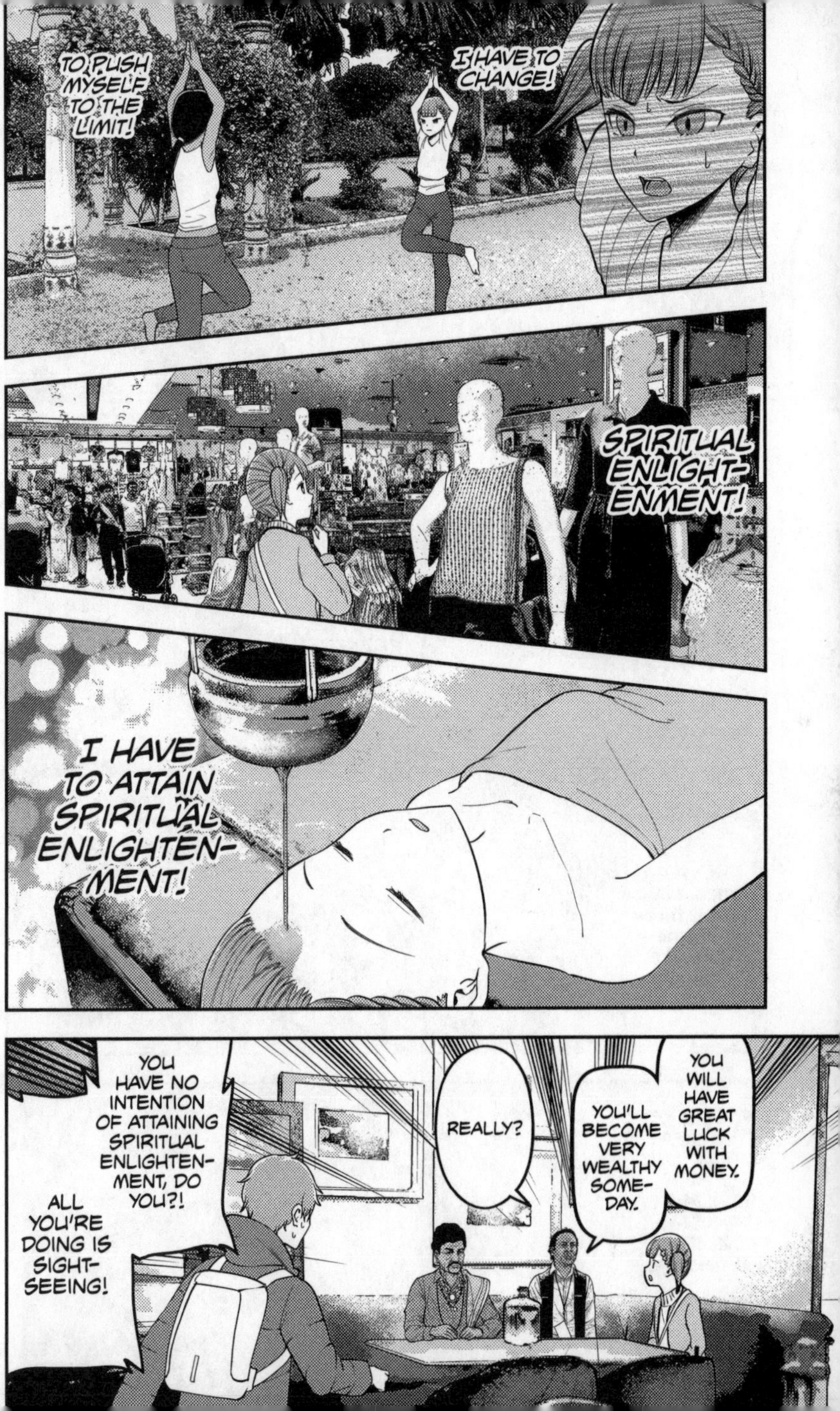

I HAVE TO CHANGE!
TO PUSH MYSELF TO THE LIMIT!
SPIRITUAL ENLIGHTENMENT!
I HAVE TO ATTAIN SPIRITUAL ENLIGHTENMENT!
YOU WILL HAVE GREAT LUCK WITH MONEY.
YOU'LL BECOME VERY WEALTHY SOMEDAY.
REALLY?
YOU HAVE NO INTENTION OF ATTAINING SPIRITUAL ENLIGHTENMENT, DO YOU?!
ALL YOU'RE DOING IS SIGHTSEEING!

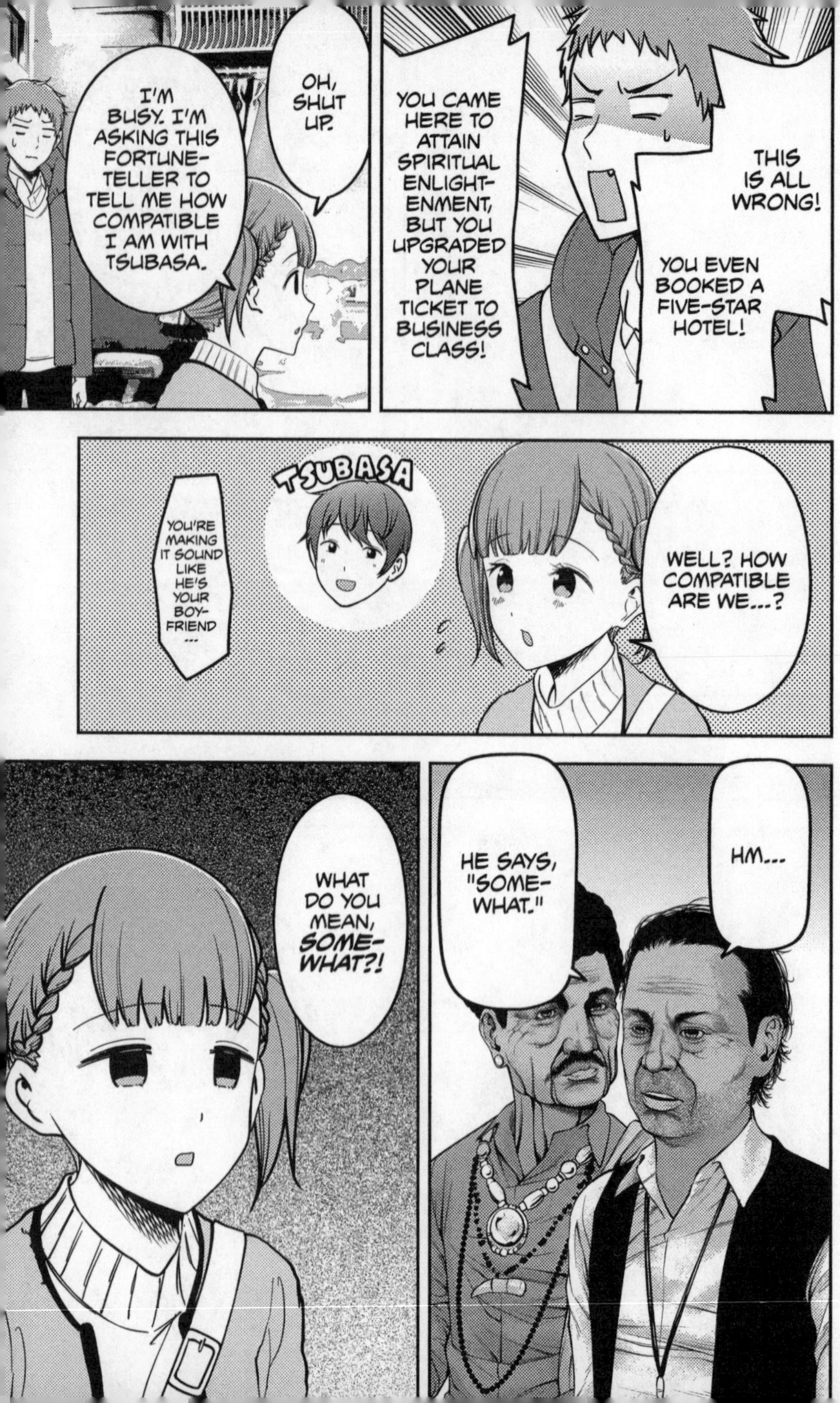
THIS IS ALL WRONG!
YOU CAME HERE TO ATTAIN SPIRITUAL ENLIGHTENMENT, BUT YOU UPGRADED YOUR PLANE TICKET TO BUSINESS CLASS!
YOU EVEN BOOKED A FIVE-STAR HOTEL!
OH, SHUT UP.
I'M BUSY. I'M ASKING THIS FORTUNE-TELLER TO TELL ME HOW COMPATIBLE I AM WITH TSUBASA.
WELL? HOW COMPATIBLE ARE WE...?
TSUBASA
YOU'RE MAKING IT SOUND LIKE HE'S YOUR BOYFRIEND...
HM...
HE SAYS, "SOMEWHAT."
WHAT DO YOU MEAN, *SOMEWHAT?!*

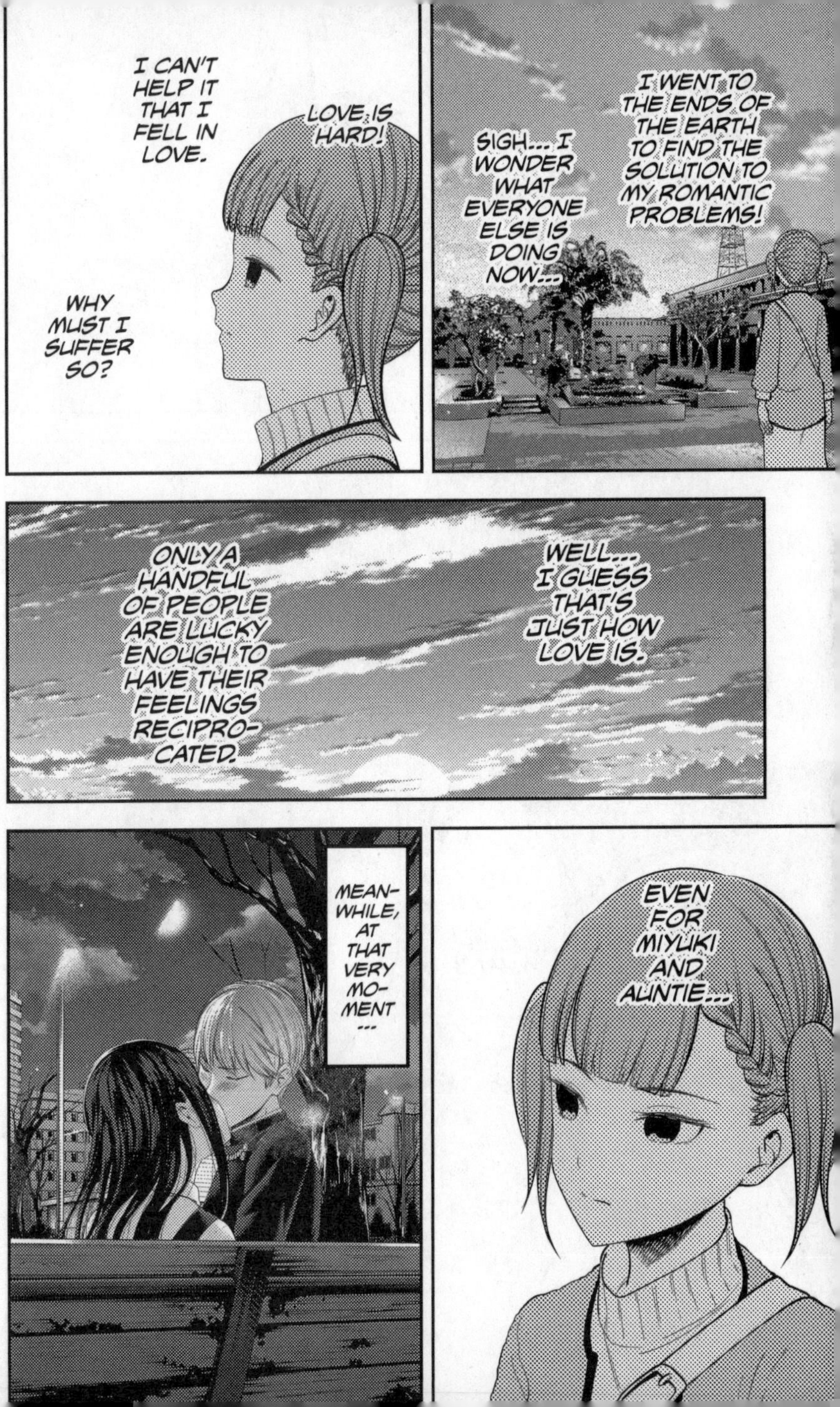
I WENT TO THE ENDS OF THE EARTH TO FIND THE SOLUTION TO MY ROMANTIC PROBLEMS!
SIGH... I WONDER WHAT EVERYONE ELSE IS DOING NOW...
LOVE IS HARD!
I CAN'T HELP IT THAT I FELL IN LOVE.
WHY MUST I SUFFER SO?
WELL... I GUESS THAT'S JUST HOW LOVE IS.
ONLY A HANDFUL OF PEOPLE ARE LUCKY ENOUGH TO HAVE THEIR FEELINGS RECIPRO-CATED.
EVEN FOR MIYUKI AND AUNTIE...
MEAN-WHILE, AT THAT VERY MO-MENT...

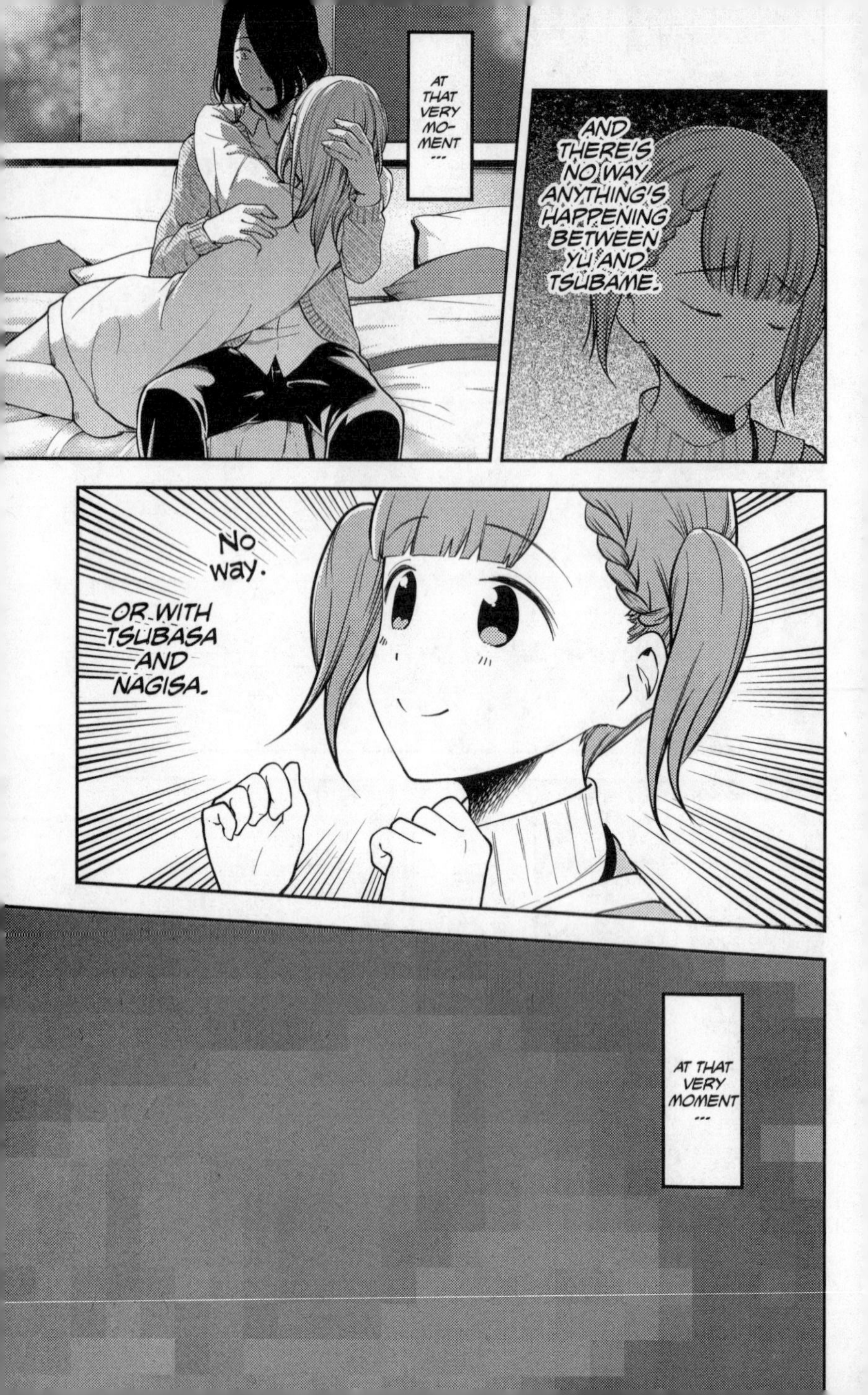
AND THERE'S NO WAY ANYTHING'S HAPPENING BETWEEN YU AND TSUBAME.
AT THAT VERY MOMENT...
No way.
OR WITH TSUBASA AND NAGISA.
AT THAT VERY MOMENT...

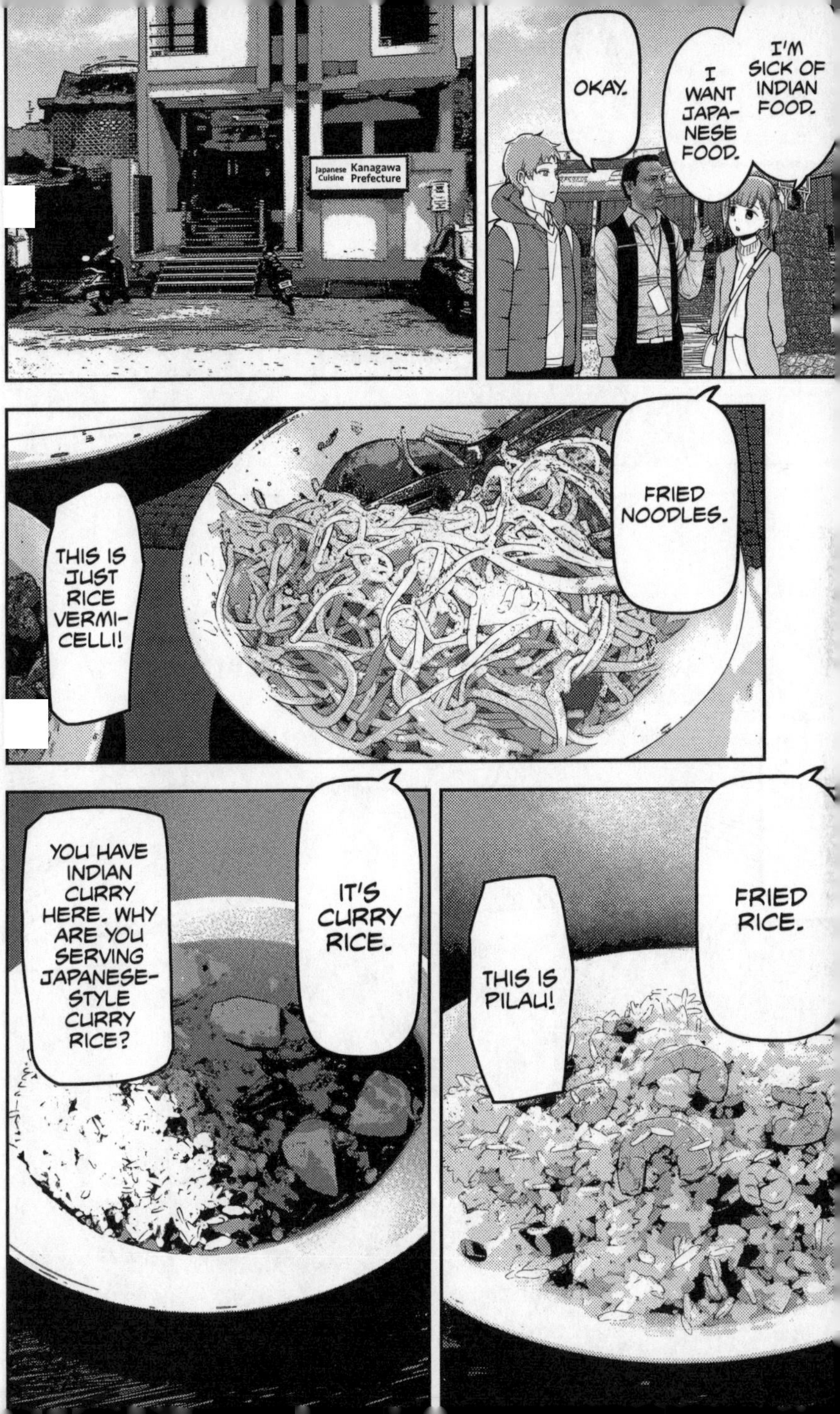
I'M SICK OF INDIAN FOOD.
I WANT JAPANESE FOOD.
OKAY.
Japanese Cuisine Kanagawa Prefecture
FRIED NOODLES.
THIS IS JUST RICE VERMICELLI!
FRIED RICE.
THIS IS PILAU!
IT'S CURRY RICE.
YOU HAVE INDIAN CURRY HERE. WHY ARE YOU SERVING JAPANESE-STYLE CURRY RICE?

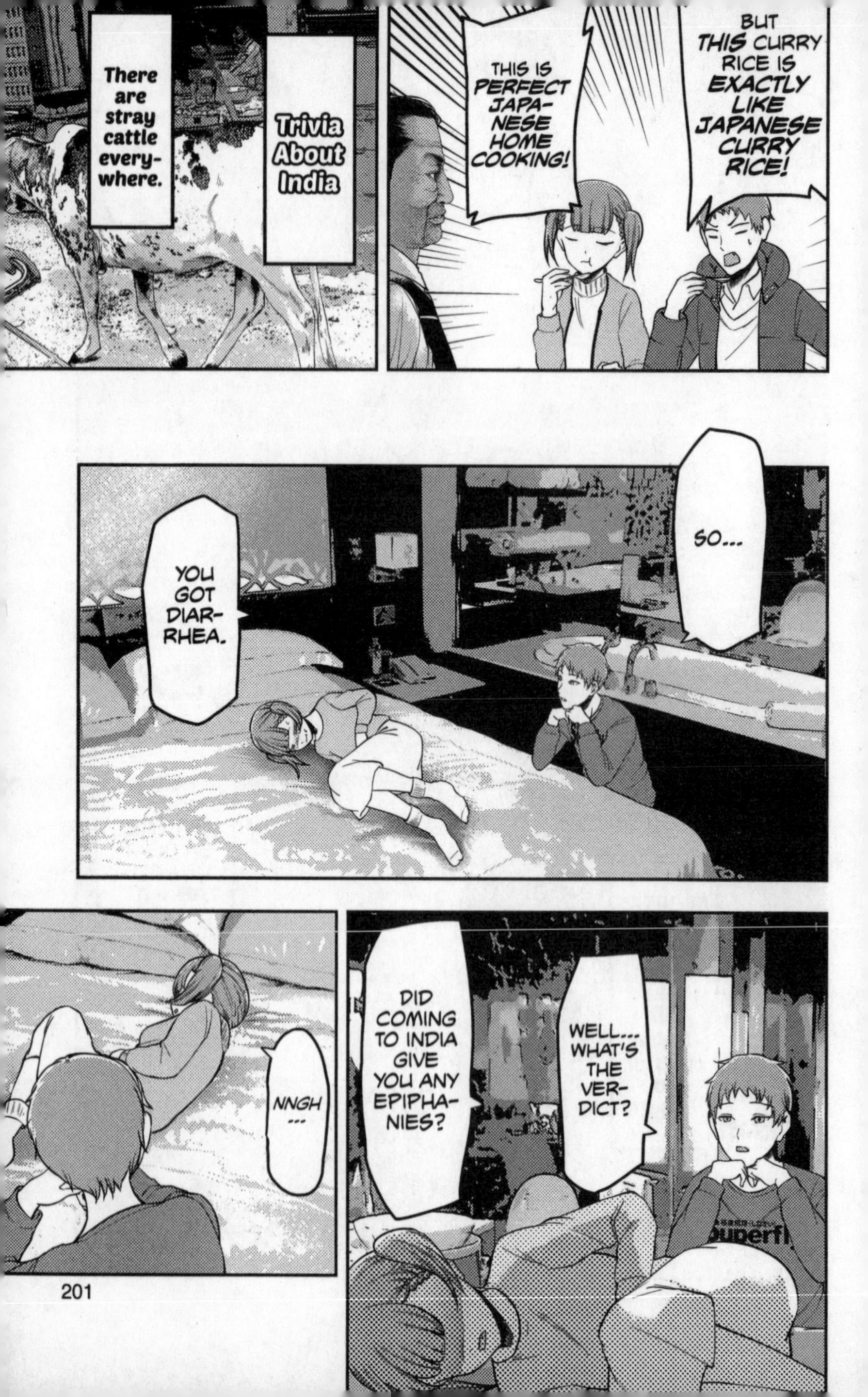
BUT THIS CURRY RICE IS EXACTLY LIKE JAPANESE CURRY RICE!
THIS IS PERFECT JAPA-NESE HOME COOKING!
Trivia About India
There are stray cattle every-where.
SO...
YOU GOT DIAR-RHEA.
WELL... WHAT'S THE VER-DICT?
DID COMING TO INDIA GIVE YOU ANY EPIPHA-NIES?
NNGH ...

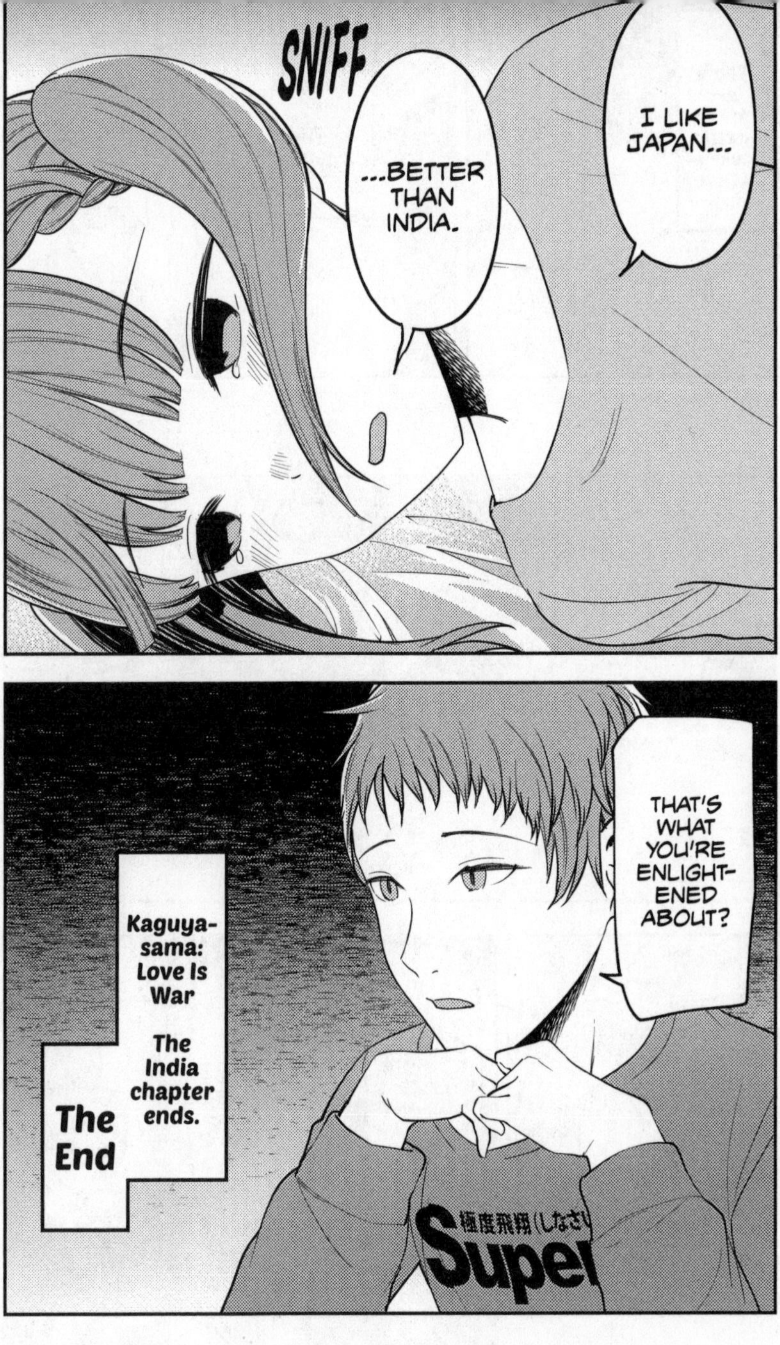
I LIKE JAPAN...
...BETTER THAN INDIA.
SNIFF
THAT'S WHAT YOU'RE ENLIGHTENED ABOUT?
Kaguya-sama: Love Is War
The India chapter ends.
The End

**To be
continued
...**

I myself enjoyed India.
— Aka Akasaka

BEING IN LOVE IS FUN UNTIL YOU ACTUALLY START DATING. THAT'S WHAT PEOPLE SAY, ANYWAY...

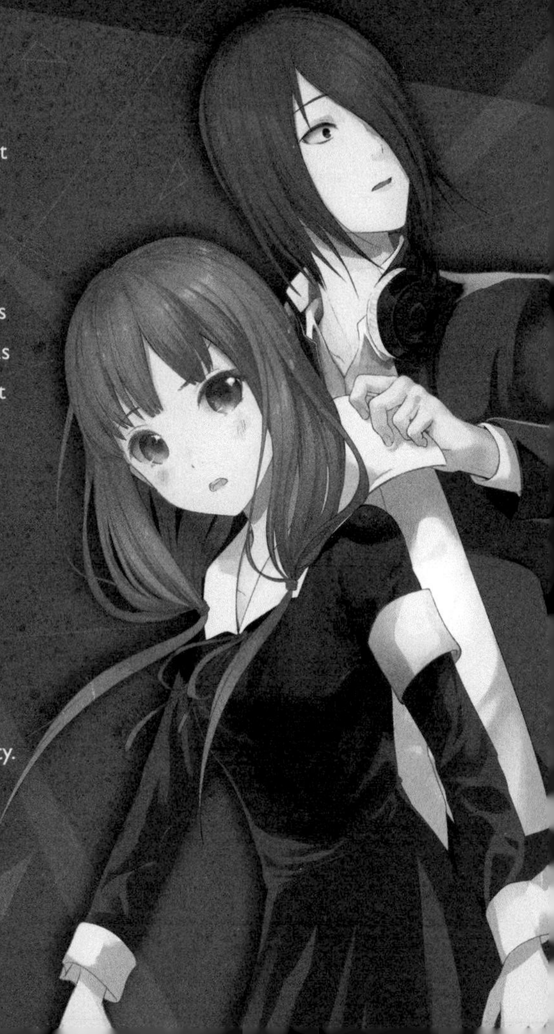

AKA AKASAKA

Aka Akasaka got his start as an assistant to Jinsei Kataoka and Kazuma Kondou, the creators of *Deadman Wonderland*. His first serialized manga was an adaptation of the light novel series *Sayonara Piano Sonata*, published by Kadokawa in 2011. *Kaguya-sama: Love Is War* began serialization in *Miracle Jump* in 2015 but was later moved to *Weekly Young Jump* in 2016 due to its popularity.

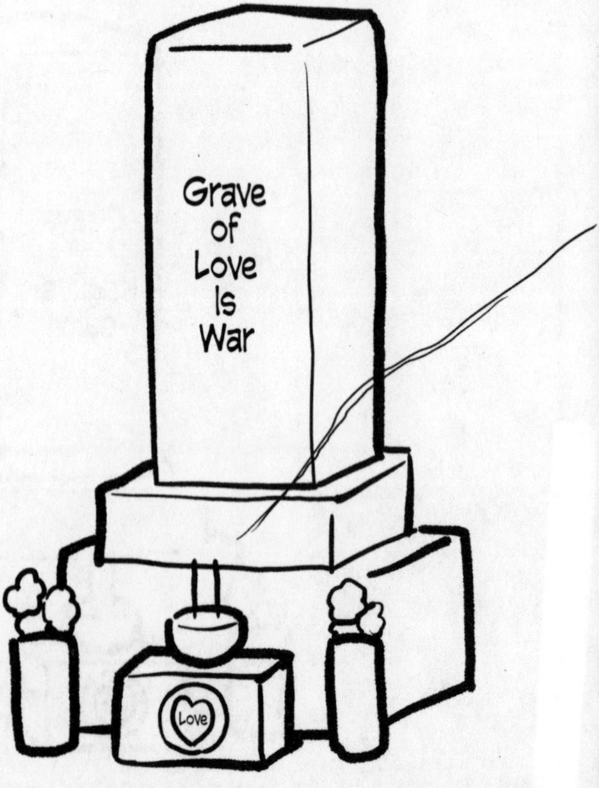
Grave of Love Is War
Love

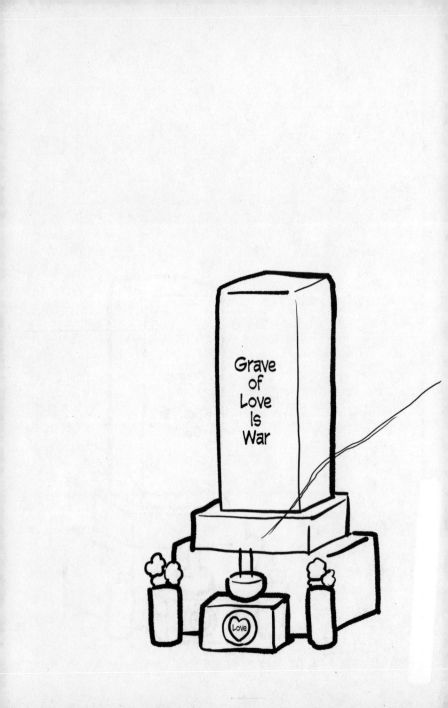

Grave of Kaguya-sama
Love

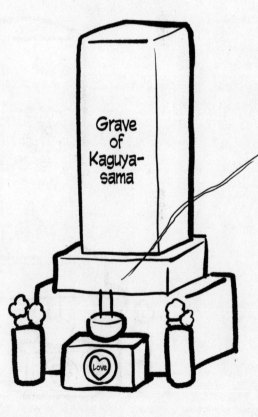

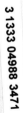

KAGUYA-SAMA
LOVE IS WAR

SHONEN JUMP MANGA EDITION

16

STORY AND ART BY
AKA AKASAKA

Translation/Tomo Kimura
English Adaptation/Annette Roman
Touch-Up Art & Lettering/Steve Dutro
Cover & Interior Design/Alice Lewis
Editor/Annette Roman

KAGUYA-SAMA WA KOKURASETAI~TENSAITACHI NO REN'AI ZUNO SEN~
© 2015 by Aka Akasaka
All rights reserved.
First published in Japan in 2015 by SHUEISHA Inc.,Tokyo.
English translation rights arranged by SHUEISHA Inc.

Printed in the U.S.A.

Published by VIZ Media, LLC
P.O. Box 77010
San Francisco, CA 94107

10 9 8 7 6 5 4 3 2 1
First printing, September 2020

viz.com

shonenjump.com

COMING NEXT VOLUME

17
KAGUYA-SAMA
LOVE IS WAR
STORY & ART BY
AKA AKASAKA

17

Will Kaguya tell her family or even her friends that she's dating Miyuki? Why is Chika pretending to be everyone's girlfriend while dressed in a bald wig? Hapless Yu gets romantic advice from recently dumped Kazeno, which he passes on to naive Miyuki. Then, repressed Kaguya gets advice from unrepressed Nagisa, and adventurous Maki gets advice from (usually) sensible Ai and tries to verify it with flustered males Miyuki and Yu. Basically, Shuchiin Academy suffers from a bad case of the blind leading the blind.

You can't learn about sex from porn.

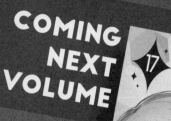

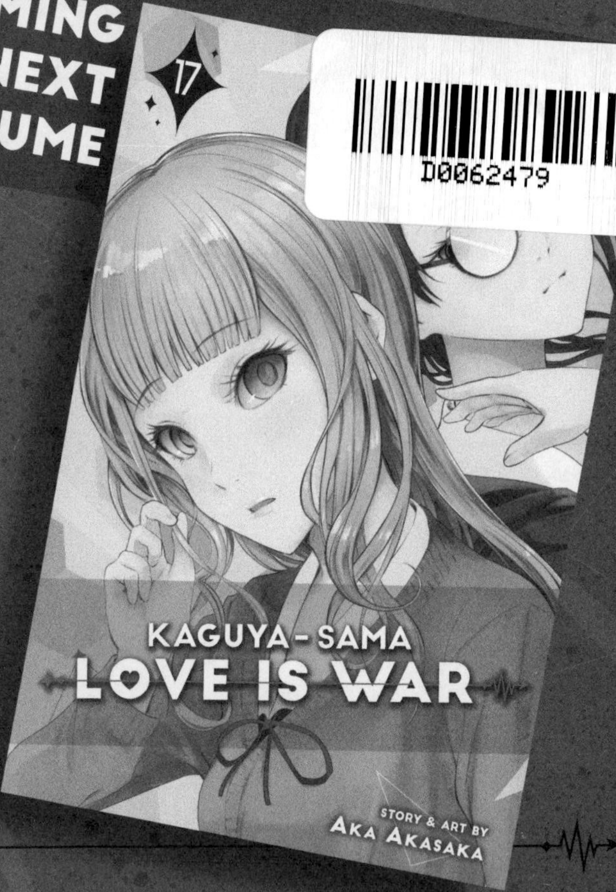